HILLBILLY HELLRAISERS

THE WORKING CLASS IN AMERICAN HISTORY

Editorial Advisors
James R. Barrett, Julie Greene, William P. Jones,
Alice Kessler-Harris, and Nelson Lichtenstein

A list of books in the series appears at the end of this book.

HILLBILLY HELLRAISERS

FEDERAL POWER AND POPULIST DEFIANCE IN THE OZARKS

J. BLAKE PERKINS

UNIVERSITY OF ILLINOIS PRESS
Urbana, Chicago, and Springfield

Arkansas
Humanities
Council

This project is supported in part by a grant from the Arkansas
Humanities Council and the National Endowment for the
Humanities.

Library of Congress Cataloging-in-Publication Data
Names: Perkins, J. Blake, author.
Title: Hillbilly hellraisers : federal power and populist defiance in
    the Ozarks / J. Blake Perkins.
Other titles: Working class in American history.
Description: [Urbana, Illinois] : University of Illinois, [2017] |
    Series: The working class in American history | Includes
    bibliographical references and index.
Identifiers: LCCN 2017009018 (print) | LCCN 2017011358 (ebook)
    | ISBN 9780252041372 (hardcover : alk. paper) | ISBN
    9780252082894 (pbk. : alk. paper) | ISBN 9780252099977
    (ebook)
Subjects: LCSH: Government, Resistance to—Ozark Mountains. |
    Ozarkers. | Ozark Mountains—History.
Classification: LCC JC328.3 .P443 2017 (print) | LCC JC328.3
    (ebook) | DDC 303.6/109767109034—dc23
LC record available at https://lccn.loc.gov/2017009018

For Jodie, Maddox, and Rylan

CONTENTS

ACKNOWLEDGMENTS

This book would not have happened without the contributions of many talented and generous people. I am deeply indebted to the helpful staffs at Lyon College's Mabee-Simpson Library, Missouri State University's Duane G. Meyer Library and its Special Collections division, the Downtown Campus Library at West Virginia University, Williams Baptist College's Felix Goodson Library, the Arkansas State Archives, the Northeast Arkansas Regional Archives, the University of Arkansas Libraries' Special Collections, the Archives at the University of Central Arkansas's Torreyson Library, the Archives and Special Collections at Hendrix College's Olin C. and Marjorie Bailey Library, the Butler Center for Arkansas Studies, the University of Arkansas at Little Rock's William H. Bowen School of Law Library, the Old Independence Regional Museum, the National Archives at College Park and Fort Worth, and the many county courthouses and local historical societies I visited for research.

I owe a lot to my many fine professors at Lyon College, Missouri State University, and West Virginia University. They include Brooks Blevins, John Wienzierl, Ed Tenace, Tom Dicke, the late Marc Cooper, Bob Miller, the late George Hummasti, William Piston, Ken Fones-Wolf, Elizabeth Fones-Wolf, Brian Luskey, Jack Hammersmith, and Mark Tauger. Certain individuals who also helped in various ways with my research or analysis deserve recognition. They include James Johnston, Lynn Morrow, Steve Saunders, Joan Gould, Patrick Williams, Lynn Gentzler, Lisa Perry, Michael Pierce, Greg Kiser, Tom Dillard, Thomas

Kiffmeyer, Bruce Stewart, Ronald Lewis, Ronald Eller, the late Lawrence Christenson, Matt Vester, Jackie Stites, Brian Jeffery, Ken Bridges, Don Cullimore, June Westphal, Mike Luster, Susan Mosier, Mildred Thomas, Joe Hodge, Jim Siekmier, Aaron Sheehan-Dean, Daniel Spillman, Ken Startup, Jerry Gibbens, Edward Harthorn, Keith McAnally, Greg French, Hal Gorby, Jenny Turman, Adam Zucconi, Jake Ivey, Josh Esposito, Karina Garcia, and Josh Howard.

My editors at the University of Illinois Press, Laurie Matheson and James Engelhardt, have been a pleasure to work with, and I thank them for encouraging this project. Thanks, too, to Jarod Roll and Jim Bissett, two of the finest historians of the rural working class, for their careful readings of the manuscript and their insightful suggestions. I also appreciate the helpful comments I received on papers related to this project I presented at conferences hosted by the Organization of American Historians, the Southern Historical Association, the Appalachian Studies Association, the Society of Appalachian Historians, the Arkansas Historical Association, the State Historical Society of Missouri, the Ozarks Studies Symposium, and the Arkansas State Archives. Constructive feedback from anonymous peer-reviewers with the *Arkansas Historical Quarterly* and the *Missouri Historical Review* also helped to sharpen my work on certain pieces of this project. I also thank those excellent journals for their permission to use material of mine that was previously published as articles.

I've had outstanding mentors along this journey, and, though I alone assume responsibility for all shortcomings and errors, they deserve much of the credit for whatever merits this book may have. Brooks Blevins first took me under his wing when I was an undergraduate student of his at Lyon College. In fact, this fellow rural Arkansawyer's example as a teacher and scholar most influenced my decision to pursue a career as a historian myself. After Lyon, I was lucky enough to continue my studies with him in graduate school at Missouri State University, where he took a new position in 2008. His teaching, guidance, and friendship—to say nothing of his pioneering scholarship on the Ozarks—have been and continue to be indispensable, to say the least. In addition, I thank him for patiently poring over and commenting on nearly everything I have ever written. When I first met my other mentor, Ken Fones-Wolf, at West Virginia University, I was immediately drawn to his enthusiasm. I have benefitted immensely from his keen editorial eye, his interpretive insights, and his ability throughout the writing of this work to help me see the bigger pictures when I was wandering in mountains of detail. Above all, I thank him for his constant encouragement.

Throughout the research and writing, several institutions provided generous funding that supported this book. West Virginia University's History Department, the Eberly College of Arts and Sciences, the Office of Graduate Education and Life, and the WVU Foundation contributed significant funding to the research that helped make this book possible. I also received helpful support from the History Department and the Office of Academic Affairs at Williams Baptist College. Finally, I thank the Arkansas Humanities Council for generously supporting this project.

Last, but most important, I thank my family for their unflagging support. My mom, Royetta, has enthusiastically supported my endeavors all my life. My dad, Jim, instilled in me through farm life at an early age a drive to work to the finish line through tough challenges. My sister, Magen, has always been there for me—and was one of my best copyeditors through college. My grandparents, Gerald and Nina Richey and Bonnie and the late Paul L. Perkins, have also given me invaluable support and encouragement. I owe my early passion for history to my fascination with their rural lives. Finally, I dedicate this book to my wife, Jodie, and our two sons, Maddox and Rylan. Words simply cannot express how grateful I am for their love, sacrifice, and support, but I'm confident they know what they mean to me. They are my inspiration, and this book would not exist without all their love and labors.

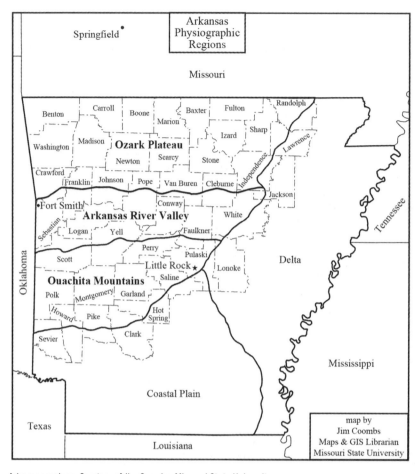

Arkansas regions. Courtesy of Jim Coombs, Missouri State University.

INTRODUCTION

On June 3, 1983, federal and local lawmen surrounded the remote home of Leonard and Norma Ginter near Smithville, Arkansas, a rural village in the Ozarks foothills. Authorities had received a tip that the Ginters were harboring fugitive Gordon Kahl, a militant tax protestor and antigovernment extremist who had recently made the FBI's most wanted list for killing two lawmen. As heavily armed officers closed in on the Ginters' house, Leonard and Norma were safely and quietly taken into custody, while the local sheriff, Gene Matthews, and a federal marshal wasted no time pursuing Kahl. Inside the house the lawmen exchanged gunfire with an obstinate Kahl, who had long promised the feds he would not be taken alive. Sheriff Matthews presumably killed Kahl with a shot to the head, but he, too, was riddled with bullets through the back and shoulder. After the federal marshal removed the mortally wounded sheriff from the house, the army of officers standing ready on the outside unloaded a barrage of gunfire and tear gas through the walls and windows, eventually sending the Ginter home up in flames. Kahl's charred remains were later recovered from the ashes, and the Ginters were sentenced to five years in federal prison.[1]

Media coverage of this violent incident put Smithville's rural community in the national headlines for the first and only time in its history. Not surprisingly, the dramatic story conjured up popular images of Arkansas's isolated hill country as a bastion of antigovernment sentiments. This perception, after all, dated at least to the legendary "wars" between hillbilly moonshiners and federal revenuers in the nineteenth century. *New York Times* columnist J. C. Barden was sure to note in his story about the shooting, though, that "far more [hill] people are unsettled by recent events than were troubled when the local criminal element turned from making moonshine to growing marijuana." In truth, Kahl was from North Dakota and the Ginters, whose Yankee accents "sounded odd" to the locals, had recently moved to the community from Wisconsin. Moreover, the radicalism of Kahl and the Ginters, who were members of a far-right-wing, white nationalist organization called the Posse Comitatus, represented no more than a tiny sliver of the rural population. When questioned by reporters about how widespread such sentiments were among the locals in the area, the proprietor of the little country store in Smithville insisted that "these [extremists] are not your average Arkansas people."[2] Still, this sensational gunfight in rural Smithville seemed too much for most journalists to resist placing it within a longstanding narrative of rural whites' hard-nosed defiance against federal power throughout American history.

Historians and social scientists have long worked to better understand the glaring and seemingly persistent conflicts—past and present—between rural white Americans and government authorities. In the wake of the 1995 bombing of the Oklahoma City federal building by "small-town boy" Timothy McVeigh, for instance, historian Catherine McNicol Stock asserted that "the recent rise of rural radicalism should not have surprised Americans so much," because "rural radicalism is in fact older than the nation itself." "The unique heritage of rural America," Stock argued, has produced a tradition of "righteous rage" against centralized authority ever since Nathaniel Bacon's rebellion in 1676, Daniel Shays's rebellion in 1786–87, and the Whiskey Rebellion of 1791–94.[3] Resistance to federal power, in this view, has been a timeless part of the fabric of society and culture in rural America.

Historians of politics have recently shown a strong interest in probing the Ozarks to locate important roots of America's modern conservatism and its rallying cry to dismantle the size and power of the federal government. Indeed, the Ozarks region today is home to some of the strongest Tea Party sentiments and antigovernment activism in America. Two recent prize-winning histories, Bethany Moreton's *To Serve God and Wal-Mart: The Making of Christian Free Enterprise* and Darren Dochuk's *From Bible Belt to Sun Belt: Plain-Folk Religion, Grassroots Politics, and the Rise of Evangelical Conservatism*, place the development of antigovernment conservatism in contemporary America on a continuum of rural white cultural traditions that date back to the nineteenth and early twentieth centuries. Looking backward from the present, they point to a "pioneering ethic," "frontier thinking," and "Jeffersonian precepts" that mixed with the "conservatism" of evangelical religion in the late 1800s and early 1900s to shape a distinct rural worldview in the western South. Then, during the second half of the twentieth century, post–World War II economic and demographic changes helped to spread and grow rural whites' conservative culture into a broader evangelical, free-enterprise, antigovernment political movement that eventually became the heart and soul of the Republican Party.[4]

This book departs from interpretations that emphasize such *continuity* of conservative antigovernment sentiments in rural American history. It argues that the particular antipathy toward the federal government that looms large in the region today, in fact, reflects far more of what is *new* in the Ozarks than what is "traditional." Rural resistance to federal power has certainly transcended time, but the specific impetuses and dynamics of that defiance have changed remarkably from the late nineteenth century to the present. This book challenges explanations that point to the exceptionalism of "rural heritage" for answers. At its basic roots the long story of rural resistance to federal power in the Ozarks is not all that different from many other working-class experiences in American history—or from other working people's experiences around the globe. In searching deeper for the roots of rural defiance and exploring its nonlinear development over time in the Arkansas Ozarks, this book asks bigger questions about why well-meaning reformers' attempts to improve human conditions in rural communities have often failed, about governmentality and the administration of social and economic programs, and about challenges confronting ordinary working people in the quest for popular democracy. *Hillbilly Hellraisers* is a work of "microhistory"—or, really, a collection of "microhistories"—that suggests many historians and "social scientists have made generalizations that do not hold up when tested against the concrete reality of the small-scale life they claim to explain."[5] It proposes that "minimal facts and individual cases can serve to reveal more general phenomena" that enable us to better understand a complex and multidimensional past that holds valuable lessons for the present and future.[6]

Cultural pundits and many scholars have long portrayed rural people—and especially the mountaineers of the Upland South—as "exceptional" and "apart" from the national mainstream and its modernizing developments. But rural experiences and aspirations embodied essential evolutions of the American story.[7] The burgeoning population and expansion of family farms in the Arkansas Ozarks after the Civil War represented the hopes and dreams of a new generation of America's yeomanry. Though "they were not a homogenous group," writes one historian, small-scale farmers commonly "engaged in subsistence and cash-oriented agricultural production[;] were subject to the power of the state and other forces; lived in small community settlements; and operated on a household basis, relying on the labor of the family with the male head as the dominant figure."[8] White smallholders in the Ozarks reproduced or created new family farms and sought modern opportunities to prosper in national and international markets and to assert their relative independence as masters of their own means of production.[9]

Many of the same forces that brought new opportunities, however, also worked to grow the corporatization of agricultural production and markets that increasingly squeezed and marginalized small-scale farms by the end of the nineteenth century, a process that would continue through the first half of the twentieth. During the 1880s and 1890s smallholder working people responded to their struggles with a determined political revolt that aimed to end rising economic inequality and defend opportunities for small producers by expanding the regulatory power of what they commonly referred to as the "people's government." This "Populist moment," I argue, despite its political shortcomings, established the primary discursive frame in the rural Ozarks in which most people viewed the legitimate roles and responsibilities of the federal government for the next six decades.[10]

Amid the insurgency and entrenchment of this Populist worldview, rural Ozarkers encountered a growing national state and its new "progressive" policies and programs, but many came to see some of these reforms as misguided or even deliberately malicious. This backcountry resistance, though, did not spring from a conservative defense of "traditionalism" or an inborn cultural suspicion of federal power. Rural folks were usually not resisting federal power per se. Rather, they defied what many called an "aristocracy of wealth" and the grip it held on the levers of governmental powers. Rural populists detested the way privileged elites controlled and manipulated federal programs to their own advantage at the expense of rural "commoners." They called for rooting out the status quo.

Neither did small farmers in the Ozarks very often resist federal power in the late 1800s and early 1900s out of a simple, parochial defense of "localism" against bureaucratic outsiders, as many historians would have it.[11] Backcountry smallholders, in fact, persistently yearned for a national government that would construct and maintain the boundaries of a democratic political economy and expand opportunities for family farmers and other laborers. They were fighting a rearguard action, though, and they primarily did so *inside* their home region. At nearly every turn it was local and regional business elites who subverted federal programs that aimed to improve rural opportunities for smallholders. The region's elites capitalized on their privileged access to federal governmentality and harnessed those powers to advance agendas that hinged on corporate industrialization and agribusiness, which, despite rhetoric to the contrary, frequently spelled increased inequalities and diminished opportunities for smallholder working families. Indeed, most conflicts between rural Ozarkers and applications of federal power during the first half of the twentieth century played out *locally*. They often pitted struggling rural smallholders against business elites who used federal authority and resources more for their own political and economic agendas.[12]

This history engages a growing body of scholarship that looks at how and why governments often fail to achieve the goals of their reform efforts. It concurs with those historians who follow social scientist James C. Scott's critique of centralized bureaucracies' "imperial or hegemonic planning mentality that excludes the necessary role of local knowledge and know-how."[13] But this book also pushes historians to think more about Scott's "high modernism" framework and its less critical analysis of the potential consequences of "local control" and decentralization in reform efforts. In the rural Ozarks most federal reforms actually adhered rather closely to the political and legal traditions of federalism and local control in the United States. That meant that federal reformers shared much of their power with—and, in many cases, outright delegated control to—comfortable local elites who generally held a large stake in the status quo and, thus, had no great ambition to promote economic democracy and independence for plain folks in rural communities.

In many ways, working people's experiences with federal power in the Ozarks paralleled those of rural populations in other parts of the world. Anthropologist Tania Murray Li, for example, shows that government interventions designed to improve the lives of rural Sulawesi highlanders in Indonesia rarely ever met their intended goals. Instead, many reform efforts exacerbated problems and produced unintended consequences that inflicted even greater detriment, prompting new crises in which the state frequently felt the need to intervene again. Li, however, locates the failures of these reform efforts less in the out-of-touch "high modernism" of distant government bureaucracies, as Scott would have it, and more in how the programs were actually implemented at the local level. Reformers negotiated and collaborated with elites who controlled the local structures of power in the Sulawesi highlands and held a vested interest in the status quo. In doing so, the actual administration of certain programs, which local elites typically controlled, inevitably strayed from the most reform-spirited aims of their designers' original intentions. Meanwhile, for their part, the rural highlanders whom the programs were intended to help exhibited a remarkable "will to improve" and openness to reform. In most cases, though, not only did the politically diluted government programs fail the rural people they were intended for, but they also wound up strengthening the elites' grip on the local structures of power. Many government interventions, then, inadvertently helped widen social, political, and economic inequalities in the Sulawesi highlands even further and, consequently, provoked stiff rural resistance.[14]

This book unveils similar patterns in the rural Ozarks. Like Li's work, this history of the rural Ozarks attempts to correct an overemphasis on the blunders of interventionist bureaucracies in studies of government reform by shifting more focus, instead, on the *local* and *regional* levels where government reform power was implemented on the ground and where its real consequences played out in people's lives. In addition to examining the goings-on in high bureaucratic offices, we ought to also look locally to find important answers that help us better understand "how certain schemes to improve the human condition have failed."[15]

Though the system often failed them, rural Ozarkers themselves were not merely passive victims of an immoveable political and economic order of American "modernity" that was somehow predestined to crush their rural communities and hopes for better economic democracy. They were underdogs, for sure, in an American electoral democracy that usually lent disproportionate influence to those with capital, but the fate of small-scale producers and their rural communities was not predetermined. Indeed, despite the Populist revolt's shortcomings, the widespread mobilization of family farmers and other working people in the late nineteenth century worked to drastically realign regional and national politics, as political scientist Elizabeth Sanders has shown. Rural grassroots activism demonstrated the immense power of collectively organized movements to challenge the control of elite "wire pullers and war horses," as populist Ozarkers were known to call them.[16] While their collective demands helped to transform national and regional political debates and forced a number of leaders to adopt new stances, however, many rural populists often failed to stand united with other working people and small producers, especially those who looked and seemed to live differently. This was a costly mistake, because it inhibited the potential for a mass working people's movement to deliver real structural changes that might have improved rural opportunities. Many Ozarkers' own flawed assumptions and misunderstandings about "others" all too often failed at pivotal moments to counter—and even sometimes contributed to—the forces working against small-scale producerism and economic democracy. Just as one historian has recently written about rural smallholders in North Carolina, "their inability to come to a common understanding of their shared problems [with others] prevent[ed] them from collaborating to change them."[17] Consequently, while many rural families mourned the demise of their communities and smallholder livelihoods and demanded change, they often could rouse only populist-*sounding* political rhetoric without forging the tight-knit, holistic "common people's" protest that would have been necessary for holding government accountable to enact meaningful reforms.

Hillbilly Hellraisers narrates chronologically in three parts the story of what were primarily local conflicts over political power and economic justice in the Ozarks during the long twentieth century. Part I, "The Populist Ethic," sets the stage for the book to show that hill folks' particular populist sensibilities are the key to understanding important dynamics of defiance against federal power in the Ozarks during the first half of the twentieth century—dynamics that have often been misunderstood. It probes the "Populist ethic" that fired up the grassroots amid the Gilded Age's growing inequalities and rural dispossession. Working-class Ozarkers did not, in fact, oppose all federal intervention. Far from it, populists hoped that a stronger national government could protect small producers from the predatory power of elites, including local elites. This working people's populism informed most rural Ozarkers' opinions about federal power and shaped their particular dispositions toward government reforms that wound up conflicting with their goals of smallholder security and economic democracy over the next several decades.

Then, part II, "Rural Resistance," presents a series of microhistories spanning the 1890s through the 1940s in which rural farmers and workers resisted certain interventions by federal power. From attempts to eradicate moonshining, to national military conscription during World War I, to efforts that aimed to develop "improved" agricultural practices, many rural smallholders saw—with logical reasoning—the manipulations of self-interested elites behind the veneer of "progressive" federal power. Even so, the Populist ethic remained alive. Most plain-folk Ozarkers supported stronger federal protections and assistance for working and poor people during the Great Depression of the 1930s. But New Deal reformers passed on most control of the federal government's new resources to regional and local business elites who had little interest in using them to help smallholders and rural farm communities. They had other plans for a New Ozarks and, instead, used New Dealers' federal power to build some "dam progress" that they hoped would spur corporate industrialization and agribusiness development.

Finally, part III, "Toward a New Defiance," takes the story of rural experiences with federal power into the transformative period that followed World War II. By the 1960s, thousands of rural Ozarkers had left their opportunity-strapped smallholder communities to join one of the largest mass migrations in American history. Many of those rural folks who stayed in the Ozarks were counted among the most impoverished people in the country, even amid postwar America's booming affluence. During the 1960s, residents' hope in the economic development programs of the John F. Kennedy and Lyndon B. Johnson administrations turned rather quickly to disappointment for poor and working people in most rural communities. Then, the federal War on Poverty's attempts to tackle poverty "from the bottom up" provoked stiff resistance. Unlike the rural working-class defiance documented in earlier chapters, though, the loudest objectors and instigators of opposition this time were New Ozarks business elites who resented federal social programs' threats to their local control and the malleable, low-wage labor force on which their new tourism-, retirement-, light-industrial-, and agribusiness-based economy depended. Reformers were unable to help re-energize a populist challenge from poor and working people in rural communities, and New Ozarks elites' new discourse of defiance went mostly uncontested. By the late 1970s the old Populist ethic had given way to a new kind of popular antigovernment sentiment that, aside from its similar anti-establishment rhetoric, had little in common substantively with the specific dynamics of rural working people's defiance of federal power in the late 1800s and early 1900s.

To tell this history, I have mindfully worked to connect local and regional history with the broader American story, to recognize change and continuity by respecting the past on its own terms, and have striven to weave together the often overly compartmentalized analytical lenses of political, social, economic, and cultural history. Still, there is no guarantee that all the microhistorical examples contained in this work represent the experiences of *all* rural Ozarkers. It seems almost cliché for authors who use "case studies" to set forth "disclaimers" up front to remind readers of their limitations, but it seems fitting to do so here as well. Historian Durwood Dunn, whose own study of a particular Appalachian community helped refocus the entire historiography of the Upland South, has rightly noted that writing case-study history often comes with "critical limitations on forming broader generalizations about the region as a whole," especially since we must consider the "uniqueness of . . . individual . . . communities."[18]

On the other hand, how can we begin to test the validity of generalized assumptions about history without zeroing in and peeling back the complex layers of specific local experiences? This is a challenge that historians of all peoples, places, and time periods face, but it is an especially tall order for historians of the Ozarks and similar rural regions whose histories have long been obstructed by "the thicket of myth, nostalgia, and stereotype." Brooks Blevins has wisely advised fellow historians not to "be held captive by generations of stereotyping and generalization" and to "avoid building our histories on a faulty foundation."[19] I see no better way to do this than by putting real flesh-and-blood people and their local experiences under the microscope of historical inquiry.

PART I

THE POPULIST ETHIC

1

THE "ONE-GALLUSED" CROWD ON GOVERNMENT

On July 4, 1899, more than three thousand Ozarkers descended on the town of Hardy in Sharp County, Arkansas, to take part in the local Independence Day celebration. Many folks undoubtedly enjoyed overdue visits with friends and acquaintances, some rare courting opportunities, an array of festivities and food—not to mention, for at least some, a good-sized swig or two, or nine or ten, of white lightning—and all the other activities that were customary of such Fourth of July celebrations throughout America. At the end of the day, rural families gathered around "a makeshift grandstand" for the celebration's main event, a rousing speech by Arkansas's attorney general, Jeff Davis—the "Wild Ass of the Ozarks," as Davis's political detractors frequently called him. In firing the opening shots for his candidacy in the next gubernatorial race, Davis lamented the injustice, inequalities, and gross imbalance of power that had come to characterize Gilded Age America and Arkansas. The toiling masses were the "wealth producers" whose hands created unimaginable abundance, "but the wealth consumers are the lawmakers," he exclaimed, who siphon off the people's riches into the hoards of a greedy few. "Under such conditions can we be free to enjoy our right to the pursuit of happiness?" Davis asked. "Do you suppose our ancestors who planted here in virgin soil the tree of liberty would recognize this country today? Would they ever have thought that the principles of this government would be so warped and distorted as to give us the miserable thing we have today?"[1]

The "Karl Marx for Hill Billies," as a noted southern scholar later referred to Davis, likely drew impassioned ovations from his rural audience as he lampooned the state legislature for always bowing to the interests of railroad companies and other corporations, and when he scolded the Arkansas Supreme Court for "rul[ing] against the people" by blocking his efforts to prosecute trusts and monopolies operating within the state. Davis likewise chastised the U.S. Supreme Court for striking down the federal income tax law Congress had passed in 1894. He charged that the court's decision was a conspiracy concocted "for the benefit of aggregated wealth . . . [so] that the wealthy should not pay taxes on their surplus incomes, although the people said they should." He also warned that the plan being drawn up by political elites in Little Rock to build a new statehouse was bound to become "the most infamous steal ever perpetrated against the people of Arkansas," because the masterminds behind it were secretly scheming a shady real estate deal to benefit one of Little Rock's wealthiest families. Davis concluded this "first speech of the most memorable political campaign in the state's history" by assuring the "crowd of leathery-skinned, one-gallused dirt farmers" that he was "in this fight for the people." "The war is on, knife to knife, hilt to hilt . . . between the corporations . . . and the people," he later told another group of rural Arkansawyers.[2]

The Pulitzer Prize-winning poet and Little Rock native John Gould Fletcher wrote nearly a half-century later that "it was the mountain people who had produced Jeff Davis; from the beginning of his career to its end, he was their spokesman and their champion."[3] Davis's popularity in Arkansas's upland counties, of course, did not alone account for all of his successes at the polls, but tapping hill folks' sentiments about government and its proper role certainly played no small part in ensuring that he would never lose another election. Davis would go on to serve three terms as governor and then as a U.S. senator until his untimely death in January 1913. Despite a much stronger penchant for campaigning than policymaking, Davis's powerful political discourse embodied a Populist ethic that had come to shape rural attitudes and ideas about government during this era of sweeping social and economic change. Indeed, popular imagery of rural isolation, insularity, and parochialism belied the fact that Ozarkers stood right in the thick of Gilded Age America's social, economic, and political developments.

The popularity of Davis's rhetoric suggests that most rural white Ozarkers in the late nineteenth and early twentieth centuries, like other rural Americans "who felt trapped in an order dominated by big business" and now found "unconvincing the old gospel of laissez-faire,"[4] championed progressive expansions of government power, particularly new interventions in the economy to ensure fairness and protection against the vagaries of capitalist-controlled markets.

Politician Jeff Davis, the "Wild Ass of the Ozarks," with his hunting dogs, ca. 1895. Courtesy of the Butler Center for Arkansas Studies, Arkansas Studies Institute, Little Rock.

At the same time, they resisted certain arms of governmental authority that they believed unjustly catered to the "special interests" of well-to-do elites. They demanded that common working folks like themselves seize control of the public realm from privileged elites in accordance with America's democratic ideals. Contrary to popular and even scholarly assumptions about tradition-bound rural folks, most small farmers and laborers were not antimodern. In fact, most rural working people supported a forward-looking political agenda of active government that would "improve the market leverage of agriculture, to strengthen the negotiating position of labor, and to address a growing crisis of economic inequality."[5] Nevertheless, a number of rural whites' own misunderstandings and prejudices—especially a suspicion of black Americans—worked to undercut significant potential for their mass democratic protest to deliver real change. The evolution of Jeff Davis's political career, in fact, would show that a rather vague and rhetorical "populist persuasion" could appeal, ironically, to both white country folks and town businessmen, poor dirt farmers and prosperous local elites alike, while doing little to produce much meaningful reform.[6] Even so, the late-nineteenth-century rural political revolt planted a Populist ethic in the Ozarks that would serve as the lens through which most rural smallholders and working families would view their experiences with government power for the next several decades. Although typically overlooked by most historians, its Populist ethic also made many rural working folks ready to direct their defiance not only against outsiders in Washington but also more radically against well-to-do *local* elites who controlled the political and economic structures within the region.

Notwithstanding popular imagery of rural isolation and quiescence, America's emerging industrialization had created major changes in the Ozarks by the last two decades of the nineteenth century. Government—federal, state, and local—had played no small role in helping precipitate these changes. Arkansas Republicans during Reconstruction, who received some of their strongest support from mountain Unionists in certain enclaves of the western Ozarks, had subscribed to a "gospel of prosperity" and worked to employ government resources to build "a society of booming factories, bustling towns, a diversified agriculture . . . and abundant employment opportunities."[7] To accomplish these ends, Arkansas Republicans raised new taxes to build the state's first public and higher education systems. They created and funded the activities of Arkansas's Commission of Immigration and State Lands, which worked to attract new labor and investors by advertising the state's abundance of land—much of it free or below market prices through the federal Homestead Act of 1862 and other government programs—and other resources available to potential developers. Moreover, Republicans during Reconstruction embarked on an unprecedented number of state-sponsored infrastructure developments, especially railroad construction.[8]

Many of these programs helped lay foundations for new economic developments in the years ahead, but state and local Republicans' affinity for the spoils of patronage and their frequent overextension of resources, as well as backroom deals between "ambitious entrepreneurs and unscrupulous politicians" amid their development schemes, opened them to staunch criticism, even within their own party ranks. Factionalism between the state's Republican machine and insurgent "native Arkansas Unionists"—initially led by Ozark native James Johnson of Madison County—combined with the federal government's waning commitment to Southern reconstruction to eventually open the door for conservative Democrats to regain control of the state in 1874. This new leadership promised to "redeem" Arkansas from Republicans' "carpetbagger," "scalawag," and "negro" rule and, thereby, to restore a *smaller* government that they argued would be run by and for "the people."[9]

"Redeemer" Democrats in Little Rock immediately distanced Arkansas from most forms of federal authority, in accordance with their "states' rights" agenda. They also went to work decentralizing the state government and slashing taxes and funding for state services—policies that "would well serve the interests of the state's landed elite far into the next century," as Arkansas historian Thomas DeBlack has written. But, as the eminent Southern historian C. Vann Woodward has noted, a "New Order" was afoot, one that ensured that government would continue playing key roles in promoting change throughout the rural South.[10] Despite such "relatively laissez-faire" and more locally controlled governance, sociologists Dwight Billings and Kathleen Blee have pointed out that "the interconnections of commerce and state making" greatly shaped the changing social, economic, and political order in the Southern uplands.[11]

Indeed, the conservative "Redeemers" proved generally unanimous in their eagerness to promote new economic development in Arkansas. They "coveted the iron horse as the key to commercial prosperity" and issued government land grants of more than a million acres to railroad companies during the late nineteenth century. Meanwhile, they fixed low tax rates and engineered favorable property assessments as parts of special-incentives packages to lure industrial investments. Railroad construction in Arkansas rose rapidly from 256 miles of track in 1870 to more than 2,200 miles by 1900, and many more miles were added during the first two decades of the 1900s.[12] Although railroad building

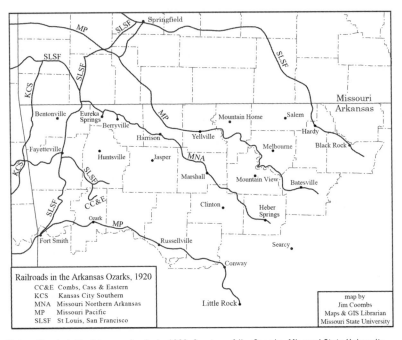

Major railroads in the Arkansas Ozarks by 1920. Courtesy of Jim Coombs, Missouri State University.

often progressed more slowly in the rugged terrain of the Upland South, five main railroads and several subsidiary lines traversed the Ozarks by 1920.[13]

"Development" connected the Ozarks more fully to the national and international economy than ever and brought new market opportunities to the region. Most rural folks hoped that the cash incomes generated from these new enterprises would help them prosper and sustain their family-farm society and the relative independence it afforded. The promise seemed rich, indeed. By 1900, "the Census Bureau found more than 35,000 farms in the fifteen Ozark counties, an increase of 90 percent in just the previous two decades."[14] Increasingly, rural people committed significant parts of farm production to raising specialized cash crops and market-bound livestock, took "off-farm" work in the region's growing timber industry to supplement farm incomes, and sold mineral and timber rights to budding entrepreneurs and investors.[15]

Industrialization in the Ozarks, however, assumed a largely "extractive" nature, as industrialists aimed primarily to exploit the region's natural resources and cheap agricultural products and labor. Though industrialists and their regional "boosters" were fond of trumpeting their contributions to job creation and expanding economic opportunities for local populations, the lion's share of industrial profits were actually carried out of the region or were unevenly distributed to well-positioned local elites. The new economic environment provided few long-term, "value-added" improvements for local communities; much like Appalachia, the Ozarks became a "periphery region of uneven economic development."[16]

Consequently, many rural folks found themselves unexpectedly frustrated and vulnerable. Some of the same opportunities that rural folks pursued as they "grasped" for yeoman independence and prosperity all too often left them marginalized amid the vagaries of market forces beyond their control. Unpredictable and speculative market prices, vicious cycles of merchant credit, exorbitant freight rates charged by railroad companies and other "middle men," and the burdens of regressive taxation soon had many small farmers in the rural Ozarks questioning the fairness of the new economic environment.

Farm tenancy in the Arkansas Ozarks rose by nearly one-fifth during the last two decades of the nineteenth century alone. Meanwhile, a handful of prosperous merchants and larger landholders came to own more and more of the region's best farm land. But tenancy statistics and the increasing redistribution of land ownership to regional elites do not tell the full story. Backcountry farmers who managed to hang on to the deeds of their farms often did so by expanding their agricultural production onto poor and underproductive lands "previously deemed unsuitable for cultivation" and continued to fight a rearguard defense for smallholder sustainability.[17] The Ozarks timber boom also provided some small hill farmers timely but only temporary relief in the form of supplemental cash incomes. However, when the timber companies finished extracting the profitable stands of timber in an area and moved on to the next, this "off-farm" income quickly disappeared. Moreover, most industrialists carried off the timber profits without investing in local communities and left behind little but a "cut-over wasteland" for struggling small farmers to try to scrape by on.[18]

It is no wonder, then, that rural discontentment arose forcefully in the region during the last decades of the nineteenth century. Thousands of small farmers began forming local "lodges" to discuss their common troubles and collectively demand change. The Brothers of Freedom (B of F), originally founded in rural Johnson County in 1882, emerged primarily in the region's western and central counties as one of the largest and best-organized "unions" of farmers in the Arkansas Ozarks in the 1880s. Committing themselves to the cause of common working people who were "gradually becoming oppressed," the B of F condemned the "combinations of capital" and the big-moneyed interests "who propose not only to live on the labors of others, but to speedily amass fortunes at their expense." Combining a "mountain-grown blend of scripture" with America's founding ideals, the organization's "Declaration of Principles" proclaimed that "God . . . created all men free and equal, and endowed them with certain inalienable rights, such as life, liberty, and the pursuit of happiness, and that these rights are a common inheritance and should be respected by all mankind."[19]

B of F organizers, led by Ozone resident Isaac McCracken, tapped into the frustrations of thousands of hill farmers and lent a new collective voice to their demands for reform. Contrary to popular portrayals of backwoods mountain folks' reflexive suspicions of all outsiders, McCracken, the farm organization's president, was a Canadian-born "furriner" who had only recently migrated to the region. As a young boy, McCracken and his family had moved to Massachusetts, where he grew up and got his first job working on a whaling ship. After three years at sea, McCracken apprenticed himself to a machinist back in Massachusetts during the Civil War. Shortly after the war, McCracken headed to Wisconsin, where he married and started a family, and then ventured to Minnesota for a brief spell. Afterward, the McCrackens migrated to the Arkansas Ozarks to homestead a small farm in the "back-country of Johnson County." Isaac McCracken worked primarily as a small farmer there, except for a two-year hiatus when he went to Little Rock to earn wages as a machinist. While in Little Rock, McCracken picked up some valuable labor-organizing skills as a member of the Blacksmiths' and Machinists' Union. Despite his outsider status, many locals in Johnson County and eventually throughout the region grew to admire and trust McCracken, who helped establish several small and independent sawmills in the area, performed dental and some other medical work in his new community, and was elected as a local justice of the peace by his backcountry neighbors. By 1885, McCracken's and other B of F organizers' calls for small farmers to unite and "stand beside each other in the right" had succeeded in enlisting between thirty thousand and forty thousand members in western Arkansas.[20]

Initially, the B of F took great pains to avoid politicization and even "banned fractious political debate within its lodges." This policy was deemed especially wise in the Ozarks, where the organization hoped to avoid competitive partisan conflicts between Democrats, Mountain Republicans, and third-party advocates. Instead, the B of F championed a "self-help" strategy that encouraged its members to essentially boycott commercial agriculture by practicing "safety-first" farming and striving toward family self-sufficiency as consumers. To obtain supplies and items they could not grow or make themselves, some local B of F lodges organized petitions that pressured some area merchants to sign contracts pledging not to charge their members more than ten percent above wholesale costs. Many others attempted to circumvent merchants and creditors altogether by forming their own local cooperatives to purchase supplies in bulk at discounted rates and to help market salable crops at better prices than farmers might otherwise obtain individually. A number of local lodges also adopted "resolution[s] to make this crop without going into debt." "We are a set of backwoodsmen out here on this mountain and do not know any better than to take each others [sic] advice, and to help each other in the right," declared one spokesman for a local B of F lodge. "Let the wire-pullers hold their wires and we the strings."[21]

While some scholars have been tempted to see rural rebellion in the late 1800s and early 1900s as antimarket or antimodern expressions, historian Charles Postel has shown that, in fact, most small farmers and rural laborers "mobilized to put their own stamp on commercial development" and ultimately to "ensure fair access to the benefits of modernity."[22] Their primary objection to recent economic developments was to the inequality produced by industrialization and capital-intensive agriculture. Rural Ozarkers' beef, then, was not generally with the market economy itself. So the B of F's "self-help" program and call to abstain as much as possible from market activities undoubtedly failed to appeal to small farmers as strongly as its architects had hoped. Moreover, the B of F and its local cooperatives also quickly ran up against the tenacious power of those local elites in the region who viewed the organization's agenda as anathema to a "land of free traders." One Pope County lodge member finally grew so disillusioned with the B of F's self-help-only approach, he told fellow members that they had just as well "bay at the moon." After all, while small farmers attempted such passive, nonpolitical resistance, the grip that greedy corporations and self-serving elites had on government power was growing stronger all the time, he argued. While farmers and other "common folks" shied away from political action, these wealthy elites were busy hijacking the reins of government to bolster their own privileges and to make "labor subservient to capital and monopolies." Rekindling a "spirit of justice" in government was urgent, insisted one leader of the farmers' movement:

> We have been keeping war hosses, lawyers, and wire-pullers in office long enough, and they are rather expensive stock, they cost more every year and do less. . . . We are going to turn it all out, root hog or die, and get a new outfit. We don't care whether they are war hosses, mules or jackasses, so [long as] they fill the place with honesty, and act fair with the farmer.

It was high time, rural working people believed, that the "industrious people" started pushing toward "purifying" *their* government. After all, it was only fair that the "people's" government step up to provide "a little 'Protection' to put him [the laboring man] on equal footing" with rich elites and corporations, as one B of F member put it.[23]

By the late 1880s the B of F and other farmers' unions in the region merged their independent organizations with the larger Farmers' Alliance that was sweeping the rural South and Midwest. Alliance organizers in the Ozarks called on hill folks to help "suppress prejudices and unite the people as a band of brothers." In July 1892 a leader of the Farmers' Alliance in Searcy County pointed to how the disasters of rising farm mortgages and indebtedness occurred as wealthy railroad magnates and other corporate interests unjustly locked in a stranglehold on government power. "Do you call this prosperity?" he asked. "Let the plutocratic eagle scream from its lofty heights . . . and 'let the people be damned' is the verdict of the capitalists," he declared. He urged fellow farmers to "grab the wheel and roll, all hands at once." As for those greedy "capitalists" who cried that the Alliance represented nothing more than backwardness, anarchy, and "destruction," the Searcy County farmer organizer retorted: "If, 'On earth peace, and good will to man,' is destruction, we'll destroy. 'Equal rights to all, and special privileges to none,' is our pass word."[24]

By 1890 an estimated one hundred thousand Arkansawyers had joined the national Farmers' Alliance, which enjoyed some of its strongest support in the uplands. The national alliance, which held a convention in St. Louis in 1889, put forth one of the most reform-spirited political agendas in American history, featuring calls for expansions of public power that might have been unimaginable only a few years before. Its list of demands included the creation of progressive income taxes to be levied on corporations and the wealthy, a government takeover of transportation and communications industries, a liberal expansion of the national monetary supply, strong regulations to curb absentee land ownership and speculation in agricultural real estate, and a "Sub-Treasury Plan" in which the federal government would build and manage a network of warehouses where farmers could store commodities for collective marketing and obtain low-interest loans through the U.S. Treasury Department. The St. Louis platform also proposed direct elections for U.S. Senate seats and endorsed an eight-hour workday for industrial laborers. Defying assumptions about rural people's "traditional" dread of federal power, thousands of rural Ozarkers embraced the national farmer movement's declaration: "We believe that the power of government—in other words, of the people—should be expanded . . . as rapidly and as far as the good sense of an intelligent people and the teachings of experience shall justify, to the end that oppression, injustice, and poverty shall eventually cease in the land."[25]

The political insurgency of the farmers' organizations made some strong showings in local and state elections in Arkansas during the 1880s. Agrarian protestors mounted their greatest challenge to conservative Democratic Party rule in the state in 1888, when they forged a political alliance with Arkansas's small but growing class of industrial workers and the Knights of Labor. Christened the Union Labor Party and chaired by old B of F organizer Isaac Mc-Cracken, the agrarian political rebels and their industrial-laborer allies put forth a slate of candidates to contest the political monopoly of Arkansas's Democratic establishment. The state's small Republican Party, which, in addition to African Americans in eastern Arkansas, owed much of its survival after Reconstruction to rural mountain voters in certain sections of the western Ozarks, endorsed many of the Union Labor Party's political positions and candidates, including its gubernatorial nominee C. M. Norwood. Mountain Republicans in the Ozarks, much like other rural supporters of the GOP "west of the Mississippi, where Republicanism remained a distinctly progressive faith," embraced the Populist ethic and rejected the conservative economic principles held dear by Eastern capitalists who dominated the national party apparatus. The Union Labor Party's 1888 platform included demands for tight government regulations on rates charged by railroad companies, a state-enforced cap of 6 percent on the profits of private utility companies, a complete ban on nonresident land ownership in

Arkansas, the abolition of convict labor, the elimination of mandatory, nonpaid road work by citizens, new tax reforms that especially raised revenue for public education, and a law preventing companies from hiring private police to use against their workers.[26]

The 1888 Union Labor ticket came closer to unseating the Democratic Party's near-absolute control of the state than any had since Reconstruction or than any would until the second half of the twentieth century. But it came up short. The September election was one of the ugliest and most blatantly undemocratic in Arkansas's history, wrought with virulent race-baiting, fraud and intimidation at the polls, and even violence and assassination. The official election count indicated that Union Labor gubernatorial candidate Norwood had lost to the Democratic incumbent, eastern Arkansas planter and merchant James P. Eagle, by a mere fifteen thousand votes. Though Norwood and fellow farmer-labor insurgents contested the election results, the Democratic-controlled legislature demanded that they pay $40,000 to finance a recount, so that "the price of justice was too high for a Party comprised of poor farmers and workers." The Democratic establishment also quickly embarked on a ruthless legislative assault that granted their party near-absolute control over local election precincts, imposed new burdens on illiterate voters, and enacted a poll tax, all in the name of "election reform." These measures stymied future attempts to forge another politically viable working-class opposition party.[27]

Some Arkansas historians have pointed to 1888 as the "high-water mark . . . for political insurgency" in the state, but, just as the far less numerous Mountain Republicans had tried to co-opt agrarian defiance, the popular rural revolt galvanized a growing economic Left in the Democratic Party to overthrow the old conservative gospel of laissez-faire, in word if not always in deed.[28] To the chagrin of many wealthy planters and corporate interests, Democrats sympathetic to the agrarian cause worked to absorb populist sentiments and muscled their way into the party's power structure. Before the turn of the century, they finally discovered their leader in the rambunctious and adept orator and politician Jeff Davis of Pope County. "Populists—why, I used to hate them," Davis remarked in one campaign speech, "but I did not know as much then as I do now; I did not have as much sense then as I have now."[29]

The ambitious Davis first erected the sail of his soon-to-be historical political career into the ferocious winds of rural populism in 1899, when, as the state's attorney general, he embarked on a merciless war against insurance companies and other corporations by loosely interpreting Arkansas's existing antitrust laws. Davis declared that his prosecutorial efforts represented "the first stroke in the great battle of the masses against the classes." "My God, if there ever was a cold-blooded, arrogant, high-handed, obstreperous, hard-to-down trust it is the insurance business," Davis quipped. When the conservative Arkansas Supreme Court—those "five jackasses" in Little Rock, as Davis called them—overruled him and virtually wiped out a year's worth of his office's work, his image as a populist defender of the meek working man and emergence as a "hillbilly folk hero" reached new heights. "Styling himself a martyr," Davis promised rural voters in his first gubernatorial campaign that "if I win this race I have got to win it from every railroad, every bank and two-thirds of the lawyers and most of the big politicians. But if I can get the plain people of the country to help me, God bless you, we will clean the thing out." After scoring the "most resounding political victory in Arkansas history" in 1900, Davis, despite stiff resistance from political opponents, went on to achieve a few important populist-progressive reforms during his three terms as governor—namely, some stronger antitrust legislation and much-needed changes to the state's prison system.[30]

Once in office, however, Davis demonstrated that his abilities on the campaign stump far exceeded his statesmanship. Indeed, much more than any meaningful policy changes, one of the greatest legacies of Davis's remarkable career was his construction of a powerful Democratic Party coalition that, notwithstanding his radical rhetoric, transcended class, the rift between town and country, and even the historically pronounced divide between Arkansas's lowlands and uplands. His new machine "brought him added power and security, but it also compromised the ideological integrity of the Davis movement" because many of his political allies "had little sympathy for and little understanding of the revolt that had brought Davis to power." "He was an innovative politician who knew how to acquire and hold power," writes his most prominent biographer, "yet his administration produced more politics than government, more rhetoric than reform."[31] An archetype of nebulous populism, Davis once contended that the "old Populist Party advocated some of the grandest doctrines the world ever new" with its proposal for a government takeover of the railroad industry and other "public franchises," and he declared that "you can legislate prosperity into a country if you have the right kind of men to do the legislating." Davis, nevertheless, effected practically no substantive change for working people during his long political career.[32]

Despite his often-rowdy rhetoric, Davis governed in a way that proved acceptable to those invested in the status quo. He continued to appeal to large numbers of the dispossessed in the backcountry, however, because he masterfully portrayed himself as one of them: a humble underdog fighting valiantly in an unfair fight against the abusive powers that be. Like an early-twentieth-century Ozarks version of David battling Goliath, Davis vowed to "let the scavengers of plutocracy howl!" and promised his rural constituents, "Insignificant as I am, if my political career be marked, let them sharpen their blade, for I will be here at the appointed hour, and while here only God can stay my voice in behalf of organized, united labor and the yeomanry of America."[33]

One of Davis's most successful tactics for building and holding together his political coalition was his exploitation of the racial fears of rural and town-dwelling whites of all classes. Davis once boasted, "I told the boys around Morrilton, Russellville, and Plumerville, that if they elected me, I would fill the penitentiary so full of niggers their feet would be sticking out of the windows." As governor, though ultimately unsuccessful, Davis also proposed a bill that would have racially segregated state tax revenues earmarked for schools, arguing that "every time you educate a 'nigger' you spoil a good field hand." Davis's race-baiting rhetoric rivaled that of any of the staunchest Southern white supremacists of his time. "We may have a lot of dead niggers in Arkansas, but we shall never have negro equality," he once bellowed in a speech, "and I want to say that I would rather tear, screaming from her mother's arms, my little daughter and bury her alive than to see her arm in arm with the best nigger on earth." Davis even made national headlines in 1905 when, in giving opening remarks before a crowd of forty thousand people to welcome President Theodore Roosevelt to Little Rock, he openly defended lynching, prompting the president to scold the Arkansas governor when he took the stage. And to top off his racist political agenda, Davis led the charge for the adoption of mandatory whites-only primary elections by Arkansas's Democratic Party in 1906, vowing that "'nigger' dominion will never prevail in this beautiful Southland of ours, as long as shotguns and rifles lie around loose, and we are able to pull the trigger."[34]

Rabid hillbilly racism, much like presumably anti-"furriner" sentiments, has long figured prominently in stereotypical accounts and imagery of rural mountain isolation and cultural backwardness. Rural racism in the Ozarks, though, as virulent and nasty as it often was, can hardly be interpreted as anything "exceptional" in late-nineteenth- and early-twentieth-century America. Moreover, while racial fear—which at times led to horrific white-on-black violence and even racial "cleansing"—pervaded the Ozarks during the era, it did not necessarily trump anti-elitist sentiments in the rural backcountry. In fact, racial conflict often blended with rural whites' antipathy for wealthy and privileged elites, just as it frequently did in urban working-class communities across America. White hill people tended to see the migration of new blacks to the region during the late 1800s and early 1900s as one of industrialization's alarming social changes, along with growing economic inequality and rural dispossession. In 1894, white working-class vigilantes in Black Rock in western

Lawrence County, for instance, protested low wages, company layoffs, and the increasingly imbalanced economic control of the area's lumber industrialists by first vowing to expel the business owners' new "cheap" black laborers and then by threatening to destroy company property. Similarly, local working-class whites in Polk County in the Ouachita Mountains, who were also joined by some Eastern European immigrants who had recently arrived to the area, kicked up in 1896 when the Kansas City, Pittsburg and Gulf Railroad Company imported thirty black laborers to help construct its new railway through the county, sparking a violent standoff between local industrial elites and working-class whites who felt that local labor ought to have been employed with decent wages to do the work.[35] Skillful politicians like Jeff Davis, then, frequently succeeded in deploying race to undercut a potentially greater populist union of a working-class economic Left that might have otherwise shattered his and his party's fragile coalitions between town and country, local elites and backcountry folks, and the lowlands and uplands.

Racial animosity, however, did not *inevitably* obstruct class-based populism in the region. While many farmers' organizations sought to avoid race or outright barred black membership, evidence suggests that in cases when agrarian leaders and organizers made the decision to take up the issue of racial inclusiveness and deliberately attempted to convince white farmers and workers that poor blacks were experiencing the same struggles against elite oppressors that they were, they could have some success in overcoming staunch racial divisions, at least politically. Arkansas's significantly disfranchised People's Party in the early 1890s openly championed major reforms to bring economic justice to "the downtrodden regardless of race," a political stance that one prominent historian has called the South's "clearest record of racial liberalism." The early-twentieth-century agrarian radical Sam Faubus of Madison County, furthermore, came around to believing that "if the powerful could keep down one group such as blacks . . . then the powerful could keep down another group such as poor hillside farmers." Historian James M. Beeby has convincingly shown that it "is striking how racism often circumscribed the limits of Populist dissent and prevented unity along class lines." But he says "it is also clear that African Americans and whites often did come together, however briefly and despite mutual suspicion, to espouse and, in some cases, enact significant economic and political change." "The Populists," writes Beeby, "were a product of their time, but . . . [they] sought to reorient southern society in a more progressive way, both politically and economically."[36] Still, rural whites' racial prejudices stood as the greatest barrier to forging a united working-class protest movement. Thus, most rural whites' unwillingness to embrace blacks and "others" who were different as fellow working people probably figures as the biggest missed opportunity of the "populist moment" and its democratic potential to reverse the deterioration of rural opportunities.

Along with race, Jeff Davis and his Democratic machine also utilized intentionally vague rhetoric and often took squishy positions that could easily appeal to the region's powerful business elites and poor backcountry folks alike, though for very different reasons. Railing against the federal government's adherence to the gold standard and lampooning giant monopolies in the Northeast, after all, scored big points with both the plain folks in the backcountry and the region's well-bred elites who envied northern industrial privilege. The populist Democrat-supporting but also local industry-boosting editor of the *Mountain Wave* in Searcy County, for instance, complained in October 1898 that "the majority of farmers and laborers throughout the country have less ready money and are living harder now than ever before—thanks to the iniquitous gold standard and the trusts." Gold-loving politicians in the East, such as William McKinley, could also make for easy targets that could command general agreement in the region: "The god of the republican party is gold," the same editor had touted about a year earlier in 1897.[37]

Many business elites in the Ozarks eventually came around to embrace even the radical populist demand to have the federal government nationalize railroads and other utility industries, but only because they believed economic development in their region had been slighted by private companies. In March 1899 the business-minded editor of Pope County's *Courier-Democrat* professed that he and other local leaders had come to "unequivocally favor" the public ownership of railroads and other utilities, insisting, "We are almost out of breath trying to catch up and climb into the band-wagon." Similarly, the editor of Searcy County's newspaper complained in October 1897 about "Mr. Morgan's railroad scheme" and explained that "we have been slow to believe that government ownership of railroads would be best for this country, but that would be infinitely more preferable."[38]

Some local elites, moreover, began to take new pains to rebut accusations by traditional economic conservatives who charged that "populism" represented a heretical slap in the face to Thomas Jefferson's founding vision of America. The *Courier-Democrat* editor printed an article in April 1901 praising the recent remarks made by New York senator David B. Hill to the Jefferson Club in Buffalo. Hill, the article reported, rebuffed conservative Jeffersonian disciples of "limited government" by pointing to the venerated president's own "extension of American institution"—namely, the Louisiana Purchase of 1803. Though sure to note that "true" Jeffersonian ideology "stands against radicalism of every description" and is "opposed to plutocracy on the one hand and to communism on the other," Hill insisted that the founding father would have certainly advocated extensions of government power that promoted "democratic expansion." "Jefferson's teachings might suggest a limitation upon the amount of dividends which could be lawfully declared," for instance, "or upon the profits which could be legally accumulated by these tremendous business organizations." "When billion dollar corporation combines are forming on every side . . . it is high time to consider whether some wholesome restrictions upon such corporate undertakings are not essential in the interest of the people." Similarly, an editorial in Searcy County's *Mountain Wave* compared populist Democrat and presidential contender William Jennings Bryan to "Thomas Jefferson, the great founder of democracy." It praised comments made by Bryan in a recent Labor Day speech in St. Louis, particularly his assertion that "not only must any real prosperity begin with those who toil, but the Nation's progress toward a higher civilization must be measured by the progress made by the producing classes." "It is the average progress, not the progress of the few, that must always be considered," said Bryan.[39]

Beneath such defiant and reform-demanding political rhetoric, though, Ozark elites' "populist" vision usually differed significantly from that of increasingly dispossessed rural folks in their locales, if the editorial positions of most county-seat newspapers in the region are any indication. While his paper was prone to scoff at the country's dominance by powerful Northeastern monopolies, the "populist"-professing editor of the *Sharp County Record* also praised in 1890 the fact that "millions of northern capital are flowing into the southern states for permanent investments." Ironically, the article was printed below a celebratory advertisement about a new edition of a popular book on the recent history of the agrarian political movement. Likewise, the editor of the *Mountain Echo* in Marion County bragged in 1898 that he had just sold the mineral rights to more than eight hundred acres of hill land at a great profit and encouraged his local readers to take notice of the potential for the area's economic growth because "the woods are getting full of men wanting to make investments."[40]

The evolving editorial positions of Searcy County's *Mountain Wave* on the politics of railroads between September 1897 and September 1899 also reveal the particularly commercial, development-oriented agenda of local elites' brand of the "populist persuasion." In September 1897 the editor excitedly reported on the hopeful "prospects" that the Frisco Railroad and a couple of other companies might be planning to construct tracks through Searcy County. "No matter what road builds into North Arkansas," he wrote, "others will be forced to follow, and whichever company does the forcing act should and will have the everlasting gratitude of the people of this country." Only a few weeks later, when company plans apparently fell through, the disappointed and likely angry *Wave* belatedly endorsed the populist call for publicly owned railroads, stating, "[Now] we see no way out of it but for the State to own the railroads." Meanwhile, however, since the nation's and state's conservative political leadership at the time probably meant in reality that "there is no longer hope" for a publicly owned railroad project in the area, at least in the foreseeable future, the *Wave's* editor encouraged the region's political leaders to "turn their attention to some other practical schemes to secure an outlet for our immense natural wealth." Namely, he called for exploring the possibilities of a government-funded "internal improvement" project to widen and deepen the Buffalo River so that it could be connected commercially to the navigable White River. The *Wave* also demanded the construction and improvement of overland roads in the region.[41]

But the *Wave* never gave up on the promise of what an iron horse might mean for the future "prosperity" of the county. Pointing to the "inter-montane" area in and around Wiley's Cove, particularly its agricultural potential and rich mineral and timber resources, one local business booster insisted that political leaders in Little Rock "should become thoroughly acquainted" with the striking similarities of this currently "undeveloped" mountainous area to that of the booming Appalachian city of Asheville, North Carolina. "Arkansas is to have here a most important mountain city," he envisioned, " . . . once the country has become accessible by means of railroads." Alas, in 1899 the North Arkansas Railroad Company revealed definite plans to construct tracks through and erect depots in Searcy County. Apparently having abandoned his former position on government-owned railroads, the *Wave's* editor now became an ardent booster for the company and even began heading up a drive to raise a "bonus of $7,000" from local citizens to provide the railroad company with some extra incentive. By September 1899, he was running a weekly column titled "Is Your Name Here? If Not, Why Not?" in which he listed the names and amounts donated for the "North Arkansas Railroad bonus," urging citizen-minded locals to contribute to the future economic progress of the area.[42]

For many backcountry Ozarkers, however, the late-nineteenth- and early-twentieth-century Populist ethic invoked very different ideas and visions. While some undoubtedly supported the "development" plans of regional elites, many others viewed the uneven realities of businessmen's visions and motives as antithetical to their goals of widely shared smallholder prosperity in the rural Ozarks. While most backcountry folks seconded local elites' complaints against Northeastern monopolies and their favoritism in most federal policymaking, many detested just as much, if not more so, the well-to-do *local* elites who disproportionately wielded political and economic control *within* the Ozarks. Sharp County farmers' movement organizer and future Populist Party gubernatorial candidate W. S. Morgan noted this more radical potential of the malleable "populist persuasion" among the rural folks he worked with and encountered in the region:

> Many persons seemed to conceive the idea that it was an instantaneous cure-all for every evil which inflicts humanity. . . . Some of them had an impression that . . . [it] had a mission to redress a specific private grievance. Some thought that the paramount object was to wage hostile war upon the one-horse country merchants, and hailed it with delight as the means by which said merchants were to be driven out of business. Others who had been swindled by commission men, conceived the idea that its special mission was to displace this class of tradesmen. Still others, who were riding some political hobby, thought they saw their opportunity . . . for . . . airing their views, and, possibly, riding into some lucrative office on this promising young steed. Many others had a vague idea that *something* was going to happen. They did not know exactly what, or how, but saw there was a great popular uprising which would revolutionize things.[43]

Tucked beneath this broad and malleable populist ethos that managed to appeal to practically all stripes in the Ozarks were intense conflicts within the region between rural debtors and their wealthier merchant-creditors, town dwellers (and their social and economic interests) and country folks (and their interests), and the agendas of larger prosperous agriculturalists and those of poor and middling smallholders. Some of the more dramatic and tragic conflicts made the local news. In November 1897, for instance, the Pope County newspaper briefly reported on a bloody altercation between a local merchant and a farmer who "became involved in a difficulty about a settlement." Claiming he acted in "self-defense," the merchant "drew his pistol and shot at [the farmer] five times, two bullets taking effect, one piercing each lung." In the same issue, the newspaper also reported that a few days earlier "some unknown person placed a stick of dynamite underneath a rail" on the railroad tracks in the area, "but it was fortunately discovered and removed a few minutes before a passenger train was due at that point." In another probable example of violent conflict between the local haves and have-nots in the region, some unknown "incendiaries" in Carroll County torched "the general store of J. N. Cardwell & Son" on the first day of February 1899, causing the merchant a "loss [of] about $10,000."[44]

Of course, despite stereotypical mountain imagery to the contrary, most rifts between backcountry folks and local elites did not end with such sensational violence. Still, rural defiance against prominent members of local establishments in the Ozarks was widespread, and regional elites hoped desperately to keep a lid on such radical populist challenges to their control. The editor of Searcy County's *Mountain Wave*, for example, cited the recent condemnation of radical resistance by one of many rural Ozarkers' greatest national political heroes, William Jennings Bryan, who warned that "those who have suggested that the burning of property and the destruction of life as a means of settling labor disputes do not understand the genius of our institutions." The *Wave* editor took the opportunity to extrapolate for his local readers. Omitting any mention of Arkansas's recent "election reform" laws that had effectively disfranchised many the region's poorest rural voters, the editor lectured that "the ballot is in the hand of every American citizen above the age of 21 years. He can use it to correct every abuse of power and every injustice imposed by the strong upon the weak." He continued:

> There is no anarchy in Democracy. There is nothing in its traditions or in its creed which councils [sic] violence for the correction of public or private wrongs. There is nothing but equal justice and good order in Democracy, and those who interpret its character in any other way do not understand the genius of the party of Jefferson and Jackson.[45]

The editor of the populist-leaning, pro-Bryan *Courier-Democrat* in Pope County also seemed to worry about *excessive* populism creeping into the established political channels. In July 1901 he reprinted some comments, with which he apparently agreed, made by former Missouri governor W. J. Stone, who had recently warned about the dangers of trusting the more rambunctious agrarian political leaders with too many leadership positions in the Democratic Party, particularly those who had "deserted their party in 1896, 1898 and 1900" to support third-party Populist candidates. "I am not opposed to the return of the prodigals, and in fact I am anxious to have them return," said Stone. "As Mr. Bryan said, I would be willing to barbecue the fatted calf when they do return," he continued, "but I would not be willing to make them a deed to the farm and I would want them to help the old hands raise one crop at least before making them the overseers." The agrarian-populist revolt had shifted the Democratic Party in Arkansas away from its old conservative laissez-faire ideology, much as it had done to its national counterpart, but many of the party's established elites and supporters clearly worried about the radical potential that the Populist ethic had stirred at the grass roots.[46]

By the 1910s, despite his inability to accomplish much meaningful reform, many rural Ozarkers continued to cast their votes for Jeff Davis and the populist-sounding allies of his Democratic coalition, confident that they were doing the best they could for the common folks against nearly impossible odds. Davis's shrinking margins of electoral victory and the gradual crumbling of his political machine, however, may indicate that some rural voters began to grow impatient with too much talk and not enough action.[47] A sizeable minority of rural working-class Ozarkers, in fact, began organizing and joining local chapters of the Socialist Party during the first decade of the 1900s, asking "By what rule of truth, right or justice has any other person a right to labor's production?" These backcountry radicals contended that "the laboring people will never be satisfied with anything less that [sic] all of the wealth they produce . . . [because] labor's share to the wealth he produces is all." In fact, drawing on a conceptual combination of "republican ideals expressed in the Declaration of Independence, the moral teachings of Jesus Christ, and the political theories of Karl Marx," these "hillbilly socialists" made some backcountry communities in the Arkansas Ozarks, along with their rural Oklahoma neighbors, hotbeds for one of "the most vigorous, ambitious, and fascinating" movements of political radicalism in American history.[48]

Many other rural Ozarkers took their populist sensibilities in a less insurgent direction. Beginning in 1906, local chapters of the Farmers' Union (Farmers' Educational and Cooperative Union of America)—probably the closest heirs to the late-nineteenth-century farmers' organizations—formed throughout the region to press for more issue-specific reforms. Local chapters of the Farmers' Union lobbied for and endorsed candidates—Democrats, Republicans, or Socialists—who would support more equitable and progressive taxation, expansions of public and agricultural education, and various forms of government protection and assistance for common farmers and other rural folks. Arkansas's new and rising cadre of more urban-oriented "Progressives" in the Democratic Party, in fact, who also determined in their own way to expand the role of government to "improve" the lives of the citizenry, began diligently to court the votes of the organization's rural members. After all, as one member put it, they "very much needed most of the Farmers Union vote" to defeat the Old Guard Democrats and remnants of the Davis machine. Knowing that the "union represented a potentially huge bloc of voters" and that "it had more members than any other organized interest group in the state," George W. Donaghey, who would be elected as Arkansas's first "Progressive" governor in 1908, gave the "welcome address" at the Farmers' Union's annual state convention in 1907.[49]

However rural Ozarkers decided to vote during the early twentieth century— that is, those who could afford to pay their poll taxes and were not too illiterate after "election reforms" were imposed in the early 1890s—it was clear that their

Ozarkers at a Farmers' Union cooperative warehouse in Springdale, Arkansas. Photo S-2006-24-54.
Courtesy of the Shiloh Museum of Ozark History, Springdale.

broader sensibilities about government were shaped by the Populist ethic that had been aroused at the grass roots during the last two decades of the nineteenth century. These were not the hard-shell antigovernment mountaineers simplistically depicted in much of Ozarks legend and lore. In this Gilded Age of concentrating wealth, growing inequality, and rural dispossession, most working-class Ozarkers demanded a good "cleaning out" of the rich and powerful from government institutions and what they called a "restoration" of the principle of "people's rule" to meet the newest challenges of modern America.

To do so, backcountry populists insisted that the "people's republic" should flex its muscles in new and unprecedented ways to protect common people against their greedy oppressors. "It was a vision informed by historical experience—by the structure and dynamic of the family farm, the shop, and the local market; by notions of government as the repository of the public will and the defender of the public good—and tailored to the exigencies of an expansive society," explains historian Steven Hahn.[50] While the populist ethos proved flexible enough to forge a rather unspecific and vague consensus of anti-establishmentarianism in the region, populism aroused radical resistance at the grass roots, particularly in the backcountry, that often turned its indictments upon local Ozark elites who disproportionately commanded economic and political power in the region as much as it did upon "outsider" oppressors. It would be this dynamic of *local conflict within the Ozarks*, more so than some supposed cultural antipathy of federal authority passed down in rural isolation by the region's earliest settlers, that shaped backcountry folks' sensibilities as they resisted their "first tastes" of the emerging American state's pro-business "reform" powers during the first half of the twentieth century.

PART II
RURAL RESISTANCE

2

FIRST TASTES: MOONSHINERS AND G-MEN

In September 1897, national and regional newspapers reported on the tragic kill-ing of two U.S. deputy marshals by moonshiners in the rugged Arkansas Ozarks. Determined to quash illicit distilling, marshals B. F. Taylor and Joe Dodson had led a small raiding party into northeastern Pope County, a place described by Little Rock's *Arkansas Gazette* as "one of the wildest regions imaginable . . . remote from the centers of civilization." There, "Desperate Mountaineers" al-ways stood ready "to resist the invading arm of the law," the *Gazette* continued. The *New York Times* reported that as the marshals came within thirty yards of "one of the largest stills in the mountains," they "walked into an ambush, and the unerring aim of the lawless mountaineers . . . made short work of them." The torrents of gunfire killed Taylor and Dodson on the spot and wounded two others before the unseen moonshiners escaped from the scene.[1]

In the ensuing days, authorities and the Taylor family offered a combined reward of $1,000 for the capture and conviction of the guilty parties. Federal, state, and local lawmen worked diligently to apprehend the suspects. More than a year later, officials finally apprehended their key suspect, a Van Buren County farmer named Harve Bruce. Bruce, who was also a Confederate veteran and for-mer deputy sheriff, at first "emphatically denie[d] his guilt" but later admitted to killing the marshals, claiming that he was the only one at the still who fired his weapon at the lawmen. But he insisted that he had done so in self-defense and had returned fire only after the feds shot first.[2]

Such widely publicized scuffles between moonshiners and federal lawmen in the southern mountains seem at first glance to illuminate an exceptional culture of unbending antigovernment attitudes—a cultural ethos assumed to have remained unchanged in rural isolation and unmovable tradition since the first pioneer settlers of the early nineteenth century. Tales of doggedly independent backwoods moonshiners resisting the feds, in fact, have probably contributed more than anything to shaping assumptions about an authority-defying rural culture. As historians and other scholars of the mountain South have argued, however, such imagined cultural imagery often tells us more about those who narrate the stories than the realities of hill folks themselves.[3]

Probing beneath the myths that have shrouded the violent 1897 affair in Pope County reveals that the burdens of an increasingly uneven rural political economy had much more to do with Bruce's and his fellow moonshiner-farmers' resistance than some timeless antigovernment culture. Rural Ozarkers like Bruce, who made moonshine, resisted specific government regulations and law enforcement because they felt unjustly prohibited from pursuing an agricultural and entrepreneurial pursuit that held the best promise for sustaining their way of life and prospering as family farmers in increasingly opportunity-strapped hill communities. As was the case for distillers plying their trade in the Great Smoky Mountains back east, "the story of moonshine," notes historian Daniel S. Pierce, "is a story of how people of little, and often worsening, means tried to find ways to cope with the difficulties of life."[4] Contrary to the dominant perception of the moonshine "wars" as primarily clashes between parochial rural denizens and government outsiders—or "furriners"—intruding into local affairs with their distant bureaucratic agendas, a closer look at the violent altercation in Pope County more accurately reflects the contest for power between *locals within the region* amid the uneven development of industrialization in Gilded Age America. Specifically, it illuminates the competing social and economic interests that frequently divided the region's supporters of an industrial and agribusiness-oriented political economy run by local business elites and small-farm families who welcomed modern opportunities but seemed to more and more find themselves with the short end of the stick as change occurred.

Harve Bruce's and other moonshiners' defiance in the Ozarks is best understood when viewed in the context of the more radical strands of grassroots resistance unleashed amid the broader and variegated populist ethos that swept the region during the late nineteenth and early twentieth centuries. In fact, these were no conservative defenders of small-government ideological purity. Most rural and town-dwelling Ozarkers—poor farmers and laborers, well-to-do landowners and businessmen, Democrats, Republicans, and third-party supporters alike—called for a pragmatic government to exert its power on behalf of "the people" and against "special interests," however differently they defined those "people" and "special interests." This general populist political culture, as we have already seen, held different meanings for different folks in the Ozarks, just as it did elsewhere throughout rural America. Well-bred and prosperous farmers and businessmen in the Ozarks tended to view "Big Capital" in the American Northeast as the primary obstacle for their vision of growing New South capitalism in the region. But struggling and dispossessed smallholders like Bruce and his fellow moonshiners resented just as much how the privileged elites *within* the region controlled and administered the arms of government power to further their own agendas. In reality, most rural working folks in the Ozarks longed for a strong, well-regulated, egalitarian republic to arise, but they detested how at that time only the well-to-do seemed able to employ the power of the American state and, in their minds, use that power at the expense of hard-working common folks like themselves.

Intra-regional conflict is usually missing in most depictions of the rural Ozarks and its troubled encounters with "modernity." Ironically, despite homogenous images of the southern mountains as the domain of tradition-defending, authority-defying, and liquor-gulping mountaineers, many Ozarkers had actually come to champion strong government regulations on the liquor trade, and, increasingly, outright prohibition by the early twentieth century. Temperance advocates in the region's towns had long crusaded against the "evil drink," since even before the Civil War, but more and more rural folks in the countryside began demanding new laws to curtail alcohol amid the social, cultural, and economic changes brought on by industrialization in the region in the late 1800s.[5] As historian Bruce E. Stewart explains in his study of the prohibition movement in Southern Appalachia, temperance reformers' "critique of alcohol culture and distilling was finally accepted because it made practical sense to many rural denizens who, adapting to a changing economic environment, discovered that preindustrial drinking mores fit poorly with the demands of life and labor in the New South."[6]

The boisterous dynamics of new railroad, timber, and mining camps and trading centers throughout the region shook the familiar social order and began to convince many white hill folks that alcohol "has been at the bottom of more crimes and heartaches than almost everything else combined," as one resident in the railroad town of Imboden put it. Many rural ministers finally began teaching about the "sins of alcohol" that evangelists in larger towns had been shouting from their pulpits for decades, appealing to the "moral side" of local citizens and "trusting and praying for the complete annihilation of the Liquor Traffic in

Arkansas." In the 1912 general election, for instance, antiliquor advocates led a flawless voting campaign—probably through local churches—among small farmers in Marion County's Bearden Township who resided just to the north of Rush, a rowdy and rapidly growing zinc-mining town. One hundred percent of the voters there opposed the state's issuance of distilling and dispensary licenses, the only legal means of buying and selling alcohol in Arkansas.[7]

Rural antiliquor sentiment, in fact, had risen rather abruptly in Arkansas during the last two decades of the nineteenth century and became the most decisive factor in the state's march toward statewide prohibition in 1915. In 1882 only 36.3 percent of the voters in Arkansas, most of whom resided in larger towns and cities, had favored a ban on the state's licensing of saloons and distilleries within their respective voting precincts. By 1894, however, a majority of voters wanted to ban liquor licenses in their local precincts. Although voting returns fluctuated back and forth by a few percentage points during subsequent elections, the polls indicated by 1904 that most rural Arkansawyers aimed to steer their state up the "progressive" road of prohibition. Indeed, for many rural folks the anti-alcohol crusade fit squarely within the broader political culture of populist reform, as temperance advocates and prohibitionists attacked America's "liquor trusts" and "King Alcohol" for filling their coffers by preying on humble families and communities.[8]

Some of the most significant political pressure for heavier government regulations on the liquor trade in Arkansas, in fact, came from the Ozarks. In January 1901, for instance, state senator N. J. Carlock of Madison County introduced a bill that, if passed, would have added to the state's existing local regulations by requiring any person who wanted to purchase alcohol to buy a $5 license from the county clerk. Violating the statute would require a $100 fine on both the buyer and the seller. Though the "Whiskey License Bill" was handily defeated the first time it came to the floor of the state senate—with some even saying that it "was considered a joke" initially—the persistent senator from the Ozarks managed to have it brought up for another vote in April. This time, much to the surprise of Russellville's *Courier-Democrat*, the senate passed "the celebrated whiskey drinking bill," and hopeful antiliquor proponents predicted that its passage in the general assembly would "virtually result in abolishing the saloon traffic in this State."[9]

Carlock's bill ultimately failed in the lower house, but the strong political support it had received further energized temperance and prohibition advocates and revealed the growth of antiliquor sentiments in many rural areas. After all, as an ever-increasing number of hill folks adapted to the new American political economy, the economic importance of alcohol manufacturing to many farm communities had waned considerably by the late nineteenth and early twentieth centuries, particularly for those with better and more economical access to improved transportation networks for shipping crops to market. Like a growing number of Appalachian "country folk" in Stewart's study, many rural Ozarkers, now "more connected to the market economy and embracing New South rhetoric, increasingly yearned to 'improve' themselves both economically and morally" and decided that government was obligated to strictly regulate or completely ban the sale and consumption of alcohol to promote their communities' general welfare.[10]

Voting returns on the local-option for liquor licenses in locales bear out the influence of agricultural marketing opportunities on sentiments about alcohol in the Ozarks. In Washington County, the home of the University of Arkansas and one of the most prosperous agricultural areas of the state, voters in twenty-six of the county's twenty-nine townships voted against licenses in 1906, and the antiliquor forces lost by fewer than five percentage points in each of the other three precincts.[11] With access to no fewer than five railroad lines (including spurs) that crisscrossed the county and a comparatively larger number of improved overland roads that ran through the gently rolling terrain, not to mention the county's relative proximity to the navigable Arkansas River, farmers working the fertile soils of the Springfield Plain in the northwestern corner of the region generally enjoyed more extensive and diverse marketing opportunities than those to their east. These farmers also tended to benefit the most from new scientific farming programs administered by the state's federally funded Agricultural Experiment Station, established in 1888 at the public university in Fayetteville. The state's agricultural commissioner, A. G. Vincenheller, bragged in October 1897, for instance, that orchard farmers in Washington and Benton Counties "have money to burn" from their "immense" sales to Kansas City, Canadian, and English firms, and this prosperity only added to area wheat farmers' lucrative marketing opportunities.[12] From the late nineteenth century through the twentieth, in fact, Washington County claimed "the highest agricultural income of any county in Arkansas."[13] Distilling and selling crops as liquor, then, made less sense to better-off and better-connected farmers on the prosperous Springfield Plain. Free from dependence on the manufacture and sale of whiskey themselves and convinced that the "liquor problem" lay at the root of new social disorder and moral depravity, an overwhelming majority of Washington County residents insisted that "sinful" alcohol had no place in their communities.

Antiliquor proponents held majorities in many other counties throughout the Ozarks by the early twentieth century as well. But sentiments were more evenly divided in more remote areas with more limited transportation networks and fewer agricultural marketing opportunities—as well as a lack of capital and resources to exploit those few that were available. Thus, in these areas, making whiskey proved economically important for some. In 1912, for instance, voters in ten of Sharp County's nineteen townships voted against liquor licenses, while proliquor proponents carried eight precincts; residents in one township, Lebanon, split their votes exactly in half. The proliquor forces also won a slim majority of the precincts in Marion County, carrying eleven townships while the antis won ten.[14] Though a railway and some limited road improvements had traversed both of these counties and several others by the early 1900s, less fertile soils and difficult terrain, poorly developed transportation networks, the vagaries of corporate-controlled national and international markets, and a shortage of affordable capital and resources to invest in improved farming methods among small hill farmers in these areas meant that most of the changing economy's new opportunities were reserved for local elites.[15] Larger landowners, prominent businessmen who owned the local mills and gins, market speculators who purchased produce from local farmers for resale to corporate firms in American cities, and, of course, the elite merchants and lenders who controlled the flow of local credit typically profited the most from new economic developments. On the other hand, the particularly uneven ways in which the national and international political economy developed in the region often brought as many burdens as blessings for resource-strapped family farmers.[16] "Like a great threshing machine," as one historian puts it, "an increasingly mechanized agriculture fueled by fluctuating export markets began chewing up and spitting out small farmers like chaff, even as it bagged and hauled off their products for profit elsewhere."[17]

Some smallholders attempting to navigate this environment found that marketing their crops as liquor made the best economic sense, despite the growing anti-alcohol sentiments among many of their rural neighbors. In his quasi-fictionalized account about life in the rural Ozarks, author Wayman Hogue recalled the economic necessities of moonshining for the farm family that he claimed to have boarded with during the late nineteenth century. In Hogue's telling, the family's patriarch, "Mr. Garrison," who was also a member of the local school board, had no choice but to distill his corn and sell it as whiskey if he hoped to prosper as a small hill farmer in his area. As Hogue explained it:

> There was no demand for corn in the valley, except a few bushels now and then. Therefore, in order to market his corn, Mr. Garrison must haul it forty or fifty miles distant to the river farms where they raised mostly cotton. The capacity of

a two-horse wagon was about twenty bushels in the ear. If he succeeded in find-ing a buyer for his corn, the price was not more than fifty cents a bushel, which amounted to ten dollars a load for his corn. He could not really make the trip for that, so the expense of marketing his corn was more than he received for it ... [but] by converting this corn into whiskey, he netted a good profit. Ordinar-ily a bushel of corn would run off about a gallon and a quart of whiskey, which he could sell for something like two dollars and a half a gallon. Therefore, Mr. Garrison's surplus crop of corn, when distilled into whiskey, brought him a gross sum of six or seven hundred dollars, which was a lot of money for one family. ... If he was able to run off ten gallons a day and sell it for twenty-five dollars, he considered he was making big money.[18]

It amazed Hogue, in fact, to see just how vital distilling was to this rural farm family and others in the area. Although he knew that a few of the men were apt to drink a little themselves, he always noticed when he visited their stills that "none of them were drunk or even drinking." "They probably considered that they were at work," Hogue explained, that they viewed making moonshine as a central part of their family business ventures.[19]

Even families in the community with no direct interest in the Garrisons' stills or those of others in the community, Hogue told, benefited from the local moonshining business. The Garrisons and other distillers frequently bought corn or other grains from area farmers, providing a dependable and profitable market for their produce. In addition, some local farmers worked for supple-mental income as part-time laborers at the stills, especially during slow periods in the agricultural cycle, or found employment hauling and selling liquor for the moonshiners. Hogue also wrote that "many of the men who worked at the stills belonged to the church." The local church even made special accommodations for its moonshining members during particularly busy times, he claimed, of-fering services on both Saturdays and Sundays to provide extra opportunities to attend.[20]

Illicit distilling in the Ozarks during the late nineteenth and early twentieth centuries had little to do with the simple persistence of an exceptional mountain culture that had remained unchanged since the earliest pioneers brought their Scots-Irish traditions with them. Far from it, the production of moonshine in the rural Ozarks appears to have *increased* and "reached its zenith," as a former U.S. deputy collector later recalled, during the late 1800s and early 1900s. This was the result of new market incentives created from the larger forces of an interdependent and government-assisted political economy that encouraged industrialization, urbanization, and more capital-intensive agriculture.[21]

Ozarks moonshiners and their distillery in Newton County. Photo S-97-145-24. Courtesy of the Shiloh Museum of Ozark History, Springdale.

While some whiskey was certainly manufactured for local consumption, Ozarks moonshiners found their most lucrative markets in rapidly developing urban centers such as Little Rock and Fort Smith, and Springfield, Missouri, in new timber and mining districts in the region, and in expanding county-seat towns and railroad centers. The federal government's opening of the Indian Territory (present-day Oklahoma) to white settlement and industrial and agricultural development in 1889–90 also provided marketing opportunities for moonshiners in the western and central parts of the region. Distillers in the eastern Ozarks, meanwhile, frequently found buyers in the lowland cotton and rice districts of the Delta region, large parts of which were undergoing massive government-funded drainage projects, road and railroad building, and other economic developments by the early 1900s.[22] Wayman Hogue wrote that "Mr. Garrison" had explained to him that illicit Ozarks moonshine also proved highly attractive to many licensed liquor dealers, because they "got it for less money than . . . from the legalized distilleries" whose prices were driven much higher by government taxes.[23] As historian Charles Thompson Jr. so deftly states it: "Choices people made when turning to liquor production have to be judged in the context of opportunities . . . [and] had a lot to do with broad national policies and economics."[24] Harve Bruce and his fellow moonshiners in Van Buren,

Pope, and Searcy Counties stood among these rural working folks who determined that making and selling liquor afforded a good chance of prospering in the Ozarks.

Born to small farmers in Georgia around 1847, a young Harve Bruce had moved with his family to Winston County, Alabama, by 1860, where his father, William, took work as a tenant farmer. When the Civil War broke out, William enlisted in the Confederate Army; his wife, Sarah, appears to have moved herself and their children to Cherokee County, North Carolina, probably to live near relatives. When Harve turned sixteen in 1863, he too joined the Confederate Army and served throughout the remainder of the war. After the war ended, the Bruce family reunited and spent some time in Tennessee before returning to North Carolina by 1870, where William either bought or inherited a small farm and Harve, now in his early twenties, worked as a farm laborer. The following year, Harve married Hannah Cotter of Sevier County, Tennessee, and they soon started a family of their own. In 1878 the Bruces headed west to settle in Archey Valley Township in Van Buren County, Arkansas, where Harve initially supported his family as a wage laborer.[25]

By the mid-1890s Bruce and his family acquired a farm of their own in Wheeler Township. In 1894 Bruce, like many other Ozarkers, took advantage of federal homesteading programs and received a 160-acre land grant on rugged Oak Mountain in northwestern Van Buren County. Bruce also supplemented his farm income by working part time as a local sheriff's deputy during the early 1890s. Bruce, unlike many of his neighbors, had managed to keep from mortgaging his farm by the end of the decade.[26] To do so, however, he embarked upon a business venture that many of his fellow Ozarkers had come to frown upon as backward and immoral.

A Sunday School man all his life who had undergone a conversion experience and "professed religion" in the early 1890s, Bruce apparently had only recently begun making and selling alcohol when he and his neighbor, Turner Skidmore, formed a distilling partnership near their homes on Oak Mountain during the summer of 1896. Just who their main buyers were remains uncertain, but Bruce and his partner likely discovered a new demand for corn liquor in the area's growing timber and mining camps, especially in the booming zinc and lead fields in nearby Searcy County. Testimony unearthed later during Bruce's trial indicates that he, Skidmore, and their moonshining comrades may have also been doing business with the owner of a wagon yard in Little Rock. In addition, they may have located profitable market connections in the newly developing Indian Territory through Bruce's brother-in-law and other acquaintances who had recently moved there.[27] Whatever the case, Bruce and several of his neighbors had found a market niche that just might make their small farms profitable. Unfortunately for them, they would have to conduct their business outside the parameters of the law.

Many Ozarkers resented Bruce's and other backcountry farmers' illicit economic activities, believing the liquor traffic to be the main culprit behind vice, crime, and social disruption in their towns and communities. The impetus for rooting out moonshining in Pope, Van Buren, and Searcy Counties during the late 1890s, in fact, came not from government bureaucrats in Washington, D.C., or Little Rock, but from concerned, well-to-do locals who were determined to clean up the "deplorable" conditions in their region. Pope County resident John T. Burris initiated the first excursions by federal marshals into the area. Born in 1849 to a prominent tanner in Pope County, Burris owned a hill farm in the northern part of the county by 1880, where he and his wife raised four young children and employed a twenty-three-year-old tenant farmer from Tennessee. In addition to his agricultural endeavors, the well-to-do Burris worked as a skilled mason and carpenter and later ran a sawmill and gristmill. At some point, he also secured a contract to carry the mail for the U.S. Postal Service and appears to have moved his family to Russellville, Pope County's seat of government, by the 1890s.[28] A devout Baptist and prohibitionist, Burris abhorred the manufacture and sale of whiskey on the rise in his section and traveled to Little Rock in November 1896 to meet with Arkansas's head collector of the federal government's Internal Revenue Service. He requested that the government dispatch a party of officers into the Ozarks to "capture the miscreants and destroy their manufacturing plants," but the collector regretfully informed him that his office lacked the necessary funds at the moment to authorize such a mission. Pleading further with the federal official, Burris even offered to "pilot the posse, and if they failed to find things just as he had described them, he would pay all the expense, thus relieving the United States of any expense whatever," but all he got was a promise to keep his request in mind. Burris left Little Rock disappointed, but by the summer of 1897 federal officials in Little Rock finally contacted him to help guide a team of marshals in a concerted hunt for moonshiners and their stills in his home area.[29]

Burris and the feds made one of their first "successful" raids into "the notorious moonshine district in the mountains north of Russellville" around the third week of August, arresting five local farmers, destroying "six illicit stills with a total capacity of 400 gallons," and disposing of "about 2,000 gallons of mash and beer."[30] Bruce's and Skidmore's distillery soon made the top of Burris's list. He and the officers enlisted the help of informant Tom Barnes, a poor resident of Snowball in Searcy County who had relocated there from Putnam County,

Tennessee, sometime during the 1880s. Barnes had known Bruce for nine or ten years and occasionally worked for him and other moonshiners hauling and selling liquor. He was also a regular customer of theirs, buying three or four gallons of whiskey at a time for his own drinking. Unbeknownst to Bruce and Skidmore, Barnes turned traitor when Burris and the federal officers offered him $10 to show them the whereabouts of their still in northwestern Van Buren County.[31]

Barnes told Burris he would only take the feds to the vicinity of the still, fearing that his old friends might see him. Once he turned back, Burris and the officers began searching Oak Mountain for Bruce's and Skidmore's still. Having no luck, Burris and the officers decided to pay Bruce a visit at his house. Burris, who knew Bruce and called him "Uncle Harve," believed that he could convince the moonshiners to surrender their still and turn themselves in. When they arrived at the farmhouse, however, only Bruce's wife and children were at home; he and Skidmore were out working at their still. The officers convinced Bruce's wife, Hannah, to send her daughter out to notify Bruce that U.S. marshals were at the house and wanted to speak with him. When Bruce's daughter found him and gave him the message, he and Skidmore quickly headed into the woods to hide.[32]

According to Bruce's own recollection, when his daughter returned to the house without him, the senior officer, Deputy Revenue Collector J. P. King—who was also an Ozarks resident from the town of Ozark in Franklin County—grew impatient and threatened to "handcuff" her. Meanwhile, Bruce's brother, Alford, arrived and discussed the situation with the officers, so he went alone to Bruce's hiding place to tell him that if he did not go talk with the marshals, they would take his daughter with them. A now-angry Bruce sent his brother back to the house to tell Burris that he would meet him out in the field to talk, but that he had better come unarmed and without any of the other men. Burris agreed, and Bruce's wife and daughter accompanied him to the field to meet the moonshiner.[33]

When they met, Bruce asked Burris if the officers had a warrant for his arrest, and Burris replied that they did not have one yet. Bruce, now undoubtedly as resentful as ever about elite Ozarkers like Burris and King using their privileged positions to exert government power against hard-working farm families like his, asked the officers what right they had to threaten to arrest his innocent daughter. "I respect Mr. King and do not want to hurt anybody," Bruce warned. Burris attempted to diffuse the situation, pleading with Bruce to hand over his still and turn himself in, because it was now a well-known fact that he and Skidmore were making moonshine and that the lawmen would not give up until they found their still and arrested them anyway. He also told Bruce "that in all probability sentence would be suspended during his good behavior" if he would willingly submit now. But Bruce refused, saying that he "would go when the proper time comes," only after he had "straighten[ed] up [his] business" and saw "what they [the authorities] did with the other boys" in the area who had already been arrested. Apparently, Burris also informed Bruce that the law would soon be after him for his and Skidmore's suspected involvement in another recent altercation between moonshiners and officers in neighboring Cleburne County, in which a local lawman was shot in the leg and later died from infection. When Bruce questioned Burris about whether they had any evidence on him, the antiliquor crusader admitted that he did not know "whether they could get enough to get an indictment." Unable to convince Bruce to surrender, Burris returned to the house to rejoin the officers and continued searching the area for the still.[34]

After his meeting with Burris, Bruce rushed to his and Skidmore's hidden distilling site to quickly disassemble the still and move its components deeper into the woods. Bruce evacuated the site just in time; Burris and the feds came traipsing into the holler later that same afternoon and discovered the manufacturing site. The officers were disappointed to find only an empty stillhouse and a few containers of beer and whiskey. They burned the wooden structure and dumped out the liquor before heading back to Russellville. Bruce remained in hiding for the next few weeks to elude Burris and the federal lawmen and even began making plans to leave for the Indian Territory.[35]

Meanwhile, federal marshals in the region ramped up their hunts for other moonshiners during subsequent weeks. One federal marshal—and another well-to-do local resident—who doubled his efforts was Benjamin Franklin Taylor of Searcy County. Born in DeKalb County, Tennessee, in 1839, a strapping young Taylor had moved west to Searcy County, Arkansas, by 1860, where he and his new wife were raising two infant daughters. The Civil War era was a pivotal time for Taylor. Local historians have credited Taylor, an unbending Unionist, with establishing the local Home Guard in the winter of 1862 to protect Searcy Countians and their property from marauding bushwhackers and pro-Confederate bands once the Union Army claimed control of northern Arkansas. He later enlisted in the Union Army's First Regiment, Arkansas Infantry, and then the Third Regiment, Arkansas Cavalry, in which he received a commission as captain in February 1864. After the war, Taylor played a leading role in Searcy County politics during Arkansas's Republican Reconstruction period. Elected to represent his county in the state legislature in 1866, he came home in 1867 to oversee the all-important process of voter registration in Searcy County.

Local lawmen destroy illicit liquor at Russellville, the seat of government for Pope County, in 1909. Courtesy of the Arkansas State Archives, Little Rock.

Eligible voters elected him to serve in the state's general assembly again in 1871. The next year Taylor helped organize a local and state campaign for the Liberal Republican-Democratic ticket and Horace Greeley for president, denouncing the corruption of the Grant administration and calling for an end to federal Reconstruction in the South. By 1870, Taylor had emerged as a powerful and prosperous man in Searcy County. While he had claimed only $350 worth of personal property and no real estate of his own in 1860, he owned $2,500 in personal property and $2,000 in landholdings and other real estate by 1870. In addition to his sizeable farming and landholding interests, Taylor opened a "large steam mill and gin" and a sawmill on Calf Creek in 1875, where he added to his growing fortune—at least by Ozarks standards—by processing and purchasing local farmers' corn, wheat, and timber for resale to urban markets.[36]

Taylor's excessive bent for profitmaking made headlines in Arkansas newspapers in January 1880 when a boiler exploded at his mill and killed four employees, including his own son-in-law. Reporters alleged that Taylor "had been informed by skillful engineers that, in its condition, the boiler of the engine used in the mill was liable to explode at any time," but he had refused to halt production and replace it. When the boiler finally exploded a few days before Christmas in 1879, his son-in-law, Wade Campbell, "was blown through the top of an apple tree, and descended into the lint-room connected with the mill" where he lay dead, and three other employees were "literally blown to pieces."[37]

Despite the bad publicity surrounding the incident, Taylor maintained his prominent and powerful stature in Searcy County. He quickly repaired and re-opened his mill, started a profitable mercantile business, and became one of the cash-starved area's most important financial creditors. He also served as superintendent for the Snowball Sunday School. Although Republicans lost the Arkansas legislature in 1874 to the "Redeemers," marking the end of Reconstruction in the state, and the Democrats even took control of unionist-leaning Searcy County during the next few years, local voters elected Taylor to the state legislature once again in 1880 and to another term in 1882. Interestingly, Taylor applied as an invalid for a Civil War pension in August 1890 after the U.S. Congress enacted a new Dependent Pensions Act, citing an injury to his right hand that he suffered while working at his mill in 1885. By the 1890s, Taylor was "the wealthiest man" in Searcy County and one of the most powerful figures in the area. Soon after President William McKinley took office in 1897 and placed Henry M. Cooper in charge of the U.S. Marshals Service, Taylor, one of Arkansas's most loyal Republicans, received an appointment as a federal deputy marshal. Upon receiving word of his appointment, Searcy County's *Marshall Republican* proudly reported the news, confidently predicting that Taylor "will make a good Marshal and should have the support of all lovers of law and order in any effort to suppress the wild cat distiller." "These individuals are becoming too numerous in this section," the paper continued, "and are becoming so obstructive to good government that many men who have heretofore held aloof and took no decided stand against them are coming out and demanding that they be suppressed."[38]

Taylor teamed up with fellow deputy marshal Joe M. Dodson—yet another native and well-born Ozarker—to begin scouring the hills for local farmers engaged in the manufacture and sale of mountain dew. Dodson was born in 1868 to a well-to-do and politically influential Ozarks family farther east. His father, John M. Dodson, a physician, farmer, and former slaveholder, was born in Georgia in 1814, and he and his family had lived in South Carolina and Alabama before his first wife died in 1846. Around 1849, John M. remarried and headed west to the Sylamore area of what was then part of Izard County but was later included in Stone County when it was created in 1873. There, Joe and several other children were born to John M. and his second wife. A staunch Democrat and local party leader, several of the prominent Stone County farmer-physician's sons and grandsons would go on to enjoy successful political careers in

Wealthy Little Rock businessman H. L. Remmel received a number of federal patronage appointments in Arkansas by Republican presidents during the late 1800s and early 1900s, including head collector of internal revenue and U.S. marshal. Remmel is caricatured here by opponents in a political postcard as an elite opportunist who exploits his privileged access to federal power. Courtesy of Special Collections, University of Arkansas Libraries, Fayetteville.

Arkansas, Texas, and Oklahoma. Though the influential patriarch died in 1889, the Grover Cleveland administration commissioned his twenty-five-year-old son Joe to a U.S. deputy marshal position in 1893. Despite the shift to Republican control over federal patronage when McKinley entered the White House, the U.S. Marshals Service kept him on its staff in 1897.[39] Interestingly, Dodson's brother, Lit, was convicted in the fall of 1897 for his involvement in a lucrative counterfeiting ring, along with Stone County physician John Tubbs.[40]

Marshals Taylor and Dodson met at Snowball in Searcy County on Saturday morning, August 28, 1897, to assemble a posse and headed south to search for distillers. Jim Kerley, Dodson's father-in-law and a friend of Taylor's, and Clay Renfroe of Searcy County and S. B. Lawrence of Stone, who were each offered $10 a piece per captured still for their assistance, joined the officers. The two marshals picked up another posseman, E. P. Schoolcraft, as they passed through Witts Spring. Just as John Burris and deputy revenuer J. P. King had done weeks earlier to help track down Harve Bruce's still site in Van Buren County, Taylor and Dodson enlisted the help of Tom Barnes—who had also worked some for Taylor in the past. This time Barnes was offered a $50 reward. After nightfall, the possemen crossed into Pope County and hid their wagon in the bushes. From there Barnes took them near the farm of moonshiner Dave Milsap.[41]

Barnes had informed the marshals that Harve Bruce, Turner Skidmore, and perhaps some other moonshiners who had been on the run in recent weeks were now hiding out and doing business with Dave Milsap and Alva Church at their distillery in northeastern Pope County. Barnes, a longtime customer, employee, and friend of the local moonshiners, in fact, had just been to visit Milsap's and Church's still on Friday night, where he also found Bruce and Skidmore. According to Barnes, he placed an order for eight or ten gallons of liquor and the moonshiners agreed to have it ready for him by Monday. Milsap, Bruce, Bruce's brother Alford, and Skidmore stayed the night at the still site—which they had started operating only about three weeks earlier—and began their day's work early the next morning. Barnes agreed to show the lawmen the approximate whereabouts of the still so long as he did not have to accompany them when they made their raid, warning the officers that Bruce was "a dangerous man" and "would hunt a fellow."[42] Before daylight the next morning, the lawmen slipped quietly through the woods until they were in view of Milsap's farmhouse. Hidden in the brush, they waited and watched for a while but decided that the moonshiners were not at home. Soon they heard some men chopping wood on a hill across the farm and realized it was the moonshiners working at their still.[43]

Over at the still, Milsap had fired up the distillery at sunup for another day's production. Bruce and Church were also there, having stayed out in the woods nearby during the night. Milsap agreed to tend to the still while the other two went to eat breakfast at Church's house about a quarter of a mile away. When Bruce made it back to the still a little while later, Milsap took his break for breakfast and headed back home to eat with his family. Church arrived back to join Bruce at the still a short while later.[44]

Meanwhile, Taylor, Dodson, and their posse snuck up the hill to a point where they could see Bruce and Church about fifty yards away sitting on a fence. Hunkering down, the possemen crawled a bit closer to make their move. Once in position, they sprang into a charge with their guns raised and Officer Taylor purportedly yelling at the moonshiners to "Hold up!" What happened next was disputed by each side during the subsequent trial. The surviving possemen testified that the moonshiners fired the first shot, while Bruce and Church contended that the raiding lawmen were the first ones to discharge their weapons. In this case, Bruce and Church probably told the truth. A county sheriff's deputy, the local justice of the peace, and other witnesses testified during the trial that posseman S. B. Lawrence admitted to them in his initial statements after the shooting that he had fired the first shot into the air in hopes of stopping one of the moonshiners who was trying to run away. Several other witnesses also testified that one or more of the surviving possemen had told them that they had shot first, including a preacher who claimed that posseman Clay Renfroe confessed to him at a gospel meeting in Searcy County a few weeks after the shooting that he and the other lawmen had "done a bad work."[45]

Bruce later confessed that he was the only moonshiner who shot at the lawmen. He claimed that Church had quickly bolted away and escaped when he saw the possemen emerge from the brush at the bottom of the hill, though the possemen swore that Church fired at them too as he hurried away. Sitting nearer to the charging possemen and with his back initially turned toward them, Bruce explained that he, unlike Church, had no chance to escape. Fearing for his life, he darted toward his .40–60 Winchester and positioned himself behind some bushes to return fire. With bullets striking all around him—one of which hit him in the leg—Bruce shot Dodson in the head, killing him instantly, and hit Taylor in the abdomen. Taylor staggered back down the hill and out of sight before collapsing. A bullet also pierced Clay Renfroe in the side, and he and Jim Kerley evacuated the open hillside. According to Bruce, the shooting ceased for a few seconds, and he prepared to make a run for it. But Bruce then noticed another man, S. B. Lawrence, lying beneath some bushes, his muzzle aimed straight at him. Bruce quickly wheeled his rifle around and shot, just as Lawrence blasted toward him. The posseman missed Bruce, but the moonshiner's bullet tore most of Lawrence's left arm from his body. Lawrence retreated down the hill to where fellow posseman E. P. Schoolcraft sat nursing the dying Taylor. Schoolcraft helped Lawrence remove his jacket to assess what was left of his mangled arm, and, after Taylor took his last breath, they and the other two possemen scurried through the woods to a nearby farmhouse to report the incident and call for medical attention.[46]

Soon after the possemen reported the shooting, local lawmen arrived to take their statements, and a doctor arrived to amputate Lawrence's maimed arm. News of the deadly affair spread like wildfire through the surrounding areas, and local and federal lawmen, as well as dozens of concerned citizens and curious onlookers, flocked to the scene, where the bodies of Taylor and Dodson were carried away. Enraged friends and members of the Taylor and Dodson families also made their way to the scene, vowing to avenge the deaths. A letter written by a citizen of Marshall to Little Rock's *Arkansas Gazette* the next day explained that some Searcy Countians were "in a high fever of excitement and in case the guilty parties are captured, Judge Lynch will probably take a hand." Marshall's postmaster, M. A. Sanders, echoed such predictions, writing to the U.S. Marshals Office that "all good citizens here are turning out to assist the officers to catch the murderers and if, under the present excitement, any of them are caught, my opinion is they will be hung without ceremony."[47]

After the shooting, Bruce had hurried ten miles east to his Van Buren County farm and stopped by his house just long enough to clean the bullet wound in his leg, shave his burly beard, and grab some food before heading deep into the wooded mountains to hide out. A few days later, Bruce went south through the Arkansas River Valley to Little Rock, and then went east of the Mississippi River. He stayed in Alabama for the next ten months, where he lived with and worked for a man named Sol Long. From there, he secretly corresponded with his wife and children and sent them money through his trusted brother-in-law who lived in the Indian Territory.[48]

It did not take long for the feds to finger Bruce as one of the key suspects, and Deputy Revenuer J. P. King, who had diligently searched for the stubborn moonshiner since his and Burris's close encounter with him several weeks earlier, led a party of officers back to the Bruce farm a few days after the shooting. Though they failed to find Bruce, King finally located and destroyed the moonshiner's distilling equipment. King convinced Bruce's wife to show them her husband's still and promised to pay her the government's $10 reward. The revenuer also probably threatened her with charges for criminal accessory in the murder case if she did not. According to the later testimony of Harve Bruce, however, King did not keep his promise to pay his wife the bounty. During the trial, Bruce denounced King for such deceit, telling the court that if the federal officer "was a gentleman he would pay it."[49] Bruce seems to have been particularly bitter toward King, who he likely felt had unfairly used his elite status in the region to acquire federal authority for exploiting hard-working backcountry families like his.

Alva Church had bolted away from the still and ran to his house when the shooting began. Finding no one home, he hurried on to his parents' place before going to hide out in the woods. Church's wife had heard the gunshots from their house and raced toward the still to see what had happened. On her way, she met a neighbor, Smith Pack, who had also heard the commotion, and the two of them went together to the still site, where they found Taylor and Dodson dead. She then rushed to the Milsap farm to tell Dave and his family what had happened. Knowing that the law would soon be on his trail too, Milsap decided to go into hiding as well. As expected, a search posse came by the Milsap house that evening and stayed the night there. When word of the shooting got around to Turner Skidmore and Bruce's brother, Alford, they too set out for the woods.[50]

The next morning, however, Milsap and Church decided to go to the authorities to report what had happened, probably hoping to clear themselves of the murder charges that were sure to come. Nonetheless, they were arrested, convicted of illicit distilling by a federal jury, and sentenced to three years in the penitentiary at Fort Leavenworth, Kansas. Charges were then filed against them for involvement in the murder of Taylor and Dodson, and the McKinley administration commuted their sentences at Fort Leavenworth after twenty months so that they could go back to Pope County to stand trial in the murder case in the fall of 1899.[51]

In the days after the shooting, federal, state, and local lawmen combed the mountains in search of other suspects and stills, making good on the U.S. Justice Department's promise to "wage war to the knife against the devotees of illicit distilling in Arkansas." The *Arkansas Gazette* predicted that "when Uncle Sam gets after the 'shiners in dead earnest, it may be reasonably expected that illicit distilling will receive its death knell in Arkansas." Authorities made a big catch on September 2 when they apprehended John Church, a relative of Alva's, who agreed to turn state's witness in exchange for immunity.[52] Two days later, deputy marshals arrested four others on moonshining charges and suspicion of involvement in the Taylor and Dodson killings.[53]

Amid the excitement of the ongoing investigation and dramatic hunts for suspects, local, state, and national newspapers closely followed the case's developments and eagerly reported the many rumors and conspiracy theories that arose as authorities unearthed bits and pieces of the puzzle. Rumors abounded that perhaps dozens of local moonshiners had conspired together to assassinate the marshals. Officials discovered that two area moonshiners, both of whom were also U.S. postmasters in their respective rural communities, had written strange letters only a few days before the tragic shooting to their distilling partners who had already been arrested and were being held in the state prison at Little Rock. These peculiar letters, which were intercepted by prison guards, stated that "there will be an earthquake in England on the 28th." Officials arrested the individuals and investigated the suspicious matter, thinking there must be a connection to the Taylor and Dodson murders. Investigators eventually concluded, however, that the letter writers were merely members of a strange spiritual group based in Springfield, Missouri, and that their curious statements referred only to their premillennialist predictions about the End Times. Still, the frustrated editor of Searcy County's *Mountain Wave* demanded that officials reopen a more thorough investigation because the religious explanation was simply too "ghostlike" to accept.[54]

Though the *Wave*'s suspicions about the strange letters never amounted to anything, other observers also speculated about a broader conspiracy. The *New York Times*, in fact, attempted to link other tragedies in the area to the violent, lawless moonshiners and the tragedy in Pope County. In September the paper reported in an article, "A Dying Man Denied Water: Friends of Arkansas Outlaws Ill Treat Deputy Marshals," that local residents—supposedly in cahoots with the Bruce gang and other area moonshiners—had refused to give water to a government search party on a scorching hot day and in a few cases even rudely chased them from their properties, causing one posseman from Searcy County to die of heat exhaustion. Keeping a watchful eye for exciting new developments in the Ozarks moonshining case, the *New York Times* ran another article in early December in which it reported that an old friend of Taylor's and a well-known enemy of local moonshiners, Albert Giles, had been assassinated from ambush by unknown vengeance-filled moonshiners tied to Bruce and a vast Ozarks whiskey ring. Less than two weeks later, the paper ran another story that told of the massacre and robbery of the prominent Patterson family in Van Buren County. "One theory advanced for the murder," the *New York Times* loosely speculated, "is that it is the work of moonshiners, who infest this section, as Patterson was hated by all of them" because he had "giv[en] the authorities information that led to the arrest and destruction of numerous illicit distilleries in the county."[55]

Despite the *New York Times*'s attempts to tie these subsequent Ozarks tragedies to the Pope County shooting and local moonshiners, government officials apparently never made the same connections in their investigations and reports. Streamlining these sensational stories into one master narrative, nevertheless, likely made for some profitable yellow journalism. It also helped to further impress stereotypes depicting an inherently backward, violent, and authority-defying mountain culture into America's urban, middle-class consciousness.

Though some observers overspeculated and embellished, there is little question that all the hype surrounding the massive searches and authorities' elevated determination to crack down on illicit distilling in the aftermath of the deadly incident in Pope County fueled a heightened sense of suspicion and distrust among locals in the region. In the weeks following the killings of Taylor and Dodson, the federal government even created new law enforcement positions to increase patrols throughout the region, most of which were filled by prominent and well-connected locals. Little Rock's office of the Internal Revenue Service, for instance, quickly commissioned John Burris with an official position as a raiding deputy collector after the shooting, "which clothed him with power to destroy wild-cat stills in any part of the state."[56] IRS officials also appointed one of the slain Taylor's own sons-in-law, W. P. Hodges, as a deputy collector, "clear[ing] the way for him to hunt down the perpetrators of the crime with all the powerful machinery of the government to aid him."[57]

As armies of federal and local officers combed the area—with a sizeable pot of reward money in hand to entice cash-starved residents to help them—some hill farmers who were engaged in the moonshining business must have begun to think twice about their friends and neighbors. They clung ever more tightly to those they could trust and at times retaliated against those who "turned traitor." Information handed over to authorities by a twenty-three-year-old northern Pope County farmer, John Vaughan, led to the arrests of a large band of illicit distillers in the Arkansas River Valley several miles to the south, including some "negro" moonshiners in Conway County, though authorities apparently never directly linked them to the Bruce gang. Several days later, Vaughan's dead body was found lying in the road near Appleton, "supposed[ly] . . . bushwhacked by the moonshiners" who feared he would spill more of the beans about the area's "whiskey business."[58] In late October the federal grand jury of Arkansas's western district filed a special report, describing the elevated sense of anxiety, distrust, and even terror that seemed to have swept the region:

> We find the unlawful manufacture and sale of whiskey enormous, and apparently on the increase. It is almost impossible to get testimony in these cases: witnesses will evade answering questions, incriminate themselves before they will answer truthfully, and will plead guilty to have committed the offense themselves in order to save large numbers charged, and who are guilty beyond doubt.[59]

Acts of intimidation by some moonshiners persisted in some places for at least another year, according to some antiliquor proponents. In October 1898 a key witness for federal prosecutors against some Cleburne County moonshiners claimed to have borne the wrath of angry nightriders. They slaughtered his livestock and dogs, torched his barn and other property to the ground, and warned him and his family to "get out of the country right away."[60]

Officers continued to make some successful raids during the weeks and months following the shootout at the Milsap farm, including one in Pope County in which authorities destroyed a one-hundred-gallon still and one thousand gallons of mash.[61] A big arrest in connection with the deaths of Taylor and Dodson came when authorities captured Harve Bruce's brother, Alford, near the cities of Fort Smith and Van Buren in mid-September.[62] With Church and Milsap already in custody, investigators had narrowed their key suspects to Harve Bruce and Turner Skidmore. Federal and state authorities, along with members of the wealthy Taylor family, issued a combined $1,000 reward for their capture—dead or alive.[63]

In late November, after finding out that Skidmore had just arrived back at his home in Van Buren County after a long stay in the Indian Territory, the local sheriff and one of his deputies snuck to his farm to arrest him. Skidmore put up no resistance, and the sheriff quickly escorted him to the state prison in Little Rock for safekeeping, arriving, coincidentally, at approximately the same time

Bruce AND Skidmore
$450 REWARD.

UNITED STATES MARSHAL'S OFFICE,
Eastern District of Arkansas,
Little Rock, September 25, 1897.

On the 29th day of August, 1897, Deputy U. S. Marshals B. F. Taylor and J. M. Dodson were killed, H. C. Renfroe and S. B. Lawrence wounded by illicit distillers in Pope Co., Ark., near Diamond Post Office.

I am authorized by the Attorney General of the U. S. to offer a reward of $200 for the arrest and delivery to me of each of the guilty parties.

Following is a description of two of the parties known to be implicated in the murder:

HARVE BRUCE: 6 feet, 2 inches high; weighs about 185 or 190 pounds; gray hair; had a long gray beard at that time; pale blue eyes; age, 55 years; wears No. 11 shoes; walks erect; carries head high and is quick spoken.

HARVE BRUCE.

TURNER SKIDMORE: 5 feet, 8 inches high; weighs 140 lbs.; dark hair; pale blue eyes; age, 45 years; wears No. seven or eight shoes; has coarse, heavy moustache, worn to cover defect—having one or two upper front teeth out; usually carries head down when walking and is inclined to be a little round shouldered.

TURNER SKIDMORE.

The Commissioner of Internal Revenue offers a reward of $150 for the arrest and delivery, to me, of each of the illicit distillers, not now in custody, who are also charged with the murder of Deputies Taylor and Dodson and the wounding of Renfroe and Lawrence.

Hon. Dan W. Jones, Governor of the State, offers a reward of $100 for the arrest and conviction of each of the murderers.

The relatives of B. F. Taylor also offer an additional reward for the capture of Harve Bruce.

Any information desired will be promptly furnished.

HENRY M. COOPER, United States Marshal.

Reward poster for moonshiners Harve Bruce and Turner Skidmore distributed by the U.S. Marshal's Office in Little Rock after the August 1897 shootout in Pope County that left two federal lawmen dead. Outlaw Reward Poster 2009-184. Courtesy of the Oklahoma Historical Society.

that a federal judge handed down prison sentences to Church and Milsap for illicit distilling. Skidmore, who denied having been within ten miles of Milsap's farm on the day of the shooting—though Searcy County's *Mountain Wave* confidently reported "that enough evidence will be produced to hang him"—pleaded guilty to illicit distilling charges and was sent to join Church and Milsap at the federal penitentiary in Fort Leavenworth.[64] Bruce, however, remained at large, and frustrated authorities continued their pursuit with very few leads.

Federal officers worked tirelessly and expended enormous amounts of resources in their search for Bruce and other moonshiners in the area during the subsequent winter, spring, and summer. By the fall of 1898, Burris and other authorities had busted up several distilleries in the region, including a noteworthy raid in Polk County in the Ouachita Mountains of southwestern Arkansas. Burris and his men captured one of the still's operators by pistol-whipping him into submission, but three of his partners escaped. A determined Burris, however, immediately "got busy" and even tracked down one of the moonshiners near Spokane, Washington, and apprehended another in Duluth, Idaho. The third finally surrendered to local lawmen at Conway in Faulkner County. Burris's ambitious efforts—or at least his heavy expenditure of federal funds to conduct these efforts—raised some suspicions among IRS officials in Washington, D.C., however. Inspector A. C. Patterson reported back to the IRS after visits to the Ozarks during the summer and fall of 1898 that he had discovered irregularities in Burris's expense accounts, in addition to some questionable conduct by him and other deputy collectors in the region.[65]

Arkansas's head federal collector in Little Rock, Republican businessman H. L. Remmel, intervened on Burris's behalf, however. Remmel complained to IRS commissioner G. W. Wilson in Washington that it "seems strange" for Patterson's charges against Burris not to come through him at the local level first. Remmel alleged that the federal investigator "is over-burdened with the consciousness of the power of his office" and was furious that Patterson had been harassing a prominent Little Rock banker and other businessmen "throughout the state who allege that they have been compelled to pay taxes which were unjustly assessed against them." Moreover, Remmel questioned Patterson's commitment to rooting out rural moonshiners, saying that local lawmen and deputy marshals had complained to him about his lack of aggressiveness in attempting to make arrests. "It is said that Mr. Patterson came here with the reputation 'as a fighter from North Carolina,'" wrote Remmel, "but his conduct upon certain occasions does not bear out such reputation." While the federal agent was apt to use "a great deal of bluster and bull-dozing tactics which are wholly unnecessary" when he examined law-abiding businesses, Remmel continued, Patterson was too soft on illicit backcountry distillers, "the class of people which have given this District a great deal of trouble." Ultimately, federal bureaucrats in Washington deferred to Remmel's "local knowledge" and "exonerated" Burris and his fellow officers from any disciplinary measures.[66]

Federal and local lawmen finally caught their break in the Taylor and Dodson case in early October 1898. During one of Harve Bruce's brief visits home from Alabama, J. W. Gist, a neighbor and regional cattle buyer, discovered that the "outlaw" was back at his Van Buren County farm. Determined to collect the large reward, Gist grabbed his rifle and snuck over to Bruce's farm, where he watched from a distance the outlaw work at his barn all afternoon. After nightfall, when Bruce returned to his house, Gist quietly slipped closer until he could see through the windows. Waiting until Bruce went into a bedroom—a safe distance away from his "trusty Winchester"—Gist stormed into the house and arrested the moonshiner at gunpoint. Gist escorted Bruce to Conway, where local police took him into custody and then transferred him to federal authorities in Little Rock. Convicted of illicit distilling by a federal court only a few weeks later, Bruce soon joined Church, Milsap, and Skidmore in the federal prison in Kansas.[67]

Not long after Bruce's arrest, the local prosecuting attorney and the circuit court judge in Pope County began preparations for the murder case, hoping to start the trial during the spring 1899 court term. But when local officials requested the transfer of Bruce and the others to Pope County to stand trial, the U.S. Attorney General's office regretfully informed them that it "has no power to interfere with the sentence of the federal court," which they were currently serving at Fort Leavenworth on moonshining convictions. Thus, they could not hand them over at the time. This disgusted the *Courier-Democrat* in Russellville, which lamented the Attorney General's decision, "because quite a large amount of costs has already accrued in preparing for the trial." In late May, however, the McKinley administration arranged to have the federal sentences commuted, "only for the purpose," wrote the attorney general, "of having them turned over to the State authorities for prosecution for a higher crime."[68]

Observers, both locally and throughout the state, eagerly anticipated the high-profile murder trial, now set to begin during the court's fall term in 1899. State attorney Lawrence Russell, U.S. attorney C. C. Waters, and Taylor-family attorney J. T. Bullock headed the prosecution, while Col. G. W. Bruce (perhaps a relative of Harve Bruce) of Conway and J. A. Gillette of Atkins prepared the defense. Interestingly, Davis and Son of Russellville, the private law firm of state attorney general—and soon to be governor—Jeff Davis, also assisted with Bruce's and the other moonshiners' defense. The "Tribune of Haybinders" himself, though, was busy at the moment using his public office to file antitrust suits against "every fire insurance company doing business in the state"—much as "Jesus Christ whipped just such a gang of fellows out of the temple," as Davis described it. After the fall term finally opened and the Pope County Circuit Court disposed of its less dramatic cases, Judge William L. Moose commenced the trial and proceeded carefully with jury selection in early November.[69]

"No case that has been tried here for many years has attracted the attention of this one," Russellville's *Courier-Democrat* noted. It and other area newspapers, reflecting the "unusual interest [in] the case," reported on the "thrill-
ing evidence" unearthed during the trial by the examinations of "[n]early one
hundred witnesses." The "most dramatic" point of the trial, of course, came
when Harve Bruce himself took the stand. Although Bruce came to court clean-
shaven—which likely disappointed a number of urban reporters hungry for
a picture-perfect mountain drama—Little Rock's *Arkansas Gazette* described
the now infamous moonshiner as "a typical mountaineer in build and character, being strong, athletic and said to be absolutely fearless and is an unerring
marksman."[70]

Standing 6' 2" and weighing about 190 pounds, the gray-headed, fifty-five-
year-old Bruce, who was said to have been known for his "quick spoken[ess],"
calmly took the stand. Never flinching as the prosecutors grilled him with tough
questions and accusations, Bruce stood ready with direct responses, his pale
blue eyes staring straight into theirs without any appearance of nervousness
or intimidation. Admitting that he had been manufacturing illegal whiskey and
eluding authorities when the deadly shootout occurred, Bruce took full-blame
for doing all the shooting at Taylor, Dodson, and the other officers at the still
that day, but he insisted that he did so only in self-defense. When asked by
prosecutors why he fired at the officers, Bruce candidly responded: "I shot to
hurt for I saw no other way to save my life." He explained that Taylor and his
men never properly identified themselves as lawmen and that they shot first.[71]

After hearing closing arguments and receiving instructions from Judge
Moose on November 17, the jury deliberated for five days. Much to the disappointment of the prosecutors, the Taylor and Dodson families, and others
who prayed for a first-degree murder conviction, the jury found Bruce guilty
of involuntary manslaughter and set his sentence at six months in the state
prison. "Bruce's statements on the witness stand," explained the *Courier-Democrat*, "made a strong impression on the jury."[72] Nevertheless, the defense, to the
surprise of many, proved unsatisfied with the verdict and appealed the decision
to the Arkansas Supreme Court. On November 23, the state's Supreme Court
notified Judge Moose that it had accepted Bruce's appeal, and his bond was set
at $4,000. The Russellville paper reported the case's new development in its
Thanksgiving Day issue:

> As soon as the necessary papers were properly executed and delivered, this
> old man accompanied by as true and loyal a wife as ever clung to man in his
> hours of trial and tribulations, passed . . . upon the streets and having received

the congratulations of many friends, entered a covered wagon and departed for his home amid the tall pines, stately oaks and towering cliffs of the Boston mountains, there no doubt to await with more or less anxiety the report of those who shall pass judgment as to what shall be the closing chapter of this most unfortunate and ever deplorable period of his life.[73]

Hoping that the Arkansas Supreme Court would overturn the ruling, Bruce and his family patiently waited for word from Little Rock, which they finally received in late June of 1900. Unfortunately for them, the state's high court affirmed the ruling. In writing the court's opinion, Justice J. Battle even went so far as to say that "the verdict of the jury is remarkable. . . . They were unreasonably lenient to him, and he has no right to complain." With his appeal for acquittal rejected, Bruce left for Little Rock to serve his six-month prison term. Soon after his arrival, Superintendent Bud McConnell assigned Bruce to guard duty, purportedly telling him that since "he could use a Winchester so desterously [sic] on marshals he would make a good guard." Luckily for Bruce, however, he had made some important connections that shortened his stay at the state prison. The owner of the Russellville law firm that had helped defend him at his trial in Pope County now occupied the state's chief executive office, and Gov. Jeff Davis included Bruce when he issued an unprecedented number of pardons after his inauguration in January 1901. "A Karl Marx for Hillbillies," as the Arkansas-born sociologist Rupert Vance characterized him, Davis later defended his controversial pardoning record against critics in typical populist fashion, arguing that at least he had "pardoned *people* while [the conservative state supreme court's] Judge Wood pardoned the *railroads*."[74]

Not long after he arrived in Little Rock to serve his time in prison, Bruce, now "one of the most noted characters in the penitentiary," received a visit from a reporter for the *Conway Democrat*, who depicted Bruce as "a typical old mountaineer and moonshine distiller" who had once "wore long flowing whiskers, which made him look about as we imagine Moses did about the time he delivered the law of the 'Children of Israel.'" Assessing Bruce's resistance through the lens of typical hillbilly stereotypes, the reporter claimed that "the mountaineer hates the marshals and the government that try to prevent him from doing with his corn as he pleases." "He thinks he has as much right to make whiskey out of it as bread," he continued.[75]

Bruce's own explanation, however, pointed more to practical economics in the rural Ozarks rather than some antigovernment culture and knee-jerk reaction against the feds telling him what he could and could not do. When asked by the reporter why he and his Ozarks neighbors had flouted antimoonshine regulations, "Bruce explained that their corn was worth only 30 cents per bushel ... [but when] they made it into whiskey the slop was worth as much as the corn to feed the hogs and they could get $2.00 per gallon for the whiskey." "This was the only way, [Bruce] explained, of getting any money up there in the mountains," wrote the reporter. It was his and his family's best chance of fulfilling the American Dream in the increasingly opportunity-strapped rural Ozarks. Nevertheless, because of the unfortunate ruckus that had left two men dead and landed him in the slammer, Bruce promised "that he would not distill any more whiskey as he wanted to live in peace now." After leaving the state prison, Bruce returned home to Oak Mountain, where he "lived the life of a respected and honored citizen" until he died a few years later in March 1907.[76]

Contemporaries such as the *Conway Democrat* reporter—and most accounts since then—assumed that moonshiners' defiance of liquor laws stemmed from a unique backwoods culture that automatically rejected any government interference. Bruce's specific ideas about the proper role of government, however, appear more complicated and complex. Like most rural commoners, Bruce left behind very little in the historical record. Important clues exist, though, which tend to suggest that he shared the typical rural American workingman's populist conviction that "yearn[ed] for a society run by and for ordinary people who lead virtuous lives," whether that meant more or less government in a particular circumstance, and not some "ancestral dread of federal power."[77]

Bruce likely supported and voted the Democratic ticket in most elections. When his third son was born on July 12, 1887, he and his wife named him Grover Cleveland Bruce, undoubtedly after the sitting Democratic president. Cleveland would eventually go down in history as a defender of "the old gospel of laissez-faire ... [and] an order dominated by big business," but his conservative legacy was not established until his second term in office (1893–1897) amid the watershed insurgency of the Democratic Party's populist wing, led by William Jennings Bryan—working-class America's "Godly Hero." Bryan's populist wing finally put the party of Andrew Jackson "on a course that led away from their laissez-faire past and toward the liberalism of the New Freedom, the New Deal, and the Great Society." Indeed, as historian Michael Kazin reminds us, Cleveland had "managed to keep his party united" during his first term amid growing fissures between economic conservatives and a rising tide of populist reformers with his appeal to rural family farmers, owners of small businesses, and urban wage laborers by touting his "anti-trust fervor" and opposition to high tariffs that benefited big business in the Northeast at the expense of common consumers. Many former Confederate soldiers like Bruce, furthermore, had celebrated Cleveland, after his election in 1884, as the first Democrat to occupy the White House since before the Civil War and applauded his appointments of Southerners to key positions in his administration.[78]

If Bruce had been a disciple of conservative laissez-faire ideology, he would have been an anomaly in the rural Ozarks during his time and would have fit in much better among the wealthy planter class of the Delta. During the late nineteenth and early twentieth centuries, populist demands for government reform spewed from the Arkansas Ozarks, just as they did from other rural regions dominated by small family farmers and laborers. Rural folks called on a government of "the people" to break apart and corral the unjust excesses of free enterprise capitalism by redistributing the wealth and power of big moneyed interests to hard-working and God-fearing commoners like themselves. Such sentiments were especially strong in Bruce's section of the rural Ozarks. The Brothers of Freedom, after all, had counted their organizing campaigns in Van Buren and Pope Counties among their most successful.[79]

The enormous popularity of agrarian Democrat Jeff Davis among rural folks in Harve Bruce's home area in the late 1890s and early 1900s also illuminates how these populist-progressive sentiments about government pervaded politics, society, and culture in the region. But the charismatic governor's political position—or lack thereof—on government-induced alcohol reform also indicates, perhaps as well as any other issue, how such a skillful politician could sometimes manage to play both sides of the fence for votes and tap broad popular sentiments that simultaneously appealed to poor backcountry folks and their well-to-do elite antagonists alike.

Davis's ambiguous stance on alcohol regulations during his tenure as governor exemplified his intentionally vague populism in general. As historian Raymond Arsenault explains, "Temperance advocates had reason to believe that the new governor would prove to be a reliable ally," because his father had been a prominent antiliquor crusader and Davis himself had served as prosecuting attorney in "the 'driest' judicial district in the state" during the early 1890s. Ever the adept politician, however, Davis realized that his "support was concentrated in the rural areas, particularly in the more isolated farm precincts," but also in those districts with small towns, villages, and better-connected farming communities. With his rural constituency largely split over the alcohol issue in many areas, Davis completely avoided the liquor question in his 1900 gubernatorial campaign. Not long after occupying the governor's office, however, the state legislature put Davis on the spot when it passed the Holt Bill, the temperance leaders' "most important piece" of legislation yet, which would have banned all liquor transportation in Arkansas's dry counties. Davis vetoed the bill, arguing that it was "too extreme" and that Arkansas had "the best liquor laws of any state in the Union" without it. Davis's decision undoubtedly set well with backcountry farmer-distillers, but disappointed temperance advocates soon forgave him too and "continued to court the governor's favor." Davis was even elected a few months later in 1901 as the vice president of the Arkansas Baptist State Convention (ABSC), "the most temperance-conscious religious organization in the state."[80] His populist magic had worked once again.

The whiskey issue confronted Davis again shortly after his resounding victory in the 1902 Democratic primary, though this time it became quite personal. Davis's political rivals attacked and accused Davis of public drunkenness, forcing his resignation as ABSC vice president in April and even prompting his expulsion from the Second Baptist Church of Little Rock in May. But Davis made the damning controversy into yet another opportunity to bolster his populist image as a victim of Arkansas's "high-combed roosters" and asked his working-class supporters to stand with him against the "pharisees who had persecuted him for his political beliefs." Davis continually "avoided the liquor issue as much as possible in political campaigns" throughout the rest of his career and "played both sides of the street consistently and sincerely."[81]

The dual legacy of the 1897 Pope County affair reflected the divided mind of the Ozarks. Local prohibitionists, business boosters, and lawmen remembered Taylor and Dodson as virtuous martyrs for the principles of "progress" and "law and order." But the tragic episode also helped confirm more radical populist suspicions about inequality and injustice for many of the area's dispossessed backcountry folks. Printed in the local Pope County newspaper, Bruce's candidness and convincing testimony at the trial—especially his claims about how Burris and King had bullied his daughter and wife and how he described Taylor's and Dodson's reckless conduct in the raid—succeeded in painting the federal officers as unjust aggressors in the eyes of many hill folks. The *Courier-Democrat* seemed to think so, commenting that Bruce's "apparent sincerity made him many friends." At least some officials confirmed these impressions on their own, even without Bruce's help. As Burris and his men patrolled for moonshiners after the shooting, for instance, they searched a small mountain farm in southeastern Newton County and encountered the farmer's wife. Before realizing that they were federal authorities looking for stills, she asked them, "Who are you anyhow?" A condescending Burris rudely responded, "I am a lady's man." Infuriated by Burris's arrogance and, in her eyes, his haughty abuse of authority, she quipped back: "G__ D___ you. You had better be at home with her instead of riding over the country destroying people's property."[82] While growing numbers of rural Ozarkers—particularly those with better market connections—championed tougher regulations by "the people" against the "whiskey interests," several others—especially in the more remote reaches of the backcountry—despised local antiliquor elites' strong-armed use of government power to enforce conformity to their vision and business interests.

The latter legacy of moonshiner-versus-government conflict outlived the former amid the evolution of the rural Ozarks during the twentieth and twenty-first centuries, weaving its way more nicely into the fabric of the region's mythical image and the purposes and tastes of its narrators. Harve Bruce went down in local lore among many rural folks as an Ozarks "legend," the nostalgic epitome of the individualistic mountaineer taking a principled don't-tread-on-me stand against the invasive and abusive arm of government. A folk ballad about Bruce and the fatal moonshine raid, sung to the tune of the popular American folk song "Cindy," passed through subsequent generations in the area into the late twentieth century:

Old Ben Taylor, he got killed
Trying to capture a wildcat still.

Taylor and Dodson got a lot of men
And thought they'd capture a wildcat den.

They went up and fired their guns
And thought them wildcat's men would run.

Old Harve Bruce, he's dead and gone
Had the best wild cat still around.

Old Harve Bruce raised the alarm
And shot Si Lawrence through the arm.

Old Schoolcraft, warn't no fool
Shot his musket and run like a mule

Alva Church was there too
Shot Joe Dodson through and through.

Old Harve Bruce he done well
Killed Ben Taylor dead as hell.

Old Harve Bruce never tried
Shot Clay Renfro through the side.[83]

In 1982 the local newspaper, Russellville's *Daily Courier-Democrat*, featured an article on "the legend of Harve Bruce" and his exceptional "pioneer" moxie. Professing that "mountain men have always been noted for their accuracy with a gun," the article recounted Bruce's larger-than-life marksmanship in the story of the deadly 1897 moonshine raid and a couple of tall-tale hunting stories, as told about Bruce by some of his "mountain friends." "According to men who knew him, he had no peer with a rifle," the paper exclaimed, and was known as "a man not to fool with," a real McCoy of mountain folklore and nostalgia.[84]

The romanticized story persisted into the twenty-first century. In 2015 *True West Magazine* ran an article about how Harve Bruce had "kill[ed] two deputy U.S. marshals and put hot lead into two posse members, while the other two scattered like quail into the wild and uncut Boston Mountains."[85] The story also became a convenient tale for America's antigovernment, anti-Obama, Tea Party culture. In 2012 Bruce's great-grandson, political activist Shane Bruce, blogged about "The Legend of Harve Bruce" on a right-wing Web site called *Bludgeon and Skewer*, an online blog "home to gun totin'; tin hat wearin'; Heinlein readin' rogue Libertarians considering HL Mencken's advice." Proudly noting that the Winchester rifle "Great Grand Daddy Harve Bruce" had used to kill the two federal marshals now "sits in my gunsafe in the position of honor," Shane Bruce boasted, "After quite a bit of noodle time on the internets [*sic*] I have come to the conclusion that I have a long way to go to measure up to Great Grand dad." "He was a hell of a guy."[86]

The myths, stereotypes, and polemical spin that have shrouded this "moonshine war" and other hostilities, however, ignore a much more complex and largely forgotten history of rural populism and intraregional conflict between the haves and the have-nots in the Ozarks. For Bruce and his fellow moonshiner-farmers, the elite favoritism and patronage-based operations of the IRS and the U.S. Marshals Service surely epitomized the unjust relationship between the privileged well-to-do and the status-quo designs of government power. As working families toiled and sweated to eke out a living on their small hill farms and thought of new ways to prosper amid a national political economy that proved to be increasingly rigged against them, the region's already-privileged business elites controlled, administered, and benefitted from the power of these government agencies whose sole purpose was to criminalize and suppress their economic activities in the name of progress, productivity, and respectability. Indeed, this was hardly a story of "furrin" government bureaucrats *invading* the isolated domains of backwoods mountaineers. Instead, it was competing *local* interests and visions amid uneven economic development in the region that concocted a very American recipe for radical populist defiance and explosive conflict.

Unfortunately for the poor and middling family farmers of the Ozarks, they would still be awaiting the fulfillment of their populist vision twenty years later. Rural populism did influence the launching of "a vigorous reform movement" during the early 1900s, and, in historian and political scientist Elizabeth Sanders's estimation, primarily "shaped the contours of Progressive Era state expansion." New roles for government in the Progressive Era included much of the populist agenda: "the redefinition of trade policy; the creation of an income tax; a new, publicly controlled banking and currency system; antitrust policy; the regulation of agricultural marketing networks; a nationally financed road system; federal control of railroads, ocean shipping, and early telecommunications; and agricultural and vocational education." Progressives' specific policy designs, however, proved to be "more attuned with the aspirations of the [industrial and agribusiness-oriented] middle class" than those of small farm families. "Progressives worked energetically for agricultural education, farm-to-market roads, tariff reduction, and some other reforms which would benefit agriculture in general," writes Arkansas political historian Joe T. Seagraves, "but not even Jeff Davis tried to alter the credit system or the landholding pattern" or other structural inequalities. "Conservative businessmen, lawyers, and large landowners still dominated the local power structure, despite the tremendous ferment and real gains won by the agrarian upheaval and the progressive movement," Seagraves continues. "At the local level, in the ordinary operation of government, the great majority of Arkansas people found the political institutions scarcely more representative or responsive in 1918 than in 1874."[87]

Thus, defiance persisted in the Ozarks backcountry as small farm families continued to struggle against the odds and searched for ways to sustain their livelihoods, propelling new conflicts and, at times, radical resistance against government authority. Though largely forgotten in the folklore-dominated "history" of the region, some of the biggest stands against the "damn-guvment" in the Ozarks would come from the backcountry hollers when local elites used the government's "patriotic" power in 1917 and 1918 to demand that rural working people and their sons put their lives on hold—and literally on the line—to go fight in what they viewed as an unjust war cooked up by greedy business interests.

3

"SILK-HATTED FELLERS" AND THEIR WAR

Sam Faubus—the father of Arkansas's notorious governor in the period after World War II, Orval Faubus—was born in 1887 and raised on a small farm in Madison County. A descendant of Scots-Irish immigrants who first settled in the Appalachian Mountains during the 1750s and who fought in the French and Indian War and Revolutionary War, Faubus entered the twentieth century working as a small farmer and timber laborer in the rural Ozarks. A product of the backcountry's more radical Populist ethic, Faubus was never shy about expressing his vision of a just government that would ensure "economic and political equality." "I'd rather be an honest peasant/ Taking my living from the soil/ Than to be a rich parasite/ Living by others toil," he once penned in poem. Faubus was a rural Socialist, as well as a member of the theologically ultraconservative Combs Church of Christ—where, in fact, he first encountered Socialist political ideas. In September 1918, during World War I, local authorities arrested and jailed Faubus for "distributing seditious literature and uttering numerous disloyal remarks concerning the conduct of the war."[1] For Faubus and many other likeminded backcountry folks in the Ozarks, the U.S. war effort represented nothing more than greedy corporate interests manipulating to their economic advantage the uneven status quo of government power, all at the expense of honest, hardworking commoners like themselves.

For good reason, many popular and scholarly accounts tend to emphasize a patriotic "tradition of soldiering" among Ozarkers, Appalachian mountaineers, and other rural and small-town Southerners. This traditional "fighting spirit" is generally assumed to be rooted in the same folk culture that is defined by uniquely rugged individualism, self-reliance, and tenacious defiance against government authority.[2] Ironically, though, some of the most vociferous challenges to federal intervention in the Ozarks during the early twentieth century involved rural working people resisting the U.S. Selective Service's compulsory military conscription in 1917 and 1918. While American soldiers were off fighting the Great War on the battlefields of Europe, federal and local officials throughout the Ozarks were engaged in battles of their own against backcountry folks who refused to have any part of what they believed was an "unjust" war.

Unlike the romantic tales of moonshiners resisting government encroachments on liberty that have long survived in popular myth, however, the stories of rural defiance during World War I have been ignored in the selective memory and lore about the region's cultural past. As Sam Faubus's son Orval later curiously said about his father's antiwar activities and arrest, "You know, I never heard it mentioned in all my growing up in that community."[3] Indeed, the memory of this incident and others like it in the region failed to serve the interests of subsequent generations who helped mold the dominant images of and ideas about the Ozarks. The fact that there are forgotten episodes of draft resistance, nevertheless, reveals a great deal about the complex, and perhaps surprising, historical dynamics of rural defiance against federal power in the region.

According to historian Jeanette Keith's study of the rural South during World War I, U.S. mobilization for the war in Europe provided optimistic leaders at federal, state, and local levels opportunities to implement new designs for a "modern managerial state."[4] In fact, as another historian reminds us, a good number of future New Dealers, including Franklin Roosevelt himself, cut their teeth in government administration during World War I and borrowed heavily from those ideas and experiences later on as they worked toward government-managed relief, recovery, and reform during the Great Depression of the 1930s.[5] But the efforts of the Woodrow Wilson administration and cooperating state and local governments to forge national unity and popular commitment to the U.S. war effort in 1917 and 1918 encountered much stiffer resistance than they had anticipated from some Americans, especially in rural regions such as the Ozarks.

While it is impossible to quantify exactly the levels of opposition to the war effort in the rural South, Keith's recent work shows that resistance, especially to the government's military conscription, was much more widespread than historians have previously assumed. This fact, she writes, adds important nuance to long-held views about white Southerners as "the nation's most militaristic people . . . always ready to fight their country's wars." Moreover, resistance against this federal intrusion did not simply stem from some unique rural attitudes about governmental authority, as some authors have suggested. Rural Ozarkers who mounted the most determined defiance, in fact, were old Populists and Socialists who otherwise demanded a strong federal government that would "fundamentally restructure the institutions of capitalist society" and help create "a more decent, fair, and just alternative to a world they knew to be fatally flawed."[6]

Rural dissent against the war and the draft emerged primarily because military conscription meant real hardships for small farm families. As they encountered these burdens, many rural Ozarkers naturally viewed their experiences through the populist ethos that had been engrained in the region during the preceding years. For many Ozarkers, it was simply not fair to have their young men sacrifice valuable time, labor, and possibly their lives fighting someone else's war. To them it was a "rich man's war" but a "poor man's fight." As Sam Faubus's personal background attests, this populist defiance also frequently merged with rural religious convictions. Many believed that the government's war effort was an unrighteous, sinful ploy designed merely to enrich greedy and powerful business interests at the expense of hardworking, God-fearing common folks like themselves. Such views should not be attributed simplistically to rural backwardness or narrow localism, however. Though major gaps in the historical record can make it difficult to probe their lines of thinking, Faubus's

Rural Ozarkers at a Socialist encampment meeting at Decatur in 1912. Photo S-2015-59-29. Courtesy of the Shiloh Museum of Ozark History, Springdale.

and other rural Ozarkers' antiwar opposition at times expressed levels of so-phisticated reasoning that fit squarely into the broader social justice critiques of a number of highly educated intellectuals in America and abroad in the early twentieth century.

Opinions about the unjust nature of the war, particularly the draft, were compounded by the Selective Service's locally run draft boards. Unlike America's first drafts during the Civil War, a man could not technically buy his way out of conscription or claim exemption based on certain indicators of wealth (in other words, the Confederacy's twenty-slave rule). Yet, in reality, class (and racial) prejudices characterized the implementation of the draft anyway, and this fact was quickly noticed by poor and middling farmers and laborers across the rural South. It would be misleading to characterize the federal government's Selective Service System as a fully top-down, statist act of "high modernism." Instead of sending bureaucrats from Washington or military bases into local communities to administer conscription, after all, the Selective Service followed a decentralized approach that delegated significant power to local draft boards. Officials in Washington, moreover, explicitly "encouraged draft boards to make decisions about exemption based on local knowledge." Yet, despite what might have seemed like a more "democratic" approach, this *local* system actually "maximized the impact of the draft on poor families." Local political and town business elites almost always dominated the draft boards. With a handful of local elites wielding such immense power over the lives of so many families in their communities, the stage was set for rural discontent and, at times, even outright rebellion. Much like the battles over moonshine in the rural Ozarks, conflicts that sprang from the World War I draft were largely *intra*regional affairs.[7]

With significant leeway for local decision making, Ozarks elites were prone to use their pull to get exemptions for their own sons and relatives, political friends and business associates, and employees whose labor they needed, while they often denied exemption requests from many small family farmers. Selective Service policies set in Washington typically allowed exemptions for husbands and fathers with dependent women and young children in their households, but these policies were designed and implemented primarily from the perspective of urban, middle-class standards. They did not, for instance, consider that drafting young men from extended families and communities in rural areas, even if they were single or had no legal dependents, often threw a wrench into small farm operations and the livelihoods of entire families. The real burdens, then, were even more irritating in light of the practices of local draft boards, which many rural working people felt favored the interests of local business elites at their expense.[8]

As the drums of war began to rumble and the U.S. government's "prepared-ness" got underway, the Woodrow Wilson administration faced some of its stiffest opposition from rural Americans and certain members of its own Demo-cratic Party in the South, especially from those leaders who had begun their political careers amid the Populist insurgency in the 1890s, or just after the turn of the century. Their positions against the war say a lot about the sentiments of their grassroots constituents, especially since many of these political leaders had witnessed the Populist revolt firsthand and knew the consequences poli-ticians could face if they ignored and angered rural voters. Notable Southern political leaders such as Tom Watson of Georgia, John H. Bankhead of Alabama, and Claude Kitchen of North Carolina railed against the "unreasonable and un-necessary preparedness" for war, brought on, they exhorted in typical populist language, for the sake of big-moneyed "manufacturers of munitions and war supplies that are being exported to Europe at immense profits."[9] By 1917 Ar-kansas had its own "progressive" Wilsonite governor in Charles H. Brough, a former University of Arkansas history and economics professor, who ensured that the president and the federal war effort had his state's full cooperation. But some of Arkansas's populist-leaning political leaders voiced loud opposition to the war.

The torchbearer of the agrarian wing of the Democratic Party in Arkan-sas, Jeff Davis, had suffered a massive stroke and died in January 1913, but his political ally and fellow U.S. senator, James P. Clarke, irritated the Wilson administration by helping stir up opposition to some of the president's early war-preparation plans until he, too, died in October 1916. Clarke, it should be mentioned, had been Arkansas's governor during the middle of the Populist revolt in the 1890s and, having read the stormy winds of popular opinion, had aligned himself with Jeff Davis and donned a populist image in his subsequent race for the Senate. His successor in the Senate, William F. Kirby, picked up right where Clarke had left off, opposing Wilson's policies of "armed neutrality" and war preparation. Kirby also questioned the wisdom of the president's decision to intervene in the Mexican Revolution, asserting that the Monroe Doctrine did "not require that we shall regulate the internal affairs of Mexico to protect any financial interest of any of our citizens." Though he ultimately relented to vote in favor of the U.S declaration of war against Germany in April 1917, Kirby noted for the record his grave reluctance by explaining, "If there was the slight-est chance on God's earth that my vote against it would defeat it, I would stand here and vote a thousand years if it might be that we do not go to war." Kirby undoubtedly made sure these comments found their way to the eyes and ears of his populist rural constituents.[10]

Opposition to foreign military intervention was nothing new in the Arkansas Ozarks. Back in April 1898, as American leaders debated about and geared up for military action against Spain in Cuba, Searcy County's antiwar newspaper, the *Mountain Wave*, had defended against those pro-interventionists who questioned the patriotism of war opponents:

> The man who hastens to answer the call of his country and fights her righteous battles is a patriot—but he who refuses to bear arms for his country in an unjust cause is a greater one. The man who respects and loves his flag is a patriot—but he who tears it from its staff when unfurled for an unholy cause exhibits a patriotism of purity. . . . This so-called patriotism [espoused by interventionists]—pure shoddy, warp and woof—that causes men to be silent and pass by unnoticed wrongs against their country because the perpetrators are high in office, have a political pull or are big guns in the community—is the veriest [*sic*] rot, the essence of anarchy and the seeds of ruin.[11]

In November 1899 the *Wave* proudly printed the remarks of the populist, anti-imperialist William Jennings Bryan, who had recently called down a prowar interventionist who supported U.S. control of the Philippines because it would best serve the interests of America's economy. Bryan's "eyes flashed fire," the paper reported, "as he thundered: 'I dare you to measure the lives of American boys and the heart aches of American mothers by the paltry dollars and cents of commerce; I dare you do it!" "You are not preaching the gospel of the Prince of Peace," Bryan continued. "You're preaching the infernal gospel of conquest and murder and death." The *Wave* applauded Bryan's passion and gladly noted that "the orator's last words were drowned in a tempest of cheers."[12] Ironically, as we shall see, Searcy County's booster-oriented paper had changed its tune about war opponents rather dramatically by 1917. Upon America's entry into World War I and in the face of continued rural resistance, the *Wave* would come to demand absolute conformity to war supporters' "over the top" patriotism for the U.S. war effort.

Despite a consensus of opposition to initial calls for war, many Ozarkers—most likely a solid majority—fell into line once their country declared war in April 1917. Like William Jennings Bryan, who had even resigned as U.S. Secretary of State in protest of the Wilson administration's drift toward militarization, many rural Americans, "now that the United States was officially, unalterably at war . . . could not imagine opposing it," especially in this total-war environment. "Few of his followers," writes historian Michael Kazin, "seemed to challenge that reasoning." But Bryan co-opted war patriotism into his broader agenda for populist reform, such as "mingl[ing] anodyne pleas for conserving food with more spirited attacks on businessmen who sought to profit from the economic boom." Like most rural folks in Tennessee's Cumberland Mountains, "regardless of whether people . . . would have chosen to go to war with Germany in 1917, once the war began and American troops were committed, many felt obligated to help 'the boys.'"[13] Still, varying degrees of opposition remained strong in the Ozarks.

It is impossible to measure just how many rural Ozarkers supported or opposed the war effort, especially since both government and private resources were heavily employed to silence critics. There is, however, ample evidence to suggest that grassroots opposition was strong in the Arkansas hills, just as it was throughout other parts of the rural South. According to a U.S. War Department report issued in 1920, 8,732 Arkansawyers, or more than 15.5 percent of the state's total military inductees, failed to report for duty or deserted during the war. This figure stood well above the national average and did not include those who had refused to register for the draft in the first place.[14]

Of course, draft evasion, desertion, or any other behavior that might be deemed unpatriotic were actions that everyone understood could have dire consequences for themselves and perhaps even their families. Some Ozarkers, then, undoubtedly complied grudgingly, and many of them did so only after applying unsuccessfully to local draft boards for exemption. By the summer of 1917, federal, state, and county governments had established "defense councils" to mobilize the population and economy for the war effort, rally patriotic support from citizens, and suppress all dissent. Powerful sources of censure bombarded and muffled voices of opposition. Federal, state, and local governments created massive surveillance and propaganda agencies. Local businessmen and politicians organized "home guards" and "citizens' groups" that dotted towns throughout the country and worked diligently to sniff out "slackers." Newspaper editors sought to instill a sense of unified patriotic fervor in their readers and to mobilize commitment to national duty. And overly enthusiastic neighbors who might have suspected that a certain person, family, or group was not going "over the top" in supporting the war effort—or who might simply have seen a convenient opportunity to settle an old grudge—commenced neighborhood campaigns of humiliation and intimidation in the name of American patriotism. Consequently, many opponents in the Ozarks, as elsewhere, must have quietly acquiesced to the demands of the war effort to avoid the ridicule that might visit them and their families, however truly resentful they may have been. As one historian puts it, "People could speak as much as they pleased in favor of the war, but dissenters faced federal prosecution." Thus, only the stories of those opponents who opted to take more overtly confrontational stances of resistance emerge from the historical record.[15]

Middle-class urbanites and townsfolk administering the federal government's war effort in the state and region typically attributed the resistance they faced to backwoods isolation and a parochial culture of stubbornness and ignorance. Nonetheless, opposition to the draft arose in the region's more "progressive" rural areas as well. In Washington County, for instance, on the fertile, gently rolling Springfield Plain in the northwest corner of the Arkansas Ozarks—the home of the University of Arkansas and one of the most prosperous and "forward-looking" counties in the state—officials, lawmen, and patriotic citizens had to work diligently to suppress dissent, especially in smaller farm communities. In May 1918, the editor of the *Fayetteville Democrat* printed a short fictional story titled "The Pacifist and His Girl," undoubtedly hoping to help quell dissent against the war in the area. The tale was about a young man who "lost both his girl and his freedom" because his "intelligence" and "personal convictions" led him to oppose the war. His disgusted girlfriend resented his cowardice and not only ended their relationship but also turned him over to federal authorities. "There's a good deal more of genuine, practical patriotism bottled up in the girl power of this country than most men imagine," the editor concluded. "And many a smart youth is learning it to his cost."[16]

Dissent against the war in Washington County continued, nevertheless. That same month, officials reported "that a nest of American Bolsheviki has been breeding in the hills along the line of Washington and Crawford counties," a dangerous group, they believed, that sought to undermine the war effort. Preston Martin, a seventy-five-year-old farmer and country storekeeper from the Strickler community, and his thirty-two-year-old son were subsequently arrested and hauled before a federal grand jury on charges of sedition.[17] A few weeks later, the county's Food Administration reported that some anonymous war opponents, supposedly out of Elkins and Greenland, were circulating deceitful, "pro-German" pamphlets among area farmers in their attempts to undermine the government's wheat drive for the war effort.[18]

Lawmen and citizen patriots stepped up their hunts for war opponents and draft evaders in Washington County over the next several months. In August, Dr. W. T. Blackburn, a civilian posseman appointed by the local Council of National Defense in the town of Lincoln, arrested a "Holly [*sic*] Roller" preacher, F. D. Davidson, for giving a speech in his community that condemned the war and claimed that President Wilson was the "beast" referred to in biblical scriptures prophesying the End Times. He had also railed that the female Red Cross workers were "no better than harlots."[19] And the following month, local deputies apprehended twenty-three-year-old deserter Albert Denny as he left his brother's farmhouse near Hazel Valley, shooting both of his legs to prevent his escape.[20] Draft resistance, then, was more widespread throughout the rural Ozarks than many liked to imagine.

The first major episode of violent draft resistance in Arkansas occurred in Polk County in the Ouachita Mountains near the Oklahoma line. Local lawmen there began hunting draft resisters in late 1917, resulting in a raid and violent shootout in December. Authorities suspected that the draft evaders in Polk County were connected to the recent Green Corn Rebellion in Oklahoma, a nationally publicized stand against the draft that had been waged by disgruntled tenant farmers and members of the Working Class Union (WCU). Most of the draft resisters in Polk County were, indeed, small farmers and rural laborers at least loosely affiliated with the Socialist Party, the WCU, or the Industrial Workers of the World. They were also suspected of having illegal bootlegging connections with their fellow rural radicals in Oklahoma. Conflict between local authorities and the draft evaders persisted during the ensuing months, including the killing of a local Council of Defense member during an altercation with some antiwar farmers when he attempted to collect crop statistics and pledges for the federal government's food census. Authorities also suspected that three recent robberies were connected to the draft resisters. The conflict came to a head May 25, 1918, when the sheriff and a posse of thirty-six men raided the draft resisters' hideout and exchanged volleys of gunfire. The "Battle of Hatten's Gap," as the incident became known, resulted in two deaths, three wounded, and numerous arrests. Ultimately, juries sentenced one draft evader to the electric chair, one to life in prison, one to a ten-year prison term, and several others to lesser penalties. In late August, about a week before the scheduled execution of draft evader Ben Caughron—a rural Socialist who said he, like "many mountain men," believed the war was "a rich man's war"—Gov. Charles Brough, announced that he would not "interfere" in the matter, "believ[ing] that an example should be made in this case."[21]

While some observers were confident that the violent showdown in Polk County and the subsequent "example" made by authorities would settle the issue of draft resistance throughout the state, such hopes proved to be wishful thinking. Reports of draft resistance continued, a significant number of them coming from the Ozarks. In early June 1918 local lawmen and a citizens' posse organized in the town of Marshall, the seat of local government for Searcy County, deep in the heart of the Ozarks, to root out draft resistance in their area. Business-minded townsfolk in Marshall had been brimming with optimism ever since certain parts of their area had undergone a lead- and zinc-mining boom in the 1890s, and then the St. Louis and North Arkansas Railroad extended into Searcy County in 1903 to stoke a bonanza in the timber industry. Supporting the war effort was their chance to demonstrate the civic virtue, patriotism, and progress of their town and area. Marshall's leaders organized several "Patriotic Meetings," inviting prominent speakers and musicians from around the state and country to drum up local enthusiasm for the war effort. They also organized various groups and committees aiming to rally the county's citizens behind the national cause. Circuit Court Judge John Worthington even found it appropriate to turn "the first day of court over to these patriotic meetings after the juries have been impaneled" so that organizers for the war effort would have unhindered access to the courthouse and the town folks' undivided attention. By April 1918, war supporters boasted that Marshall had gone "over the top" in raising $16,050 in liberty bond subscriptions, a figure that exceeded the town's quota by $4,050. The town's high school also held its own fundraising rally and contributed an additional $1,250. "Tomorrow your neighbor or your neighbor's boy may give his life for our country," read an ad in the *Mountain Wave* for a series of "Patriotic Rall[ies]" to be held throughout the county in March 1918. "Are you a Patriot or a slacker? If you are a Patriot, rally around 'Old Glory.'"[22] Visions of business progress and development combined with American patriotism to have the *Wave* singing a new song; its attitude about antiwar dissent had changed remarkably from the positions it had once taken during the Spanish-American War.

Unfortunately for the "Patriots" in Searcy County, there were more "slackers" in their midst than they cared to admit—or cared to put up with. Antiwar sentiments in their county had even attracted the attention of the Little Rock office of the federal Bureau of Investigation, the U.S. Justice Department's surveillance agency charged with monitoring and investigating individuals and groups suspected of seditious behavior. In the summer of 1917 the Bureau had obtained a copy of a Searcy County newspaper, the *Leslie News*, which had published material critical of U.S. involvement in the World War. One article, titled "The United States Has Placed an Order for 200,000 Coffins!" received top billing on the front page of the paper's June 22 edition and warned readers that "those coffins are to be occupied—by somebody's boys!" The paper also printed a letter that urgently called for "the total defeat of the Allied Money power" and proposed that the U.S. government's massive war spending be redirected toward "conserving human life instead of destroying it." Offering $3,000 apiece to any German soldier who would voluntarily surrender, it proposed, would surely bring a rapid end to the war. These German "prisoners" of war, it continued, now "with hands washed pure from blood," could then be employed by the U.S. government and supervised by "American boys" no longer needed on destructive battlefields to begin amassing a "Grand Army of the World" that would dig canals, build roads, reclaim desert lands, work to eliminate hunger, and develop fair and secure employment for people around the world. "Who will combat this solution of the war, this solution that would heal every wound, banish all hatred, that would establish charity for all and malice toward none, as in the great American melting pot the races met on common ground?" the letter asked. "The Money Power, the Money Power, THAT DOES NOT WANT THE WAR TO END."[23]

After an investigation, however, bureau agent C. M. Walser reported that, while he would be sure to keep an eye on its future activities, the Leslie newspaper no longer appeared threatening. Walser had discovered that the owner of the paper, E. B. Bedford, was a native-born American and a member of the Christadelphian Church, "whose teachings he claims are against war." His investigation also found that the paper's editor, J. L. Barnett, also a native-born American, was a member of the Socialist Party. Nonetheless, Walser reassured his superiors that he had been "informed by subscribers . . . that they have ceased publishing such articles," and he was confident that the "postmaster and other loyal citizens" would let the Bureau know "if any more should appear."[24]

But if such vocal opposition to the war effort had mostly fallen silent in Searcy County by 1918, compulsory military conscription ensured that dissent would not go away. In early June, Sheriff J. H. Barnett received a tip that "Pet" Goodman was harboring draft evaders at his farm near Oxley. According to lawmen, word had circulated that the Goodmans had vowed they would not be taken without a fight. One of the Goodman boys, it was reported, had even committed suicide some months earlier "rather than enter military service," after he had been drafted by the local board and was ordered to report to Marshall for a medical examination. Expecting a confrontation, the sheriff and his posse left Marshall late in the night and surrounded Goodman's farmhouse, where they waited until daylight to conduct their raid. When the time came, Sheriff Barnett shouted to Goodman and his guests to surrender themselves. According to the lawmen, Levi Goodman, Pet's oldest son and a deserter, reached for his gun, and one of the officers opened fire, killing him instantly. Pet Goodman, his other son and draft resister Eli Goodman, and a neighbor and fellow deserter Wesley Passmore subsequently surrendered and were hauled to the county jail. The next day, officials took the Goodmans to Harrison in Boone County and held them there for a federal hearing, and they escorted Passmore back to military officials at Camp Pike in Little Rock. In August, Eli Goodman was ordered into military service at Camp Funston in Fort Riley, Kansas.[25]

Press reports revealed little about the Goodmans' and Passmore's motives. The *Fayetteville Democrat*, though, believed that the Goodmans' and their neighbors' "pernicious Socialis[m]" best explained their antiwar positions and bullheaded defiance.[26] Indeed, since agrarian Socialism had a particularly significant presence in Searcy County among small farmers and rural laborers during the early twentieth century, the Fayetteville newspaper, despite its unsympathetic hyperbole, may have been on the right track. The lives and experiences of the Goodmans and the Passmores, after all, were not unlike those of the thousands of other small farmers and rural working-class folks in the western South who joined the ranks of the Socialist Party during the early twentieth century. Rural Socialists championed what they believed would be a more just political economy, one that would curtail unfair exploitation by wealthy and powerful capitalists and rightfully return the fruits of productive labor to hardscrabble farmers and workers. They refused to stand for a horrific war that they believed had been primarily orchestrated by and for capitalist profiteers.

Hardscrabble farming was all Pet Goodman had ever known. He was born in 1867 to William E. and Martha Goodman in Searcy County. Several years before his birth, William and Martha had begun their lives together on a small farm in Lewis County, Tennessee. By 1860, though, William had given up farming to become a blacksmith. Sometime during the tumultuous decade of the 1860s, the Goodmans headed west to Big Flat Township in Searcy County, Arkansas, where William worked in a blacksmith shop and his four eldest sons, ranging in age from eleven to seventeen, worked as farm laborers. By 1880, with young Pet now twelve years old, William had quit blacksmithing, and the family ventured across the county line to settle on a small, rugged farm in Stone County.[27]

By the turn of the century, Pet Goodman had married a young woman from Kentucky, and the couple had settled on a small farm of their own in Searcy County, where they were raising three young boys. Ten years later, the Goodmans had added three more children to their family, and their three eldest sons, now ages sixteen, fourteen, and twelve, were old enough to provide valuable labor on the farm, especially during this era of increasingly commercial-oriented agriculture in which more and more small farmers found it difficult to compete. In 1911 the Goodmans owned one horse, three cattle, one mule, twenty-five hogs, one wagon, and $50 worth of equipment and other personal assets, for a combined personal property assessment of $330.[28]

Pet Goodman's sons were apparently still living in his household when the government initiated the military draft in 1917, and all three were called up by the local draft board in Marshall. This without a doubt placed major strains on the Goodman family, just at a time, in fact, when farmers in the Ozarks and elsewhere in rural America were beginning to hope for a better economic future, as international demand for American farm products during the war drove agricultural prices upward. Like many other hill farmers who sought to take advantage of these new opportunities, it appears that the Goodmans had started to expand production on their family farm during the war. By the end of the war, they had purchased a second mule, a relatively expensive investment for a poor hill farmer, indicating that they were probably tilling more land and producing more crops than before. They also appear to have sold off several hogs and some other assets and reinvested in a few more cattle, a move made by a number of hill farmers during the war years to capitalize on unprecedented beef prices.[29] The government's military conscription, then, which promised to strip away the family's most important labor source and strap them with huge burdens, probably only further validated for the Goodmans and several of their rural neighbors the persuasiveness of Socialist critiques and claims that this was truly a "rich man's war, and a poor man's fight."

The Goodmans and their neighbors also lived in an area that had a strong historical precedent of opposition to seemingly unjust wars conjured up by "elites" for their own selfish interests. Some of the Passmores, one of the largest extended families in the community who had deep roots in Searcy County's early settlement, had participated in the Arkansas Peace Society's objections against Arkansas's secession and the Confederacy back in 1861. A secretive organization of loosely affiliated anti-Confederate groups, composed mostly of small hill farmers, the Peace Society was eventually quashed by the Confederacy and local militias; many of its members were pressed into Confederate military service.[30]

The Passmores, like the Goodmans and many other Ozarkers, were also struggling in the face of confusing economic and social changes that increasingly stacked the odds against them. Back in 1892, John Passmore, the father of deserter Wesley Passmore, owned no horses, no mules, eight cattle, fifteen hogs, one wagon, $5 worth of gold or silver, and $20 worth of equipment and other personal assets. By 1911, he owned two horses, one mule, fourteen cattle, thirteen hogs, one wagon, and $150 in equipment and other assets. Vital to Passmore's small farming operation, especially by 1918, was the labor of twenty-three-year-old Wesley, two other sons who were either already eligible for the draft or would soon become eligible within a few months, and two younger sons just entering adolescence. The government's burdensome draft for a seemingly unnecessary war, then, must have appeared to the Passmore family as an intrusive, unwanted obstacle inhibiting their quest to get ahead and stay ahead in rural America.[31]

While none of the brief newspaper reports mentioned the families' faith in explaining the Goodmans' and Passmores' actions, their religious convictions may have nevertheless played a significant role in their decision to resist the draft. According to local historians and family descendants, most of the residents in the Oxley area were members of small, independent Baptist churches, many of whom considered themselves nondenominational Christians. While mainline denominations, especially in towns, often counted themselves among the most supportive of the war effort, a number of dissenting Christians in the region and throughout the rural South, including many members of the Churches of Christ, Holiness and Pentecostal churches, independent Baptists and Methodists, and nondenominational groups, considered the military conflict an unrighteous, "unjust war," at times even going so far as to condemn U.S. military action in Europe as "murderous."[32] Furthermore, members of such "churches of the disinherited" were frequently drawn to populist and Socialist politics, basing their political beliefs, in large part, on their interpretations of Scripture and the message of love and peace exhibited by their savior Jesus Christ. They viewed Jesus as the greatest advocate for social justice the world had ever known and held up his defense of the poor and downtrodden as the "Real Gospel of Christ."[33]

There is no question that religion figured prominently in the Adkisson family's and their Cleburne County neighbors' opposition to the war effort and military conscription. On July 6, 1918, Cleburne County Sherriff Jasper Duke organized a posse in the county seat of Heber Springs to hunt down draft resisters in his county, offering $50 apiece to the four "patriotic" citizens who joined him. Their sights were set on the Adkisson family and their rural neighbors between the villages of Pearson and Rose Bud near the White County line. The family's patriarch, Tom Adkisson, had been a thorn in the side of the local draft board since at least the previous October, when his son Bliss refused to report for military service, and many of his neighbors had also refused to comply. The Adkissons were premillennialist Russellite Christians (known today as Jehovah's Witnesses) who believed that the war represented the Satanic conspiracy long prophesied to usher in the biblical Apocalypse. While the Adkisson sons and several of their rural neighbors had registered for the draft, many of them had requested religious exemptions on the grounds that they were members of the International Bible Students Association and, thus, conscientious objectors to the war. Their requests had been denied by the local draft board.[34]

When Duke and his posse made their move at the Adkisson farm early on the morning of July 17, a brief gunfight ensued, leaving one of the sheriff's possemen fatally wounded. Duke and his small posse retreated to Heber Springs to gather reinforcements and returned with twenty-five men to the Adkisson farm later in the day. Meanwhile, the Adkissons had rounded up several neighbors to help mount a defense, and they stood ready when the posse returned. Another shootout erupted—this one lasting for forty-five minutes. The draft resisters, despite being outnumbered, were well-positioned around the farmhouse and surrounding structures, in the nearby woods, and even in treetops. Realizing the numerical odds were against them, however, the Adkissons and their comrades eventually escaped into the woods, where they would elude authorities for more than a week. They were finally taken into custody, but only after a dramatic manhunt conducted by local lawmen, volunteer "home guards," and even a unit of the 4th Arkansas Infantry, National Guard.[35]

For Russellite Christians, the World War seemed to confirm the prophesy of their recently deceased leader, Charles Taze Russell of Pittsburgh, Pennsylvania. Russell had predicted since the 1880s that the millennium would come after 1914 and had described how the nations of the world, long corrupted by sinful and self-serving religious and secular officials, would crumble into destruction and disorder before ushering in the biblical Second Coming of Christ and his thousand-year reign and Final Judgment. Only Christ's few true followers—themselves and fellow Russellites—would inherit God's heavenly reward, while the evil—nonbelievers and those so-called Christians who had diluted and tainted the purity of Scripture—would suffer eternal damnation. By the outbreak of war, Russellites believed "that the spirit of selfishness and ambition, which is driving the nations insanely to war for commercial supremacy, will increase more and more, and will involve everybody."[36] Thus, the pure had to stand firm. When the Selective Service called up the Adkisson boys and other young Russellite men in 1917, they viewed their experience as nothing less than a struggle between the righteous and unrighteous, between Godly virtue and the forces of evil in Armageddon.[37]

To gain a better understanding of this episode and the attitudes that led to such determined resistance, however, it is important to note that the elder Adkissons and their neighbors had not simply inherited a tradition of Russellism from their forefathers, for this was a relatively recent religious movement, especially in Cleburne County. Rather, social and economic conditions and personal experiences in the Ozarks during the late nineteenth and early twentieth centuries likely drew them to this new religious faith. Amid their struggles in the rural Ozarks, they likely found comfort and promise in this new doctrine that assured them their earthly hardships would soon be rewarded. Their faith promised the greatest of all populist justice. As historian Edward H. Abrahams explains, such dispossessed rural folks were drawn to Russellism because it "satisf[ied] their political, social, and emotional needs" by promising to "those who listened that their present trials would soon cease, that literally within a single day all the power and status that society had denied them would be theirs and theirs alone." Russell's teachings ultimately taught that "not until the kingdom of God is established can the rights of men be properly adjusted" and that no earthly political action could bring complete justice. Even so, some Russellites endorsed much of the agrarian-populist political agenda in the late nineteenth and early twentieth centuries for temporary, earthly relief and "clearly indicated where their sympathies lay."[38]

Tom Adkisson, the community leader and founder of Russellism in the area, was born in the fertile Arkansas River Valley in 1859 to Sampson and Martha Adkisson. His parents had moved from Tennessee to Arkansas in the 1840s and enjoyed rising prosperity and upward mobility farming the valley's rich soils. Between 1850 and 1860 the Adkissons saw the value of their real estate holdings grow from $500 to $4,500. In 1860 they claimed an additional $2,000 in personal property, including two slaves, making them one of seven slaveholding families in Muddy Bayou Township. Within a decade, however, just as young Tom began to come of age, the Adkisson family's fortune had reversed course. The Civil War and emancipation appear to have leveled major blows to the Adkissons' relative prosperity. By 1870, the value of the family's real estate property had plummeted by more than half to $2,000, and they had lost 75 percent of their previous personal property valuation. Sometime during the next decade, the Adkissons left their valley farm and headed north to the Ozarks to settle in the rugged hills of Van Buren County. Like many other hill farmers during this era, Sampson Adkisson joined the budding commercial timber industry in the region, undoubtedly hoping to restore the prosperity his household had enjoyed before the war. In 1880 the U.S. Census listed Sampson's primary occupation as a lumberman, while Tom, now age twenty-one but still living with his parents, was listed as a farmer, probably assuming most of the agricultural responsibilities on the family farm.[39]

Sometime during the next few years Tom left his parents' home and took up residence near Rose Bud along the Cleburne-White County line. In 1887 the twenty-eight-year-old Adkisson married twenty-year-old Alice Conner of Cleburne County, and the new couple set out to start a family and make a life of their own in the rural Ozarks.[40] Since the 1890 manuscript census records are not extant, not much is known about their lives during these years, but it was sometime during this period when Tom, as he himself later explained, embraced Russell's religious teachings. We can only speculate about Adkisson's conversion, but, having grown up amid his family's declining fortune and difficult struggles to regain their lost prosperity despite their hard work and entrepreneurial spirit, it may be that a disillusioned Adkisson found security in this doctrine of faith that promised justice, peace, and reward in the very near future.[41] After all, Adkisson, in addition to his own struggles, was witnessing the uncertainties and confusion of Gilded Age America all around him. Railroads had begun penetrating the region, new towns popped up seemingly overnight and out of nowhere, new and strange people came while some familiar neighbors were beginning to leave, and small-farm families' livelihoods became evermore subservient to unpredictable national and international market forces controlled by corporate interests. Confusion and frustration spawned resentment and strong feelings about injustice. Comments made later by Tom Adkisson after the shootout reveal a good deal about his thinking. When questioned about why his family had continued to use sugar and flour during the war despite other Cleburne County residents' patriotic pledge to consume only necessities such as corn meal to do their part for the country, Adkisson responded in typical populist language: "Lots of people don't deserve anything but corn bread, don't do anything to earn it. . . . I worked and earned it."[42]

By 1900, Tom, Alice, and their five young children were living on a farm of their own in Cleburne County, where Tom was running a small sawmill, probably harvesting the virgin timber on his own farm and perhaps that of neighboring farmers and selling the lumber in regional markets. Since the children were still too young to work at their father's sawmill, the Adkissons boarded two day laborers in their home, one age eighteen and the other nineteen. Within the next ten years, however, Adkisson quit his sawmilling operation, probably having exhausted most of the marketable timber resources in his area. Perhaps more important, Cleburne County had undergone major changes after the Missouri and North Arkansas Railroad snaked its way through the area in 1908. The population of Heber Springs, which would become the location of "one of the largest depots on the railroad," more than doubled by 1910, and the timber industry rapidly came to dominate the county's economy. Consequently, small independent sawmillers like Adkisson frequently found themselves crowded out once larger, more highly capitalized and technologically equipped operators set their sights on new timber areas that could now be harvested and shipped in profitable mass quantities by rail. By 1918, the old sawmilling site on the Adkisson farm was barely recognizable; an old rusted boiler and decaying sawdust piles were all that remained.[43]

With Adkisson's short-lived stint in the local sawmilling business over by 1910, the federal census now listed him as a general farmer. By then, Tom and Alice had eight children. Their two eldest sons, Bliss and Hardy, ages sixteen and fifteen respectively, were finally old enough to provide much-needed labor on the family farm. Gone were the two day laborers who had boarded with the family before, though another laborer, thirty-five-year-old Sam Bates, was living with them and working for wages on the farm. The Adkissons were clearly engaged in commercial agriculture. In 1915 Tom Adkisson owned two horses, two mules, eighteen cattle, five hogs, and $50 worth of equipment and other personal assets, all of which was assessed at $525 in taxable personal property. In 1918 Adkisson owned one horse, two mules, twenty cattle, seven hogs, and $70 worth of equipment and other personal assets, an assessed value of $540. In addition to marketing livestock and probably other surplus farm products, the Adkissons grew cotton and sold it to buyers in regional commercial centers such as Conway and Searcy.[44]

Like many other Ozarkers who raised livestock in numbers above subsistence levels, grew cotton as a cash crop, or sold other surplus farm products on the market, Tom and Alice Adkisson probably hoped to help reproduce their rural way of life for their children, six of whom had reached adulthood or were in their teens by 1918. In fact, by 1918 their twenty-four-year-old son Hardy, who was now married and the father of an infant child, had established the modest beginnings of his own household, having built a small house on the family farm about a hundred yards from his parents' home. That year he reported four cattle, three hogs, and $20 worth of equipment and other personal assets of his own, which amounted to a total personal property assessment value of $90. Hardy continued to work on his father's farm as well. Tom and Alice's daughter Pearle and her new husband, Leo Martin, were also beginning their life together. Martin, a Tennessee native, was earning wages working for a local farmer named E. A. Fisher, but he and Pearle continued to live with Tom, Alice, and their younger children in 1918, a living situation that likely helped precipitate a denial by the local draft board when Martin requested exemption. Another daughter of the Adkissons, Ila, had also recently married into a neighboring farm family, the Simmonses.[45]

The odds seemed to be stacking higher against these families and other small farmers throughout the Ozarks, especially for this next generation. In 1918, though, farm prospects seemed to look better, as wartime demand drove up the prices of American farm products in European markets. If the government and its war would only leave them alone, many must have believed, this might finally be the chance to improve their families' prospects in the rural Ozarks. But the interests of privileged, ungodly elites seemed to be standing in their way once again. This probably came as no surprise to the Adkissons. The Bible plainly told them, after all, that the privileged and ungodly of the world would reap their reward on earth but not in heaven; the righteous and just, on the other hand, would endure long-suffering in this dispensation before inheriting the Kingdom of Heaven in the next.

The Adkissons' neighbors and co-religionists undoubtedly shared this frame of mind as well. Despite their own struggles, the Adkissons were better off economically than most of their impoverished neighbors, such as the Sweeten and Simmons families. In 1918 E. J. "Jack" Sweeten, whose son Amos had deserted from Camp Pike in Little Rock and was also evading authorities by the summer, owned two horses, two cows, two mules, seven hogs, and $25 worth of equipment and other personal assets, for a total personal property assessment of $200, which was $340 less than Tom Adkisson's. Similarly, Matt Simmons, who would be Tom Adkisson's son-in-law and fellow draft-evasion accomplice by the time of the altercation with local authorities, owned no horses, one mule, four cattle, one hog, one $10 wagon, and $20 worth of equipment and other personal assets, for a total personal property value of only $120. Despite the small size of his farm, Simmons, like most others in his neighborhood, grew cotton as a cash crop and probably sold other surplus farm products on the market.[46] Sweeten, Simmons, and other poor hill farmers in the community may also have supplemented their meager farm incomes with part-time timber work or seasonal jobs. Merely scraping by, however, was about all it seemed they could muster. Adkisson's faith in Russellism apparently appealed to several of these neighbors.

It is unclear how Adkisson went about spreading his doctrine of faith in the area. Many conversions to Russellism were undoubtedly the consequences of intermarriage with the Adkisson family, which may also have won over some other extended family members. The number of Russellite Christians in the area is unknown, but press reports about the shootout indicate that adherents probably numbered more than just the Adkissons and their extended family network. Their religious community had apparently grown large enough by 1918 that they were able to hire a new Russellite preacher, former Baptist preacher Houston Ausburn, who brought a family of nine to the community. Others in the area probably adopted the faith through their economic and social dealings with the Adkissons. In 1903 Russell's organization, then headquartered in Pennsylvania, commenced its campaign of door-to-door evangelism and tract distribution that would come to characterize the Jehovah's Witnesses, so perhaps Adkisson and his Russellite brethren may have been employing these aggressive recruiting tactics during the years preceding World War I—tactics that may have been unwelcome and irritated some Cleburne County residents. If that was the case, though, Adkisson and his co-religionists do not appear to have been stigmatized in the area as dangerous or obnoxious religious radicals before the draft-resistance affair occurred. During the subsequent trial, several prominent citizens, including some Heber Springs townsfolk, testified that they had long known Tom Adkisson and had generally known him to be "all right, quiet, peaceable and honest, and a good fellow" before the draft incident.[47]

The only real question to surface in the case about Tom Adkisson's reputation dealt with his apparent thirst for the hard stuff, a chink in Adkisson's armor that the prosecution hoped would cast doubt on his character. Several witnesses said that "he used to drink right smart," though most qualified their statements by adding that Adkisson's occasional drinking sprees and rowdiness were nothing out of the ordinary and that he had simmered down since his younger days. Adkisson himself confessed that he had "paid a few fines for being drunk" in his younger years but insisted that he had not "ordered any whiskey I reckon for ten years"; he had "quit before the bone dry law came" to Cleburne County because he decided "it was best for me too." In 1906 Adkisson had been arrested and pleaded guilty on charges of disturbing the peace. Unfortunately, since the case file is missing, details of Adkisson's offense are unknown, though it probably involved one of these drunken escapades. Co-religionist Columbus Blakey was likewise arrested and convicted for disturbing the peace in 1915, despite a not-guilty plea. He was indicted again the same year, along with Harry Potey, though the specific charges were not recorded in the docket and the case was apparently dropped the following term.[48] It is possible that Adkisson and his neighbors had already ruffled some feathers in Cleburne County by 1918, but their religion does not appear to have branded them as undesirables before the conflict over the draft.

Still, some in Cleburne County harbored intolerant attitudes toward dissenters during the late nineteenth and early twentieth centuries, as did many of their counterparts throughout a rapidly changing America. A couple of conflicts between the town-dwelling "better sorts" and dissenters in the area even made national news. Even before the railroad came to transform Heber Springs in 1908, the town had long prided itself on being a lively, progressive tourist attraction built around the area's beautiful natural springs that had become popular health spas back in the 1880s. Local businessmen and boosters worked diligently to build and protect their town's New South image, especially at a time when the Ozarks, like Appalachia back east, increasingly became associated with the "dim-witted hillbilly and the noble hillman" in America's popular consciousness.[49]

Russellism was not the only "strange sect" to crop up that threatened the county's respectable image. The *New York Times* had reported in 1897 that a "state of panic" had arisen among the town people of Heber Springs over the birth of a new movement of dissenting Christians in the area who referred to themselves as "The Order of Holiness." "The carousals of the holiness camp shocked the community," the paper reported. Alarmed Heber Springs residents sought to suppress these "crazed" people and their teachings, even with the use of local law enforcement.[50] Many townsfolk also proved ready to stamp out anyone who bucked the political and economic ideals of town "progress," even if it required extralegal means. Less than five years after the draft resistance affair, a self-appointed "citizens' committee" was formed to supplant anyone in the county suspected of participating in or sympathizing with the Great Railroad Strike that had recently swept the nation. On a cold January night in 1923, they captured two men, whipped them, and forced them to leave the area. This act of intimidation and other "investigation[s]" and "question[ing]" by the "citizens committee" succeeded, according to the *New York Times*: "Virtually every striker or strike sympathizer was reported to have either left that vicinity or was preparing to leave."[51] Like other boosters and residents in budding towns in the region, Heber Springs townsfolk were not about to allow their county's reputation to be called into question and risk ruining their quest to become the New South's next success story.

When the United States went to war in 1917, local businessmen and officials in Heber Springs determined to demonstrate exceptional commitment to the national cause, and no "slackers" refusing to comply with military conscription would dare spoil their mission. As Jeannette Keith explains, "Mobilization put considerable if unspecified power into the hands of members of the town elites," and sincere patriotism frequently blurred with economic interests and boosterism.[52] It is no surprise that many who joined the citizens' posses in Heber Springs and the nearby towns of Searcy, Pearson, and Quitman to go after draft resisters were local businessmen and professionals. S. A. Turner, one of the original four possemen who accompanied Sheriff Duke and took part in the initial shootout, was a physician in Heber Springs. Porter Hazlewood, the posseman who was killed in the shootout, appears to have been an aspiring gunsmith or a firearms dealer in town, though the only personal property he reported in 1917 was $10 worth of firearms. J. R. Chesbro, who joined Sheriff Duke's posse for the second shootout, was a town merchant whose entrepreneurial ambition would land him a conviction and a $10 fine for illegal cigarette sales. The leader of another citizens' posse, Arthur Frauenthal, was a thirty-two-year-old jewelry salesman in Heber Springs and the chairman of the County Council of Defense. Frauenthal, ironically, was the son of a German Jewish immigrant, the late Max Frauenthal, a prosperous merchant, Confederate veteran, county political leader, and the original founder of Heber Springs. In addition to his stake in guarding the town's image, Arthur Frauenthal may also have been self-conscious, despite his prominent standing among local elites, about leaving any doubts regarding his allegiance to the Red, White, and Blue in the fight against his "dreaded Hun" kinfolk.[53] For these men and other local boosters filled with wartime patriotism, it was their time to shine and prove to any naysayers that their county was as progressive as anywhere else America—indeed, "100% American." The Adkissons and their neighbors would pay for their un-American "slacking" one way or another.

After the shootout at the Adkisson farm, more than one hundred armed men began searching the countryside for the draft resisters and their supporters, and this number grew within a couple of days to more than two hundred. Governor Brough dispatched a contingent of National Guard troops armed with machine guns. Local officials and town businessmen even petitioned the governor to declare martial law.[54] Family members and neighbors suspected of sympathizing with or aiding the draft evaders were arrested and detained in a Heber Springs hotel for questioning. Among those arrested were Ila Simmons and Pearle Martin, the daughters of Tom Adkisson and wives of draft evaders. They told authorities that their family and neighbors were, in fact, loyal Americans but were "conscientious objector[s] to war." Fearing for the lives of the evaders, Ila and Mrs. Blakey, the mother of three draft resisters, convinced federal officials to allow them to try to contact the evaders and ask them to surrender, though their efforts to find them were unsuccessful. Authorities also arrested Russellite minister Houston Ausburn and his family, after they found him hiding under the floor of his home. They suspected Ausburn was a key instigator, because he had been preaching that the "world is coming to an end as a result of the world war, and that all men participating in the conflict will be doomed to eternal hellfire, that those who do not engage in war will be spared and that therefore men should not put on a uniform."[55]

Jack Sweeten, the father of two resisters, was also arrested, but he promised officials that he knew the whereabouts of one of his sons, Amos, who had deserted from Camp Pike. He thought he could talk this son into surrendering if they would release him. But when Sweeten returned that night to Heber Springs without Amos, an angry mob seized him and "threatened to lynch him." Luckily for Sweeten, one man intervened to prevent the lawless act. But news of the old man's harsh treatment somehow quickly reached his son, and Amos rushed to town to turn himself in about an hour after midnight. Amid the "feeling of intense indignation" and the potential for "mob law" in Heber Springs when Amos surrendered, he and his father were quickly escorted to the county jail.[56]

Meanwhile, heavily armed possemen and soldiers hunted for the draft evaders and worked to "dry up" any supplies, food, or shelter that might assist the "slackers." Plans to isolate and squeeze the resisters out of their wooded hideouts and into submission eventually succeeded, though it took much longer than expected. Four days after the shootout, lawmen spotted George Burleson and his stepson walking along a dirt road near Rose Bud. When captured, Burleson was said to have been carrying a copy of *The Finished Mystery*, a volume of Charles Taze Russell's writings published after his death in 1917 that had been banned by federal authorities. One federal judge had claimed the book was more dangerous than "a division of the German army" because it denounced patriotism, war, and "civil governments of the earth" that rule in contradiction to "the law of heaven."[57] The next day, the National Guard troops and other lawmen conducted their most thorough search yet. Faulkner County Sheriff W. W. Bishop took prisoner Ila Simmons and her Uncle Tobe Adkisson, who had recently arrived from Conway, on a long drive through the area, hoping to find their kinfolk and convince them to surrender. But the Adkissons and other draft resisters remained at large.[58]

The National Guard unit packed up its machine guns and returned to Little Rock the following day. But local law enforcement and citizens' posses remained determined as ever. Tom Adkisson's son-in-law Leo Martin, who told officers he was "tired of being hunted," finally surrendered on Saturday morning in White County. On Sunday, after surviving for a week on water and peanuts, four more draft resisters, Jim, Jess, and Columbus Blakey and John Penrod, turned themselves in to the Searcy-Judsonia Home Guard at Rose Bud. Bliss Adkisson surrendered at the same place the next day. Finally, on Tuesday—nine days after the shootout—Hardy Adkisson turned himself in at the town of Cabot in Lonoke County, and Tom Adkisson went to Conway in Faulkner County to give himself up. He told authorities that he and the others would have surrendered to federal officials earlier had it not been "for fear the other [local civilian] mob would cut us off."[59]

As the spectacle of draft resistance in Cleburne County drew to a close, observers weighed in to explain the Adkissons' and their neighbors' stubborn defiance against the government's draft. Charles T. Davis of the *Arkansas Gazette*, in a lengthy article on July 14, attributed the Cleburne County affair to a backward rural hill culture:

> To one who sees the mountains from afar off it would seem that the mountain people should be God's chosen people, that their souls should be great with the vast distances they view, and their hearts in harmony with the marvelous beauties of nature. . . . But this is not so. It is not so in the Swiss Alps, nor the Balkan mountains, nor the Himalaya piedmonts, nor the Ozark foothills. Geographically the mountains have always bulked against the progress of industrial advancement,

and sociologically their people have always stood against the forward movement of national betterment. There are probably many reasons, not the least of which is the law of heredity.

The "Heritage" of the hill folks' pioneer "ancestors," Davis surmised, had been fully preserved "in the sanctuary of the mountains," which explained why mountaineers even in the twentieth century "still carry an inborn hatred of the law, inbred and interbred through generations." Isolation had created "a simple inability to comprehend . . . the primal causes of the law, the changed conditions which made it necessary." Davis wrote that the rural Ozarker had long been "afflicted with a mental myopia." "Out there lies a big land, he knows, but its existence affects him little." "He limits his gaze to the close drawn horizon of the hills which gird him round," the journalist stated, "and he cannot vision the high, ineffable stars nor that which lies beneath beyond." Ultimately, because these backwoodsmen had "little sense of any geographical limits more than purely local," Davis argued that "the very limitations of their information render them an easy prey to fanatics or renegades of their own people who take up the preaching of sedition under the guise of religion," such as "the subtle, sapping dogmas of the Russellite[s]."[60]

Yet Davis's use of mountain stereotypes and rural parochialism to diagnose the Cleburne County affair proved overly simplistic, even among at least some contemporary federal officials. In early August an officer of the Fourth Arkansas National Guard unit completed an official investigation and, in shifting at least part of the blame to the local draft board and law enforcement, concluded that the whole incident might have been avoided if local authorities had been more sensitive to the resisters' religious objections and taken better care to explain noncombat alternatives that were available. Federal authorities, then, seemed to demonstrate far greater empathy for the rural resisters than the local administrators did, notwithstanding assumptions that local control was inherently more democratic.[61]

Despite the U.S. military investigation's findings, a court martial sentenced four of the deserters, Jesse and Columbus Blakey, John Penrod, and Leo Martin, to five years of hard labor in the military barracks at Fort Leavenworth, Kansas, with dishonorable discharges once their time was served. Several of the resisters were also indicted by the circuit court in Cleburne County on charges ranging from assault (with intent) to kill to first-degree murder. The Adkissons, of course, received the harshest sentences. Tom Adkisson attempted to take the rap for killing posseman Porter Hazlewood, but a jury convicted his son of second-degree murder and sentenced him to eighteen years in prison. The defense appealed the case to the Arkansas Supreme Court but lost. Tragically, during a jailbreak at the state prison in Little Rock in September 1921, an escaping inmate killed Bliss Adkisson, who was on guard duty. Meanwhile, Tom Adkisson was convicted of voluntary manslaughter and got two-and-a-half years in prison. A jury also found his other son, Hardy, guilty of the same charges and gave him two years behind bars. Gov. Thomas McRae paroled Tom Adkisson in May 1921 for good behavior but then "ordered his re-arrest and return to prison" to serve the rest of his time when the American Legion of Arkansas and its local members "protested vehemently" against the "slacker's" release.[62]

The drama in Cleburne County was not the last explosive encounter between rural draft resisters and authorities in the Arkansas Ozarks. Another incident of armed resistance broke out deep in the heart of the Boston Mountains—the most rugged subregion in the Arkansas Ozarks—in the Cecil Cove community near Erbie and Wilcockson in Newton County. (The latter locale was the future home of Dogpatch, USA, a theme park founded in 1967–68 and based on Al Capp's popular hillbilly comic strip). There, amid "nearly impenetrable mountains, ravines and tangles of timber and underbrush" that one newspaper said would "fill a stranger's soul with trepidation," local authorities estimated that as many as thirty-six evaders and their family members had organized in armed defense and signed a "covenant" to resist the draft. Several young men in Cecil Cove had been eluding authorities since September 1918. But the "belated call" to Arthur Keeton, the son of Bill Keeton—a former justice of the peace in the community and, ironically, a member of the local draft board—appears to have precipitated the resisters' collective action. Bill Keeton sought his son's exemption by citing the need for Arthur to carry the mail for the U.S. Postal Service in his rural neighborhood. Apparently, other members of the draft board in the county-seat town of Jasper had overruled Keeton's attempt to have his son and other neighbors exempted.[63]

Newton County Sheriff W. J. Pruitt prepared to arrest the "Cecil Cove Slackers" but quickly decided against risking the lives of his deputies when, according to one newspaper report, he received a threatening notice from the draft resisters that read, "Come on, but look out for yourself." The evaders had a clear tactical advantage, positioned high and well-fortified in the cove's steep, mountainous terrain. Indeed, a few outspoken war supporters near Cecil Cove also reported that they too had experienced dangerous run-ins with the draft resisters. Joe McFerrin had wanted to check on some of his cattle that were feeding on the open range in the cove but said he was warned not to "come down to look after 'em." The resisters had also rounded up "a drove of hogs" in the cove, animals owned by Levi Smith, a merchant in the small town of Compton, and took them to his place one night, leaving a note that read: "You don't need to come down into the Cove." Another resident of the area, Alex Biggs, an itinerant preacher who championed the U.S. war effort, even decided to leave the community altogether because of his neighbors' antiwar positions, stating, "I couldn't stay there and think the way I do."[64]

"Uncle Jimmy" Richardson, the preacher at the Chapel Church just west of the cove, probably received the most serious threat. A Confederate veteran who had come to the Ozarks from central Tennessee during the late 1800s, the elderly Richardson was an avid supporter of the war effort and had outspokenly condemned the "gang of yellow bellies" in Cecil Cove. Richardson had chastised the resisters' fathers, telling them: "If you got any manhood in you them boys will be made to go serve their country." It's no surprise that the families in the cove did not take kindly to Richardson's neighborly advice. When the preacher traveled into the cove one day, he claimed that a concealed gunman fired at him, the shot coming so close that "the bullet whistled past his ear." "In the old days of the Civil War," Richardson told a newspaper reporter, "them kind was swung up to the nearest tree." He was frustrated with the sheriff's reluctance to confront "the cowardly hounds," complaining, "I'm 73 now, but I'd have got down my rifle and gone in with anybody that would have went after them." "I don't like to live near folks who ain't Americans," he said. Paradoxically, by 1918 this old Southern rebel had become "100% American."[65]

By the mid-September, local authorities pleaded with Washington officials to declare martial law in their county and begged for federal lawmen to come deal with the draft resisters. Col. Mark Wheeler, the second-in-command at Camp Pike in Little Rock, arrived to meet with local authorities in Jasper and told them, "If you fellows don't round these men up soon I think we'll let our boys come up and clear out these slackers." He seemed sure that his troops "would like the job." But after further assessment, Wheeler apparently changed his tune. He and other federal authorities determined that "it would take a regiment of soldiers months to comb the country, which is so rough that . . . [it is] doubt[ful] the search could be undertaken with horses." More important, they concluded that any attempt to arrest the draft resisters would be "nothing short of suicide," as Deputy U.S. Marshal Jim Holt put it.[66]

Interestingly, the U.S. War Department directed local authorities to try negotiating with the "Cove gang" and to assure them that desertion charges would not be filed if they surrendered peacefully. According to locals interviewed after the affair ended, federal officials also promised the resisters that they would arrange it so that the young men would be "gone only from sixty to ninety days, [and] that they would all get a suit of clothes and a dollar a day." In the meantime, Newton County swore in a new sheriff, Frank Carlton, who was born and raised within five miles of Cecil Cove, had taught school in the area, and was well acquainted with many of the families who lived there. Carlton was confident that he could convince the resisters to surrender and went to the cove to meet with the families. He promised to arrange to have the evaders turn themselves in at a remote crossroads, assuring them he would come unarmed and with no other lawmen or local citizens' posses; he alone would escort them to federal authorities at the military base at Camp Pike. The draft evaders agreed, and the potentially explosive affair ended peacefully. "Uncle Sam's Little War in the Arkansas Ozarks," as the *Literary Digest* labeled the Newton County incident, ended with only one casualty, in fact. One resister's twelve-year-old brother had been traipsing through the cove and, mistaken as a local posseman, was shot in the leg by friendly fire.[67]

Despite its anticlimactic ending, the story of "How the Hill Billies of Cecil Cove Defied Uncle Sam" drew the attention of the *Kansas City Star's* yellow journalism mill, which tended to keep a watchful eye on its peculiar rural mountain neighbors to the south for scoops that could be whipped up into sensational stories.[68] The *Star* found it amusing that "Cecil Cove, in the most remote [v]astness of the North Arkansas Ozarks, [had] baffled the United States government where the Wilhelmstrasse failed at the job." "Bernstorff, Von Popen, Dernburg and their like couldn't fool Uncle Sam's agents," the paper remarked, "but [the cove's] old Lige Harp and their boys could and did." Framing the story with typical rural stereotypes, the paper commented that "time swings far backward" in this rugged and isolated community:

> The little log cabins that house families of eight and ten seem to belong to another era. Hogs, dogs, cats, chickens, geese, turkeys and children run riot in, around and through these houses. Rifles of several stages, from the long-barreled muzzle-loader to the most modern repeater, hung above the open fireplaces. Corn pone, corn fed hogs and sorghum molasses are the culinary standbys. "Pa and Ma" and the majority of the kids smoke corncob pipes, sometimes use snuff and always are unerring spitters. The youngest of the family is considered deserving of a reprimand if he cannot hit the fireplace at ten paces. The mountain folk are suspicious of strangers and are exceedingly reticent in their presence, but are peculiarly hospitable. It is something akin to an insult if the wayfarer does not stop and partake in their hospitality, but he will find difficulty in getting questions answered.

Hill folks' clannishness and their exceptional intimacy with the forbidding terrain were what allowed them to elude one of the most powerful and resourceful governments on the planet, the *Star* explained; "News travels by strange and devious processes in the mountains" through close-knit family networks. Paradoxically, while the paper depicted a primitive rural community frozen in time, the pervasive use of telephones somehow proved especially useful, allowing the families to know the minute a stranger set foot in the cove. The *Star* also suggested that a peculiar mountaineer physique provided advantages over the authorities: "Bent forward, walking with characteristic shuffle, he can scurry over boulder and fallen log like an Indian."[69]

"What caused the rebellion in Cecil Cove?" the *Star* asked. "A combination of plain ignorance, Jeff Davis politics, the *Appeal to Reason*, and mountain religion," it explained. The paper employed mountain stereotypes and caricatures and portrayed their resistance against the draft as backward and irrational, but it was closer to the mark in pointing to their political and religious dissent, despite a clear lack of empathy. "Same stuff that Jeff Davis created about all those years the 'hill billies' were electing him to the United States Senate.... He is dead now, but his teachings live in the activities of these mountain people," the paper remarked. "Uncle Lige" Harp, a small farmer and one of the cove community's most respected patriarchs, told a reporter, "We didn't have no right to send folks over to Europe to fight; tain't a free country when that's done." "Wait till them Germans come over here and then fight 'em," said Harp. "If anybody was to try to invade this country ever [*sic*] man in the hills would get his rifle and pick 'em off."

The war probably irked the Harps even more because sending off their son Wesley and other young men to serve in the military brought immense burdens upon their small farm community. The descendant of antebellum-era Ozarks pioneers and son of a Union veteran of the Civil War, Lige Harp was born around 1860 and appears never to have ventured far from Newton County. His family entered the twentieth century toiling as small farmers in Cecil Cove. By 1918, his eldest two sons had left the community, and an aging Harp depended on his twenty-five-year-old son Wesley to help operate the family farm, especially since his teenage son Garrett suffered from a disabling mental illness and his other son was only about nine years old. Receiving the local draft board's orders for Wesley to report for military duty, then, must have been particularly troubling, if not downright devastating, for the Harps, just as it was for other small farm families in similar situations.[70]

Family farm problems also mixed with deep religious convictions to rally resistance in Cecil Cove. The local church leader, Holiness preacher and farmer George Slape, told reporters that "the good book says: 'Thou shalt not kill.'" "We didn't want our boys takin' nobody's life," he explained, ".... 'cause it's contrary to the Bible and the good Lord's teachin's." When one reporter questioned Slape about why the evaders could violently take up arms against the authorities, he responded: "The boys wasn't goin' to kill nobody unless they had to. It's different killin' a man who tries to make you do wrong and killin' somebody in war."[71]

Brother Slape and his family were also rural Socialists. The son of a Confederate veteran and small farmers, George Slape was born in Boone County around 1855. In 1877 Slape married a local woman, Mary, and they settled on a small farm and began raising a family in the same county. Unlike the Harps, though, the Slapes were quite mobile during the next several years. By 1900, the family, now with eight children, had moved a few miles south to a farm in Newton County. Sometime during the next decade, the Slapes, including the young family of their eldest daughter Rosa and her new husband Thomas Edwards, left for Cherokee County, Oklahoma. They worked as tenant farmers and wage hands and probably became involved in the growing agrarian Socialist movement in the new Sooner State. Another daughter, Elsia, married Georgia native, Oklahoma farm laborer, and fellow Socialist Jim Blackwell, and they, too, began raising a family. The Slapes and their extended family left Oklahoma sometime after 1910 and returned to Cecil Cove. The Slapes rented a house north of the cove in Boone County, where George apparently farmed his own land and preached on Sundays at the local church in Cecil Cove. The Blackwells and their young children lived with the Slapes and worked on the farm, while the Edwardses settled and farmed a place of their own. When questioned about why they and their neighbors had resisted the draft, Jim Blackwell and his friend France Sturgil stated that the U.S. war effort was nothing more than a scheme "for the benefit of them silk hat[t]ed fellers up in New York." "We don't want our boys fightin' them rich fellers' battles and gettin' killed just to make a lot of money for a bunch of millionaires," they explained. "Why they own most of the country now." According to the *Kansas City Star*, Blackwell and Sturgil were "reputed to have been the circulators of the covenant [to defy the draft]" and to "have read scattering copies" of the *Appeal to Reason*, the prominent Socialist newspaper published in Girard, Kansas.[72] Despite its overriding theme of isolation-induced ignorance and rural anti-modernism, the *Star's* own reporting belied the reality that these small farmers in Cecil Cove were taking part in a broad international ideology and criticism of the political economy of war.

The rural Ozarkers who resisted the U.S. government's military conscription, then, did so because the draft violated their populist sense of justice, fairness, and morality and imposed unique burdens on their small farm families. The federal government's Selective Service system delegated much of the real administration to local draft boards, which handed immense power to local elites who made decisions based on their own points of view, visions, and interests. The particular needs of poor-to-middling backcountry families often went ignored in the process. Draft evaders in the Ozarks were not the ignorant rural parochials depicted by town dwellers and newspaper reporters. Far from it, many embraced "modern," progressive political ideas that aimed to foster a more democratic political economy and corral the power of business elites and corporate interests. They despised U.S. military intervention in Europe in 1917 and 1918 because they deemed it to be yet another contrivance by well-to-do business interests to conduct a "rich man's war" with "a poor man's fight."

The struggles of small farmers in the Ozarks continued after World War I, as did populist resistance against government policies that seemed to favor "elites" and "special interests" at their expense. The ultrapatriotism and demands for conformity during World War I and the anticommunist Red Scare hysteria that followed, however, stigmatized as "un-American" many of the traditional populist expressions against inequality in the region, just as they did throughout the rest of America. When a young Independence County hill farmer sat on the stand in a courtroom in 1922 to defend himself against murder charges, for instance, the prosecuting attorney found it useful to bring up the fact that the suspect had dodged the draft back in 1917 and 1918. When asked why he had refused the local draft board's orders to report to fulfill national duty, the defiant Ozarker cussedly responded: "That is for me to know and you to find out." The prosecuting attorney moved on, confident that this exchange about draft resistance had painted the defendant as a dangerous and subversive character.[73] Due to such powerful stigmatization, then, the more vocal rural criticisms of economic and social injustices had quietened, as had the kinds of collective rural political action that had been prolific in the late 1800s. Rural draft resistance was quickly buried and forgotten in regional memory, and its history has been omitted from the dominant narratives of Ozarks culture ever since.

Nevertheless, populist sensibilities and the determined resistance they produced persisted in the Ozarks backcountry. Small farmers continued their struggles against a political economy that seemed constantly to work against them but helped their local elite antagonists instead. The Independence County farmer just mentioned, in fact, was standing trial, along with several of his neighbors, to determine his role in one of rural America's most violent cases of resistance to a federal farm policy that they felt burdened small farmers for the benefit of well-to-do business elites.

4

THE DAMN GOVERNMENT'S TICK TROUBLE

On a cool Monday morning, March 20, 1922, Charles Jeffrey left his home near Jamestown, Arkansas, to begin his week's duties as a federal cattle tick inspector in the hills of Independence County. The prosperous owner of two farms and a blacksmith shop, Jeffrey had been hired to inspect quarantined cattle and enforce local compliance with the U.S. Department of Agriculture's (USDA) tick eradication program designed to eliminate Texas fever, or *babesiosis*.[1] En route to supervise a cattle dipping, Jeffrey met local farmer and fellow inspector Lee Harper on Hutchinson Mountain around 7:30 A.M. Harper expressed concern to Jeffrey about rumors of antidipping threats in the community that he had just heard while quail hunting with some friends. Despite threats that he himself had recently received, Jeffrey intended to carry out his duties, and the two proceeded toward the dipping vat.

Trekking along a wooded farm road, Jeffrey was suddenly cut down by a thunderous shotgun blast. Harper, who was slightly wounded in the right arm, begged the concealed assassin to spare him and scurried to a house nearby to report the incident. Jeffrey lay gasping for his last breaths, his lungs filled with buckshot. Within an hour Jeffrey was dead, and the county sheriff and a local posse led by Jeffrey's eldest son, Sherman, and brother, A. L., soon arrived at the murder scene, bent on hunting down the assailant. By the next day, local, state, and federal lawmen, with assistance from bloodhounds, had apprehended

six suspects and continued to hunt for more. They believed tick eradication opponents in the community had organized a "conspiracy" to murder Jeffrey.[2]

The Jeffrey murder was a particularly horrific instance of a broader challenge to the federal government's tick eradication program. In her history of
the federal tick program in the South, historian Claire Strom seeks to explain
the widespread resistance to tick eradication from small farmers, especially
those in relatively isolated places such as the highlands, marshes, and piney
woods—what she calls "the few remaining outlying bastions of southern yeomen."[3] Southern farmers opposed the program, according to Strom, because it
infringed on their Jeffersonian political ideals and traditional allegiance to local
democracy and because it burdened without benefit "semisubsistence" farmers
who, she claims, "rais[ed] cattle largely for themselves" or for local trade only
and had no stake in national markets. Likewise, local historians have argued
that fiercely independent and authority-defying farmers in the Ozarks "saw the
[tick eradication] law as too much government interference in their lives."[4]

An examination of Ozarks smallholders and the murder of Charles Jeffrey, however, warrants a more nuanced treatment. Rather than a high-statist
program imposed from bureaucrats in Washington, it was local and regional
elites who instigated and administered a remarkably decentralized tick eradication campaign in the name of "efficient" and "improved" agriculture. Small,
less-capitalized farmers who received few or no benefits from the program,
meanwhile, resented the burdens and expense it placed on them and viewed it
to be yet another ruse cooked up by self-serving elites. This resistance to federal power was, in their minds, another case of populist backcountry defiance
against "well-bred" locals, their competing agribusiness interests, and their
privileged position in the regional political structure.

Most backcountry farmers, furthermore, were in no way isolated from national, or even international, market forces—nor, apparently did they want to
be. As we have already seen, despite relative geographic isolation, small farmers still participated in national markets and, these market trends affected their
lives in significant ways. The mast and greenery of the open range of the Ozarks
were well suited for raising cattle, and many hill farmers used these resources
in their entrepreneurial efforts not simply to sustain their families but to get
ahead in a commercial economy. To borrow the words of Appalachian historian
Robert S. Weise, "Economically, localism did not at all imply an anticommercial
or antimarket attitude."[5]

While some smallholders raised only one or two cows for strictly subsistence
purposes (mostly for milk and butter), cattle represented the most valuable
cash commodity for many others, even if their herds were much smaller and

comprised poorer stock than those of more prosperous cattlemen. Indeed, it was their connection to national market forces, rather than their disinterest in or isolation from commercial farming activities, that brought their opposition to dipping laws to a boil. Although there had been discontent over, and resistance to, the tick program in many parts of the South since its inception in 1906, the deadliest incidents of resistance occurred amid the agricultural crisis of the early 1920s. Many small farmers had benefited from high cattle prices driven by increased international demand during World War I and had accordingly suffered from the market fallout of the postwar years that sent cattle prices spiraling to their lowest points in more than a decade.[6]

Chiefly orchestrated by Southern agribusiness and political elites, the eradication program had its origins in a congressional appropriation to the USDA in 1906 to combat Texas fever. A quarantine that roughly followed the northern border of the old Confederacy but also included southern California had been established at the behest of Northern beef producers in 1891 by the USDA to protect Northern cattle from Texas fever, caused by protozoa hosted by ticks. This deadly and contagious disease carried by Southern cattle bound for slaughter and meatpacking houses in the North and Midwest threatened the herds of Northern and midwestern cattlemen, whose higher-grade breeds were vulnerable to the fever. While native "scrub" cattle in the South had developed immunity to the fever, the quarantine line posed a disadvantage for the increasing number of wealthier cattlemen in the South who were attempting to emulate the more capital-intensive, midwestern-style cattle business and sought to participate in more profitable higher-grade beef markets. Although there was an "open season" in the winter during which Southern cattle could be shipped above the quarantine line without restrictions, the quarantine hindered Southern cattlemen's access to ship their stock to Northern markets. Southern cattle had to be either slaughtered in the South and then shipped out (which proved problematic since there were few meatpacking houses in the South) or shipped in special quarantine-marked railroad cars and slaughtered immediately when they reached their Northern destinations. Either way, the extra expense and hassle cut significantly into profits, particularly for those bigger cattlemen investing in higher-quality livestock to sell to Northern slaughterhouses for choice-grade beef markets.[7]

But Texas fever also posed a more immediate threat to larger cattlemen attempting to raise top-quality, pure-bred stock in the first place. Just as the disease was proving deadly to cattle in the North and Midwest, the fever tick was taking its toll on high-grade purebreds imported by more prosperous cattlemen in the South. These well-to-do livestock growers, their political representatives, and the scientific experts promoting their interests at agricultural experiment stations and the USDA were the key figures in the establishment of the tick eradication program in 1906.[8]

Assuming that tick eradication would receive nearly unanimous support as a "progressive" measure that benefited all farmers, the USDA initially embarked on a voluntary program. Placing the tick program under the charge of its Bureau of Animal Industry (BAI), the USDA sought to work closely with state experiment stations and with county governments, offering matching funds for voluntary local programs and leaving the planning and administration mostly to local officials. The program's supporters and the BAI soon found, however, that farmers in only a few locales were willing to join their effort, and those tended to be the likeminded cattlemen in more prosperous agricultural areas—those who, not surprisingly, stood to gain the most from tick eradication.[9]

In Arkansas, eradication began in the northern part of the state, with special interest given to the relatively prosperous counties of the Springfield Plain subregion of the Ozarks. Washington and Benton Counties, the former the home of the state's flagship university, had long set themselves apart from the rest of the rugged Ozarks as a "progressive" agricultural center. These counties were at the forefront of the state's efforts to establish an improved cattle industry. Generally better-off farmers there heeded the suggestions of agricultural scientists and experts at the nearby Agricultural Experiment Station at the University of Arkansas who claimed that "in no other State is there greater need of improvement of the native cattle or greater prospective profits from the importation of pure bred males of the beef breeds."[10] While opposition to tick eradication in Washington and Benton Counties was not entirely absent, the program "was more favorable among the prosperous farmers of the Springfield Plain," as historian Brooks Blevins puts it, "which was the birthplace of such progressive intervention."[11] Progressive Washington and Benton County farmers and their prominent cattle growers' associations answered the call. "The better class of intelligent and up-to-date farmers and stock owners was willing and eager to do all in their power, both by precept and example, to forward the important work of tick eradication," commended the director of the Agricultural Experiment Station in 1907. By 1914, Washington and Benton Counties, along with several others, had been declared tick free and were lifted from the federal quarantine.[12]

Eradication was less successful in other parts of the region. Whereas more prosperous cattlemen in the business of raising purebred cattle for choice beef markets embraced and encouraged the eradication program, smaller farmers raising "scrub" stock on the open range were less inclined to see any benefits from the program. Even in counties that had been declared tick free by 1914, eradication efforts had had to overcome the grumbles and groans of opponents. In rugged Newton County, for instance, tick inspectors faced "some trouble here at first, as many refused to dip cattle," but the program prevailed, nonetheless. Once local eradication supporters and the BAI realized that many small farmers were unwilling to cooperate with the federal program voluntarily, they abandoned their "carrot" approach for the "stick," working through state and local governments to force mandatory dipping by law.[13]

Historians have viewed the conflict over tick eradication as part of a broader dispute between "progressives" and "traditionalists."[14] These labels, however, run the risk of oversimplification and of misunderstanding the real dynamics of the disputation. As the recent works of historians such as Charles Postel and Elizabeth Sanders have shown, small farmers—the so-called "traditionalists" in many historians' accounts—often stood among the most determined "progressive" champions of government-supported educational advancements and scientific farming improvements during the late nineteenth and early twentieth centuries.[15] In Arkansas, for instance, many resented the University of Arkansas's and the state Agricultural Experiment Station's relatively inaccessible location in Fayetteville in the extreme northwest corner of the state. As Blevins has noted, the presence of the state university and experiment station in Fayetteville "provided farmers of northwestern Arkansas with valuable scientific information and helped spur the development of a prosperous and diverse agricultural community; conversely, the station's isolation and subsequent narrow subregional focus denied farmers elsewhere in the Ozarks and in much of the state the benefits of research results and information until the establishment of the [federal] extension service on the eve of World War I."[16] Though his own political agenda aimed more at fiscal conservatism than a "progressive" expansion of state services, Gov. George W. Hays attempted to tap populist grumblings in Arkansas about the uneven benefits of the state's university. In a public address in August 1916, "George the Wobbler," as the infuriated *Fayetteville Democrat* called him, "attack[ed]" the university as "a complete failure located where it is, principally because of its geographical situation." Though the governor declared that he was "in favor of removing the state university to some central location in the state," he never took any action. His rhetoric and its populist appeal, nevertheless, are revealing. Rural folks demanded more equitable benefits from their government institutions.[17]

Small farmers in the Ozarks objected not so much to the federal government's expanded role in economics and education but more to how better-off agricultural interests—those with the "clout"—pulled the strings and shaped the designs of government programs for their own ends. The Smith-Lever Act of 1914, engineered primarily by congressmen representing predominantly rural districts in the South and West, created the USDA's Extension Service and provided federal funds for farm agents in counties that agreed to cover one-third of the administrative costs (states were also expected to contribute one-third of the expense). Many small farmers, however, resented the regressive taxes imposed by state and county governments to raise the local matching funds, especially when they became convinced that the local "big shots" would control the programs and benefit the most anyway. In July 1918, for instance, small farmers in Boone County circulated petitions to demand that the USDA fire their county's agricultural agent, S. D. Carpenter. Though Carpenter denied their accusations, backcountry populists there claimed "that he took an active part in the recent movement of the thresher owners of Boone County to charge an exorbitant price" to local farmers for processing their grain.[18] Instead of helping improve the viability of their farms, these rural folks must have believed that this government program was helping those who needed it the least and, in doing so, only made their own situations worse. Similarly, to many poor and middling hill farmers, the USDA's tick eradication program seemed unnecessary and unfair.

While most dipping opponents merely grumbled or simply refused to dip their cattle in defiance of the local and state mandates until they were slapped with fines or had their cattle confiscated, others expressed their anger more forcefully. Some angry farmers in Izard County destroyed dipping vats with dynamite at Guion and Lunenburg in 1912. Although no one was ever charged, the tick inspector at Lunenburg reported that he had been chased by about twenty-five night riders and barely escaped their wrath by hiding out in a remote hollow. Such intimidation of inspectors and destruction of dipping vats was repeated on numerous occasions throughout the South. The dynamiting of vats became, in the words of Claire Strom, "the most common form of [violent] resistance." Cheap and readily available dynamite gave dipping opponents the publicity and attention they desired, as local and state newspapers generally covered these dramatic episodes.[19]

Eradication officials and supporters were appalled at such resistance. Only backwardness and narrowmindedness could explain such obstinate behavior in their eyes. Officials simply could not understand why anyone would oppose such a progressive measure. Although it is unclear how he derived his statistics, Arkansas's state veterinarian W. Lenton claimed that ticks were costing the South "forty millions of dollars annually," which was inexcusable given that the problem "[could] be entirely eliminated with little expense and a little trouble on the part of cattle owners." For Lenton, ignorance and indifference toward the common good were the obstacles. "If every farmer understood this question and was willing to spend a few cents and a few minutes' time each week," he wrote in his attempt to strike a chord of public duty, "between now and the first of next November, every tick in Arkansas could be killed."[20]

But for many small farmers, tick eradication was more trouble than a "few cents and a few minutes' time each week," and they remained unconvinced that it truly benefited the "common good." As Strom explains, tick eradication worked for the interests of prosperous cattlemen and mostly against the interests of smallholders. Prosperous cattlemen emulating midwestern stock raising, who reaped the benefits of tick eradication, were in much better shape to treat their animals for ticks. They were equipped with corrals and pens, neat fences and pastures to manage their herds, and the money and labor to invest in eradication methods. Smallholders, on the other hand, had to round up cattle that roamed free on the open range and drive them to dipping vats through forests and difficult terrain, a "nearly impossible" task. Eradication laws required farmers to dip their cattle bi-weekly until inspectors declared their district tick free. For small farmers who usually relied on family and occasionally neighbors for labor, this almost always consumed valuable time and resources and distracted them from other important farming ventures that were necessary to make ends meet. Furthermore, the flat tax of five cents per head on cattle that was levied to help finance the program in Arkansas also proved a much bigger thorn in the side of poorer yeomen than more well-to-do cattlemen who believed the tax was well worth it.[21]

Even more significant, perhaps, than the greater inconvenience and cost of tick eradication for small farmers was the fact that the program stood to benefit yeomen scarcely, if at all. This was not, however, due to their isolation from and disinterest in national and international markets. Rather, a closer look at the differentiation within the national and international beef market reveals that well-to-do cattlemen and smallholders generally targeted different sectors of that market. While wealthier cattlemen who possessed the capital to invest in higher-quality breeds, fenced grazing pasture, and nutritious feeds aimed at the choice-grade, top end of the beef market, backcountry farmers' native "scrub" breeds were generally bound for the low-end, canned beef market.[22]

For small farmers lacking the necessary land and capital to invest in high-quality breeds for choice-grade beef, raising lower-quality breeds for the low end of the market was most feasible and profitable. Raising native "scrub" cattle on the open range required smaller investments. Aside from occasionally penning calves up for some last-minute fattening before sending them to market, smallholders allowed their cattle to subsist mostly on the grasses and forest mast of the open range at little cost. They usually sold their cattle to drovers or drove their small herds themselves to the nearest railroad town to be loaded onto livestock cars and shipped to market.[23] Farmers in the Arkansas Ozarks frequently shipped their cattle to Missouri. John Quincy Wolf remembered his uncle selling open-range cattle raised in the White River hills of Izard County during the late 1800s. "Very early Uncle saw the profit in raising cattle, for they ran on the free ranges all the year, finding abundant forage in the winter on the south sides of the hills, up the coves, and along the creeks and the river valleys where cane was abundant," recalled Wolf. "In the spring Uncle sold from ten to twenty-five head of cattle to Missouri buyers and in the fall two or three bales of cotton, which brought in more than enough money for the family needs."[24] Ozarks smallholders continued to see the economic benefits of open-range grazing well into the twentieth century. Yellville's *Mountain Echo* reported in early June 1921 that local farmer George Roberson had "shipped a car load of fat cattle to butchers at Springfield, Mo., the first of the week." "These cattle," the paper noted, "had grown fat on the open range.... Here in the Ozarks where our range is fine, and where cattle have free access to all the pure running water they

Hill farmers with calves from "scrub" stock. Courtesy of Special Collections, University of Arkansas Libraries, Fayetteville.

take on flesh very fast, and make the very best of beef."[25] In addition to requiring little land, raising cattle on the open range demanded minimal labor, allowing farmers to devote their time and energy to other farm endeavors. Thus, even with "canner" beef usually bringing less than half the price of top-grade beef, small farmers enjoyed significant profits from "scrub" cattle that best suited the resources at their disposal.

Although well-to-do cattlemen and agricultural experts insisted that ticks were costing the cattle industry millions of dollars each year, backcountry farmers rarely saw any benefits from dipping their cattle. State Veterinarian W. Lenton claimed in 1908 that even low-grade canners were losing about twenty-five to fifty cents per hundred pounds under the quarantine. But while the quarantine may have shaved a few dollars off the market price of an animal, the costs of eradication typically outweighed its benefits in their eyes. After all, ticks were not killing their cattle or making them ill, and the costs and inconvenience of dipping were great enough for them that earning a few dollars less could be overlooked.[26]

Perhaps, if it were not for agricultural experts telling them so with statistical analysis, small farmers would hardly have noticed any real negative impacts on cattle prices caused by the tick quarantine. Such nuances were hardly distinguishable from typical market fluctuations, especially after the various middlemen took their cuts. As cattle prices in Arkansas more than doubled between 1912 and 1918, it is likely that many who were being forced to dip their cattle dismissed eradication officials' and supporters' claims that ticks were significantly hurting market prices; their tick-infested cattle were bringing more than ever.[27] Furthermore, evidence suggests that successful eradication and lifting the quarantine did not necessarily result in the improved prices that officials promised. According to USDA statistics, although South Carolina had been completely freed from the quarantine by 1921, average cattle prices in that state fell from $20.30 per head in 1921 to $13.80 in 1922. Similarly, although a few of its counties were requarantined later, Mississippi's average cattle prices fell from $14.10 per head in 1921 to $10.80 in 1922, after that state had been released from the quarantine.[28] Many Ozarkers, then, must have had a hard time buying into officials' claims that tick eradication was necessary and urgent for the economic betterment of all cattle farmers.

Exaggerated claims made by frustrated agricultural officials in their attempts to educate farmers probably led some smallholders to question the validity of the tick program as well. State Commissioner of Agriculture Clay Sloan went so far as to claim that "one tick can draw 200 pounds of blood from one animal in a season." The editor of the *Batesville Guard*, Independence County's leading newspaper, who supported the "progressive" tick eradication program, was utterly disgusted at such a potentially damaging statement by an "expert statistician." "Why, the dreaded blood-sucking vampires of India, or the gorgeously and most stupendously advertised blood-sweating 'behemoth' of olden circus fame, would have no odds on one of the hideous [tick] monsters with a capacity of a pound of blood a day," retorted the editor. "Frankly we do not believe in such far drawn and imaginative arguments," he asserted, "and it is just such 'freak' statements which have caused so much ridicule and opposition to an otherwise intelligent campaign of education."[29]

In addition, small farmers' suspicions of the program surely rose as it became obvious that tick eradication was inherently designed to benefit more-prosperous cattlemen's broader agenda for an "improved" agricultural industry. This became more than clear when eradication officials and supporters increased their longtime calls to close the open range in order to accelerate and ensure the success of the tick program. The director of the Arkansas Experiment Station pointed to the open range as "the main factor in propagating and distributing the tick," arguing that "were a general herd law in force, the [tick] question would become, if not a simple one, at any rate a much less difficult one than it is at present."[30] Eradication officials' advocating to close the open range undoubtedly struck a sensitive nerve with small farmers who counted on the free range for a vital source of farm income; closing the range would likely mean running them out of the cattle business altogether.[31]

Feeling wrongly disadvantaged by the tick program, a few disgruntled Ozarkers took their grievances to the courts in hopes of redress. While some local officials occasionally sided with rural dipping opponents, such as in Van Buren County, where the elected county judge refused to enforce mandatory dipping until a majority of citizens demonstrated support for the program, small farmers typically did not fare so well in the courtroom. In 1916, the Arkansas Supreme Court upheld the constitutionality of the state legislature's Act 86 of 1915, which had authorized the enforcement of mandatory dipping and prescribed penalties for noncompliance. And the next year, the court upheld the constitutionality of penalties for violators of cattle quarantine orders.[32] These rulings confirmed that law-abiding smallholders had no choice but to dip their cattle, in compliance with the federal program.

Most smallholders grudgingly obeyed the law and took their cattle to the dipping vats every other week, many undoubtedly grumbling to themselves and their neighbors about what they perceived to be a ridiculous and unfair program. Other less scrupulous farmers continued to refuse to dip their cattle and risked being fined or having their cattle taken from them when they were finally caught by inspectors. But during the World War I years, tick eradication was a little easier pill to swallow for most farmers. They still resented the difficulties of rounding up their cattle and paying the dipping tax for no apparent benefit, but the record cattle prices they were receiving during those years likely helped offset the hassle and expense.

Although Southern newspapers naturally devoted most of their attention to the great surge in cotton prices during the war years, the increased international demand for nearly all American farm products during the war drove other prices, including beef, to unprecedented levels. The war and consequent food shortage in Europe happened also to coincide with a devastating drought in Texas, which hurt that important beef-producing state but boosted demand even higher for cattlemen elsewhere.[33] Whereas the annual average of prices Arkansas cattle farmers received fluctuated around $3.50 per one hundred pounds between 1909 and 1912, prices rose to a three-year average of about $4.50 between 1913 and 1915, climbed to $4.90 in 1916, and then shot up to $6.40 in 1917, peaking at an annual average of $7.00 in 1918. In May 1918, average cattle prices in Arkansas hit a whopping $8.00 per one hundred pounds, a level that would not be matched again until 1942.[34]

Such an increase in cattle values did not go unnoticed. In an editorial on November 8, 1916, titled "Meat Prices are High," the *Batesville Guard* sought to draw its Independence County readers' attention to the tremendous rise in livestock prices and encourage farmers to diversify. Citing an agricultural official in Texas, the editorial commented that "meat animals are more likely to be higher next year than cotton is likely to remain high." Warning readers not to become too comfortable with good cotton prices, the Texas official explained that "in one year cotton has risen from 10 to 18 cents; it can fall in another year back to 10." Referencing the increased demand in war-torn Europe, he assured readers that the cattle market promised to be a much safer and stable market than cotton, since "people can economize in the use of cotton goods . . . [but] cannot economize much in the matter of food."[35]

Analysis of personal property records of Independence County farmers involved in the Charles Jeffrey murder case suggests that many smallholders responded to these market incentives. Although most backcountry farmers lacked the capital to greatly expand the size of their herds, many did find ways to seize the opportunity in hopes of improving their farms' profitability. Many who lacked the capital to greatly expand their small cattle operations still enlarged their herds when possible by buying a few head from neighbors when they had extra cash to invest or by keeping some of the heifers (female calves) from natural reproduction to add to the next year's stock of breeding cows. Even for those who did not expand their herds, the high prices they received by selling each season's naturally produced calves put more money in their pockets than most had ever imagined before the war.

But while smallholders enjoyed the record prices of the war years, they also suffered the consequences of the agricultural market crisis that ensued when such high demand for American farm products wore off after the war's end. In fact, as historian James H. Shideler has pointed out, weakening livestock markets were the first indicators of the general postwar farm crisis to come, claiming that the "declining European market for meat coupled with continued high-level American production brought about a crisis in livestock, which was a foretaste of what was later to come to the rest of agriculture."[36] In Arkansas, the prices cattle farmers received per one hundred pounds fell from the $8.00 peak in May 1918 to $5.80 by the end of 1919. At the end of 1920, prices had fallen to $4.40 per one hundred pounds, plummeting to a mere $3.20 by December 1921.[37]

In the words of historian Gilbert C. Fite, "Farmers were not only discouraged over low prices, they were downright angry." Historians have given most of their attention to discontented farmers in what are usually considered "commercial" agricultural areas during the post–World War I farm crisis, such as the retaliation and destruction caused by angry "night riders" in Southern cotton and tobacco regions.[38] But it is important to situate the escalation of small

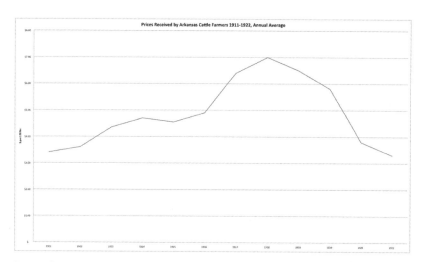

Source: USDA, "Prices Received by Farmers for Beef Cattle: United States and by States, Monthly and Annual Average, 1909–1959." *Statistical Bulletin No. 265* (Washington, D.C.: Agricultural Marketing Service, 1960).

hill farmers' violent resistance to federal tick eradication within the context of postwar agricultural panic, rather than just explaining it away as a simple continuation of rural Jeffersonian ideology and inborn resentment toward the federal government's encroachment upon local rights.[39] While small farmers in the Ozarks may have been able to endure complying with tick eradication amid the high prices of the war years, the postwar beef market fallout fully restored the sharper-than-ever pains of forced cattle dipping—pains that some backcountry folks were evidently no longer willing to tolerate.

The dynamiting of dipping vats picked up significantly not long after cattle prices began to dip, becoming a fairly regular occurrence in the hills of Independence County by 1922. The first government-built vat in the county was blown up near Hutchinson Mountain in 1919, and four others were destroyed in the area before Charles Jeffrey was murdered in March 1922. Another vat was dynamited near Locust Grove in 1921, and a deputy sheriff went to that community to force twenty-two farmers to dip their cattle afterward. To compound the problem of falling cattle prices, eradication officials decided to stiffen regulations. It appears that officials and the tick program's supporters may have realized that their message about the tick problem damaging cattle prices had been undermined during the war years, as "ticky" cattle were bringing more than double what they had when the program first started. New regulatory revisions in Arkansas went into effect in March 1919 that outright prohibited farmers from selling any cattle from a quarantined district that had not been completely declared tick-free and issued a signed certificate by a federal inspector.[40] Thus, no longer could farmers even sell cattle simply marked "quarantine," since they now had to possess an inspector's certificate to sell them at all.

With farmers' ability to sell cattle greatly impeded and with prices plunging to $3.10 per one hundred pounds in January 1922—the lowest they had been at any point since 1911—panic spawned a surge in violence against tick eradication.[41] As blowing up and burning dipping facilities became evermore widespread, disgruntled dipping opponents' retaliation also became more personal. Threats and intimidation against inspectors were nailed to trees and fences at dipping vats throughout the hills of Independence County. Hoping to break the resolve of eradication officials, threats against law-abiding farmers who sought to comply with mandatory dipping were also reported.[42]

It was in this atmosphere of boiling tempers that an unknown assassin gunned down Inspector Charles Jeffrey on Hutchinson Mountain on March 20, 1922, resulting in the eventual arrest of nine suspected "conspirators." Questioning revealed that these suspects and about thirty other men had attended a "secret" meeting on the tick question at one suspect's farm after church services on the Sunday afternoon prior to the murder, where officials believed the dipping opponents had plotted to kill Inspector Jeffrey. The six suspects initially arrested, who the press reported "refused to talk," were held at the county jail for a hearing before Justice of the Peace J. A. Holmes to commence on March 24. Meanwhile, law officials and their bloodhounds searched for co-conspirators and reported that unknown murder accomplices had been attempting "to throw the hounds off the trail by firing the woods" near the murder scene.[43]

Like the "wild rumors" of communist conspiracy that circulated during Arkansas's infamous Elaine Race Riot of 1919, Red Scare hysteria found another outlet in the press coverage of rural whites' antidipping defiance. Just as Georgia's state veterinarian had condemned what he called a "Bolsheviki contingent" for dynamiting dipping vats in Lowndes County, Georgia, in the summer of 1917, the *Arkansas Democrat* linked dipping opposition to Socialist anarchy, claiming that one of the suspects arrested for Jeffrey's murder, James McGee, was "a Socialist leader in his section of the country."[44] Indeed, there is good reason to speculate that McGee may have been a Socialist. Sometime after 1910, McGee's family, along with the families of his son and brother, had come to Hutchinson Mountain from Kiowa County, Oklahoma, a well-known stronghold of agrarian Socialism in the Southwest.[45] Moreover, the Socialist Party had been considerably active in Independence County, especially between 1908 and 1912, when it "ran a full slate in each election." Under the leadership of the populist Farmers' Union member W. P. Datherow, the local party organization sought to appeal especially to discontented small farmers and tenant farmers. Socialists in the western South—particularly the "secret, direct-actionist" Working Class Union, which, according to historian Jim Bissett, "claimed as many as thirty-five thousand Oklahoma and Arkansas farmers among its membership in 1916"—counted themselves among the most aggressive opponents of the government's cattle dipping mandate as part of their broader stand "against the farmer who farms the farmer."[46]

An examination of 1920 election returns, however, reveals that if McGee was a Socialist organizer, he had yet to win over very many votes for his party on Hutchinson Mountain. Of the twenty-seven votes cast in Relief Township in the presidential election, only four went to Socialist Eugene Debs, while one of twenty-six votes went to the Socialist gubernatorial candidate, Sam Busler, and those votes were probably cast by McGee and his family. Instead, most of the township voted Republican, but this in itself might have been an expression of political protest against the Arkansas and local political establishment.[47] Granted, Independence County and other parts of the Ozarks had once had an unusually large Republican presence by Arkansas standards that dated back to old Unionist sympathies during the Civil War, but the county, like the rest of the Solid South, was firmly Democratic by the 1920s. Discontent and defiance, then, appeared strong among the smallholders on Hutchinson Mountain.

The stigma of "anarchy" attached to dipping opposition could be seen clearly in the strategies of both the prosecution and defense in the hearing held by Justice of the Peace J. A. Holmes on March 24–25. The prosecution set out to show that angry dipping opponents on Hutchinson Mountain had called the "secret" meeting to organize Inspector Jeffrey's assassination as an act of lawless rebellion. Defense attorney Earl C. Casey, who was fully aware of the incriminating image of tick eradication opposition, sought to portray the suspects not as dipping opponents but as upright citizens who were simply confused about the technicalities of the law. Casey argued that their "tick meeting" was not as a secret gathering of raging dipping opponents but rather a gathering of law-abiding men discussing and informing one another about the "dipping question."[48]

The prosecution suggested that dipping opponents at the tick meeting had paid off local riffraff Paul Curtis to do the shooting. Bloodhounds had led lawmen to the home of farmer and fellow suspect Aaron Strothers, where Curtis admitted he had stayed the night before the shooting. Curtis had earned a reputation as a lawless character in preceding years. In the spring and fall of 1915, he had pleaded guilty on charges of disturbing religious services. He was also sentenced in 1916 to a year behind bars for stealing two mules. Even more important, only months before Jeffrey's murder, Curtis had been indicted in another murder case, though he was acquitted for lack of evidence. Curtis, a sharecropper who lived with his elderly mother and had no property of his own, also testified that he had recently been looking to hire himself out as a farm laborer, but with no success. The prosecution argued that Curtis, whose boots matched tracks found near the murder scene, must have taken the cash from tick opponents at the Sunday tick meeting and then shot Jeffrey in cold blood. It also suggested that his fellow antidipping conspirators had secretly paid Curtis's attorney fees.[49]

Although Justice Holmes was convinced enough to hold the defendants without bail for a grand jury proceeding, the prosecution got very little help from tight-lipped witnesses. The *Arkansas Democrat* reported that most of those "placed on the stand by the state made poor witnesses, plainly showing signs of fear . . . [and] 'lapses of memory.'" Witnesses, most of whom admitted they had attended the tick meeting, usually kept their statements brief and vague, showing a clear reluctance to say anything that might implicate someone. Such timidity on the part of witnesses only bolstered the prosecution's certainty that some sort of an organized murder plot had been schemed, but it also frustrated efforts to pin down hard evidence to convict the suspects beyond a reasonable doubt.[50]

For the defense, tight-lipped witnesses were a blessing. Attorney Casey's attempt to draw attention away from the fact that most of the men present at the meeting were dipping opponents was unsuccessful. When questioned by the prosecution about their opposition, the defendants and witnesses who attended the tick meeting tried to elude the issue by stating that they were law-abiding citizens. For instance, when questioned about his views on tick eradication, farmer J. W. Burnett, who was also a justice of the peace in Relief Township, claimed that he had actually voted for the dipping tax and "dipped every time they notified me." When pressed further, however, Burnett finally admitted, "I can't say that I loved it. . . . [I am] opposed to it if I can get around it without disobeying the law." S. D. Lambert, the suspect at whose residence the tick meeting had been held, even went so far as to claim that he supported the eradication program, although he received no support for this claim from the other defendants or witnesses, who were more open in admitting that they opposed dipping when pressed by the prosecution but were sure to state that they respected the law. Still, despite its failure to dodge the antidipping issue, the defense benefited from witnesses' reluctance to provide convicting testimony.[51]

For most observers, there was little doubt that some, if not most, of the men placed on the stand at the preliminary hearing had been involved in some way or at least knew who killed Charles Jeffrey. The day after the hearing concluded, on Sunday, March 26, an angry lynch mob assembled in Batesville and threatened to inflict vigilante "justice" on the defendants, despite pleas from Jeffrey's eldest sons to allow the legal system to run its course. Sheriff Noah Harris took no chances and quietly transferred the suspects from the county jail to the state penitentiary in Little Rock for safekeeping.[52]

The prosecution proved unable put its finger on any undisputable evidence to discern just who the guilty parties were. The *Arkansas Gazette* remained confident that the antidipping assassins would be brought to justice, though, and assumed that the prosecution was just awaiting the proper time to show its winning hand: "It was evident throughout the trial that the prosecuting attorney was holding back most important and damaging evidence for use in the higher court, and seeking only to have the men held without disclosing the principal evidence and without producing the most important witnesses."[53]

Ultimately, however, the prosecution failed to come up with any new evidence strong enough for a conviction, and its principal evidence, the bloodhound trails and boot prints found near the murder scene, had too many holes to stand alone. The Independence County Grand Jury indicted Paul Curtis for first degree murder and six others as accomplices: George and J. W. Scoggins, Alfred Martin, James Lambert, Aaron Strother, and James McGee. But the prosecution could not unearth the smoking-gun evidence needed to put the suspects away. Vying for more time, prosecutors managed to postpone the trial, originally scheduled for November 1922, until the following April, but the case was dropped from the docket afterward.[54]

Just who pulled the trigger and who was involved in Jeffrey's murder will forever remain a mystery. Local tradition has reached several different verdicts, from beliefs that Curtis was hired by dipping opponents, as the prosecution argued, to claims that Curtis acted alone simply because he was a depraved character who was believed to have murdered before. Others offered completely different explanations, such as one that said the dipping altercation had only escalated a deeper personal grudge between one suspect's family and Charles Jeffrey over a sexual-affair rumor. Still others attributed the murder to simple jealousy over Jeffrey's coveted federal inspector position. According to Jeffrey family lore, Curtis eventually confessed to the shooting years later on his death-bed and asked for Jeffrey's widow to beg for her forgiveness.[55] But what is not disputable is the fact that the murder occurred amid heated and passionate re-sentment toward mandatory tick eradication during desperate times for small farmers in the Ozarks.

Even as the jailed murder suspects awaited their trial, violent resistance to cattle dipping persisted in Independence County. Three days after the murder, the federal inspector at Union Hill, located about fifteen miles southeast of Jeffrey's district, reported that his own barn had been torched and burned to the ground by night riders. He also turned over a threatening notice that had been posted at a local vat by dipping opponents and several other anonymous letters warning him that his life was in danger. Fearing for their lives, all federal tick inspectors in the "rebellious" mountains south of the White River in Independence County temporarily resigned their posts, and the county tick eradication supervisor suspended mandatory dipping in the area until federal marshals could arrive to quell the violence.[56]

But before the nine federal ex-servicemen requested by local officials and the BAI arrived to restore order and resume dipping, more violence erupted. On April 2, a few days after another dipping vat had been destroyed, a band of about fifteen or twenty night riders set fire to the barn of a well-to-do farmer, the brother of a prominent local merchant and a vocal tick eradication supporter, Dave Wyatt, in the Rosie community. Although a night watchman and several alarmed neighbors were able to fire off about thirty shots at the fleeing bandits, only one horse was apprehended. Forty-eight hours later, the belligerent night riders struck again. This time Wyatt and his brothers discovered the intruders before they could damage any property and unloaded a barrage of gunfire in their direction as they fled. One vigilante appeared to have been hit but was rescued by a fellow night rider before Wyatt and his men could capture him. Local officers arrested five suspects within the next week, and they received grand jury indictments for night riding.[57]

The initial presence of federal marshals slowed violence considerably but did not end it entirely. The *Arkansas Gazette* printed a hopeful headline on April 12 that read, "Anti-Dipping War Crisis Is Passed," although this turned out to be a premature claim. However, it seems that many dipping opponents who had previously formed large bands of "night riders" were no longer willing to risk being arrested or shot up by federal marshals. Ten days after the last encounter at the Wyatt farm, another tick eradication supporter in the Rosie community, Ira Castleberry, had his property targeted by what appeared to be a lone marauder. A federal marshal, accompanied by Castleberry and Wyatt, discovered the bandit slipping through some bushes on his way to set fire to Castleberry's barn; they opened fire, but he escaped into the hills and eluded arrest. And a lone "firebug" returned to Dave Wyatt's farm several days later, the sixth attempt to destroy his "large barn," an area newspaper reported. A local policeman and Wyatt's two sons who were standing guard attempted to apprehend the man, but the surprised would-be arsonist bolted over a nearby gate and escaped, though not before ripping half his jacket from his body on the barbed wire as he barely escaped a bullet from the officer's revolver. With this incident, violent resistance petered out, and the federal marshals oversaw the resumption of tick eradication in the area.[58]

Amid the chaos of the Independence County tick rebellion, observers attempted to probe the reasons for such violent behavior in the rural hills. The *Arkansas Democrat* attributed the violence to a backward mountain culture. In this "rebellious district," claimed the *Democrat*, "live a great many mountaineers, not a few being emigrants from other states, who up to a certain point are illiterate, and do not keep abreast of the times." "They apparently have not learned to adapt themselves to new conditions and new customs," it continued. Again referencing a claim that Socialism predominated in the area, it charged that many of the dipping opponents "spend a large part of their spare time in preaching their Socialist doctrines to their neighbors and friends." Ultimately, "living in the mountains . . . they oppose a great many laws of the state and federal government, and especially such laws as interfere with their own personal freedom and bring extra expense or work upon themselves," the paper argued. "They feel that the [dipping] law places a restriction on their personal freedom."[59]

Perhaps there is reason to assume that dipping opponents in Independence County and elsewhere had come to resent federal intervention and its seemingly unjust intrusions into their lives. Frustration over tick eradication may have built upon considerable resentment toward the draft during World War I. Jeffrey's accused murderer, Paul Curtis, had unsuccessfully requested exemption from the draft on the grounds that his mother depended on him for her livelihood. Another murder suspect, J. W. Scoggins, outright dodged the draft and had hidden out during the war.[60]

At the root of such objections to overbearing federal authority, however, was their perception that the prosperous and well-to-do were using this power for their own gain at the expense of ordinary people like themselves who were working hard to prosper from new farm opportunities. A close analysis of the dynamics of society and economy in the Hutchinson Mountain community suggests that the high cattle prices of the war years brought high hopes to many small farmers and their families. Historians have broadly defined smallholder yeomen as farmers who "filled the social and economic space between large commercial farmers and tenants." The common thread, they say, was that yeomen "bas[ed] their livelihood on subsistence agriculture" and "self-sufficiency."[61] But the small farmers on Hutchinson Mountain defy such simplistic characterization. While subsistence-oriented farming may have been the top priority of some, many more smallholders saw economic opportunity in the cattle market and speculated accordingly.

Historian Altina Waller notes in her study of the post–Civil War period in the Tug Valley of southern West Virginia and eastern Kentucky—the setting of the infamous Hatfield-McCoy feud—that "the most important function of a father" in smallholder agricultural societies was "economic and social support." Fathers felt obligated to provide their sons at least "a modest start in life," and sons expected it of them. In this age of increasingly bleak prospects for smallholders in America, high cattle prices during the war years afforded farmers and their sons on Hutchinson Mountain hope against "a frustratingly barren future."[62]

Such prospects may have brought a few farmers into the community in the first place. S. D. Lambert, one of the murder suspects, had sold his row-crop farm in the lowlands of Randolph County and purchased a small farm on Hutchinson Mountain in 1910, where he would move permanently around 1916 and become the community's largest cattle farmer. Lambert's eldest son, twenty-two-year-old James—also a murder suspect who was eventually indicted—had recently married and moved to a place of his own on the mountain by 1920. According to the 1920 census, James owned his new home, and personal property tax records show that he had three head of cattle, though he undoubtedly continued to work for his father on his farm too. Lambert also had two other sons, ages twenty-one and nineteen, still living with him but soon to be leaving the nest, not to mention four younger children. So for Lambert, who, it is worth mentioning, had taken out a mortgage on his own home by 1920, the cattle industry was vital to his family's economic security and dreams for the future.[63]

Lambert sought to capitalize on the record cattle prices of the World War I years. Although personal property tax records do not provide a full picture of market transactions, an analysis of herd sizes and assessment values of cattle reveal a great deal about yeomen and the national cattle market trends of the years during and after the war. In 1917 Lambert owned thirty cattle assessed at $300. Plainly more than he needed for subsistence, they accounted for 38 percent of his $790 total personal property value. In 1918 he enlarged his herd to forty cattle, listed at $600, representing 67 percent of his $900 total valuation. And in 1919 Lambert had sixty cattle assessed at $900, which made up 78 percent of his $1,150 total worth. Doubling his herd in just three years and putting a disproportionate amount of his personal assets into cattle, Lambert was clearly banking on the beef market.[64]

But as the market plummeted after the war, Lambert felt the pinch. In 1920, Lambert's continued investment in the cattle market backfired. He had enlarged his herd to eighty cattle, but with the major decline in prices, the assessed value of his cattle had fallen from $900 to $800, even though his herd consisted of twenty more head than it had the year before. The following year, after an apparent effort to trim back a bad investment, Lambert owned sixty cattle that were only worth $450, and his total personal property valuation now slumped to $690.[65] Although Lambert testified that he supported tick eradication and that others in the community were just "pushing" him, it appears that he was simply attempting to save his own skin. Justice of the Peace Holmes was not convinced that Lambert favored dipping or that his arrest had been a mistake. Lambert, in fact, had organized the tick meeting in the first place and held it at his residence, and while other witnesses and defendants were careful not to implicate Lambert, no one supported his claim that he actually favored dipping. Although the grand jury apparently acquitted Lambert himself, his son James was one of the seven eventually indicted for the murder. Indeed, the Lamberts, who were probably the hardest hit by receding cattle prices, had the biggest and most expensive job of dipping their sixty-plus cattle that roamed the open range, and were undoubtedly among the most resentful toward tick laws.[66]

Other local farmers felt the squeeze of declining cattle prices and felt the sharper pains of dipping by the 1920s. Even though they apparently did not have the capital to invest in the cattle market to the extent Lambert did, they felt the crunch anyway. George Scoggins, who was eventually arrested along with his brother and son for involvement in the murder, seems to have welcomed the opportunity to capitalize on higher cattle prices, possibly needing to help his son J. W., who was in his early twenties, get a start in his adult life. In 1917 Scoggins owned twenty-four cattle assessed at $300, which represented just under half the value of his $610 total in personal property. With higher offers from cattle buyers, Scoggins appears to have sold not only his calves but also a few cows as well, as his herd was reduced to eighteen head in 1918. With the increase in cattle values, his reduced herd was still listed at $270. By the next year, Scoggins may have begun attempting once again to build up the size of his herd, either by purchasing a couple of cows or by keeping a couple of heifers; he owned twenty cattle, which he reported (conservatively in light of cattle values reported by other local farmers) to be worth $300, accounting for 56 percent of his total personal property.[67]

But Scoggins, who was significantly poorer than Lambert, seems to have been more concerned with immediate cash returns, despite slumping prices by 1920, than with looking ahead to long-term investments in cattle. Tax records in 1920 show that Scoggins's herd reduced to fifteen head, now worth only $150. By the time prices bottomed out in 1921, Scoggins had eighteen head of cattle assessed at only $135.[68] Although Scoggins did not risk as much—perhaps because he was less able—as Lambert in the cattle market, falling cattle prices adversely affected him and must have made the trouble and expense of dipping his now-less-valuable cattle all the more irritating.

The trends of the international beef market also affected those farmers who had only a few head of cattle or had begun with none at all. Aaron Strother, who was indicted as an accessory for harboring suspect Paul Curtis the night before the murder, owned four cattle in 1917, assessed at $50, which accounted for nearly half of his $120 total personal property valuation, and in 1918 Strother had five cattle worth $75, representing exactly half of his total valuation. These numbers were the same in 1919, but in 1920, Strother had increased his small herd to eight cattle, although their assessed value grew to only $80 as postwar demand contracted. In 1921 he had accumulated eleven cattle, but they were now worth only $60.[69]

Like Strother, C. W. Hembry, who was arrested but not indicted by the grand jury, attempted to improve his economic prospects by investing in cattle but came into the game too late for it to pay off. In all likelihood, poorer farmers like Strother and Hembry decided to try to invest their meager resources in cattle when the market slumped and cattle could be purchased more cheaply in 1920 and 1921, expecting that the market would soon rebound. Hembry, a poor farm laborer with no personal property to assess in 1917 or 1918, appears to have saved some of his wages and bought his first three cattle, worth $45, in 1919. He increased his holdings to ten cattle in 1920, but more than tripling his herd only slightly more than doubled his cattle value to $100. Tax records from 1921 suggest that he had stopped investing in cattle, but his ten head were now assessed at only $70. Even the suspected Socialist leader of the community, James McGee, who had only one cow in 1917, owned four head by 1921, indicating that he was probably now selling at least a couple of calves for cash.[70]

Young smallholder Alford M. Martin, who was also indicted for Jeffrey's murder, had likewise invested his limited resources into raising cattle. Martin had six cattle in 1917 worth $75 and enlarged his holdings to eleven head worth $165 in 1918. The next two years Martin apparently took advantage of high offers from cattle drovers and sold not only the calves but a few cows as well, as he reported only seven cattle in 1919 and six in 1920. But Martin sought to reinvest his profits the following year as prices slumped. In 1921 Martin owned a much larger herd of eighteen cattle, but the continuing dive in beef prices meant that his much larger herd was now only assessed at $125, which was $25 less than what his seven cattle had been worth in 1919.[71]

As for the most prosperous resident of the community, former Justice of the Peace W.F. Grady, while he may not have particularly liked dipping, his anger toward tick eradication appeared less intense. Grady attended the tick meeting but claimed that he took a neutral stance toward dipping and favored adhering to the law. The prosecution discovered that Grady had, in fact, been on his way to speak with Charles Jeffrey the morning he was killed and suggested that the intent of his visit must have been to warn Jeffrey that his life was in danger. Although Grady denied this assertion, insisting that he just wanted to "talk to him about some rules about dipping," it seems that he was less militant toward compulsory dipping than others in the community.[72] The greatest difference, it seems, is that unlike others in the community, Grady's economic situation had improved significantly by 1922 despite the farm crisis.

By community standards, Grady had been a little-better-than-average farmer until 1920, when he opened a local mercantile. By 1922, Grady had also been appointed postmaster at Hutchinson. Personal property tax records show that Grady owned thirteen cattle worth only $85 in 1921, but they represented only 12 percent of his $720 total value. While neighbors struggled with declining cattle prices and the trouble of dipping in 1921, Grady was doing well enough to purchase the first automobile in the community.[73] Unlike his smallholder neighbors, Grady had much less to panic about.

For disaffected farmers in the community, there was a great deal to resent about Charles Jeffrey. The owner of two farms in the area, Jeffrey, while apparently never expanding the size of his livestock herd, must have enjoyed the unprecedented prices he got for his calves during the war years. But the pressure of falling beef prices after the war did not affect him as it did poorer neighbors who depended on cattle for an essential part of their families' income. In addition to his farms, Jeffrey owned a blacksmith shop in Jamestown and a sawmill. He also held a federal contract to carry the mail from Batesville to Heber Springs for the U.S. Postal Service. During the war, Jeffery had also managed to obtain a lucrative government contract to provide lumber for the U.S. war effort. Ironically, versions of local tradition say that Jeffrey's initial opposition to cattle dipping had been widely known throughout the area. Jeffrey's opinion on the matter changed abruptly, however, when the county's federal tick eradication supervisor, W. H. Lendreth, offered him a salaried position as inspector in his locale.[74]

Already enraged over the pains of dipping, tick eradication opponents likely despised taking orders from a "well-connected" man who had only recently sided with them against an unnecessary law that stood to benefit only the prosperous and well-to-do. Such antipathy toward eradication officials was widespread anyway. The *Arkansas Democrat* noted that "one of the public arguments made by those who oppose and fight against the dipping law is that it is gotten up to give a select few good paying jobs."[75] A Stone County man also mockingly detested the greed and corruption of the tick program:

> This will be a lonesome old place to live when the tick eradicators get all the . . . ticks eradicated. They may eradicate for a thousand years and there will not be any difference in the amount of ticks. The one Tick they are after is a big round tick. I call it a Dollar. When they are all eradicated, then the ticks [money] will be gone. . . . The poor we have with us always.[76]

Resentment, then, must have been especially strong toward Jeffrey, the man after the "ticks" in their Independence County community. This truly made him a walking bull's-eye among desperate and furious smallholders.

The myth of a distinct culture of feuding and violence in the Southern mountains has been largely laid to rest by historians. "Vigilantism," however, "had long been part of the fabric of rural America," including the Ozarks.[77] Indeed, evidence suggests a significant presence of vigilante activity in the Hutchinson Mountain community even before the dipping rebellion in the early 1920s. In 1915 "an organized band known as Night Riders" on Hutchinson Mountain set their sights on one Charley Gilbert, a "loafrer [*sic*]" and violator of community mores. In a threat letter signed by the group, including George Scoggins and W. F. Grady, the vigilantes scolded Gilbert for accusing the Scogginses of stealing a pig and "tell[ing] things that you no is a dam lye." The vigilantes also warned Gilbert, who "don't do anything but loafrer and round over the woods and cuting peoples . . . trees," that they "came dam near catching [him]cutting some bodys fence line." Like other contemporary vigilante groups such as the Ku Klux Klan, these "Night Riders" also appeared to be the self-appointed moral police in their community. They warned Gilbert, "The next time we catch you fucking old red Elembrough we are going to shoot your god dam ass off of you." Accompanied by some "drawings of vulgar pictures" and their signatures, the vigilantes issued their final warning: "Now the shot gun boys are coming after you and you had better stay out of the woods here . . . unless you take some of them hoars along with you to pick the shot out of your dam ass."[78]

Given the circumstances of the Hutchinson Mountain community during the 1910s and 1920s, the presence of "vigilante justice" is not surprising. As Waller has observed in the Hatfield-McCoy affair, Southern mountaineers who had previously been almost exceptionally apt to take their grievances into the courtrooms might decide to take extralegal measures when they felt alienated from the legal system and feared that justice would not prevail.[79] For small farmers in the Ozarks, the legal system appeared rigged against important aspects of their livelihood. In addition to tick eradication and the military draft, the issues of hunting, fishing, and trapping regulations and enforcement against moonshining, as we have seen, also confronted hill farmers in the 1910s and 1920s.[80] They may have felt justified in resisting dipping laws by extralegal means as a necessary fight against well-to-do, selfish interests who were denying their rights to participate on even ground in an agricultural market and undermining their quest for a more democratic political economy.

Examining the changes wrought in the community during the 1920s after federal force overpowered and quelled dipping resistance leaves little reason to wonder why so much passion and emotion surrounded the hopes of cattle farming and the obstacles of mandatory tick eradication. Determined efforts to eradicate ticks continued after resistance culminated in Jeffrey's murder in 1922, but the prices that Arkansas cattle farmers received continued to fall even lower, bottoming out at $2.80 per one hundred pounds in October 1924. Prices gradually rebounded in the final years of the decade, climbing over $7.00 in the fall of 1928—just in time to be sapped by the Great Depression of the 1930s and long after a great many young farmers had likely been forced to flee the economically distressed community.[81]

The decade of the 1920s was a period of significant population exodus from the rural South, including the Ozarks. Small farmers were typically "pulled" by urban opportunities and "pushed" by agricultural distress.[82] Typical outmigrants from Hutchinson Mountain were young men whose hopes of settling down near their families on farms of their own had likely been crushed by their and their fathers' inability to profit enough from cattle farming to give them a secure start—a hope they had fully come to embrace during the prosperous World War I years. By 1930, although the community's largest cattle farmer, S. D. Lambert, had been able to hold on to his farm and home that was mortgaged in 1920, all but one of his older sons, including murder suspect James, had left the community. Even though he still had enough room on his small farm for one twenty-eight-year-old son, Lambert was apparently unable to help this son build or buy a place of his own, as he still lived with his parents in 1930. In addition, Lambert also had a twenty-five-year-old daughter at home in 1930, which may also reflect a lack of men of marrying age in the community.[83]

Census records for 1930 indicate that usually only those young men who could step in to fill the shoes of deceased or retiring fathers on small farms were able to stay in the community. J. W. Scoggins, for instance, was still listed as a farm laborer in the community in 1930 but had likely taken over the leading role in running the family farm from his aging father. Paul Curtis also appears to have taken over his mother's small farm after his stepfather died and his mother went to live with her daughter and son-in-law. By 1930, Curtis had married a widow, had two young children, and was renting a house in the community.[84]

Other young men appear to have realized that they would have to leave the community. Alford M. Martin, a murder suspect and a young, up-and-coming farmer who had invested a great deal in the cattle market, had moved his family from their small Hutchinson Mountain farm by 1930. But the young farm laborers who counted on their fathers and families to help set them off on a secure and successful farming career likely suffered the worst. Frank Holland, a key suspect in the night riding activities and property destruction at the Dave Wyatt farm in Rosie, was undoubtedly feeling desperate in the early 1920s. To make ends meet, Holland and his wife and two children were living with his wife's parents in 1920, where Holland worked for wages on his father-in-law's small farm. By 1930, with hopes of making a good life in the hills of Independence County snuffed out, Holland had moved his family to a rental house in White County, where both he and his wife worked for wages as farm laborers in the cotton fields.[85]

The antidipping rebellion and assassination of Charles Jeffrey in the hills of Independence County in 1922 was the culmination of anger over what small farmers perceived as an unjust and abusive federal program during a period of great desperation and anxiety. Small farmers struggled to ensure their families' economic security and relied greatly on the profitability of cattle raising to do so.

The high cattle prices of the World War I years gave them high hopes, but these were shot down as beef prices plunged below prewar levels after international demand subsided following the war.

The panic and desperation that resulted from the post–World War I agricultural recession had coincided with stepped-up efforts by the region's elite supporters and administrators of the federal tick program. For small cattle farmers, the mandatory dipping laws administered by and for local elites were costly and troublesome, made all the worse because they stood to reap none of the benefits. Dipping laws had always impeded their ability to fully enjoy the commercial rewards of raising cattle, but an increasingly stringent policy that prevented farmers from selling their "ticky" cattle during the dire postwar years transformed resentment into violent hostility. Most backcountry farmers seem to have rebelled against the federal program because it obstructed their ability to participate in the national cattle market at a time when their hopes were high and because it benefited only elite cattlemen at their expense. They rarely resisted out of some authority-defying cultural impulse or because they had no stake in commercial agriculture. Inequality spawned desperation, discontent, and resentment to create an explosive environment of resistance that was ripe for tragedy.

Despite their efforts to adapt, backcountry Ozarkers continued to confront the uneven consequences of efforts to remake the region in accordance with regional elites' visions of corporate industrialization and agribusiness development—and the government power that typically underwrote these visions. Like the rest of America, the Roaring Twenties aroused ever greater enthusiasm for the potential of business growth and economic development in towns, commercial centers, and more prosperous agricultural locales in the Ozarks. For a moment, it seemed that business-minded elites might have triumphed over backcountry populism.

Regional and local elites worked hard in the 1920s to promote business development and vigorously defended against anything they feared might impede their vision, sometimes even by extralegal means. In Harrison, the seat of government for Boone County, for instance, local businessmen and their supporters under the banner of the Ku Klux Klan intimidated and violently assaulted striking railroad workers and local sympathizers in the area. Klansmen in the Ozarks also set their sights on rural moonshiners, bootleggers, and other "irreputable" locals.[86] Klan activity was generally centered in towns and led by local business elites, but it seems that most rural people's responses usually ranged from indifference to endorsement. In such instances, it appears that most backcountry Ozarkers fatefully chose not to stand—at least not openly—against local elites and their antidemocratic structures of power. They seem to have dismissed many fellow working people in nearby towns as "strange" newcomers whose plight had little meaning for their own lives in rural communities.

Some smallholders confronting the anxieties of waning opportunities and rural dispossession in the 1920s seem to have veered, at least for a time, from their old populist demands for economic democracy. For the most part, the decade witnessed an eclipse of rural working-class populism by a primarily town- and business-led discourse that blamed "dangerous" sociocultural changes for the region's misfortunes—and America's writ large. This discourse particularly lamented a perceived departure from America's "Anglo-Saxon" ethnic foundations and "traditional [Protestant] Christian morality." While regional and local elites continued working diligently behind the scenes to advance their industrial and agribusiness agendas against the interests of smallholder farm communities, efforts to safeguard purported "Christian principles" and "traditional morality" dominated Arkansas politics. Attempts to combat the teaching of evolutionary theory and to mandate daily Bible readings in the public schools, to prop up old Sunday "blue laws," and to enforce the prohibition of liquor and other "moral vices" preoccupied local and state political endeavors.[87] To be fair, rural working people in the 1920s received little encouragement from most reform-minded intellectuals who claimed to champion working-class democracy. "Secure in their urban enclaves," writes historian Michael Kazin, "[intellectual reformers] convinced themselves that pietistic Americans of small means were ignorant foes of social reform."[88] Still, the rural Populist ethic for economic democracy seemed to recede into the background.

Even so, despite the seemingly dormant status of older working-class sentiments, the Populist ethic about the roles of government remained alive in the rural Ozarks. Notwithstanding promises to the contrary, the decade's "business prosperity" failed to reach most poor and middling backcountry folks; their struggles to sustain smallholder farming and to halt the deterioration of their rural communities continued largely unabated. Thus, when the bottom fell out of the broader national economy in 1929, unleashing widespread cries across the nation for new government interventions to promote greater economic democracy, Ozarkers attempting to survive the deepening crisis of the Great Depression would join the popular demand for a New Deal. With national political leaders more receptive than ever to new roles for government that promised to bring greater fairness and security to the American economy, many populist Ozarkers hoped that the more powerful liberal state might finally help bring justice and opportunity to the rural backcountry.

5

BRING ON THE DAM PROGRESS

Local spectators gathered on the hills overlooking the White River near the Baxter-Marion County line on a hot July morning in 1952. President Harry S. Truman had just arrived to formally dedicate two hydroelectric dams that had been authorized by the Flood Control Acts of 1938 and 1941 and constructed by the U.S. Army Corps of Engineers at a cost of $134.6 million. Truman and his entourage first stopped for a smaller ceremony at the Norfork Dam, the Corps' pilot project in the region that had been completed in 1943. Then they headed to the more recently finished Bull Shoals Dam for the main event. Sporting a white suit and a panama hat, Truman commended his and his beloved predecessor Franklin D. Roosevelt's progressive supporters for their valiant efforts in seeing these government projects to completion.

The Missouri-born president spared few words in blasting the conservative political detractors and lobbyists of corporate power companies who had long fought these public projects, which promised to bring much-needed flood control, affordable electrical power, and economic development to the rural Ozarks. Despite the "private selfishness" of business conservatives and special-interest lobbies, said Truman, the "people" and their government had prevailed. "These dams belong to the people and we are here to dedicate them to the service of the people," he exclaimed. Truman promised the region's residents more of these kinds of "people's" projects from their federal government in the coming years, vowing that "some time or another, we're going to get it done, in spite of all the opposition." "If it hadn't been for the New Deal and Fair Deal of the last 20 years," he reminded the audience, "you wouldn't have these dams and these improvements. . . . Put that in your pipe and smoke it."[1] Truman's rhetoric and its popular reception indicated the persistence of the Populist ethic in the rural Ozarks. Yet his speech also hinted at watershed changes that government had helped create in the region by midcentury. Notwithstanding the president's populist-sounding oratory, his speech signaled a victory for local elites' corporatist vision of New Ozarks business growth over rural working-class hopes for smallholder opportunities and economic democracy.

Like most Americans, rural Ozarkers had remained cautious about government power as they entered the dreary 1930s. This held especially true for many rural families in the Ozarks where, as the novelist Daniel Woodrell puts it, "there has never been much belief in the essential fairness of a social order that answers most readily to gold." Some Ozarkers, scarred and weary from troubled encounters with various tentacles of government in the past, undoubtedly harbored no hope for change, "assum[ing] the installed powers were corrupt and corruptible, hence to be shunned and avoided, except when you couldn't and must pay them."[2] Like most other Americans, however, a majority of hill folks

President Harry S. Truman and local political and business leaders catch a train in Cotter bound for the public event to dedicate Bull Shoals and Norfork Dams in July 1952. Courtesy of the Baxter County Historical Society.

demanded reform and insisted that their public institutions cease catering to "special interests" and start serving "the people" instead, whether this meant drastic and unprecedented expansions of government or not.

Thousands of hill people hoped that Franklin D. Roosevelt's and his liberal successor's promises of economic justice might finally reverse the deterioration of family farm life, supporting most of the groundbreaking growth of federal power that occurred during the Depression. Despite drastic expansions of federal authority that vowed to defend a more egalitarian "cooperative commonwealth," however, New Dealers and Fair Dealers generally adhered to the American political traditions of "federalism" and "local control," vesting most new power and resources in the hands of local elites. These local elites had little interest in expanding smallholder opportunities for the rural working class but, instead, employed their leverage on federal power to promote corporate industrialization and agribusiness through massive infrastructure projects like dam building.

More desperate than ever, most rural Ozarkers, except some who stood to be forcibly uprooted from their land, ended up backing federal dam-building schemes. Many were eager for the public-works jobs they provided, however temporary they would be, for much-needed income to supplement their distressed family farms. Local elites promised, moreover, that the completion of the giant hydroelectric dams and sprawling lakes would bring transformative opportunities to the Ozarks that would raise all boats, including the revival of a vibrant small farm economy. This proved to be wishful thinking, though. The government's dams and lakes remade a handful of towns into prosperous tourism, retirement, and light industrial centers. But the prosperity failed to ripple out into the countryside, where depression persisted even through America's booming World War II and postwar eras and thousands of Ozarkers fled their rural communities each year.

Already in the throes of rural depression since the agricultural market collapse of the early 1920s, backcountry Ozarkers saw their situations deteriorate even more with natural disasters and the bust of the national economy between 1927 and 1930. Disastrous floods swept the broader Mississippi River Valley in 1927 and decimated many farms in the narrow creek and river valleys in the Ozarks. Then, after national markets tanked in the fall of 1929, devastating droughts arrived to wreak even more havoc in the Ozarks and the western South during the early 1930s. The editor of Searcy County's *Mountain Wave* sought to lift the spirits of benighted Ozarkers with a joke about a conversation between two poor corn farmers. "Well, John . . . is your corn sufferin' because of the heat?" one of them asked. "No," said the other, "it ain't suffering now, but it suffered a lot before it died."[3] His dry humor aside, everyone realized that the crisis for small farmers had worsened. It was high time, many believed, that their government help to do something about it.

At the state level, rural economic populism resurfaced as political leaders waged a major battle over tax reform in 1929. Gov. Harvey Parnell, under pressure from the Arkansas Education Association and its plan to provide state subsidies to help poor and cash-strapped school districts in rural areas, proposed that the state legislature adopt a progressive income tax and other "privilege taxes" on corporations to raise revenues primarily for a school-equalization program. Faced with heated opposition from Arkansas business interests and their political representatives, Parnell and the plan's supporters in the state legislature compromised to pass a less progressive measure, but one that included a limited income tax and a school-equalization fund, nevertheless. Despite the compromise, conservative political leaders and industrialists claimed that "Arkansas Cannot Go Forward under Socialistic Taxation Dictated by the Organized State School Group" and kept up their fight to repeal the tax altogether. Populist rural voters, however, finally defeated conservatives' efforts to repeal the state income tax at the ballot box in a statewide referendum.[4]

The battle over progressive taxation hinted at rural populism arising more forcefully as the pains of depression mounted nationwide calls for economic and political reform. In 1932 the *Arkansas Farmer* featured an article proclaiming that "Prosperity Must Start at the Bottom," demanding a greater role for government to ensure that farmers get "a just share." "Will we stand by our time-worn prejudice that supply and demand must rule agricultural prices (when we know that it does not) and thus permit a complete collapse?" it asked its rural readers. Most rural Ozarkers applauded Franklin D. Roosevelt's New Deal and his liberal-progressive supporters' calls for relief, recovery, and reform, hoping the new designs of federal power might ensure better security and opportunities for working families.[5]

Stronger regulations in the economy and a more just redistribution of wealth and power, many Ozarkers believed, were the right courses not only for political action but also for the greater cause of moral decency and Christian principles. As national observers offered various autopsy reports to explain what had happened to the economy and what was needed to fix it, one Ozarks newspaper printed a "Two-Minute Sermon" by minister Thomas Hastwell, who declared that the sin of "Greed" had caused the Great Depression. "Because of greed there has grown up in this country an autocracy of wealth by which a few control and manipulate the business of the nation to their further enrichment," he explained. "The only lasting remedy," said Hastwell, "is the curtailment of greed—the larger flow of the national wealth into the hands of the mass purchasers, a more liberal application of the live and let live doctrine, a closer adherence to the tenents [*sic*] of the Golden Rule." Many rural Ozarkers undoubtedly agreed with Hastwell's motion to "go back to the teaching of Christ to find the permanent remedy for the depression."[6]

Even those areas that had remained strongholds of Mountain Republicanism since the Civil War showed significant support for the New Deal and its supporters across party lines, bucking against, as they typically had in the past, the national GOP's conservative Eastern establishment. In 1932 Roosevelt carried Searcy County, home to some of the most loyal Republican voters in Arkansas, where many applauded his plans for "corralling the bulls of Wall Street" and compared him with his fifth cousin, the "progressive" Republican Theodore Roosevelt. Even the liberal Democratic nominee for the Senate, Hattie Caraway of eastern Arkansas, who became the first woman ever elected to the U.S. Senate, made an impressive showing in Searcy County against the more local Republican candidate, John W. White of Russellville. Caraway's narrow loss in Searcy County by a mere thirty-five votes is noteworthy, especially since her campaign tour with the nationally known Louisiana populist Huey Long skirted only a few towns along the southern rim of the Ozarks. Caraway appealed to rural and laboring voters who saw her as a "great champion of the rights of the little man" and a leader who would stand "against encroachments upon their rights by the more privileged." Economic populism tended to cut across party lines in the 1930s rural Ozarks, just as it had in the past. Even many of those who refused to vote for FDR and his New Dealers demanded that the federal government step up to take on "this combine of money grubbing hogs and for God sake do something to remedy this situation," as one loyal Republican put it.[7]

More praise than criticism chimed from the Arkansas Ozarks in response to the ambitious and unprecedented efforts of FDR's first hundred days in office in 1933. In late June, local newspapers remarked about the "Splendid Record" achieved by the special session of the Seventy-Third Congress, "passing every vital bill submitted by the President and starting the government on new enterprises." Reports on the removal of the U.S. dollar from the gold standard, "far-reaching" regulations on the banking industry, the imposition of progressive taxes to raise federal revenues, the creation of the "country's biggest public construction program," the "first federal large scale direct relief grants," and the granting of new authority and money "to boost farm prices" and provide much-needed agricultural relief must have sounded promising to rural populists in the Ozarks who had long called for such reforms. To be certain, some in the Ozarks remained suspicious. The editor of Yellville's *Mountain Echo*, for instance, had warned his readers during the devastating drought of 1930 to "make every effort possible to take care of [themselves] before assistance from any source is given," because "[t]he individual who sits down for this relief will doubtless have a long, hungry wait." Considering the vast blunderings and inadequacies of federal and state relief in 1930 and 1931, this was probably sound advice, regardless of politics.[8] But even the most skeptical of rural Ozarkers, as historian Brooks Blevins points out, "seemed quiet, forlorn, and resolved to accept" the new actions taken by Washington.[9] More optimistic Ozarkers hoped that the government's new measures might finally help bring security and opportunity to their rural communities. The New Deal's promise even inspired the radical agrarian Sam Faubus, who had revived the local Socialist Party chapter in Madison County in the early 1930s. According to his biographer, Faubus "became a Democrat in the 1930s and remained loyal for the rest of his life."[10]

Early New Deal programs provided significant relief for many families in the rural Ozarks. A few days after Christmas in 1933, Marshall's *Mountain Wave* proudly reported that "Your Uncle Sam Plays Santa Claus" and commended "the exhilarating effects of the CWA [Civil Works Administration] program . . . throughout the state." These included twenty-two projects already approved for Searcy County, which were set to spend more than $73,000 to employ local labor.[11] In addition to a host of public-works projects, including a popular Civilian Conservation Corps camp that provided much-needed employment for young men, the Searcy County newspaper and others throughout the region hailed the important relief that new agricultural programs were bringing to the region. By November 1934, federal programs had contributed more than $100,000 in benefits to farmers in Searcy County, though uneven distribution of the funds soon became a point of contention among rural folks.[12] Despite the heavy spending that these programs and others required, the FDR administration's progressive taxation policy typically met with rural populists' approval because it "plugs loopholes by which many rich tax dodgers have heretofore escaped" and "really lightens the tax on the little man, but puts a higher rate on large incomes." After all, as one local newspaper put it, since "more than one hundred thousand millions of dollars" had already been lost since the Depression began, the United States "can well afford another hundred thousand millions to get out of the depression, if that is necessary." Even though the Depression had devastated the national economy, the paper explained that "this isn't any little country or any poor country"; while it might seem like a lot of government money, it was only a drop in the bucket for big wheels like "John D. Rockefeller" if they were only made to pay their fair share.[13]

Some Ozarkers passionately defended the administration against conservative criticisms about the government's increased role in the economy. Wayne Phillips, a former Ozarker who had relocated to Stigler, Oklahoma, penned a letter back to the newspaper in his home county in 1934 in which he praised the New Deal's "entirely new concept of the function and duty of government." "Traditionally, our government was supposed to do little in time of depression except keep the tracks clear for such revival as private industry might be able to bring about," wrote Phillips, but "[n]ow its responsibility is to provide jobs for the people." "While our Federal, or central government, is growing stronger," he thought " . . . it may be correct to say that we shall have to admit that the old Jeffersonian concept of government no longer is applicable." "At least we are getting better adjusted to our environment," Phillips concluded. He even wondered if it might work best for the federal government to take over America's public education system from the states and localities.[14]

In response to conservative claims that an expanding government was creating a culture of dependency and destroying Americans' work ethic, one local newspaper editorial assured readers that "the aid that these men received during the hard times is not the thing that spoils them." There had always been those who "were of little use before the depression came," after all. "The depression is merely going to develop the qualities that are already there the same as any adversity does." Another editorial commented, "We don't think much of the complaint of the fellow who insists that the government should not get into business and at the same time uses a government envelope in the conduct of his business."[15] One reader of Searcy County's *Mountain Wave*, furthermore, wrote to the editor hoping to set the record straight against those who charged that the United States was headed down a liberty-stifling path to communism, "just like Soviet Russia." "In the United States," he contended, "it is sweet, soft paternalism. In Soviet Russia [it is] a stern, hard unsympathetic dictatorship. There is plenty of difference."[16]

Though most Ozarkers evidently supported the New Deal's general idea for a "cooperative commonwealth," one that "champion[ed] both the individual and big government—the latter to serve the former"—a number of backcountry folks soon felt the impact of the unevenness and limitations of many of its programs as they were implemented by state and regional elites.[17] Local farmers generally heralded the aims of the USDA's corn-hog program, for example—which sought to improve market stability and prices by reducing the supply of pork, instituting a government purchasing program, and regulating sales by issuing permits to shippers and buyers—but some farmers complained that corporate speculators and middlemen in Springfield, Missouri, had managed to secure most of the buying permits at the expense of cooperatives formed by local farmers in the region. These and similar complaints from other small-farm regions in America prompted the USDA program's chief to promise that he would work to correct this "preference . . . being shown to buyers and speculators," but the unforeseen and unintended unevenness of the federal hog program typified most other New Deal farm policies as well.[18]

Historians have thoroughly documented the adverse consequences promoted by the Agricultural Adjustment Administration's cotton program for poor farmers in the South, particularly for sharecroppers and tenants. Big planters and large-scale farmers, those who least needed help but generally exerted the most powerful political influence, received the lion's share of the benefits, while the federal cotton program helped encourage the dispossession of poor farmers.[19] Tenancy rates in the Ozarks remained far below those in the Delta (although farm tenancy had risen dramatically in the hills, too, since the late nineteenth century), but the unintended consequences of locally controlled federal farm programs also burdened many landless hill farmers and elevated tensions with their landlords. Though many of the details went unreported, a deadly conflict ensued in October 1933, for instance, between native sharecropper Monroe Mathis and his landlord, F. M. Robinson, in Searcy County. A dispute between Robinson—a newcomer to the region who "owned a large farm" near Zack— and Mathis had resulted in the sharecropper's eviction. But Mathis insisted on returning to the farm to tend the crop he had raised since the spring and had apparently determined that he would harvest it, whether Robinson approved or not. When the landowner and the sharecropper "resumed their quarrel," Mathis gunned down his former landlord and was subsequently arrested on murder charges.[20]

In general, most farmers with small landholdings in the Ozarks wound up faring little better than tenants in the broader scheme of New Deal farm programs. In December 1933 more than two hundred hill farmers met at the Searcy County Courthouse in Marshall "to discuss the benefits that are being afforded" by the federal government. The meeting, which had been called by the Searcy County Farmers Independent Association, erupted into "a heated discussion," according to the local paper, in which a number of rural folks expressed "considerable dissatisfaction." Contending that "the small farmer needs relief, too," the farmers appointed a three-man committee to draft a petition aimed to awaken government officials to "the needs of the common people." In it these Ozarks farmers—who hailed from a county divided about evenly between Democrats and Republicans—resolved that "we are all loyal to the relief work program of the Roosevelt administration [even though] many of us differ on the policy thereof." But they explained that they "ha[d] not been able to participate" or benefit enough from agricultural programs because such initiatives had favored mostly large and highly capitalized producers and firms. With many small farmers on the verge of or already facing foreclosure due to delinquent taxes and their inability to make mortgage payments, their current situation was "rendering farm life intolerable," their petition continued. This was grossly unfair, they argued, since "the town and city men are given higher wages than we ask for man, wagon, and team." These Searcy County farmers stated their case simply: "[We] ask that we be permitted to share in the relief to such extent only as to enable us to maintain our families and save us from sacrificing and exhausting" the resources needed to make ends meet on small farms.[21]

Rhetorically, at least, New Deal officials such as Henry Wallace sympathized with small family farmers and advocated returning agricultural profits "back to the mass of people." Shortly after Roosevelt's reelection in 1936, Wallace toured parts of the rural South, including the Ozarks, where he saw firsthand the plight of small farm families. After returning to Washington, Wallace disgustedly remarked in an article he penned to the *New York Times* that "city people of the United States should be thoroughly ashamed" of how they had passively allowed their rural American brethren to suffer in such deplorable circumstances.[22] Despite stiff resistance from Big Agriculture and political conservatives, the Roosevelt administration embarked on greater efforts to address rural poverty during its second term. The Bankhead-Jones Farm Tenant Act of 1937 led to the creation of the Farm Securities Administration (FSA) in September of that year, which reorganized and built upon the programs of its predecessor, the Resettlement Administration. "Rural rehabilitation" became the FSA's most significant program goal, which was "centered on the concept of government loans and grants providing or returning security to small-scale and impoverished farmers." From its inception, though, the FSA "stumbled" because of the "vagueness in its goals and methods," according to historian Charles Kenneth Roberts.[23]

For a handful of rural Ozarkers, assistance from the FSA helped save their farms, at least for a few more years, though it typically tried to do so by bringing them more thoroughly into the agribusiness political economy promoted by local elites. By the end of 1942, Boone County farmer Oscar Conner, for instance, had become an FSA success story. In 1929 Conner and his family had left their 117-acre farm on Gaither Mountain and spent four years in another state hoping to make a better living. In 1933 they returned to their Ozarks farm with little to show from their hiatus as migrant workers. Back on the farm, they struggled to scrape up a "bare existence." Between 1936 and 1942 the Conners received six small loans from the FSA and its predecessor, ranging from $125 to $285 each. By late 1942, the Conners had succeeded in hanging on to their farm by selling calves, hogs, lambs, wool, tomatoes, and a colt and had repaid all their FSA loans in full, including the 5 percent interest owed on them. Now that the farm seemed secure, the Conners "centered" their agricultural ventures on growing chickens in a new "14x40 house of logs and lumber" and selling poultry and eggs "on the commercial market," joining the proto-factory-farming trend that would eventually give rise to Don Tyson's Fortune 500 poultry empire. The Conners, a Kansas City newspaper reported, had "rise[n] above the plane of bare existence."[24]

For most backcountry farmers, however, small loans and grants from the FSA made little difference. Though 155 families in Izard County received federal farm loans in 1936, only seven of them ended the year with even "sufficient supplies and food," let alone the resources to make their farms profitable.[25] Though the FSA was generally flexible and lenient in collecting payments from rural debtors, some Ozarkers, nevertheless, found themselves facing court orders that required them to settle their accounts with the FSA. In April 1940 the U.S. District Court at Harrison ordered J. N. and N. E. Pangle to sell two horses and two colts at a public auction in order to make a payment on their past-due FSA loan. Similarly, the federal court at Harrison issued a "Decree of Foreclosure" against Floyd and Argie Pumphrey of Lead Hill in October 1941 to help satisfy the $392.78 debt they owed on a loan from the old Resettlement Administration.[26]

Boone County farmer meets with local officials in Harrison about agricultural debt adjustment in 1939. Courtesy of the Arkansas State Archives, Little Rock.

The FSA, despite its sincere intentions to help alleviate rural poverty, was fraught with shortcomings, due most notably, Roberts points out, to its "vague" and conflicting policy prescriptions, "which combined modern scientific farming techniques with an old-fashioned, even nostalgic, view of the family farm and the rural community." The FSA proved unwilling or unable to challenge the structure of agricultural capitalism that lay at the heart of the decline of family farms, such as the gross inequalities in profitable landholdings and market opportunities. Instead, it focused mainly on "retraining farm families in improved farm and home management" and instilling the "right mindset" and "right attitude" in its clients. Then, the FSA assumed that rural poverty could be solved with small loans and grants—distributed through and managed by local elites—that would rescue rural families from outdated farm practices and bring them into the prosperity promised by corporate agribusiness. Its limited impact created a large bull's eye for Big Agriculture and conservative critics as they continued their political assaults on the program. By 1943, opponents had successfully "gutted" the FSA.[27]

"No matter how hard they worked," writes historian Charles Thompson Jr., small farmers in the Mountain South "couldn't make it in the farm economy structured as it was": "No matter how skilled they were, no matter whether their rows of corn were straight and their grain cradle swings true, there was a lot about farming they couldn't control, particularly the price" of their products. "As the government pushed modernization, farm youths on the smallest of holdings would know there was no future for them in agriculture."[28] Fingering federal bureaucrats and their "high modernism" alone for the shortcomings and failures of government assistance to small farmers, however, overlooks the fact that local leaders who were in the best positions to influence policies offered no serious attempts to help save family farms and rural communities. No matter how much they might rail against national economic injustices and promise to bring Wall Street and Big Money to heel, most of the region's political elites (whether they actually said so or not) generally concurred with USDA economists, who "believed the small farmers would ultimately need to leave their farms to improve their lives."[29]

Instead, Ozarks political elites used their power to tap government resources for promoting corporate industrial and agribusiness growth, brimming with confidence that such development would stem the tide of massive rural outmigration and alleviate poverty by raising all boats. By the late 1930s, the region's New Deal–supporting political leaders, like most other liberal-progressives throughout America, had begun shifting their priorities away from public relief and the regulatory reform of capitalism and toward the Keynesian pursuit of programs aimed to assist the growth of private industry.[30] In the Ozarks, this transition undoubtedly reflected, at least in part, the growing demands of some of the region's most powerful political constituents. As early as the summer of 1934, for instance, disgruntled merchants from six Ozarks counties met in Harrison to draft a resolution "protesting Federal relief authorities against the free distribution of commodities in the drought areas of the mid-west" and insisting that the "distribution of such commodities should be handled through the regular channels of business."[31] With such pressure mounting, political leaders tailored new plans they hoped would also appeal more broadly to their distressed rural constituents as well, most of whom were desperate for any form of assistance that would somehow help their economic survival—no matter how short-term it might be. Writing in December 1933, a "hill farmer" and rural school teacher in Searcy County complained that, although the "New Deal has done many things," it had "benefitted the small hill farmer but very little." As a solution to rural problems, however, he did not call for a restructuring of the agricultural political-economy but recommended, instead, an even greater increase in government funds for infrastructure projects, such as more "road improvement," to put local boys to work earning much-needed supplementary incomes that would help sustain their families and farms.[32] Faced with both town businessmen's growing resentment of government interference and the persistent desperation of rural working families for any kind of immediate help they could get, infrastructure development seemed to be the most politically viable solution.

Congressman Clyde T. Ellis, representing northwestern and north-central Arkansas's large Third District, led the charge to tap federal resources for massive infrastructure projects. He and his supporters promised "the dawning of a new day in Arkansas," because the projects, they said, "should considerably stimulate business" so that "thousands of people will be given work." Ellis was the son of a Benton County farm family, a former teacher and school superintendent at Garfield, and had been an attorney at Bentonville. Once elected to congress, he worked diligently to add provisions to the 1938 Flood Control Act for the construction of a series of hydroelectric dams on the White River. Inspired by the Tennessee Valley Authority (TVA) in Appalachia and the extensive federal reservoir projects in the West, Ellis called for the creation of a White River Authority (WRA) not only to promote flood control but also to provide public electrical power and spur economic development in the Ozarks. "While the Government for years has been spending millions out West" and in Appalachia on such projects, dam supporters in Arkansas announced that "this part of the Southwest should now glory in the fact that it, too, is getting Federal money." "The far reaching potentialities of this program now at last definitely launched are so extended," they extolled, and "the benefits to come to the present and more to the future generations [are] well nigh incomprehensible." After the House of Representatives passed a flood control bill in June 1938, R. E. Overman, the chairman of the Arkansas State Flood Control Commission, boasted that "it may be stated, earnestly and candidly, that Arkansas today is 'sitting in the lap of the Gods.'"[33]

Hardly had the ink of Roosevelt's signature dried on the Flood Control Act of 1938 before local elites excitedly proclaimed the victory of their long-held visions to transform the Ozarks. After introducing a bill in January 1939 to establish the WRA, Ellis declared that its passage "would mean the difference between poverty and prosperity" in the region. The dams, he claimed, would achieve much-needed flood control, "provide for the agricultural and industrial development of the White river valley," generate cheap electricity for "every home in my district, both rural and urban," and "provide jobs for everybody in my district who wants to work." Local supporters echoed the enthusiasm. At a public hearing convened at Harrison by the U.S. Army Corps of Engineers' Little Rock office in September 1940, engineer Col. Stanley L. Scott "declared that he had never attended a public hearing at which such unanimous approval of a project was voiced." According to Ellis, "more than a thousand" people "from all parts of the White River basin" attended the hearing at Harrison.[34] Mrs. C. W. Gray, a former schoolteacher in Baxter County who now resided in Apache, Oklahoma, wrote Ellis to thank him for his hard work on behalf of the region and its people. "That part of Arkansas has always been sadly neglected, always lived on promises," she wrote. "You probably have you a life job if that Dam on Norfork is built," she guessed. But Gray strongly advised Ellis to stay on top of "push[ing] the project . . . to actual construction," because rural Ozarkers "have had so many promises that they believed nothing until its [sic] done."[35]

Despite mounting efforts—or, as the White House put it, the "reactionary trend"—from conservatives in Congress to "doom . . . administration plans for developments similar to TVA" in the Ozarks, President Roosevelt approved the Corps of Engineers' feasibility study and its recommendations for the construction of hydroelectric dams in the region in August 1940. He then urged Congress to act. By the summer of 1941, however, Ellis's bill still had not passed, even though the Corps had already started the "first phase of the dam and reservoir" of this pilot project on the North Fork River in accordance with the 1938 Flood Control Act. Frustrated by Congress's foot-dragging on Ellis's provisions for the WRA and hydroelectric power, delegations of local businessmen, including one group of "more than forty men," began making trips to Washington in

U.S. Congressman Clyde Ellis with a live 'possum sent to him by some of his Ozarks constituents. Courtesy of Special Collections, University of Arkansas Libraries, Fayetteville.

the summer of 1941 to lobby Congress. One Baxter County advocate, who was losing all patience with Congress, framed the fight as a "modern version" of the battle between "David and Goliath"—"Congressman Clyde Ellis vs. a Congress that hasn't thrown us anything but table scraps for the last 50 years." Urging fellow Ozarkers to raise their voices, he argued, "The least we can do is to chip in, buy Congressman Ellis a new sling and some ammunition." Likewise, Kansas City native and Mountain Home resident Tom Shiras, the editor of the *Baxter Bulletin* and chief spokesmen for local dam and business boosters, wrote Ellis in February 1941 to tell him, "We are all pretty well sunk down here over the Northfork dam situation," because, even though "the president endorsed power for the dam when we were up there a year ago," Congress had authorized "no power yet." "If this thing goes on as is," he continued, "we will have only a frog pond instead of a lake."[36]

Ellis's proposal faced stiff opposition from a coalition of political conservatives in Congress, the strong lobbies of private power companies, and a small cadre of environmental conservationists. Frederick Sullens, a conservative columnist for the *Daily News* in Jackson, Mississippi, alleged that Ellis's proposal was "just a plan to sell power and costly electric gadgets to squatters and shanty dwellers who subsist on corn pone and sow belly."[37] Democratic congressman John J. Cochran of St. Louis helped lead the opposition against Ellis's "lavish program," contending that the Corps' dam projects and the creation of a WRA were far too costly and altogether unnecessary. Moreover, he complained that the expensive dams would inundate valuable farm land and "strike a critical blow to state conservation." The St. Louis *Globe Democrat* believed that Cochran was "dead right," asserting that "such a program would be additional encroachment of national government upon private industry." The paper called on Americans to help "arrest this federal invasion of Missouri and Arkansas by a little TVA." The Missouri Conservation Federation also drafted a resolution against Ellis's proposal for publicly built dams in the Ozarks, claiming that their construction would result in "a needless, shameful spoliation of nature." Ellis responded directly to the Missouri Conservation Federation's attacks, alleging that this "so-called" environmental organization was not really "what it professes to be" but rather "an organ of the already repudiated Missouri power-trust and speaks the voice only of that gang."[38]

The most powerful obstacle proved to be the lobbies of private utility companies. Once their fears of competition from public utilities were at least partially allayed—for the time being, that is—Ellis's proposed hydroelectric dam projects moved forward. The privately owned Arkansas Power and Light (AP&L) company, which held a monopoly on electrical utilities in the state, temporarily backed away from its "unremittingly hostile" position against federal dams when it worked out a plan to "purchas[e] power at beneficial rates from federal facilities" rather "than sinking [its own] investment capital into large-scale dam construction." The company had already reached an agreement with the TVA to import power to eastern Arkansas from public facilities in Memphis. Indeed, AP&L went on to become the main distributor of the Norfork and Bull Shoals dams after their completion. After securing these federal contracts, however, the company revived its political opposition to the creation of public electrical cooperatives and their use of dams built by the federal government in the 1950s and 1960s.[39]

When Ellis dropped his proposal for a federally managed WRA in 1941, his agenda for a series of dams in the Ozarks—a list that would grow longer and longer over the next few years to include almost every free-flowing river in the region—finally received authorization and appropriations from Congress. Ellis's proposal for a "little TVA" and government planning in the region had never been his main priority anyway. Not long after submitting his White River bill to Congress in 1939, Ellis had candidly admitted to a St. Louis attorney that "the WRA was introduced by me upon the suggestion of the anti-power trust leaders here." "If we can get the dams without having an authority," he continued, "it will not be necessary to go ahead with it."[40] For Ellis the TVA model had merely been a political means by which to secure federal approval and funds for hydroelectric dams and large reservoirs for the economic development and jobs that his constituents clamored for. After scrapping the WRA, Ellis's provision for hydroelectric power finally passed the Senate in a new flood-control bill, and Roosevelt signed it into law on August 22, 1941.[41]

Before the Senate finally passed his measure, Ellis had argued that *all* opposition to his bill came from selfish interests outside the region. "In my district," he declared, "there is not a single person opposed to these projects that I know of."[42] Despite solid evidence indicating a groundswell of support for the dams in the region, it seems that Ellis had to stretch, to say the least, to claim absolute unanimity among his constituents. Support certainly outweighed opposition, but at least some rural Ozarkers remained suspicious, particularly some rural families who were trying to remain anchored amid the waves of farm failures and outmigration in their small communities. Their vastly outnumbered voices failed to make it into the region's booster-dominated press, but the discourse of dam-supporting newspapers even suggested that some important "persuasion" remained to be effected locally. In March 1940 Tom Shiras's *Baxter Bulletin* attempted to convince its most skeptical readers that everyone, rural and town folks alike, would see their lives improved by the construction of the Norfork Dam and reservoir. Not only would struggling families find work on its various construction projects, but the county's overall population could be expected to swell by "several thousand people" during the building of the dam and lake alone to create whole new market opportunities, not to mention what was sure to come after the projects were completed. "Many of the men will be employed on the dam and will have no time for gardening or raising chickens and will buy most of what they and their families eat," the paper explained. "This will open a new market for . . . all kinds of produce for our farmers if they take advantage of it," it continued. "Those farmers who get set for this new market will no doubt make money from it."[43]

The *Baxter Bulletin* continued its efforts to "sell" the dam's promise for prosperity to uncertain locals in July 1941. "Some see a dark side, others a bright," it acknowledged, indicating at least some degree of skepticism in the region, "and we cling to the latter." The paper argued that the "precedent" of the construction of Powersite Dam and Lake Taneycomo in the Missouri Ozarks back in the 1910s and that area's subsequent development ensured that "the same thing will happen in Baxter County when Norfork lake is created." "Looking into Baxter County's future," the *Bulletin* envisioned that tourism, manufacturing, mineral resources development, and agriculture would all work together to promote regional economic growth for everyone. "The opportunity to make this county one of the best in the state is here . . . [but it] rests with our citizens as to what they will make of it." The *Bulletin* implored those narrow-minded and hardheaded political leaders in other parts of Arkansas to open their eyes to the region's potential. More liberal state funding for highway improvements, it reasoned, would complement the federal "progress" in the central Ozarks and assist economic growth that would benefit the whole state.[44]

The economic boom that accompanied the Corps of Engineers' groundbreaking for construction projects on the Norfork Dam proved convincing enough for most rural folks. By the third week of March 1941, the *Baxter Bulletin* reported that "hundreds rush here in hope of getting work," even though "it will be at least 30 to 60 days before there will be any work opportunities available on the dam." Rural workers eagerly awaited the construction projects on the dam itself to begin, but ancillary projects such as clearing, grading, graveling, road and railroad building and rerouting, constructing workers' camps and living quarters and managerial and government offices, clearing rights-of-way and erecting power lines by AP&L, and work by private developers on future town sites were already well underway by April. Even before the dam itself began to go up, Marion County's *Mountain Echo* marveled at how "the area around

Construction at the Norfork Dam site in February 1942. Courtesy of Special Collections, University of Arkansas Libraries, Fayetteville.

the Northfork dam site, which a few weeks ago was a stretch of rough, primitive Ozark mountain wilderness, is developing fast into a modern industrial picture."[45]

The jobs created by the construction of Norfork Dam provided timely opportunities for struggling working people in the area. Letters poured into Congressman Ellis's and other leaders' offices from constituents requesting assistance in getting work on the federal project. Cecil Keiter of Searcy County asked Ellis to help him get a job on the Norfork Dam working as "a Tool checker or Tool Room Man," though he certainly "would take a Watchmans job" if others were not available. "I own 40 acres of Land and pay taxes . . . went over to France [during the First World] War . . . and also [am] a Christian man and my family needs my help badly," Keiter explained. Similarly, Marvin Morgan of Marion County informed Ellis, "I need work and shall appreciate anything you can do to get me a job . . . [because] I have a family to support and it seems there is no work to be done."[46]

Local elites also petitioned Ellis and other officials for help to obtain certain benefits from the federal project. Ben Dearmore, a Mountain Home real estate agent and one of the most outspoken proponents of the dam projects, asked Ellis to do what he could to help him secure the federal contract to conduct the land and property appraisals for the acquisitions area. John Q. Adams, the superintendent of Yellville-Summit High School in Marion County, also asked Ellis to use his influence to help his nephew and "some of our boys to get jobs as truck drivers" on the federal construction project.[47] Though Ellis explained that many of these types of decisions would ultimately be up to Corps bureaucrats, District Engineer S. L. Scott of the Little Rock office assured Ellis that "wherever it is possible under the regulations to hire a man in whom you are interested, I shall be glad to do so, provided, of course, that he has the necessary qualifications to perform the work to which he may be assigned."[48] Like most other government projects in the past, federal officials agreed to delegate most of the decisions on the ground to local officials and elites.

Despite the Corps' deference to the local political structure, area elites encountered some challenges to their control that their plans had not foreseen. The Corps and its private contractors promised to prioritize hiring local residents to work on construction crews. But after sifting through hundreds of applications and soliciting recommendations from Congressman Ellis, Corps officials failed to find enough locals who were qualified for some of the more skilled and best-paying jobs. Area businessmen were concerned that the Corps and its contractors might begin importing outside laborers to fill these jobs, which might mean that many of the project's payroll checks would wind up being spent elsewhere. Rex Bodenhammer, one of Tom Shiras's business partners in Mountain Home, asked Ellis to persuade Corps officials and its contractors to loosen their hiring qualifications, since "anyone who has been or had experience as a mechanic" or "a background of work in mines" could "easily" do the work.[49]

At least some intraregional conflict also arose over which towns and locales would receive the greatest benefit from the economic boom created by the dam's construction. In February 1941, Marion County Judge Earl Berry of Yellville complained that "an injustice is being done to the people of his county" because the Corps was deliberately favoring Baxter County in its hiring "method." This put Ellis, who explained that Berry "is one of our best friends in this fight and who was my campaign manager two years ago," in a rather uncomfortable predicament. So the congressman wasted no time in requesting that the Corps' district engineer at Little Rock "give the matter your attention and see if an adjustment can be made."[50]

One of the greatest fears among local elites emerged when the Brotherhood of Carpenters, an affiliate of the American Federation of Labor, and other labor unions arrived in March 1941 to begin organizing construction workers on the Norfork project. The *Baxter Bulletin* and local businessmen strongly objected, insisting that "the sentiment in this section is for an open shop, and that the unemployed men in Baxter and adjoining counties build the dam." The *Bulletin* speculated that "if the job was unionized local men would be shoved off the job and that a labor racket . . . would be inaugurated." Mountain Home mayor and automobile dealership owner Hugh Hackler quickly convened "an impromptu meeting . . . to discuss the situation" with other local officials, area businessmen, and the union representatives. Hackler vowed "that any attempt to bring in outside labor that would conflict with local labor would be resisted and that any racket would be immediately protested." The union representatives assured Hackler and other area elites that they had no intention to steal jobs from locals and would continue prioritizing the employment of area residents. Nevertheless, the alarmist discourse over organized labor at the dam persisted.[51]

Local elites petitioned Ellis to intervene, so the congressman called on the Arkansas Department of Labor to open an investigation of the unions' activities at the Norfork Dam in June 1941. But Labor Director Eli W. Collins replied that his office had "no definite information upon which to base an investigation." With collective-bargaining rights protected by the National Labor Relations Act of 1935, little could be done to halt organized labor at the dam. Collins assured Ellis, nevertheless, that he had "instructed one of our most reliable office managers to make a general checkup during a visit to the dam site on June 13." The inspector reported back that "Baxter County folks are getting most of the jobs on that project" and that the labor unions, as far as he could tell, were otherwise conducting their affairs in a lawful manner. Not quite sure what he thought Ellis expected his office should do now, Collins continued: "As I wrote you previously, if you will give me definite information as to what your friends deem to be wrong we will make a serious effort to straighten the situation out."[52]

To the chagrin of many local business elites, the Utah Construction Company and the Morrison-Knudsen Company (the Corps' main contractors) signed an employment agreement for common labor with the American Federation of Labor's Building and Trades Council on June 11, 1941. They also signed contracts with the Union of Electrical Workers and the Brotherhood of Carpenters for skilled "branches" of labor.[53] The disappointed *Arkansas Gazette* worried that "the project has been turned into a card job," though it acknowledged that a small wage increase for workers had gone into effect, that "seventy-five per cent of the labor being used is from Baxter and adjoining counties," and that "the pay roll gradually is increasing" from the nine-hundred men already employed.[54] The *Baxter Bulletin* maintained that the "sentiment over the entire county had been strong against organization of the job because people here feared that it would result in a 'racket' such as reported on other large construction jobs." Though the greatest tensions on the ground, it admitted, seemed "to a large extent [to have] died out" during the weeks following the labor agreements, the paper suggested that "some laborers still maintain that the Unions are doing little except collecting dues while others seem well satisfied."[55]

The *Baxter Bulletin* reported that the simmering controversy, which the paper claimed still lingered over organized labor at the dam, appeared to have ignited a violent incident at the construction site in August 1941. During the wee hours one Friday morning, some unknown vigilantes exploded dynamite under the floor of the Building and Trades Council office, shattering all the windows and destroying much of the floor. The explosion also broke out several windows and damaged some plumbing in the state employment office building next door and inflicted some collateral damage on a nearby café. Investigators "found no clues" to determine who was responsible, the paper reported. Though union representative M. S. Lee claimed "he knew of no reason for the blast," the anti-union *Bulletin* speculated that tensions between the union and resentful workers had probably caused the drama. "A persistent rumor" that the union "planned to hire labor other than men in this county" may have led to the incident, the paper suggested, though it admitted that its theory "could not be verified." "Another speculation" posited by the Mountain Home paper held that new workers' hostility toward the expiration of the union's thirty-day "special" on "initiation" fees may have prompted the incident, because those who joined after August 1 saw their membership dues rise from $5 to $10.35.

But the union-versus-laborer conflict at Norfork, the *Bulletin* surmised, did not end with the destructive blast at the union office. Undisclosed "witnesses" stated that a "street fight" between Carpenters Union leader John Mullins and two "workers," Ray Amyx and Burnice Martin, broke out several hours after the dynamite incident on Friday evening. Martin had been a local farm laborer in Baxter County and probably was a common laborer on the Norfork project, but Amyx was likely a contractor and not an ordinary "worker," as the *Bulletin* suggested. Blows from Amyx and Martin "knocked down" Mullins "several times" before they "submitted" to local lawmen and received small fines from the local justice of the peace for assault.[56]

The voices of rural workers themselves regarding organized labor at the dam are absent from the historical record. The *Baxter Bulletin* undoubtedly exaggerated in claiming that people "over the entire county" were "strong[ly] against organization of the job." After all, as historian Michael Pierce points out, "labor and anticorporate radicalism was endemic in hills and valleys of northwestern Arkansas" during the first half of the twentieth century. As working-class Ozarkers attempted to navigate the depression of the 1930s and early 1940s, however, local elites' warnings that organized labor would create "rackets" to steal jobs from locals may have alarmed many rural people. As Orval Faubus, Sam Walton, and Don Tyson would do in the region during subsequent decades, anti-union local elites in Baxter and surrounding counties portrayed themselves as populist "defender[s] of Arkansas's white working class, protecting it from a labor movement dominated by outsiders and intent on undermining traditional values." In 1943 and 1944, the Arkansas legislature, under pressure from the conservative corporate lobbies of the Christian American Association and the Arkansas Free Enterprise Association, passed an "anti-labor violence" bill and proposed the nation's first "right-to-work" law, barring closed-shop agreements in the state. Arkansas voters approved the "right-to-work" initiative 105,300 votes to 87,652 at the polls in 1944.[57]

Though much of the opposition to Arkansas's "right-to-work" law came from citizens in the uplands, even some of the most dedicated prolabor advocates in the Ozarks seemed torn and confused over the debate about unionization. Robert Blecker, a Baxter County resident and a worker on the Bull Shoals Dam project, wrote to Gov. Sid McMath in January 1949 to voice "the side of the laboring man." Blecker explained that he initially had "complete confidence in the Taft-Hartley Law," the federal legislation passed in 1947 over President Truman's veto that revised the National Labor Relations Act of 1935 to strike a major blow to organized labor by allowing federal deference to state "right-to-work" laws like the one in Arkansas. Blecker had at first believed Taft-Hartley to be a progressive, worker-friendly law. Since its passage, however, Blecker had "been told by un-reliable sources that there is a provision in the Law that says State Laws will supersede it," and now it seemed that they were right. Earlier concerns had focused on the threat that labor unions would harm local employment opportunities. But now it was "this company, The Ozark Dam Constructors, [that] is importing workers to take the jobs which we are trying to stay out on in order to get some sort of recognition," he explained, and the state's "right-to-work" law was enabling it. "We were told that it would take a strike to start the [National Labor Relations Board] on the job of settling the case, but now it seems that not much can be accomplished even by them because of our Arkansas Labor Laws." Wondering whether McMath had "considered the plight of Labor under these present labor laws," Blecker urged the "progressive" governor to prioritize "build[ing] Arkansas first!"[58]

Blecker's confusion over the unionization debate illustrates how pragmatic working folks tried to decide how new political and economic developments might best benefit their families in the rural Ozarks. With little assistance from government to help their smallholder farm economy otherwise, most rural Ozarkers came to support the federal dam projects—much as they had the Works Progress Administration, the Civilian Conservation Corps, and other New Deal relief programs. They seem to have reasoned that the temporary construction jobs would provide timely sources of income for rural working families. Many undoubtedly also hoped that the dams, once they were finished, would spawn the plethora of opportunities that local business boosters had long promised and that affordable rural electrification might make their small farms more profitable. In a substantial show of support, about ten thousand Ozarkers gathered to celebrate the beginnings of the Norfork project—"the fulfillment of their dream," as Tom Shiras interpreted it—on May 22, 1941. They watched construction crews dynamite the majestic bluff that would help hold the massive concrete dam in place. Afterward, Shiras recalled that the lyrics of "America" echoed proudly through the hills and hollers, "sung by the voices of 10,000 and accompanied by four bands."[59]

Only a handful of disgruntled rural folks who stood to lose their farms to the government's eminent domain for the construction of the dams and lakes remained standing to carry the old torch of populist resistance against this particular agenda. In doing so, ironically, their protests joined those of a small group of business conservatives who dreaded the changes and loss of property that the Corps' dam projects entailed. On October 1, 1944, the more conservative of Little Rock's two major newspapers, the *Arkansas Democrat*, ran an article opposing plans for future dam construction on the White River at Wolf Bayou between Guion and Batesville, which was expected to cover 40,800 acres, primarily in Izard and Stone Counties. "Not only would the fertile White River Valley, [the] chief agricultural source for the two counties and one of the most scenic areas in the South, be obliterated," the *Democrat* pointed out, "but also one of the best timber areas in this section would be covered with water." The proposed dam "probably would do away with" area mining industries such as the Guion Silica Company, too, the paper guessed. Several established towns "would be wholly or partly submerged," it noted, and the "present route of the Missouri Pacific Railroad" would have to be "realigned," creating heavy burdens for even those established towns, businessmen, and property holders outside the Corps' land-acquisition area.[60]

Some rural opponents voiced similar concerns about federal dam construction. Reverend John Zachary of rural Johnson County wrote Gov. Ben Laney in May 1945 to protest federal flood-control projects along the Arkansas River. Zachary claimed that these projects would "cause Millions of dollars [in] Property Loss," not to mention that they would destroy two of his home area's most important highways and force the railroad to reroute its tracks. Most important, the government's land confiscation would "plac[e] a number of good farmers on the unemployment list" in Pope, Johnson, and Franklin Counties. In Johnson County, Zachary complained that the Corps' plans would ruin "some of the finest orchards" in the region. "I ask as a minister of the Gospel trying to hold our people in Peace and good will . . . that you Protect our state from this great Loss," the minister pleaded with the governor. Laney wrote back to assure Zachary that he was "aware of the many conflicting interests concerned" but also to advise him "that the people in the affected territories will be the ones who will determine whether or not this engineering project is accepted or rejected." As for the governor's own position, Laney told Zachary, "I have determined that the will of the people shall prevail."[61]

Backcountry folks who stood to have their lives uprooted by the dam projects also protested. One elderly farmer's wife from Pope County, Mrs. George W. Scott, wrote to the governor's office to request help in saving her family's farm from the Corps. "This [farm] is all we have for a life time of work and we aren't young people any more and don't want to have to start all over again at our age," she explained. "They are trying to take our land and push us out because we are the poores [sic] and less educatid [sic] and don't know what we can do," Scott lamented. "So I am beging [sic] you please if there is nothing you can do to help us let us know whom we can find out from [because] we don't want to loose [sic] our place and have to move and start again."[62]

In another letter of protest in March 1941, Baxter County farmer J. M. Gasset wrote Congressman Ellis urging him to consider the detrimental effects of a depreciating tax base on local residents that the construction of Norfork Dam posed to the area. Gasset stood to lose fifty-five of his 160 acres because of the project, and, aside from his likely resentment over losing a big chunk of his farm, he said he "want[ed] to know when this Dam is completed and the Good . . . land is tuck [*sic*] out of Taxashen [*sic*] what will be the Results in taxes in Baxter County[?]" "Will it Rase [*sic*] the Revenue of the Land to Equal the Present taxes or not [?]" he asked. According to Gasset's figuring, "it look[s] very much like the taxes will be about 4 times more after than now . . . and that will mean a lot to us Hill Farmers."[63] Ellis's response to Gasset acknowledged that "in the readjustment that must come with such a big development as this there will be many headaches just as there have been many headaches in every step of progress that has been made in our country up to now." "If our forefathers had been unwilling to endure those headaches," lectured the congressman, "we would have been as backward as Old Mexico." Nevertheless, Ellis assured Gasset that "all the figures show plainly that the over-all benefits from this dam will far outweigh the various costs." He continued:

> What actually will happen is that you will have a new economy in Baxter County. It will be a new day. There will be work for farmers and farm boys to help round out there [*sic*] income. There will be better markets and better roads and better living conditions and people will be better able to pay taxes. There will be more property to tax and it will not be necessary to raise taxes anywhere but on the other hand taxes are paid for the benefit of the people and more taxes will mean more benefits.[64]

Moreover, the congressman encouraged Gasset to view his situation as a glass half-full instead of half-empty. "I think you are very lucky to have a farm that will be partly covered by the lake for you will have considerable acreage along the water's edge," he explained. "It is a good guess that the 105 acres which you have left will be salable for more than the entire 160 acres which you had originally." Should Gasset consider putting his property on the market, Ellis told the farmer that he would gladly refer him "to several people who are interested in land bordering the lake." The congressman then sent Gasset some Arkansas real-estate bulletins in case he decided to sell the remainder of his farm and purchase property elsewhere.[65]

After reading Ellis's reply, Gasset's outlook appears to have changed remarkably. Gasset wrote the congressman again a few months later to thank him for the real-estate bulletins, explaining, "[I could] get a lot of Real Good From this as I can lurn [*sic*] a lot about How to take the advantage of a lot of things by this." So grateful was Gasset, in fact, that he urged Ellis to run for a U.S. Senate seat in the next election, assuring him, "You Will Go Over big in My Part of the country."

With this transformation in sentiments, Gasset even asked Ellis to help some of his neighbors turn their disadvantages to advantages. One impoverished neighbor who lived on forty acres about a quarter of a mile from the dam had in fact asked Gasset to see if the congressman could also help him find a buyer for his farm. Gasset explained that this destitute neighbor was especially desperate to sell his place because he had "a Wife that needs to Go to a Hospital For Treatment" and could not afford the costs.[66]

While Ellis apparently managed to calm Gasset and some of his rural neighbors and convert them into dam supporters, at least some Ozarkers remained unsatisfied with such assurances of "progress" and a "new economy" for all, believing that the benefits promised could not offset the life-changing sacrifices they and their families were being forced to endure. In the Norfork project, the Corps removed about four hundred residents near Henderson alone to take possession of land needed for the reservoir, and local officials held a public auction to sell the "school building, houses, fence wire, roofing and everything of value" in the "one-time cotton-gin town" and small trading center. In addition to the many farms, homes, schoolhouses, and church buildings lost to eminent domain, an Indiana-based company received a federal contract to disinter and relocate a total of 1,848 graves in twenty-six cemeteries.[67] Clearly, many rural families suddenly found their communities, their heritage, and their entire lives uprooted.

The Corps took steps it hoped would help minimize hardships. In an effort to reduce excessive real-estate speculation and private profiteering at local residents' expense, the Corps tried for as long as possible to keep a relatively tight lid on the official surveys and plats that charted the lands scheduled for condemnation for the reservoir project. Consequently, however, the government's policy for land acquisitions frequently allowed landowners as little as thirty days to vacate the premises, leaving some rural folks' whole lives hanging in question with little time to plan what they would do next. Shortly after early announcements were made about the future construction of Norfork Dam, some farmers began writing letters to political leaders to inquire about how they might be affected. Anticipating that the lake might inundate his Baxter County farm, G. H. Hand wrote Ellis in May 1939, demanding "to know what the prospects are at once so I would know what to do about other arrangements." Though the congressman assured his anxious constituent that "it will be some time before land very far from the dam will be flooded," Ellis attempted to deflect the problem onto Corps bureaucrats. He told Hand, "Your guess as to how long it would be [before they issued condemnation notices] is perhaps as good as mine."[68]

Farmer R. E. Rand of the Rodney community expressed similar concerns. The location of Rand's 442-acre hill farm left no doubt that the government would soon take more than half of his land for the reservoir, so he had already started looking to buy a new farm and relocate. Writing in July 1941, Rand asked Ellis to find out what the government would be paying him for his land so that he could start making arrangements to purchase another farm elsewhere, especially since "land values seem to be going higher all the time." The Corp's district engineer concurred with Rand's speculation, saying, "It appears that a portion of your land will be needed," but he wrote, "I regret to advise you that we are not yet in a position to furnish you with a plat . . . or negotiate with you for its sale to the United States." Though he patiently insisted, "I don't want to pester you so much about my place," Rand wrote to Ellis again in November 1941 to explain that he was "not able to buy a farm and pay cash for it" and didn't "want to pay inerest [*sic*] on one very long." He needed to know, he said, "about when they [the government] would pay for this one [so] I would know what to do" about future plans. In the meantime, Rand said he and his neighbors also needed the government to notify them about whether they would "get another crop after this one" before they had to move, so they could begin making preparations for the spring planting season. Ellis forwarded the letter to the Corps' Little Rock office, but Maj. J. R. Crume Jr. replied that the government was "still not in a position to negotiate." However, though he made no definite promises, Crume advised Rand to proceed with plans "to cultivate and use [his] land" the following year, since his farm's "relatively high elevation" meant that "its possession by the United States [would] not be necessary before next fall."[69]

Belated changes made by the Corps after its initial surveys of acquisition areas and first rounds of land condemnation compounded rural residents' uncertainty and hardships. After federal officials acknowledged that they might possess more land than they would need in some areas but still had not obtained enough in others, former Baxter County judge R. M. Ruthven and other local business boosters sought to capitalize on the Corps' excess land holdings. Ruthven lobbied Ellis to pressure the government to turn over "all lands not needed for the reservoir" for private sale as soon as possible, believing that the ensuing real-estate frenzy would create "a financial boom to Baxter County." While District Engineer Maj. T. F. Kern noted that the "importance of Judge Ruthven's suggestion is appreciated," he ultimately decided "it does not appear advisable to release any of the lands now," because the Corps might later discover that it needed some of the land after all.[70] But ambiguous acquisition schemes meant much more than simply the loss of potential development profits for rural folks who abruptly received notice that the government planned to take their farms.

R. S. Hensley's sudden discovery that the Norfork project would turn his life upside down is a case in point. Hensley had moved to the Gamaliel community during the 1930s and settled on a small piece of land that was still in the public domain, where he claimed he had made about $300 worth of improvements to the land, including "a nice orchard . . . and some fencing." While securing the legal title to the land had not seemed so urgent before, all the buzz aroused by the Norfork Dam project apparently prodded Hensley to file a formal homestead claim in February 1942. He had heard that the reservoir would inundate only a small corner of the general area where his farm was located: "The way they [the Corps] have it sayrvaied [sic] out and of corse [sic] will not no way interfear [sic] with me." The federal government rejected Hensley's homestead claim, however, and explained that it had already transferred the land to the Corps. A desperate Hensley asked Ellis to intervene, to "get it where I could Home stead it." Though he said he was "terribly sorry to learn" of Hensley's predicament, the congressman referred him to the Corps' Little Rock office and regretted to tell him, "I just don't know whether there is anything at all you can do about it."[71]

The construction of the dams and reservoirs also placed unforeseen burdens on some rural folks who remained on their backcountry farms after the Corps finished its condemnations. The Corps did not condemn George Bell's farm for the Norfork project, which was located about four miles from the reservoir. But Bell complained that the filling of the lake would isolate and make inaccessible his and other backcountry farm communities more than ever by inundating and dividing important parts of the area. Deploring the region's poor and inadequate country schools and the lack of decent roads, Bell claimed that his rural community of Elizabeth "mite have had" better educational opportunities and roads "by now if it had not been in the Reservoir." Though he was no fan of the government's dam project, Bell explained that he had "5 children that needs a better chance at school than they have" and, since the reservoir promised to divide and ruin his rural community, he wished now that the Corps would just take his land too so he would have some money to move his family elsewhere. The Corps informed Bell, however, that it was "not in a position to negotiate . . . at this time."[72]

Tempers boiled among some dispossessed rural folks, and a few angry opponents resorted to violence. Though Baxter County Sheriff Harvey Powell "found no clues of value" with which to make arrests, some angry arsonists set fire to a "recently erected" store building at the dam site in late August 1941, not long after workers had finished diverting the flow of the North Fork River from its original channel and started building the massive concrete structure that would become the hydroelectric-power-generating dam. Luckily for the building's owner and the rest of the new properties under construction at the newly platted town, workers and Corps officials staying at the site noticed the blaze and "extinguished [it] before it got well underway." When local authorities arrived at the damaged building to investigate, they found a back door busted open and an empty kerosene jar "lying open in the rear room" with its contents "poured over the floor." Though the unknown arsonists inflicted far less damage than they had hoped, the store's owner suffered a significant financial loss because he had not yet purchased fire insurance.[73]

The clear majority of rural folks disaffected by the dams eschewed such violent retaliation, however. A handful of more prosperous and better-connected hill folks filed or threatened lawsuits and circulated petitions objecting to what they deemed to be unfair treatment by the government's land acquisition schemes. In the fall of 1940, sixty-eight-year-old S. J. Hutcheson, a prominent landowner, stockman, and retired Main Street merchant at the old town of Norfork, filed a suit against the government in the U.S. District Court at Harrison. The Corps had offered Hutcheson $1,250 for a 129.3-acre tract of condemned riverside land located upstream from the dam site, but he insisted that it was worth much more than that. A few years before, Hutcheson had rented this part of his large farm to the AP&L, which had considered constructing a small power-generating dam on that section of the North Fork River before the Corps' project was approved by the federal government. Hence, Hutcheson claimed the land held a special "availability" value, along with its agricultural value, and was worth at least an additional $10,000. Still, he proposed to settle with the government for $4,300. When the Corps refused his counteroffer, Hutcheson sued. Hutcheson died about a month before the October court term commenced, but his heirs pursued the case. On October 9, federal judge Harry J. Lemley and the jury traveled by bus from Harrison to visit the disputed land in Baxter County to determine whether the government had made a fair offer to the landowner. The following day, the court ordered the Corps to double its original offer, awarding Hutcheson's heirs $2,500 for the land.[74]

The Hutcheson heirs, led by Jack Bonner, sued the government again the following spring. This time the family disputed the government's offer to compensate them for the acquisition of rights-of-way through other parts of their land for a new highway and a new eight-mile railroad spur to connect the dam site to the main tracks in the town of Norfork. Bonner and some of the other heirs had already invested in and begun developing the Hutcheson lands near the dam into a new lakefront town site, and they had told local reporters in April 1941, "Our lots are selling well and we expect to build up a good town on the site." The Hutcheson heirs likely welcomed the decision to route the new highway and railroad through the family's booming property, but they hoped that holding out in federal court would force the government to fork out more money for the rights-of-way. Their efforts paid off. In October 1941 the jury once again made the trip from Harrison "to personally view the site," and the court required the government to increase its purchasing price and pay an additional 6 percent interest to the Hutcheson heirs, since it had taken possession of the land from them a year before the case was settled. [75]

A few other better-off landowners also embarked on a litigious path of resistance. As late as the fall of 1942, S. R. Seward, Don Chapin, Lon Jones, and a few other farm owners organized a petition to challenge the Corps' land condemnations above the Norfork Dam to make way for the area that would contain the twenty-two-thousand-acre lake. They acquired an attorney and threatened to slow the construction of the reservoir by filing for an injunction and tying the matter up in court. They sent the petition straight to their powerful local political friends, Tom Shiras, Rex Bodenhammer, Tom Dearmore, and other Mountain Home boosters, and "insisted" that these men pressure federal officials to do something about the landowners' "troubles." They primarily complained that the government was shorting them with lowball offers for their land. Bodenhammer wrote Congressman Ellis "to find out whether [he] could and would try to get an adjustment made without their going into court." While he "realize[d] that any improvement will cause a hardship on someone" and did not believe "it is the intention of the Government to damage anyone," Bodenhammer admitted that his farmer-friends "are justified in asking" for more just compensation, because "some of these petitioners' farms have been appraised way too low."[76]

Though they occasionally invited poorer neighbors to join their lawsuits, the few wealthier landowners in the area were typically the only ones with the resources to follow through with their threats to challenge the federal government in court, and they usually did so only to hold out for more money. Instead, the responses of most poor and middling hill farmers dispossessed by the Corps' dam projects probably resembled that of Billy D. Potter's family in the Higden community in Cleburne County.

Billy Potter's farm near the Little Red River had been in the family since his grandparents had migrated from Tennessee and settled the small tract of hill ground in the 1880s. Born in 1918 in the original house his grandparents had built, the young Billy later helped his family survive the Great Depression and maintain the farm by supplementing the family's scanty agricultural income with part-time work at a local sawmill and employment with the Civilian Conservation Corps. In April 1942 Potter's father died unexpectedly from a massive stroke after he and Billy had finished clearing some new farm ground. The family's loss left the twenty-four-year-old Potter "the full responsibility of making a crop, running the farm, and taking care of his mother and younger sister." Potter married the following month, and he and his new bride, Claudia, conceived their first child a few weeks later. That summer, Potter received word from Uncle Sam that he had been drafted for military service in World War II, but the army granted him a discharge so he could return and care for his family after his son was born in late January 1943.[77]

Back in Cleburne County, Potter supported his family with a combination of semi-subsistence farming, raising livestock for the market, and growing corn and cotton as cash crops. To keep the family farm viable in America's postwar agricultural economy, Potter significantly expanded production during the 1940s and 1950s. In addition to maximizing production on the family's modest hill farm, Potter rented several acres of fertile bottom ground in the area's narrow river and creek valleys from three different landowners, where he also grew corn and cotton for the market. By the late 1950s, after many of their neighbors and extended family members had packed their meager belongings and fled the opportunity-strapped community, the Potters had managed to preserve the family farm and sustain their smallholder livelihood in the rural Ozarks.[78]

In the summer of 1959 the Potters' lives suddenly changed when the federal government notified them that they must turn over their farm to the Corps of Engineers for the construction of the Greer's Ferry Dam and Lake. The Corps later made its offer to compensate them for the land, but the family believed that "there was no way the amount of the settlement could replace what was being taken," especially since it included only a "minimal allowance for the improvements on the land." Potter's daughter, Karen, who was a high-school sophomore at the time, remembered the stress her father and the rest of the family endured as they attempted to navigate the dislocation. Karen explained that although they considered fighting the government, "Dad knew the only other option was a formal appeal, which would tie up any settlement until all court proceedings were completed, a minimum of several months, could be years." The family simply could not bear the expense and uncertainty. Her father "could not afford to miss planting a crop in the Spring," she recalled, "so he reluctantly accepted the Corps' settlement offer and began to focus on getting relocated."[79]

By the fall of 1959, while they scrambled to harvest their crops and keep up with other demands on the farm, the Potters arranged to purchase a lowland farm in Craighead County in northeastern Arkansas near the home of some relatives. Then they began transporting corn, hay, and other farm products and equipment to the new farm in Craighead County, a round trip of about three hundred miles. In all, Karen remembered that her father made "about forty trips moving everything he needed to move," mostly at the family's own expense, because "the Corps' monetary settlement included only a very small allowance for moving expenses." Except for a few cows—"enough for a small herd at the new farm"—Potter sold most of his "100 head of Hereford cattle," in addition to all but "a load of hogs." After Christmas—which Karen later described as "the saddest Christmas I've ever experienced"—the Potters started moving their household items. Though they had "procrastinated even acknowledging the reality of it as long as possible," the Potters finally vacated the family farm a few weeks later.[80]

Soon after the Potters arrived at their new lowland farm, Karen remembered her aging grandmother, whose parents had originally homesteaded the family farm in Cleburne County in the 1880s, sitting on the porch swing one rainy day and remarking as she peered out across the flat and treeless terrain: "It ain't the same, is it?" Though the Potters soon became "very busy with the demands and activities at the new place," Karen recalled that "the move was very traumatic for all of us, heart-wrenching, actually." By the time they returned to Cleburne County in May 1960 to attend a relative's high-school graduation, their "former community was only a skeleton of itself." "So many houses and barns were gone that you could barely tell where families had lived only a short time before," she recollected. During another visit "home" in August 1961, shortly after the Corps began filling the new lake, she remembered her resentful father commenting as the family drove across a new bridge overlooking the flood zone: "They took our farm and made us move, but I don't believe that lake will ever cover as much ground as the Corps says it will." "Dad's doubt was soon proved wrong," she explained. President John F. Kennedy arrived in Cleburne County on October 3, 1963, to dedicate the Greer's Ferry Dam (which turned out to be Kennedy's last public appearance before his assassination the following month) and to applaud these public "investments which will make this a richer state and country in the years to come." But the Potters continued their struggles to "recover" from this "painful" and "transitional time" and to remake their lives.[81]

The plight of the Potters notwithstanding, dispossession by the Corps' dam projects typically spelled the end of family farming altogether and brought about even greater transformations for most rural folks who were forced to relocate. The small cash payments distributed by the federal government to compensate rural families for their "poor hill ground" prohibited most from buying farms elsewhere that were large enough to provide an adequate income to survive as smallholder producers. Most joined the mass exodus from rural communities to start life anew in places like the sprawling industrial zones of California and Illinois or more urbanized regional centers in Arkansas and other parts of the western South. Even those backcountry folks whose farms were not taken by the government and who stayed attached a while longer usually underwent similar

President John F. Kennedy talks with Corps of Engineers officials at the dedication of Greers Ferry Dam in October 1963. This was his last appearance at a public event before his trip to Dallas where he was assassinated the following month. Courtesy of the Cleburne County Historical Society.

experiences. Indeed, the vibrant opportunities for small hill farmers that local business boosters had promised would emanate from the growth created by the Corps' dams never materialized. Even Tom Shiras had to admit in 1945—two years after the completion of the Norfork Dam—that "no extensive boom took place around the dam," as many had envisioned, though he continued to insist that "opportunities are here for a long-neglected section of the United States."[82]

The federal government began building the even larger Bull Shoals Dam on the White River in 1947, so hundreds of rural locals in Baxter, Marion, and surrounding counties—many of whom were returning World War II veterans— temporarily benefited once again from the decent-paying construction jobs it created. Most of these government-funded paychecks ended, however, after contractors finished the biggest part of the project in 1952. Marion County native Doyle Hurst remembered that, though the "rural Ozark area thrived" around several small towns in the vicinity of the dam while it was under construction, "there was a severe job shortage" after the Corps and its contractors finished the project and moved out.[83] Ultimately, dam "progress" failed to stem the flow of rural decline and outmigration.

The lion's share of the permanent economic benefits generated by Norfork and Bull Shoals Dams went to the town of Mountain Home in Baxter County. "Ideally situated about midway between the two projects," Mountain Home rapidly transformed from a small county-seat town and local trading village with fewer than six hundred people in 1930 into a blossoming tourism, recreational, and retirement center of more than twenty-two hundred people by the 1950s. Even before the full impact of the new Bull Shoals Lake materialized, the town had become "the third most popular destination for retirees in Arkansas, and Baxter County boasted over 150 resorts, lodges, hotels, and restaurants." In keeping with the national trends of postwar suburbanization, Mountain Home continued growing its tourist- and consumer-based economy during the ensuing decades and reached a population of more than eight thousand by 1980 and almost 12,500 by 2010.[84]

Similarly, the town of Heber Springs harnessed most of the economic growth fueled by the Greer's Ferry Dam. While economist Christopher Garbacz claimed in a 1971 article in *Land Economics* that the Greer's Ferry project had contributed "substantial benefits" for "economic development in this depressed area" of the Ozarks in Cleburne and Van Buren Counties due to rising levels of per capita income and job creation, he had to admit that there were "certainly complex analytical problems" in gauging costs and benefits. Based on statistics for 1969, Garbacz estimated that the ripple effect of the dam's economic impact after its completion had "directly" or "indirectly" created about 1,253 new jobs, accounting for more than 26 percent of the total employment in the two-county area. He confessed, however, that these statistics did not disclose the fact that "certainly some of the new employment was absorbed through in-migration" and that a disproportionate number of the jobs was subject to "seasonality of employment and low earnings potential." Garbacz also acknowledged that "non-residents" and recent in-migrants now owned a large portion of the local wealth. In 1970, for instance, nonresidents (not including recent permanent in-migrants) owned $11.25 million of the $27 million value of housing properties "adjacent to the lake." Furthermore, Garbacz noted that residents of communities in the area "have not prospered equally." A comparison of per capita personal income in Cleburne and Van Buren Counties between 1960 and 1967 revealed this unevenness, not to mention the marked disparities from community to community within the two counties. While Cleburne County, mostly reflecting the growth of Heber Springs, had climbed the ladder in Arkansas's per capita income rankings from number 56 to number 35 out of its seventy-five counties, Van Buren County actually fell from 67 to 70 on the list. Another study of similar dams and lakes in the Missouri Ozarks, moreover, indicated that "in many cases, poverty had increased in counties with dams even though there had been immigration by higher income government workers and well-to-do retirees."[85]

As Ozarks historian Brooks Blevins puts it, "The dams would bring prosperity to the region, though not always to its people." In writing about the impact of the Corps' pilot project in Baxter County, Blevins explains that "the long-term effects on the human community in the Norfork Dam area in many ways paralleled the effects on the fish community," after the government constructed a new fish hatchery to introduce nonindigenous trout species into the cold-water stream below the dam. "Retired and entrepreneurial midwesterners poured into the Mountain Home area, replacing those uprooted by the dam and the hundreds more whose agricultural pursuits failed to support them after World War II." "The newcomers, like the brown and rainbow trout," Blevins suggests, "were and are most often non-reproductive; they lived out their lives in an environment quite different from the one heritage had provided until they were replaced by another Midwestern retiree at death. But they came to northern Arkansas in large numbers" seeking comfort and prosperity in a New Ozarks, while hundreds of capital-strapped natives exited the region's rural communities en masse.[86]

The experiences of many native-born rural Ozarkers who managed to stay in their home areas during this era of regional transformation resembled those

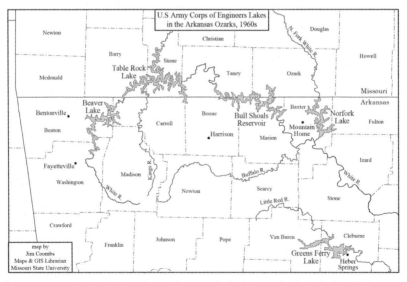

Lakes constructed by the U.S. Army Corps of Engineers in the Arkansas Ozarks by the late 1960s. Courtesy of Jim Coombs, Missouri State University.

of Harlin Pierson, Jewell Tilley, and Doyle Hurst of Marion County. Pierson had helped his family during the Great Depression by supplementing their small farm income with part-time work for a local dairy farmer and by cutting stave bolts for extra cash. He then took a job with the Civilian Conservation Corps at Dierks. During the late 1940s and early 1950s, Pierson worked as a rotary driller on the Bull Shoals Dam. After that job ended in 1952, he scraped by, raising livestock for a few years before the government placed him on its payroll as a local park ranger. He later received a promotion to become a park superintendent. Thus, Pierson managed to remain in his home area and retired comfortably with a government pension after eighteen years.[87]

Jewell Tilley remembered that the Depression "was dang hard" and that he had helped keep his family's farm afloat with extra "cotton pickin'" wages and a WPA job during the late 1930s and early 1940s. Though that "bunch of Republicans . . . By God . . . starved us out," Tilley explained, Roosevelt "started all that work" and "got things to goin'." "A lot of people forgot that, but by gosh we didn't," the loyal Democrat continued. The jobs provided by the dam projects "helped out a whole lot," he explained. After the Corps and its contractors finished the Bull Shoals project, Tilley went to Washington State and found work with a giant corporate farm and seed company, which he recalled had a "big orchard," "900 acres of potatoes," a large alfalfa and clover ranch, a bee farm, and other sectors of agricultural production. Having made "pretty good money" there, he returned to Marion County a few years later and bought two hundred acres on the "mountain" to add to the family farm in the Rea Valley, where he primarily raised livestock. He supplemented his farm income by guiding trout fishermen below the Bull Shoals and Norfork Dams for Elmo Hurst's recreational guiding and outfitting business. Though he later sold much of the farm when he and his wife divorced, Tilley retired on his forty-acre homeplace and continued raising "a few cows" into the 1990s.[88]

Doyle Hurst was born only a few months before the United States entered World War II, but he remembered his working family's struggles in rural Marion County. His father worked a construction job on the Bull Shoals Dam, but the subsequent "change in the supply [of local employment] forced the Hurst family to move frequently in the summertime" after the project ended. The Hursts kept their small farm in the Ozarks but went to Texas and Montana to find work between spring planting seasons and fall harvests. During one summer in Montana, the young Doyle worked at a grocery store to contribute to the family's income. With the help of this seasonal employment as migrant workers, the Hursts maintained their place in the rural Ozarks. After Doyle Hurst graduated from the local Flippin High School, he went to the University of Arkansas in Fayetteville. Then he attended Oklahoma State University, where he earned a doctorate in education. Upon completing his education, Hurst "came back to his roots" in the rural Ozarks to teach at the local high school.[89] While many hill folks were unable or unwilling to stay in the rural Ozarks, those like Pierson, Tilley, and Hurst who did usually had to turn to economic endeavors off the farm—and often outside the region altogether—to survive during the second half of the twentieth century.

The region's predominantly rural areas remained some of the most impoverished locales in the nation, but life had changed dramatically in the Ozarks between the 1930s and 1960s. Ozarkers had continued to demand that their government intervene to promote economic justice during the Great Depression and supported political leaders who promised to redistribute American power and prosperity to hardworking common people. Armed with the unprecedented powers of an expanded federal government, New Dealers provided much-needed relief to desperate hill folks, but most of their programs only temporarily assisted rural families and wound up mostly serving the interests of the local elites who ran them. In the long run, many of the government's rural programs actually exacerbated the extinction of smallholder farming.

Nevertheless, as rural depression reached new depths in the 1930s and 1940s, fewer backcountry Ozarkers opted for the paths of defiant resistance that some hill folks had taken during the moonshine wars, the controversial military draft of World War I, and the government's burdensome agricultural "improvements" over the previous three decades. Most struggling rural folks pragmatically welcomed any help they could get. Aside from the handful of hill folks literally displaced by land condemnations, most rural Ozarkers joined with regional business elites to support federally funded infrastructure projects such as the Army Corps of Engineers' dams. Many likely agreed with one liberal-progressive's assertion that, since there was "no ongoing or planned program to upgrade the mobility of the labor force," and because a "direct subsidy to improve employment prospects in the rural underdeveloped regions [was] not likely on any large scale," the benefits from these dams and similar government projects, however limited, "may be at least a partial solution to underdevelopment in rural areas."[90] Indeed, despite their limited benefits—or, perhaps, *because* of their limited benefits—dam building and other such development projects in the Ozarks became "addictive."[91] At last, local businessmen's vision of corporate development and its favored status in exercises of government power had won the Ozarks. The liberal state's yielding to local elites and their ideals would effectively pitch rural populism's quest for working-class democracy into the dustbin of history.

During the post–World War II era, as smallholder farming headed toward extinction, working families in the rural Ozarks became more thoroughly hitched than ever to America's corporate development-oriented political economy. Meanwhile, the national liberal state's continued delegation of authority to local political regimes ensured that powerful local business elites controlled the ground-level administration of most federal programs that intended to help the working poor. This also meant that these local elites held a nearly uncontested position from which to shape political discourse in the region about federal programs and their effectiveness, especially in the absence of working-class voices from small farmers' organizations and their Populist ethic of economic democracy that had once been so prolific. Consequently, a New Ozarks began taking shape during the post–World War II era that spurred a marked shift in the dynamics of defiance in the region away from its rural working-class roots. Increasingly, many of the most impassioned expressions of "damn guv'ment" resistance in the region would now be instigated by New Ozarks elites who were determined to fight all federal interventions that might impede their local control and compromise their prospects amid America's bustling corporate growth.

PART III

TOWARD A NEW DEFIANCE

6

GROWTH POLITICS AND RURAL DISAPPOINTMENT

Martha Wagner was dismayed at what she saw happening to her rural community in 1952. "Just a little old woman here on Pryor Mountain" in Cleburne
County, where she had lived for "most of 50 years," Wagner felt helpless because
"ever-Body is leaving here to hunt work." She decided to write Gov. Sidney Mc-
Math and "put in a plea for my good neighbors and friends," feeling, as she said,
"[that] I just had to do something if I could for our People here." Small farmers
in Cleburne County who typically owned "from 3 to 120 acres" of "Just Plain
Hill land," she told the governor, "will grow eney-kind [*sic*] and all kinds of
vegetables—from corn to pumpkins." "[I]f we had a Big government Canner or
Compney [*sic*] Canner here that would Can and Buy what they Raise," Wagner
thought, "People could stay on their homes and Raise stuff and have a good income to [*sic*] and not half [*sic*] to leave and go to Calif. or Mich. to work." "Please
Mr governor," she pleaded, "will you help us . . . so folks can keep their homes
and at the same time Help enable them to feed the World?"[1]

Wagner must have figured that if any political leader would listen, it would
be McMath. Sidney McMath stood as the torchbearer of New Deal liberalism in
postwar Arkansas, having ridden into the governor's office in 1949 as a "popular
progressive" reform leader. McMath and his liberal allies had managed to keep
conservatives and race-baiting Dixiecrats from dominating Arkansas's Democratic Party as they had in most other Southern states. During his two terms in
office the "reform-minded" governor oversaw several measures, including "an

unprecedented highway-construction" program, "improved health care," educational reform, and critical "support for the rural electric cooperative movement" in the face of corporate obstructionism. Moreover, the McMath-sponsored "legislation that more than doubled the annual budget of the [state] labor department, increased minimum-wage laws, and strengthened industrial-safety codes" helped boost the governor's image among Arkansas's working class.[2]

McMath's brand of "progressivism," however, remained in stride with most other postwar liberals who stood committed to the promise of business prosperity—and not so much redistributive and regulatory policies—as the key to solving social and economic problems, including rural decline. In his reply, McMath assured Wagner that the rural "problem" she spoke of "has come to my attention many times since I have been Governor of this State." He explained, however, "There is no provision whereby a state can provide a market for the fine products which are raised in your community and many others in America." Still, he was confident that his state-sponsored development programs would spur new business growth in Arkansas that would help fix the rural crisis and encourage future prosperity for all. "I am doing everything possible to provide a good improved highway system in the state," he told Wagner. "I feel that once this is done that private industry will come into Arkansas and will set up factories and processing plants thereby providing a market for the natural products of Arkansas." "I assure you," the governor pledged, "I am doing everything possible to provide a better life for the ordinary citizens of Arkansas."[3]

Wagner's letter to McMath represented many rural Ozarkers' continued conviction during the post–World War II years that a just government ought to help provide opportunities and security for working families and communities. Despite unprecedented economic growth in the United States after World War II, depression remained fixed in rural communities across the Ozarks. Folks like Martha Wagner, however, hoped that the same "peoples' government" that had so successfully mobilized its collective commitment and resources to guarantee Americans' security and prosperity in war could also help protect and promote opportunities for America's rural working families.

McMath's reply, however, also represented the persistence of American progressives' delegation of the liberal state's power and resources to local elites and their visions. Postwar reformers, both locally and nationally, aimed not to revive what they believed to be a worn-out and outdated smallholder farm economy but, instead, to bring "modernity" to the Ozarks and other depressed regions by opening the door of "opportunity" afforded by corporate industrialization. They sought to use government power to break down barriers of "isolation" and to pump resources into "lagging areas" left behind in an otherwise affluent

America. Leaving the applications of federal power and resources in the hands of local elites who presumably "knew best" about how to deal with specific circumstances on the ground, the postwar liberal state set out to "grow" and "uplift" rural communities out of their antiquated "exceptionalism" and "otherness" by integrating them more fully into mainstream America's burgeoning industrial economy.

Many rural Ozarkers hoped that the John F. Kennedy and Lyndon B. Johnson administrations' federal programs would help their region "grow" and "develop" its way to newfound prosperity. By 1966, federal, state, and local officials had created the Ozarks Regional Commission (ORC), one of five commissions in the United States authorized under Title V of the Public Works and Economic Development Act of 1965. The mountainous, "underdeveloped" Ozarks seemed the logical choice to follow the government's larger pilot program in Appalachia. The story of federal development efforts in the Ozarks, however, was one of initial high hopes that turned rather quickly to disappointment. The ORC and the other Title V commissions, unlike the independent Appalachian Regional Commission, operated within the Department of Commerce and never transcended their secondary status in the broader regional development program. The later formation of the Title V commissions amid the escalating war in Vietnam and conservatives' increasing assaults on social programs ensured that the ORC would be a low priority. In Appalachia, some level of regional coordination had already established roots among political and economic leaders before 1960. But calls for a regional program in the Ozarks came only after the announcement of the Appalachian program aroused concerns about federal favoritism from political and business leaders in Arkansas, Missouri, and Oklahoma who wanted their piece of the pie. State and local leaders who controlled most of the ORC's projects advanced a "trickle out" vision that helped promote an uneven process of development that aided already more prosperous "growth centers" at the expense of the opportunity-strapped rural areas that had been held up as examples to justify federal regionalism in the first place. Most rural working people, then, received little but disappointment from postwar liberals' economic reform efforts.

In a November 1965 article titled "Echoes of Appalachia," *Wall Street Journal* reporter James C. Tanner drew national attention to the "Poverty-Ridden Ozarks." Pointing to distressed Newton County in northwest Arkansas, where more than one-third of the citizens were on welfare and per capita income was less than one-third the national average, Tanner described "a land characterized by out-migration, a rising median age of residents, depreciating tax bases, inadequate schools, few public facilities and a limited road network." Tanner continued:

"If all this sounds like Appalachia, the Ozarks . . . have much in common with that 11-state mountain area. . . . But while Appalachia draws the headlines and massive doses of federal aid, the economic situation in the Ozarks continues to deteriorate." "Stirrings of hope" were in the air, though, because President Johnson had recently signed a major public-works bill authorizing economic programs for the Ozarks modeled on the Appalachian Regional Commission's (ARC) $1 billion federal aid program. "Much of the new hope," Tanner explained, " . . . rests on the prospect of help from Washington." Against the backdrop of postwar liberalism's heyday, many comfortable, yet compassionate, observers felt confident that rural poverty might be solved with government assistance to help pour the blessings of corporate investments into the region.[4]

In the words of historian Godfrey Hodgson, "The United States entered the 1960s in an Augustan mood: united, confident, conscious of a historic mission, and mobilized for the great task of carrying it out." The World War II era had produced "an economic leap forward, which gradually engendered a new social optimism," an unwavering faith in American capitalism that promised to "produce abundance on such a scale that social problems would be drowned under a flood of resources."[5] Amid the excitement, however, a few keen observers such as intellectual and social activist Michael Harrington helped turn the nation's and its political leaders' attention to "another America" that existed within the country's borders. Harrington exposed an "invisible land" in rural and urban places where a "culture of poverty" had been left behind. Affluent America, he insisted, was obligated to reach out to these forgotten people, for "society must help them before they can help themselves." Moreover, lifting these areas out of poverty would present yet more opportunities for American industrial expansion, a win-win for everyone.[6]

No people better epitomized the "Other America" than residents of the southern highlands. "There's nothing wrong with hillbillies—a description which Mountain people loathe—that a strong dose of equal opportunity wouldn't cure," wrote Harry W. Ernst and Charles W. Drake in *The Nation* in 1959. "Applying every yardstick of social well-being, their Appalachian homeland emerges a sordid blemish on the balance sheet of the wealthiest nation in the world."[7] Unemployed coal miners, dispossessed small farmers, and generally impoverished families of Appalachia reminded middle-class America that the promise of unbounded prosperity was still a work in progress. Thousands of rural folks had already hit the migrant trails to northern or western cities to escape their depressed communities, and destitution and desperation engulfed too many of those who remained. Confident that this "blemish" could be healed, however, policymakers and activists made Appalachia a central battleground in a national antipoverty crusade.

John F. Kennedy's campaign for the Democratic primary in West Virginia in 1960 cast the spotlight on Appalachia's poverty. His campaign through the Mountain State drew significant attention to rural poverty, and it left a major impression on his ideas for future policy. In the words of journalist Theodore White, "Although Kennedy's background of wealth and privilege provided him with little understanding of poverty and the struggles of less affluent Americans, his time in West Virginia had awakened in him sympathy for the unemployed coal miners and rural poor of Appalachia." Kennedy promised that, once elected, he would put forth a comprehensive program to improve West Virginia's and other depressed areas' economic suffering.[8]

Despite the immense changes it had undergone since the 1940s, the Ozarks was one of the other areas suffering intense poverty and a dearth of economic opportunities. But as historian Brooks Blevins notes, "Unlike Appalachia, which became a cause célèbre during the 1960s' war on poverty, the Ozarks never entered the mainstream consciousness as a region racked by unbelievable poverty and distress." For one thing, the Ozarks did not have a Harry Caudill, the Kentucky lawyer and activist whose widely read *Night Comes to the Cumberlands* (1962) exposed the blatant exploitation that industrialists, especially coal companies, had wrought upon Appalachia, leaving chronic poverty and dependency in their wake. While industrialization, as we have seen, had certainly brought significant change to the Ozarks since the nineteenth century, the clearly visible scars on the land and people that corporate exploitation had left on Appalachia were less obvious at first glance in its sister region to the west. With the help of romantic travel writers and tourism boosters the Ozarks actually seemed like an unspoiled land of rural simpletons living in the bygone years in mainstream America's popular imagination. "Whether consciously or unconsciously," writes Blevins, "the Ozark region had been relegated to almost pure image, a land that apparently embodied the rural and pastoral virtues of a largely mythological American past, yet one not worthy of serious thought or respect." With only a few exceptions, such as Tanner's 1965 *Wall Street Journal* article, the Ozarks was mostly viewed as a beautiful and quaint travel destination, and not a "wretched" and impoverished region like Appalachia.[9]

Nevertheless, this image overshadowed the serious poverty that truly plagued rural Ozarkers outside the resort towns. In 1959 the annual per capita income in the region stood at only 67 percent of the national average; while the nation's average per capita income was $1,850, it was only $1,242 in the upland counties

Scenic View of Norfork Dam and Lake Norfork in the Arkansas Ozarks

Post–World War II era tourism postcard. Courtesy of Special Collections, University of Arkansas Libraries, Fayetteville.

of northern and western Arkansas, southern Missouri, and eastern Oklahoma. With the region's population at about 2.5 million in 1960, a federal report in 1967 indicated that the per capita income gap represented about a $1.5 billion income deficiency in the Ozarks.[10] More than 44 percent of Ozarks families had annual incomes of $3,000 or less in 1960, a poverty figure more than double the national average. Interestingly, the Ozarks poverty rate was nearly 14 percent higher than the aggregate rate of Appalachia's (as defined broadly by the ARC), the symbol of rural poverty in the nation.[11]

The corporatization of agriculture in the postwar years had profoundly hastened the demise of rural communities and smallholder economies of the Ozarks. Adding to the rapid decline of family farming that had already begun during the 1940s, the percentage of Ozarkers employed in agriculture fell from 28.2 percent to 13.4 percent between 1950 and 1960. The loss of opportunities for small farmers put many working families on the migrant trails. During the 1950s alone, the region experienced a net loss of 431,000 people, most of them young adults. Consequently, older residents disproportionately populated the Ozarks. In 1960, while people sixty-five years and older accounted for just over 9 percent of the national population, senior citizens made up 13 percent of the Ozarks population.[12]

Some rural folks who remained in the region found new advantages in the New Ozarks economic and social environment. Some who happened to have good rapport with local bankers and were deemed "safe" to receive federal loan assistance were consequently able to buy cheap land from neighbors as their rural communities emptied. A few, like my grandfather, Paul Perkins, and his brother Earl, eventually amassed farms large enough to compete in an economy dominated by Big Agriculture. Their grandfather had been among several small farmers during the agrarian cooperative movement in the 1890s who helped found a local bank in the rural trading village of Smithville, and the family had managed to hold on to its modest stake in the twentieth century. The small bank at Smithville, in fact, was the only bank in the county that remained solvent during the Great Depression. This longstanding relationship with the local bank came in handy when, after returning from military service in World War II, Paul and Earl began working to expand the three-hundred-acre family farm in western Lawrence County. The family's good standing proved vital as local bankers made important decisions about the distribution of the federal government's low-interest loan programs during the postwar era. Stamps of approval on their applications for federally subsidized credit through the Farmers Home Administration helped enable the Perkins brothers to grow a profitable commercial cattle and hay farm comprising more than two thousand acres by the 1970s. Earl also bought the local feed store.[13] Similarly, some other rural Ozarkers with "connections" managed to secure enough capital to start small and midsized businesses that thrived in the light industrial-, agribusiness-, and tourism-oriented political economy or found off-farm employment subsidized by local, state, or federal governments.

The vast majority, however, gave up farm life altogether or attempted a part-time, "one-foot-on-the-farm strategy" to now rely primarily on company paychecks in a low-wage, non-union economy controlled more and more by recent in-migrants and corporate business interests. Some rural Ozarkers hung on to their family farms by converting them to "factory farms" in the employment of large agribusiness corporations, particularly poultry-processing companies. In doing so, however, they were "deprived . . . of the independence traditionally associated with Ozark agriculturists" and became "little more than temporary caretakers of the company's valuable property." "Ozarkers who were able to stay on the land in the post–World War II era had to adapt and evolve," Brooks Blevins writes. "But they were a minority. Most farm families eventually left their fields and barns behind."[14] Rural dispossession created ripe opportunities for some well-connected Sun Belt entrepreneurs like Sam Walton and Don Tyson who adeptly channeled the region's social, cultural, and political circumstances to their advantage, helping to further transform not only the Ozarks but America as a whole.[15] Poverty, scant economic opportunities, and vulnerability, however, kept a dark shade over most working-class people in the Sun Belt's rural heartland.

Although the region's poverty and outmigration disturbed many postwar leaders, both locally and in Washington, they tended to view the decline in smallholder farming in a positive light. Amid burgeoning national prosperity, agricultural and other government officials under the sway of powerful organizations such as the Farm Bureau and other Big Agriculture lobbies looked for ways to replace the small farm economies of such regions as the Ozarks. But it would be overly facile to suggest that high-handed federal bureaucrats in Washington imposed their centralized agendas in a simple top-down fashion. As historian Elizabeth Brake explains, postwar farm policies, in fact, generally worked hand in hand with local elites' interests and plans for rural industrialization. Leaders of programs such as the Agricultural Stabilization and Conservation Service (ASCS), the successor of the New Deal's Agricultural Adjustment Administration, exalted their agencies as "commendably democratic" and "intensely practical" by highlighting how "grassroots democracy" and local control shaped most of their programs' decision making and administration. Brake's study, however, finds that local elites, many of whom were close partners with area banks and local chambers of commerce, dominated the elections and administration of ASCS committees and used their power to advance their industrial and agribusiness visions, as well as to influence broader policymaking in Washington.[16]

Accordingly, the U.S. Department of Agriculture classified 46 percent of farmland in the Ozarks within the "worst" four categories of land capability. Agricultural experts condemned small Ozark farmers' damaging and "wasteful practices," such as the plowing of hillsides and slash-and-burn grazing techniques.[17] Much of family farming's history in the region, most local and federal officials believed, had largely been a mistake, at least in the modern era. The valiant and independent yeoman farmers of the nineteenth and early twentieth centuries might nostalgically remind Americans of their virtuous past, but small farmsteads had no place in the postwar world of progress and prosperity. The solution seemed simple: the region needed to be more closely integrated into the national corporate economy to catch up with the rest of the "modernized" nation. Local, state, and federal officials advised the vast number of rural folks displaced from small farms to seek off-farm industrial work.[18]

Amid postwar affluence, the Kennedy administration embarked on a mission to tear down the barriers that seemed to be preventing corporate investment from pouring into lagging areas.[19] Soon after his election, Kennedy established a task force to study economic conditions and develop a plan for proposing legislation to address the needs of impoverished areas. Its recommendations significantly influenced the passage of the Area Redevelopment Act in May 1961. Designed to pump federal money into depressed areas, the Area Redevelopment Administration (ARA) subscribed to a "trickle down" approach that mostly funded low-interest business loans, public facilities grants, and job training programs, all through the channels of local business and political establishments.[20]

The Southern states and Appalachia received a disproportionate amount of the ARA's limited funding.[21] Within these regions, however, depressed-area aid was unevenly distributed and tended to go to more urbanized and industrialized areas that needed it least. Appalachian historians, for instance, have noted that the thinly spread ARA program did little for rural communities that lacked the personnel to draft aid proposals, the required matching funds, and the profitable industrial and business prospects that were necessary for application approval.[22]

The development program had a similar impact in the Ozarks. The ARA's first project in the nation, in fact, provided the town of Gassville in Baxter County a $17,000 loan for a community industrial facility and a $133,000 grant for a municipal water system. This funding was intended to assist local boosters' efforts to bring in a new shirt-making factory, a subsidiary of the Capital Shirt Company of New York.[23] Gassville was situated within the greater Mountain Home area, the budding tourism, recreation, and retirement center that had undergone a major transformation since the early 1950s when the city became sandwiched between the Norfork and Bull Shoals Lakes. The *New York Times* noted the raised eyebrows that might accompany the ARA's decision to conduct its "pilot" program of depressed-area aid in this "Resort Region." "At first glance," the *Times* remarked, "no outsider would guess that this tidy Ozark Mountain resort region is a depressed area and will get the first aid under the recently passed Federal assistance program." After all, the already thriving Mountain Home area "is a hybrid of Main Street and suburbia," where "housewives in shorts gossip over coffee in Cooper's Drug Store . . . [and] pastel motels and ranch houses bake in the summer sun on what was once pasture land on the fringes of town." But local businessmen and civic boosters convinced the ARA that the new shirt factory would provide much-needed employment opportunities for the impoverished rural hinterlands that surrounded the resort area, where the average family struggled to survive on an annual income of less than $2,000.[24]

Local political and business leaders, led by Mountain Home Ford dealer T. J. McCabe, and the Arkansas Industrial Development Commission—one of the first state development agencies of its kind in the South—had offered the shirt company numerous incentives to bring its new plant to Gassville.[25] McCabe donated twenty acres of land himself to the company for its new factory. Furthermore, despite spirited opposition from a group of Baxter County's "modest-income retired folk" who opposed "being taxed for the benefit of private business," local boosters managed to convince voters to pass a five-mill increase on local property taxes to finance a $350,000 bond issue to build the company a new production facility. The company would then lease the plant for $18,000 a year for thirty-five years. Baxter County and Marion County leaders also promised they would put up the money to double the size of the plant once the company employed at least six hundred workers. Company president Donald Cooper could not refuse the offer, conceding in a benevolent tone that "we wanted an area that needed us." County officials also offered the company special tax exemptions, vowed not to bring in other industries that might compete for the company's labor force and drive wages up, and promised to keep labor unions from organizing in their areas, although the Arkansas Supreme Court struck down these latter provisions of the local bond issue.[26]

The ARA's pilot project in Gassville brought disappointing results and became a source of controversy among national policymakers. The project had promised to create about twelve hundred jobs, but reports in 1964 showed that employment was far below the projected level. Reports that year conflicted, with one showing employment numbers at only five hundred workers and another claiming that 737 were employed at the shirt factory. Either way, the Gassville project had failed to live up to its promise. Furthermore, almost all of the factory's workers were women who were initially hired for $0.85 per hour as trainees and were told that they could eventually earn up to $1.75 per hour, though they would have to do so at piecework pay rates. Although several poor rural women gave the new factory's impact a positive appraisal—one commenting, "We wouldn't have made it last winter if it hadn't been for my working"—the fact that the ARA's pilot project helped promote low-wage employment for women ran counter to policymakers' priority to "create good jobs for men" and preserve traditionally gendered family economies.[27] These "shortcomings" in Gassville gave the ARA's national conservative political opponents potent ammunition for their charges that the depressed-area aid program was wasting taxpayer dollars. They also undoubtedly disappointed many working-class Ozarkers who had high hopes for the project.[28]

It became increasingly clear to policymakers that the ARA was insufficient to seriously address the problems of regional poverty and underdevelopment. Governors from the Appalachian states in particular had already begun putting more pressure on President Kennedy to support more concerted regional development strategies. Arguing that rural underdevelopment required specific multistate coordination that the thinly spread ARA could not provide, they prompted Kennedy to establish the President's Appalachian Regional Commission (PARC) in 1963. Over the next several months, PARC worked with economists and federal, state, and local agencies to discuss strategies for addressing the region's problems. It recommended core infrastructure improvements, resource management and industrial development, flood control and hydroelectric power, and human-resource development to boost economic growth. The Kennedy administration began moving forward on a program specifically for rural Appalachia, but the assassination of the president on November 22, 1963, left the future of the regional agenda in question.[29] Fortunately for Appalachian development proponents, the new president welcomed their proposal into his broader Great Society agenda. Although the Appalachian bill was largely eclipsed by Lyndon Johnson's separate "War on Poverty" program and bounced around in Congress for nearly a year, the Appalachian Regional Development Act (ARDA) finally became law on March 9, 1965, creating the Appalachian Regional Commission (ARC).[30]

Not surprisingly, the creation of the ARC aroused loud complaints from political leaders outside Appalachia. A number of them objected to giving Appalachia special help while there were areas within their districts that were just as distressed. The *Tulsa World* noted that Sen. John McClellan of Arkansas was among the loudest objectors. McClellan and Oklahoma senator Fred Harris, who pointed to the plight of nineteen counties in the eastern part of his state, called for an amendment to have impoverished areas in their districts included in the ARC. Congressmen in rural New England, the Great Lakes area, and elsewhere also insisted that their impoverished locales needed special programs like Appalachia's.[31]

Theirs were not the only complaints. Conservative journalist Jenkin Lloyd Jones condemned the ARC's creation and warned of "The Spreading 'Appalachia Disease'" in a February 1965 article in *Human Events*. "Like the hogs grunting to the trough," he wrote, "congressmen are clamoring to get their districts declared 'Appalachias.'" Citing a county judge in Kentucky who remarked that "you'll find about 80 percent of our people just looking for another handout," Jones asked, "Are Americans going to put on their dirtiest shirts and ragged fishing pants and go crying their deprivations and disadvantages to Washington?"[32] Conservatives lamented the federal spending on depressed rural regions. Responding to a constituent who wondered why parts of rural Texas were not being included, Sen. John Tower lectured that "[w]e should attack poverty not by creating a new tax-absorbing bureaucracy, but by encouraging creation of new jobs in private industry and business." "Catchy political slogans and expensive Federal programs won't create jobs," he continued. Claiming that the Johnson administration was simply trying to dust off failed New Deal programs from the 1930s, Tower quipped, "We have already tried and found wanting the CCC and the WPA and the prepetuation [*sic*] of tiny farms without the resources to compete . . . [so there] is no reason to try these things again." Similarly, back in September 1964, Republican presidential candidate Barry Goldwater had denounced proposals for a regional program to help rural areas, along with President Johnson's other Great Society measures, as a Marxist scheme taken from the Soviet Union's playbook. Such a program was altogether unnecessary, he said, because citizens in a free enterprise system always "took care of their brothers in need, but not their brothers who refused to work and wanted to live off of them." In the 1960s, though, most working folks in the Ozarks still expected their federal government to play an important role in contributing to the economic well-being of their rural communities.[33]

Although the Senate rejected McClellan's and Harris's proposed amendment to add counties in Arkansas, Missouri, and Oklahoma to the ARC, congressional supporters and the Johnson administration promised to include a provision for other regional commissions in a separate bill. McClellan remained suspicious and voted against the Appalachian bill, although Harris seemed content with the offer and voted for it.[34]

Johnson signed the Public Works and Economic Development Act in August 1965, replacing the old Area Redevelopment Administration. Under Title V of the act, the secretary of commerce was authorized to establish multistate regional commissions in parts of the country that lagged behind national economic norms. The Ozarks Regional Commission, created in March 1966 and officially organized in September, was the first of five Title V commissions established. The designated ORC region initially included 125 counties in northern and western Arkansas, southern Missouri, and eastern Oklahoma, although nine impoverished counties in southeastern Kansas were included at the request of that state's governor in September 1967. Like the ARC, the ORC and the other commissions were designed as "equal" partnerships between federal and state governments, with each commission's membership composed of a federal co-chairman and the governors of the states included in the designated region. William McCandless, ORC federal co-chairman, "emphasized the new, imaginative nature of the regional commission, especially its special feature of including state governors as commission members." Such local control, he suggested, explained why "Ozarks governors have . . . devoted substantial time to commission matters because they have seen in the commission a vehicle to bring about decentralization of Federal decision making." Any "excessive Federal discussion on controlling regional commissions," McCandless warned, would mean that the "commissions will not be sufficiently productive to warrant continuance."[35]

There appears to have been considerable stirrings of hope for the ORC among mid-American cities such as St. Louis, which saw the Ozarks as a backyard of potential development. The *St. Louis Post-Dispatch* attempted to draw attention to the real economic plight of the rural region that was often hidden beneath Ozarks tourism promotions. Most Americans—even many of those middle-class residents who lived in the region—"are inclined to look upon the Ozarks as a fishing and boating mecca, with some neon-lighted, chromium-plated honkytonks thrown in to enliven the tourist's vacation activities," commented the *Post-Dispatch*. This image overshadowed the fact that as many as 60 percent "of the region's young people packed their bags and left because of chronic underemployment and low incomes" during the preceding ten years, the paper reported, saying also that the new ORC "offer[ed] hope for dynamic rejuvenation of a region whose economic potential too long has been bypassed."[36]

Political leaders in the region also exalted the great promise of the new ORC. Missouri governor Warren E. Hearnes, elected by other governors as the ORC's

Governor Orval Faubus signs forty-four Arkansas counties into the Ozarks Regional Commission, March 1, 1966. Behind him are (from left to right) U.S. Secretary of Commerce John T. Conner, Sen. John McClellan of Arkansas, and Rep. Wilbur Mills of Arkansas. Courtesy of Hendrix College Archives and Special Collections, Conway.

first state co-chairman, helped fuel the hype when he told news reporters, "We are witnessing what might be a new era." "The vast potential of the commission," he boasted, "has raised the hope of all of us who are committed to bringing greater prosperity and a better life to the citizens of the three states."[37] Commenting on the proposed ORC when the commission's application was under consideration in December 1965, Arkansas governor Orval Faubus, the notorious defender of school segregation in the Little Rock integration crisis of 1957, assured a Department of Commerce official, "When you and President Johnson approve our regional applications we will provide and furnish you with the most successful program in the nation." Faubus later wrote to Secretary of Commerce John T. Conner in March 1966 to say that he believed "this [ORC] program has more potentialities for bringing about greater progress and development for this economic region than any program that has been established in my lifetime."[38] Along with other congressmen and senators from the area, Sen. Fred Harris of Oklahoma promised that the regional program "can make this area synonymous with 'opportunity,'" exclaiming, "We have always had the people, the natural resources, and the potential, and now we have the Organization to get the job done. . . . We have now decided to reverse the out-migration of our people and capital, high unemployment, low family income and inadequate use of our natural resources."[39]

There was excitement about the new ORC at the local level as well. Upon hearing about the new program, locals such as Kenneth Hurst of the small town of Evening Shade wrote their congressmen for information about how they could benefit from the ORC's development activities.[40] In rural Sharp County, where Hurst resided, annual per capita income was only $723, and 60.9 percent of the population was underemployed. Hurst and others like him saw potential in the federal regional program to help revive their decaying communities. Indeed, twenty of Arkansas's forty-four counties initially included in the ORC had populations in which more than half were underemployed, such as Stone and Newton Counties where, respectively, 65 percent and more than 70 percent were underemployed.[41] The ORC seemed to offer hope amid increasingly grim prospects for rural folks in the New Ozarks.

In Perry County, where underemployment stood at nearly 60 percent in 1960, a civics teacher, Mr. Neal, asked his students at East Bigelow High School to consider the recent news about the ORC's creation and what it might mean for their rural community. They were then asked to write letters to Congressman Wilbur Mills expressing their and their families' opinions of the new regional program. All the students concurred with Judy Dickens who, although she admitted that she did not know much about the details of the program, wrote that

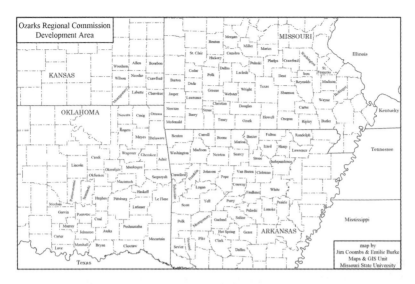

Counties that originally made up the Ozarks Regional Commission's development area upon its organization in 1966. Courtesy of Jim Coombs and Emilie Burke, Missouri State University.

she and her family believed "it will mean a great deal to my county and town." Specifically, because her town's 237 residents "need[ed] a sewage system badly," Dickens and her family hoped, she said, "[that] the Ozarka program will enable my town and others to have the facilities we need."[42]

Ninth-grader Joyce and her family likewise believed that the regional program was a "very good and intelligent thing." But they also had doubts about the fairness of the ORC's future activities, since, as she mentioned, "it looks like Missouri and Oklahoma are going to get the best part of the deal." Joyce and her family insisted that ORC projects "should be divided equal between the states."[43] Many of the region's political and business elites, such as Mayor Jan M. Bullock of Eureka Springs, also expressed concerns about the ORC's fairness. Bullock shared the suspicions of Arkansas's State Planning Commission, which was "gravely concerned that the State of Oklahoma expects to receive the vast majority of the $3,000,000 planning fund." The mayor proposed instead "that the vast majority of the planning funds need to be expended in Northwest Arkansas on the planning of new highways and other public facilities feasible under this program" because eastern Oklahoma, she said, had already received a good deal of federal aid for highways through other programs in recent years.[44] Despite such concerns, and perhaps in light of them, Ozarkers appear to have seen important potential in the regional program as long as their areas received a fair share of the funding.

It did not take long, however, to realize that the ORC was strapped with major limitations. Just as funding issues were being worked out for the new commission, the Johnson administration and the Office of Emergency Planning (OEP) announced concerns about growing inflation and asked federal agencies and state governments to limit spending on construction and development projects that might add to the problem, in addition to asking American businesses to reconsider investment plans and housewives to practice frugal consumption. In April 1966 Arkansas governor Orval Faubus publicly objected to the administration's anti-inflation policies, arguing that they had "stymied the three-state Ozarka Regional development program" just as it was getting off the ground. The OEP assured the regional commissions that funding applications would still be considered as usual, but Faubus and other members of the regional commissions saw the logical consequences that the administration's anti-inflation worries posed for the young regional development programs and began blaming federal bureaucrats in Washington for the problems.[45]

The new ORC's timing proved a major impediment because of the United States' escalating war in Vietnam. President Johnson himself later regretfully described the war's detrimental impact on his broader domestic agenda: "I left the woman I really loved—the Great Society—in order to get involved with that bitch of a war on the other side of the world."[46] As the demands of the war, along with heightened conservative criticism, took their toll on practically all Great Society programs, the new Title V commissions received an especially hard hit, since the initiatives just getting started were easier to put on the back burner. Just as news of the new regional commission had stirred optimism in the Ozarks, disappointed ORC officials were left to explain the federal budget problems to hopeful constituents. When Rep. Wilbur Mills wrote to ORC federal co-chairman William McCandless in October 1967 on behalf of a constituent who had inquired about the program's opportunities for his rural community, McCandless had to reply that the ORC "has not received at this date any money with which to fund specific projects, and the realities of the war in Vietnam and the pressure on the federal budget would suggest that we cannot expect any substantial appropriation by the Congress until these two conditions have changed."[47]

The early disappointment in the ORC was perhaps best expressed in 1967 by an unknown staff member of Arkansas's new governor, Winthrop Rockefeller—the state's first Republican governor since Reconstruction.[48] Upon entering the governor's mansion, Rockefeller received a briefing on the ORC and was advised to "cover 'Local Expectations' with McCandless." "This program has been badly oversold on the local level," the staff member wrote: "There will probably never be the money from Congress that has been envisioned; at least not in the foreseeable future." It was suggested that Rockefeller "put the burden on McCandless [and other Washington bureaucrats] to bring local expectations more in line with reality."[49]

Budget problems were, indeed, compounded by the Title V commissions' bureaucratic organizational structure. Unlike Appalachia's commission, which held an independent status within the Executive Office of the President, the ORC and other Title V commissions were given a "stepchild status" under the Department of Commerce.[50] While the ARC reported directly to the president, enjoyed direct lines to the Office of Management and Budget, and was authorized to both set regional development policy and directly fund its projects, the ORC and the other commissions merely served in a planning and advisory capacity and answered to the Secretary of Commerce. Initially, the ORC's funding could only be used for research, planning, and administrative costs, though Congress passed an amendment in 1967 that allowed the Title V commissions to issue small supplemental grants (usually no more than 20 percent of total costs) for projects in which state and local governments could not come up with all of the matching funds required for grants from the Economic Development Administration, the Farmers Home Administration, the Federal Aviation Administration, and other federal agencies. The Title V commissions' status within the Department of Commerce meant that they collectively competed, along with the department's other agencies and projects, against the ARC for funding. And, as one observer put it, all the ORC's "recommendations must be sent through bureaucratic channels for approval before they can be implemented."[51]

This secondary status frustrated commission officials and their constituents who felt entitled to a larger slice of the pie. In February 1969 senators representing the Title V commissions confronted the Senate Public Works Committee chairman Jennings Randolph of West Virginia and other sponsors of the ARC about the seeming unfairness of the other regions' secondary status. Randolph justified the ARC's preeminent position by arguing that its domain served nearly the same number of people—approximately sixteen million—as the other regional commissions combined. More important, however, Randolph argued that the older and more experienced Appalachian program was intended to serve as the pilot project for the other regions. Sympathizing with the distressed conditions of the other regions, Randolph claimed, "Our [ARC's] experiences will help them . . . [because the] few errors that we have committed in part will be their successes." The senator vowed to continue supporting the other regional commissions, but he was unwilling to relinquish Appalachia's favored status in the federal regionalism policy.[52]

Commission officials and the state governors and local supporters in the region all agreed that the program had great potential but was simply too limited to live up to its promise. Missouri governor Warren E. Hearnes praised the thoughtful planning and limited work the commission had accomplished, claiming that several development projects would have failed if not for ORC support. But he told reporters that "if the commission program [were] ever to become effective," it would have to be freed from its bureaucratic position under the Department of Commerce because "funds from that department alone cannot carry the commissions."[53] Arkansas's new Democratic governor in the early 1970s, Dale Bumpers, issued a more stinging appraisal of the commission's organization, calling it a "cruel hoax" because it had given Ozarkers false hopes that it would transform the region's economy. Testifying before a Senate subcommittee in 1972, Bumpers demanded that the ORC and other Title V commissions be either restructured as independent agencies equal to the ARC or at least be given a higher status within the Department of Commerce. "If we are going to meet even the basic needs," urged Bumpers, "we must make the same billion dollar effort that has been made in Appalachia."[54] One federal official claimed, however, that, despite the exceptional level of shared power that already existed in the program, what the governors really wanted was "to minimize the role of Commerce, keep the Federal Co-chairman out of their hair in Washington, dominate the Executive Director on the scene, thus hopefully capturing the Commission staff for themselves." "They also want more money that they can control [locally]," he believed.[55]

By the early 1970s the regional commissions and their supporters found themselves merely trying to survive under President Nixon's hostile administration. Nixon had proposed that the commissions be phased out and their funding integrated into his broader revenue-sharing program in which he issued federal block grants to individual states and cities. But the Senate voted 77–3 in March 1971 to extend the regional aid program, an outcome that one political observer called Nixon's "first legislative setback." Fellow Republicans who defended the regional programs, such as ARC supporter Howard Baker Jr. of Tennessee, argued that the commissions, in fact, could work hand in hand with Nixon's new revenue-sharing plan. Nixon came to accept the continuation of the thirteen-state ARC, which was backed by several of his strongest campaign supporters, but his administration continued its efforts to eliminate the other Title V commissions, including the ORC. The president even cancelled all funding for the Title V commissions in his 1973 budget proposal, although there was "a change in the White House viewpoint" when legislators from the other distressed regions lashed out at the unfairness of Nixon's support for the ARC.[56]

By the mid-1970s the ORC had also decided to include entire states within its domain, instead of just its underdeveloped Ozark counties, a move that ultimately fit better with Nixon's federal revenue-sharing plan with the states. Before, state governors were often in the uncomfortable position with their constituents of favoring certain counties and found it politically advantageous to call for the inclusion of their entire states. By 1974 the ORC's boundaries had greatly expanded beyond the 125 counties in southern Missouri, northern and western Arkansas, and eastern Oklahoma that were originally designated in 1966 to now include the entire states of Arkansas, Missouri, Oklahoma, Kansas, and even Louisiana. The decision to include entire states helped to keep the commission alive temporarily by giving more political constituencies a stake in the program. Like the ARC, however, which had also enlarged its boundaries to obtain wider political support, the expansion of the ORC's borders spread resources even more thinly and undermined any remaining hopes for regional development in the rural Ozarks.[57]

From at least 1972 on, when President Nixon vetoed an amendment that would have given Title V commissions more autonomy to fund regional development projects beyond their supplemental grants, high hopes that the ORC would pump new life into the region's economy mostly dissipated. The commission and its supporters struggled just to survive.[58] The program would fare a little better under Jimmy Carter's Democratic administration, but even then it seemed to most observers that the ORC and the other Title V commissions were just "part of the price for winning Senate support for the Appalachian program," as *New York Times* journalist John W. Finney put it.[59] Feelings of disappointment in the Ozarks, meanwhile, increasingly lent a popular air of credibility to many frustrated local business elites' and political conservatives' fiery charges that "limousine liberals" and Big Government bureaucrats were inherently guilty of mismanagement and cronyism for "special interests."

State and regional ORC officials and their supporters may have been at least partially justified in condemning the commission's organizational and funding restrictions as key reasons for the program's inability to fulfill its promises. Like much of the American liberal state's ambitious domestic social agenda in the 1960s, the ORC and other development programs had declared a war to eradicate poverty but never obtained sufficient federal commitment and resources and to carry out a full-scale fight. Local officials' tendency to place full blame on the blunders of the federal government, however, belied their own roles in the program's disappointing effects. An examination of regional leaders' planning activities and the projects for which the ORC provided supplemental grants suggests that a stronger and better-funded regional program like they wanted would likely have only promoted more uneven economic development in the region, much like the ARC did in its region. State and local leaders maintained a narrow vision about how to address rural economic problems, namely their unshakable faith that corporate business growth would lift all boats. In fact, to borrow the words of Appalachian historian Ronald D. Eller, their vision was "a value-laden political act, complete with winners and losers."[60]

Upon first hearing about the new ORC, some rural folks had hoped the program might help them revive a viable smallholder farm economy in their communities. "As we understand [it]," E. A. Emerson of Van Buren County wrote in a letter to Governor Faubus, "the [regional development] idea should originate at the 'grassroots' of the local area." Emerson, who spoke on behalf of a newly formed rural "Steering Committee" in his home area, proposed a three-step plan that might provide "the means for the development of an economy for this area that can be permanent and self-sustaining." First, the new regional commission should conduct an "intensive survey of agricultural possibilities" that best suited specific areas and should establish plans for "specific development projects." Then the ORC would begin "building . . . warehouse[s], processing plants, [and] freezing plants" and assist with "road development," "power development," and other projects to upgrade the region's infrastructure. The commission's new federally constructed and federally owned agricultural facilities could be "leased or rented to private companies" at rates that would eventually raise enough revenue to repay project costs, administer the programs, and even provide agricultural education and other services for local farmers. Finally, the commission, which would establish a "central advisatory [sic] office" and several "sub-offices" throughout the region, would be charged with "finding markets, obtaining price information, advertising commodities . . . [and] working with state and national governmental agencies" to secure grants and develop initiatives to promote smallholder opportunities for working families. Emerson was confident this was "something that [would] provide future jobs at home, here, and overcome the need for these people to have to search for part time jobs . . . or . . . to leave the state permanently in order to secure a reasonable livelihood."[61]

ORC officials and local business leaders made it clear from the start, however, that their aim was to transform the region's rural economy into a thriving "modern" industrial one. The ORC asserted in its first published mission statement in 1967 that "the Ozarks Region, still with a substantial percentage of its people living on farms or in rural non-farm communities, must make even greater economic development advances than other areas to achieve a healthy economy." "This is not being done now," the statement continued, "and it cannot be done by relying on the traditional ways of making a living in the Ozarks, such as agriculture."[62]

Business boosters, especially, held up their region's "unique" labor advantages to prospective industrial investors. "Accustomed to eking out a living from worn-out farm land," Tanner noted in his 1965 *Wall Street Journal* article, "[Ozarkers] know the value of a job and don't treat one lightly." He pointed to companies like Daisy, an air-rifle manufacturer, that had seen the advantages in the region's labor force and decided to relocate their plants. Daisy's president claimed that he moved his company from Michigan to the city of Rogers in northwest Arkansas because he wanted a place "where people were interested in doing a day's work for a day's pay." It is important to note as well that Daisy had successfully resisted five efforts by unions to organize its Arkansas plant.[63]

Regional business developers were convinced that federal aid could be used for incentives that would attract more industries to the region. Governor Faubus, believing "that the first thing to do is development work down to the grassroots," had initially argued during the ORC's early startup phase that the primary focuses should be on highway building and basic infrastructure improvements. Even so, as regional leaders and U.S. Secretary of Commerce Maurice Stans hashed out the ambiguous meaning of "economic development" in 1969, they decided that they "should *switch the emphasis* from the *current infrastructure Public Works approach* that has been followed by . . . the Commissions to development of jobs in the *private sector*." Stans, agreeing with the sentiments of most state governors and commission supporters, sought to move away from "providing roads, schools, utilities, etc." because "the thrust should be upon reaching potential employers and persuading them to come in." Once they entered the region, he claimed, in the typical language of supply-side economics, "the streets and schools will follow." Stans concluded: "'Economic development' means the expansion of income-producing activity, aimed at growth in output and in income and employment. It is not . . . oriented toward upgrading the general welfare of the region." Instead of worrying so much about "lagging areas" that had no realistic hopes for revitalization to begin with, the regional commissions should prioritize "the bird in the hand" and focus on those better-off areas with the greatest potential for more growth.[64]

Most commission members, including Gov. Winthrop Rockefeller, promoted what became known as the "growth center strategy," which prioritized "natural" centers that promised high levels of growth and good returns on public investments. During his gubernatorial campaign in October 1966, Rockefeller issued a plan for regional development in which he argued that there were fourteen "natural" subregions in Arkansas. Each of these subregions, he suggested, contained "capital cities" where development efforts should be directed because economic prosperity would surely radiate outward into the opportunity-strapped hinterlands.[65]

The ORC's emphasis on growth centers, however, helped produce results that mirrored the path of economic development in Appalachia. Historian Ronald Eller's study of the ARC shows that the "growth center strategy . . . exacerbated the poverty and depopulation of rural areas."[66] Ironically, although the federal government's regional program had been initially justified by underscoring the severe poverty of rural communities, the growth-center strategy ensured that most projects ignored those areas that needed assistance the most. To be sure, ORC planning and supplemental grants for such projects as hospitals and vocational and technical colleges (many of which have now become important community colleges in the region) provided much-needed aid for healthcare and educational opportunities in the Ozarks. These were benefits that generally reached beyond the growth centers where the facilities were located, although in the case of vocational and technical education, Ozarkers frequently just stepped from these schools into low-paying job markets or wound up leaving the region in order to put their newly acquired skills to work for decent wages. "The jobs are not out there," one disillusioned agency director remarked. "What good is it to sit here and train our people for its own sake?"[67] In general, most development projects failed to live up to the promise that benefits would radiate outward from growth centers to uplift the whole region—rural hinterlands and all.

Between 1968 and 1979 the ORC spent $69,647,418 on 660 supplemental grants. Of those, 424 went to industrial parks and industrial water and sewer systems, ninety-two to vocational and technical schools, forty-nine to small airports, forty-three to industrial access roads and railroad spurs, thirty-four to community facilities projects, nine to hospitals, and nine to port facilities.[68] Many of the commission's projects in the Arkansas Ozarks benefited the already-prosperous Springfield Plain subregion in extreme northwest Arkansas, the home of the state's flagship university and the birthplace of Fortune 500 companies such as Wal-Mart, Tyson Foods, and J. B. Hunt Trucking. Several others went to resort and recreational areas near lakes built by the federal government. Most of the poorest areas in the region, however, including Fulton, Sharp, Searcy, Stone, and Newton Counties—the latter, of course, was the primary subject of Tanner's 1965 *Wall Street Journal* article—received no supplemental grants at all. As was the case in Appalachia, federal regional development resources in the Ozarks were designed "to flow to more populous and politically powerful counties."[69]

Many residents in smaller communities in the Ozarks grew frustrated at the difficulties in obtaining assistance for even the most basic needs, while larger towns and cities grabbed up the federal funds. W. R. Braden of the rural Muddy Gap community complained early on to Governor Faubus, a fellow Madison

County son, about the ORC's neglect of rural communities. Braden said it appeared to him and many of his rural neighbors that "most of the Ozarks plan money will be spent a long ways from the Ozarks and in heavy populated [and] prosperous areas to get votes." Braden, a Mountain Republican, warned Faubus, a Democrat, that "unless you plan to spend the money in the Ozarks your days as the governor is fast ceasing."[70] Similarly, in December 1975 Sen. John McClellan wrote Secretary of Commerce Rogers Morton to get answers for "some of the tough questions which have been addressed to me" by rural constituents on why federal development programs neglected many of Arkansas's most needy areas. "The decisions . . . have resulted in raising false hopes about assistance which might be available," he wrote, "and have contributed to the credibility problem which all of us in public service must deal with constantly." Despite these qualms, the growth-center strategy remained at the center of regional development efforts, and local leaders passed the buck to federal bureaucrats in Washington to bear the complaints of disappointed rural folks.[71]

Most of the ORC's planning projects and supplemental grants were actually implemented locally through the Economic Development Administration's (EDA) area development districts, which were run by multicounty boards generally comprising county judges and commissioners, town mayors, and the heads of local chambers of commerce.[72] These area planning districts and the local officials controlling them, and not the federal government, usually took most of the credit for any development efforts that seemed to succeed. The town of Harrison in Boone County—the federally designated growth center for its subregion—even made national news in 1973 for its "striking" economic progress amid the rural "razorback ridges of the Ozarks." Failing to even mention an $89,400 federal grant from the ORC for an industrial park the town received in 1970 or other federal assistance, the *New York Times* article, drawing from interviews with local officials and businessmen, attributed the town's "turn-around" to the local chamber of commerce, entrepreneurs, and county development leaders, claiming that the town had "pulled itself back from . . . stagnation and decline."[73]

On the other hand, local elites tended to deride the broader scheme of federal regional development when proposals emerged that threatened their local control. The experience of Ozark County, Missouri—located just across the Arkansas line—is a case in point. County leaders had been reluctant to join the seven-county EDA planning district and leery of the regional program in the first place, probably feeling subordinated to the subregion's growth center at West Plains, Missouri. Nonetheless, they hoped to bring valuable federal funding to their county. Indeed, Ozark County secured an EDA grant to purchase two ambulances and received federal funding to run water lines to industrial sites in the county-seat town and a $51,600 ORC supplemental grant in 1971 to help build an industrial park in Gainesville. But local leaders became highly suspicious about the broader regional program and the seeming threat that it might eventually pose to their control over local affairs. Ozark County officials attended only one ORC meeting and refused to participate afterward. They even withdrew from the seven-county EDA planning district in 1974, claiming that local government "would lose its authority in a seven-county bureaucracy and that [federal] land control, at some time or other, would be implemented through the commission."[74]

The growth center strategy also spawned conflict between local leaders who vied for "capital"-center status in their subregions, realizing that most federal funding would be funneled into places receiving that designation. Town booster and businessman Thomas Tinnon of Mountain Home in Baxter County wrote EDA field coordinator John Opitz in March 1967 to demand a realignment of the local multicounty planning districts so that his town could have its rightful place as a growth center. Complaining that federal officials had wrongly placed his town and county in the easternmost part of a planning district centered at Harrison in Boone County, Tinnon insisted that it was only logical to redraw the lines and create an alternative district with Mountain Home at its center, citing common socioeconomic and political factors, the town's status as a center of employment, and the resort area's importance in facilitating tourism. "By any criteria," he wrote, "Mountain Home, Arkansas should be designated an Economic Center . . . for the purpose of planning and developing the economy around common interests for the common welfare of all concerned."[75] Tinnon fully understood the implications of a growth-center strategy that would mostly reward Harrison with federal dollars at Mountain Home's expense. Faced with such frustrating dilemmas, local leaders typically lambasted a "stubborn" and "out-of-touch" bureaucracy in Washington for their and their constituents' problems.

The problem of encouraging uneven development grew even more when the ORC added entire states by the mid-1970s. Though President Nixon's revenue-sharing plan encouraged this approach, state officials were the most vocal advocates for including entire states, especially since "governors find themselves in the difficult position of pleading the special interest of [certain] counties." Some federal officials, including EDA field office director John Opitz, warned that expanding the commission's boundaries would necessarily require increased funding and personnel if it hoped to fulfill its mission, funding that Congress and the administration almost certainly would not approve.[76] The governors and other regional officials determined to expand the ORC's borders anyway. By January 1969 metropolitan developers in large cities outside the region were also pitching arguments that their cities should be included in the ORC since "it would be beneficial if the Commission could tie St. Louis and Kansas City to the hinterlands of the metropolitan areas" and produce "more bang for the buck" on public investments. Other Title V commission members, particularly from the Upper Great Lakes commission, objected to including large metropolises such as Detroit, arguing that such an approach defeated the whole principle of providing aid to depressed regions, but Ozarks governors' calls to include entire states became the norm in federal regionalism by the mid-1970s.[77]

By the late 1970s, despite the ORC's failures to live up to the promises that had been made when it began, the commission still had some supporters within the region, mainly chamber-of-commerce types in larger urban centers. J. William Perry, president of the Little Rock Chamber of Commerce, for instance, complimented the ORC: "I do not know of a 'better run' agency and an agency that does more for our region." Similarly, in January 1981 the enthusiastic chairman of the board of a Little Rock–based advertising and business consulting agency urged the ORC federal co-chairman to "Keep the faith, baby . . . [President] Ronnie needs all of the growth centers he can get out here in the boon docks!" "Stimulating private-sector growth has got to be his 1981 theme song!" he continued. "We just need to keep the growth music flowing [because it's] an economic fox-trot we're after!"[78] Ironically, "Ronnie" Reagan's decision that same year to terminate the ORC along with his other social-spending cuts in the name of promoting private-sector growth may have caught this pro-growth business booster off guard. He had apparently found appealing Reagan's conservative political ideology and campaign promise to shrink the federal government but seems to have expected important exceptions, particularly when it came to federal spending for business development.

Such compliments on the ORC from the rural hinterlands—those that had been held up in the mid-1960s as examples of the great needs the federal regional program would address—were few and far between, however. Indeed, by the late 1970s the ORC came under stinging criticism in some small towns and communities. After the ORC published its annual report in the spring of 1979, the small-town newspaper editor in Iola, Kansas, published an article titled "Expensive Vanity," blasting the federal government's "conspicuous waste of the taxpayers' dollars . . . [for its] overblown, expensive annual report which will never be seen by the public the commission was created to serve." The editor complained about the fancy, high-quality pictures that appeared on ten of the report's twenty-four pages when a basic, inexpensive "summary report" issued on standard typewriter paper would have sufficed. "Such a utilitarian, economical approach would never do, however, because an opportunity to puff up the ORC staff and the elected officials would go unseized," he continued. "It is a small matter. Only a few thousands of dollars were wasted," the editor admitted. "But it is another example of government for the sake of government rather than government with the public in mind." This Kansas newspaper editor likely represented the feelings of many Arkansas Ozarkers as well.[79]

When a copy of the Iola newspaper editorial reached the desk of one ORC staff member a few days later, he cussedly scribbled in the margins, "You can't win an ass-kicking contest with a skunk!" But most rural Ozarkers had experienced little but disappointment from the ORC, a federal program that had promised to bring economic opportunities to their distressed communities.[80] The regional commission, especially for the working Ozarkers it was designed to serve, had for the most part been the "cruel hoax" that Arkansas governor Dale Bumpers described, and had only further contributed to the uneven economic development that already characterized the region. Thus, when Ronald Reagan entered the White House with his budget-cutting ax in 1981, bent on slashing social spending and lowering taxes, it is doubtful that many rural Ozarkers objected too strongly when he felled the ORC.

Disappointed Ozarkers came to believe more and more that a bumbling and faceless bureaucracy in Washington was keeping their region from America's unbounded prosperity. Ironically, though, even more than most federal reform programs in the past, regional development efforts had put most control into the hands of state and local elites. Local leaders held a virtual monopoly on framing public debates and explaining the program's limitations and failures in rural areas. Conversely, they took all the credit for federally assisted successes that did occur in the region's growth centers. In this elite-controlled discourse, the unevenness produced by regional and local boosters' plans for growth centers and "trickle-out prosperity" remained hidden beneath complaints against an inept and out-of-touch government in Washington.

Parts of the Ozarks—particularly its more prosperous "growth centers"—received large doses of federal assistance and rose to bask in America's thriving Sun Belt economy.[81] In the mainstream political discourse of the New Ozarks, local elites argued that if federal bureaucrats would simply allow it, other towns and communities could also "pull themselves up" as Fayetteville, Bentonville, Harrison, Mountain Home, and other bustling locales had. This meant that, as one regional industrial development proponent put it, "in all fairness, it is time the Ozarks received its 'fair share'—nothing more, but hopefully nothing less"—of federal funding. At the same time, though, they insisted that Washington should stay out of the way and leave local leaders, businessmen, and boosters in full control to administer the designs of economic development in the region.[82]

Local elites had helped construct a New Ozarks political economy built on a combination of cheap and relatively docile labor, strong doses of government assistance, and the balance sheets of local and outside business owners that shifted with the winds of a national and increasingly global corporate climate. Economic growth during the postwar decades brought new prosperity to some people and places in the region, but it also worked to magnify the vulnerability and poverty of many others, particularly in small rural areas. The Ozarks—notwithstanding its new leaps of "progress" and "modernity" in certain growth centers—remained one of the most impoverished regions of the country. Other federal efforts in the 1960s and 1970s to eradicate poverty from the bottom up, however, would also fail to win the hearts of most rural Ozarkers. Far from it, reactions to the federal government's War on Poverty would actually help set in motion a new style of "damn guv'ment" defiance in the region, a culture of defiance far removed from the old Populist ethic that once pervaded the rural Ozarks.

7

THE WAR ON POVERTY
AND A NEW RIGHT RESISTANCE

In late 1978 the Ozark Institute (OI), a federally funded antipoverty agency in Eureka Springs, began hosting "public forums" in six counties in northwest Arkansas to encourage community discussions about rural poverty, particularly the drastic decline of small farm communities. An OI staffer noted the diverse backgrounds of the rural whites who attended the meetings, ranging from small part-time farmers and country working people to agribusiness operators and town businessmen, as well as midwestern retirees and other recent in-migrants—a diversity that reflected the immense changes of a New Ozarks since midcentury. Crowds at every meeting extolled the distinctive pride, dignity, and independence that rural life provided, virtues they felt most urban Americans failed to appreciate. In what must have been a rebuttal to neoprogressive views about rural poverty, one defiant Ozarker proudly exclaimed: "Everybody [who is still] on a small farm in Newton County wants to be on a small farm in Newton County."[1]

A significant number of attendees at the meetings thought the region would benefit greatly from a revival of smallholder farming and reinvigorated rural communities. Some "asserted plainly that small farmers can make it," if only they were afforded a fairer playing field. Others disagreed, suggesting that small-scale agriculture ought to stay relegated to the bygone years. They contended that the future of the Ozarks hinged instead on what they called "modern" economic growth. One Madison County resident even condemned the

OI for organizing the public meetings in the first place, because he thought the endeavor was a waste of taxpayer resources. Small farms, he said, have an "abysmal success rate" on repaying bank loans and contributing to economic growth. Promoting business investments and "developing service jobs for the current residents," another believed, ought to be the aims of public policy. As for the farm economy: "Let supply and demand take care of it, and let our taxes go down. I can't see taxpayers supporting a lifestyle some people enjoy but can't afford." Others, however, complained that the recent trends of low-wage service jobs offered little hope for truly expanding economic opportunity for rural Ozarkers and thought that a comeback of viable family farms might hold some promise.[2]

Despite such major differences of opinion, the OI reported that virtually everyone at the meetings "commonly criticized" the federal government and "[expressed] a strong sentiment against government programs." Distrustful residents in Newton County even objected to the OI's filing any reports with federal agencies about opinions they expressed at their meeting. At another, when an economic historian from the University of Arkansas reminded participants that federal programs to help rural areas dated "from the time of Teddy Roose-

Local residents at a public forum on improving rural communities hosted by the nonprofit Ozark Institute in the winter of 1978–79. Courtesy of Special Collections, University of Arkansas Libraries, Fayetteville.

velt," one man interrupted to say that the persistence of rural poverty, despite more than seventy-five years of federal involvement, ought to be proof enough, then, that "government programs are a failure." Another participant favored the revitalization of small farms in his home area but rejected any programs from Big Government liberals: "If the small farmer is left alone, he can do it. Family farm survival is not dependent on the federal government. It depends on whether you have a fair amount of intelligence, a pretty good back, and strong determination."[3]

The discussions among Ozarkers at these public forums about rural opportunities and the role of government in the late 1970s told an important story. Attitudes had apparently moved a long way from rural working-class sentiments during the Populist era of the Gilded Age. The particular loathing for the federal government revealed a new ethic of defiance in the Ozarks, one actually more akin to an "Anti-Populist Legacy" than the Populist ethic that had once been the wellspring of rural working people's resistance to elite power.[4] If the federal government's regional development scheme had disappointed most rural Ozarkers, its separate War on Poverty, which aimed more to tackle poverty from the bottom up, ironically, had provoked bitter resentment and helped effect this change in attitudes. But the impetus for resistance to federal power was very different this time. Unlike rural working folks' grassroots defiance in the late 1800s and early 1900s, now it was local business elites who led more of an "Astroturf" charge to defend "local control" and "local heritage" against federal power.[5]

Local elites in the region initially responded with enthusiasm for the War on Poverty programs. But they soon learned that the poverty programs would work differently than the ORC's economic development initiatives. While the ORC functioned as a literal "partnership between local, state, and federal governments to channel designated federal resources . . . [for] strategic development," the poverty programs aimed, instead, to spur "community action" at the grass roots and "encouraged low-income participation." Concerned primarily about the need to help poor blacks living under a Southern political structure controlled by segregationists, the Lyndon Johnson administration originally designed its poverty programs to circumvent state and local political establishments in order to take assistance directly to the poor themselves.[6] When it became clear, then, that "community action" would spoil Ozarks elites' expectations for local control, they quickly mobilized a stiff political resistance against what they viewed as "federal intrusiveness."

At the same time, liberal reformers who came to work in the region through federal poverty programs, most of whom hailed from the urban North, failed to understand and tap into the long Ozarks tradition of poor and working-class populism that might have won grassroots support for their rural improvement efforts. While reformers missed what might have been another "Populist moment," an elite-led New Right vocabulary helped to stoke new expressions of antigovernment defiance. The targeting of Big Government as the number-one *problem* for rural communities amid the anxieties of New Ozarks transformation and the controversial War on Poverty, even among those Ozarks leaders who had initially supported federal action as a legitimate effort, proved pivotal for molding future political discourse in the region. For their part, many working-class Ozarkers suspected that federal poverty programs were little more than special-interest doles for black Americans in other parts of the country. As we have seen, rural whites' inabilities to see common cause with blacks and "others" during the Populist era of the late 1800s often obstructed efforts to unite for working-class reforms at that pivotal moment, though it did not crush their overarching ethic for economic and local political democracy. This time, however, with national liberals' federal programs actually assisting America's black communities amid the tumultuous Civil Rights movement, many rural Ozarkers apparently felt too threatened by the unknowns of such social and cultural change and cast their lots with local elites—their old regional nemeses— who promised to stand against any hazards that distant outsiders might pose to the "way of life" in the Ozarks. All told, the dynamics of defiance against the War on Poverty in the New Ozarks would help begin to bury the working-class populism of the region's forefathers, particularly the old notion that government *could* serve as an effective counterweight against inequality, injustice, and deteriorating opportunities for rural Americans.

Ozarks political leaders watched closely as the Johnson administration and Congress worked up legislation after the president declared an "unconditional war on poverty" in his first state of the union address in January 1964. With Appalachia standing as the national symbol of rural poverty and the central battleground of federal reform efforts, regional and local leaders in the Ozarks hoped the War on Poverty programs would bring in valuable federal funds for economic "modernization." In April the *Arkansas Democrat* reported that Gov. Orval Faubus had "put his enthusiastic stamp of approval on President Johnson's war on poverty program." While the governor believed that "the Ozarks are not as bad off as Appalachia"—or, he clarified, at least "as they write about" that region—Faubus initially believed that the mountain region of Arkansas should be an important priority as well. "All through the mountains here," Faubus explained, "there [is] what is termed underemployment . . . [and] people whose family income is below what is termed poverty level." "Prosperity is at an all time high," the governor said, echoing President Johnson, "but there are still pockets of poverty and many individuals even in the most prosperous areas who are not sharing in the wealth." Though Faubus admitted that his administration would still need to give the matter more thought, he stated, "We especially are going to emphasize projects of employment for youth," such as "improvements of the parks and beautification of our cities and highways." When asked to respond to conservative critics who warned of the "danger of the president's program" in returning to the wasteful federal spending of the New Deal era, Faubus "reminded the reporters that there are monuments existing today and will last our lifetime that came from President Roosevelt's anti-depression program."[7]

Various local officials also jumped at what they thought would be a prime opportunity to bring federal poverty money into their locales to stimulate industrial growth. In June 1965 local officials in Pope, Yell, and neighboring counties in western Arkansas with mountainous areas straddling the Arkansas River formed the Arkansas River Valley Area Council (ARVAC), expecting the multicounty agency to capitalize on federal poverty grants requiring localities to put up only 10 percent in matching funds. Chickalah native Bob Adkisson, executive director of ARVAC, remembered that initially the "group leadership . . . thought they were getting an economic development grant." "We realized," he said, "if Appalachia could get federal money, why couldn't we?" Local officials soon discovered, however, that the grant "was really anti-poverty money," and not economic development funding. When President Johnson's poverty program chief, Sargent Shriver, arrived in Little Rock to "finalize" ARVAC's first grant application, Adkisson recalled that the Washington official "was met by a contingent of bankers and power people" from the region, prompting Shriver to ask them "where the poor folks were." "Our leadership was thinking economic opportunity," Adkisson explained, and "didn't realize focus was going to be soley [*sic*] on poverty."[8]

Congress passed the centerpiece of the War on Poverty in the form of the Economic Opportunity Act (EOA) in August 1964, which established the Office of Economic Opportunity (OEO). Title II of the EOA announced that its programs, unlike federal economic development efforts, would be administered not by state or local governments but by newly created Community Action Program (CAP) agencies that required "maximum feasible participation of the poor." After state and local leaders eventually grasped the seemingly ambiguous meaning of this clause in the federal law—in fact, the CAP concept "was initially misunderstood" even by President Johnson himself—it became clear that their ability to control the programs would be limited. About a month after Faubus's ringing endorsement of Johnson's War on Poverty initiatives, he changed his tune and told Arkansas's four U.S. Congressmen, "I don't want to see any federal program set up where the states are bypassed." He urged them instead to support a much more decentralized antipoverty measure that adhered to the American traditions of states' rights and local control.[9]

The requirements for community action and "maximum feasible participation" irritated most local officials who felt entitled to manage federal poverty programs in their areas as they saw fit. One of the most controversial programs created by the EOA was Volunteers in Service to America (VISTA), which, modeled on President Kennedy's international Peace Corps, deployed federally trained "volunteers" to America's needy areas with a mission to help energize poor people to improve their lives and communities. "For those already in power, those who resisted change," writes one historian, "VISTA was nothing short of subsidized anarchy."[10]

Storms of protest against the federal War on Poverty arose almost immediately as well from Arkansas business interests and Big Agriculture. Mrs. Arthur Alexander of the Little Rock area sent a telegram to Governor Faubus in May 1964 to warn him that he was "losing hundreds of votes from the farmer, the planter, [and] the big and little business man" by endorsing President Johnson's

Political cartoon printed in the *Benton Courier* in 1971. The powerful Arkansas Farm Bureau staunchly opposed the federal Volunteers in Service to America (VISTA) program in the state. Courtesy of the *Saline Courier*.

antipoverty agenda. "There are more of us than there are of the no work, all play, group," she said. Instead of participating in a wasteful government program, Alexander advised the governor to "have jobless men register with the employment agency." After all, she and her husband were "looking for tractor and transport drivers and men for other jobs." The Arkansas Farm Bureau's hostile opinion of the federal government's War on Poverty, moreover, quickly prompted that powerful agribusiness lobbying organization to issue petitions "requesting its removal from the state."[11]

A few days after Alexander mailed her letter, William P. Rock, owner of a business consulting firm based in Little Rock, wrote Governor Faubus to likewise protest the federal War on Poverty. "Basically," he wrote, "poverty elimination is impossible in view of the way the departments of the Federal government restrict industrialization." "They are strictly power-grabbing groups and cannot do anything of the nature that the President seems to think he can convince the people that he can do," Rock continued. "The truth of the matter is that industry's viewpoint is being completely ignored," which he believed was absurd because "industry is the only force which can go into an area and truly relieve the poverty condition." "We are constantly aware . . . from all of our 30,000 industrial contacts," Rock argued, that "labor costs" were the real impediment to growing the economy and, thus, solving the poverty problem, "such as [in] West Virginia where the mining unions under Mr. Lewis priced coal out of the fuel market." He was certain that all the meddling government was doing with these programs, "thru such concentration of power at Washington," was "verifying . . . that the union bosses will move in behind the expansion and force those wages up." "This is what is holding up the full movement of industry today" and causing the persistence of poverty, Rock concluded.[12]

Similarly, the executive vice president of the Arkansas Chamber of Commerce asked fellow members in the May 1964 edition of the chamber's *Arkansas Newsletter* whether "this great big, prosperous, booming America of ours really need[s] to embark on an enormously costly and paternalistic spending spree to 'wipe out' poverty among the less affluent of our society?" "All over the world for the last two decades," he regretted, "the initials U.S. have stood for Uncle Sugar, that incredibly rich Croesus with an inexhaustible bag of golden gifts for all 'under-privileged' and 'emergent' peoples wherever situated." "As a matter of fact," he claimed, "many Americans didn't know the situation had changed greatly until all the anti-poverty promotion got underway." Only then did they begin "to learn that vast areas of dire need and human want existed throughout the Nation and that the critical urgency of this lamentable development necessitated the immediate appropriation and expenditure of billions of dollars by the

Federal government." Despite all the talk about severe poverty in such states as Arkansas and West Virginia, the chamber of commerce spokesman wondered:

> Well, really how poor are we? . . . So far as Arkansas is concerned, the fact remains that there were more than 420,000 Arkansans holding non-farm payroll jobs in March at an average of $75 a week or $3,800 a year; fewer than 35,000 (including fringers and loafers) were out of work; 62,500 were employed in Arkansas's great agricultural industry which had a cash production in excess of $862 million last year; and more than 115,000 self-employed and others were busy making a living.

And as for the Johnson administration's claims about the needs for new job-training programs, he reminded his readers that the "American public school system is open to all." "Anyone who wants to go in business for himself finds the way open," and "those who want to work, who want to make a life for themselves and their families, are doing it," he contended. "The question is," he rhetorically asked: "Will the lavishing of taxpayers' dollars on all sorts of visionary schemes . . . be likely to inculcate in such persons habits of industry and thrift and thus eliminate improvidence from the American Scene?"[13]

The widely read national publications of the War on Poverty's conservative opponents also helped color the thinking of at least some rural Ozarkers. In November 1964, A.F. Burgess of rural Pope County mailed Governor Faubus three articles he had torn out of his copies of the *Reader's Digest* that warned of the bloated federal bureaucracy's dangerous urban renewal, infrastructure development, and antipoverty projects. One of the articles, a reprint from the *Wall Street Journal*, objected to the government's "underlying theme" about poverty, which held that "society is the real villain, that all of us are jointly responsible for the plight of the poor." It declared that this line of thinking "is bad history and worse sociology." "Almost none of our forebears," the article stated, "considered it anybody's responsibility but his own to see that he got up." "It was a lot of individual hard work and a great deal of freedom to move and act and think," the writer continued. "Henry Ford," after all, "did more to bring abundance to the majority than any amount of doles or vote-getting programs," which proved "that a free economy and society expands the opportunities for all its members but leaves it largely to the individual to decide what he will do about them." Burgess was bitter about the New Deal farm programs he had experienced during the Great Depression and the failed federal development efforts since, which had apparently destroyed any faith he might ever have had in the government's reform efforts. He also resented liberal reformers' condescending views of rural people. "We are not paupers and resent being treated as such, but with the war on poverty we cannot help ourselves," Burgess told Faubus.

"The only thing we [rural people] can do is to do as we did when crop control was put on us [which] is just get up and leave this area and start all over again." He challenged the governor, "[S]ee if you can see any gain to the ones affected, not even the towns, and most people in them are against it."[14]

Despite local elites' misgivings about the intentions of federal poverty programs in western Arkansas and the fact that "poverty was sort of incidental in [their] minds," they went forward with the newly formed ARVAC, which qualified as a CAP agency and "became very poverty conscious." According to director Bob Adkisson, though, the agency's compliance with the "maximum feasible participation" mandate "created a power struggle" with area elites. The county judges and local chambers of commerce heads reluctantly "agreed" to adhere to the government's terms, he recalled, "but [they were] always trying to 'back door' [to] get the money for their use." The organization's use of federal VISTA workers proved especially divisive, so Adkisson explained that he "had to convince [the] power structure to let Volunteers come into communities and not put a muzzle on them . . . had to tightrope that thing." Luckily for local elites, most of ARVAC's earliest volunteers were older and "well accepted" reformers who worked on nonthreatening projects like tutoring at local schools and organizing community art shows. At least one volunteer, a retired Kansas schoolteacher in her seventies, even joined the local chamber of commerce and said that she believed America's biggest problem was that "we are losing our heritage of a strong moral people, becoming a nation of curs." Eventually, though, like many other CAPs, ARVAC began to get some younger, "anti-establishment" volunteers who were "having a field day with their idealism." Adkisson recalled that "there was some struggle between them and the county judges." Still, ARVAC and its poverty warriors "never got as radical here as elsewhere" and managed mostly to "appease local power entities." Even so, local officials remained on their guard, especially as troubling news about poverty programs arrived from other parts of Arkansas and the nation.[15]

Contrary to Faubus's initial assumption that the white rural Ozarks would be the focus of federal poverty initiatives in Arkansas, many national reformers determined to connect the War on Poverty with African Americans' struggles for civil rights. "The War on Poverty has usually been seen as distinct from the southern civil rights movement," writes historian Annalise Orleck, "but the two historic movements were inextricably tied together."[16] The black communities in the lowlands of the eastern part of the state, then, became a focal point in Arkansas, and it did not take long for controversy to brew among resentful whites.

Even in the Ozarks, where whites made up well over 90 percent of the population, the image that the national War on Poverty was ostensibly a "special interest" program for blacks and social radicals alarmed a number of rural whites. In September 1964, Mrs. Cyrus Stutchman, the wife of a retired coal miner and small farmer in Franklin County, complained to the governor about federal poverty officials' plans to establish a youth-training center in her county. "I think it would be a bunch of red trained youths of course," she wrote, and "there will be niggers in the crowd." "I think we should keep such out of our state," Stutchman continued. "Our Government is so set on tearing up our way of life so do not let the Government put another one over on us." Governor Faubus responded to assure her: "I will consider carefully the establishment of any camp in Arkansas . . . before giving my approval." Then, after thanking Stutchman for her letter, Faubus worked to appeal to her populist sentiments. "I need all of the help I can get to defeat the millionaire candidate [Republican Winthrop Rockefeller]," he pleaded, and urged her and her neighbors to make sure to pay their poll taxes before the deadline.[17]

Faubus won the 1964 gubernatorial election but opted not to run for re-election in 1966, ending his unprecedented twelve-year tenure in office. His final opponent, liberal Republican Winthrop Rockefeller, who had served as a chief economic advisor in the Faubus administration, won the governor's office in the 1966 election. The new governor (whose nephew Jay Rockefeller—the future West Virginia governor and U.S. senator—had worked in the VISTA program in Appalachia in 1964) endorsed the federal War on Poverty when he took office in 1967. OEO head Sargent Shriver even wired Rockefeller a telegram to give him his "most sincere thanks for your public endorsement of the War Against Poverty in the *Washington Evening Star* last night." Arkansas's recently enfranchised black voters had cast the deciding votes for Rockefeller's election, so the new Republican governor prioritized using federal poverty programs to assist his African American constituents in the eastern part of the state.[18]

Nevertheless, like Faubus before him, Rockefeller also resented the federal government's efforts to bypass state and local power structures. In October 1967 Rockefeller wrote to the National Governor's Conference's Office of Federal-State Relations to complain: "It alarms me that even though most of the Governors have stated the need for an increase in state involvement, OEO insists on giving the states such a minor role."[19] Congress responded to state and local political leaders' loud protests by passing the Quie and Green Amendments to the EOA that same year, which gave "local officials the power to designate which community organizations were eligible for federal money" and stipulated that "elected officials would now comprise a third of the local poverty boards and could fill another third of the seats with welfare professionals and representatives of the private sector."[20] These changes, according to historian Ronald Eller, "effectively eliminate[ed] maximum feasible participation of the poor."[21] After Congress granted states and localities more authority over federal poverty programs, Rockefeller even used his veto power to block a food stamp supplement program in black-majority Phillips County.[22]

Negative publicity about antipoverty projects and community action in black communities of eastern Arkansas spread to help color many white people's perception of the federal government's War on Poverty throughout the whole state. White animosity raged in the Delta: in June 1969 an angry mob beat two VISTA volunteers "with coffee cups and other items" at a café in Hughes, an assault that severed one of the victim's arteries. In November 1969 white planter T. H. Barker penned an angry letter to the *Arkansas Gazette* in which he claimed that "Lee County did not acquire this poverty status until a group of bureaucrats decided we should wear this label. . . . I hope the Volunteers have been frustrated by the farming empire . . . for we have been frustrated by many bureaucratic mandates . . . that you and your kind have administered on an unsuspecting community." Milton Davis, another Lee County white, contended, "This is nothing short of socialized anarchy" and insisted that "it is about time we all stopped and took a good look around and demanded that our government put these funds to better use." Not surprisingly, the (White) Citizen's Council in Lee County also issued a statement condemning the "NAACP (National Association for the Agitation of Colored People), OEO, VISTA (Vipers in Subversion to America), and other trouble making organizations." "These same Communist organizations," the council claimed, "are the cause of the population ratio in Marianna to change" to a black majority in recent years. "Are you going to join with others NOW or AFTER they burn your business or home or assault your wife or daughter?" asked the Citizen's Council.[23]

Even in the Ozarks, which by the mid-twentieth century was comparatively one of the whitest regions in the country, black activism stirred some controversy over federal poverty programs. One of the region's few black communities resided in East Fayetteville near the University of Arkansas. When the federal government's War on Poverty began, Bobby Morgan, a native son of the black neighborhood, became interested in helping to start a community action agency for his home county. He wrote the new Washington County Community Action Agency's first successful grant application for job-training assistance in 1965. As federal money started to come in, however, Morgan remembered that "local politics got involved." Despite the federal mandate for "maximum feasible participation" before 1967, he claimed that "only the power people had the power—judges, mayor, sheriff." Morgan drafted one of the agency's largest funding proposals for a "mobile social clinic" to help serve all of Washington County, but especially the black community, with supplemental services such

Bobby Morgan, a Fayetteville native, wrote the first successful application for a federal poverty grant for the Washington County Community Action Agency in 1965 and later worked for the federal Office of Economic Opportunity's (OEO) Rural Training Center in Little Rock. His reform efforts often raised the ire of many local political and business elites. Courtesy of Marvin Schwartz.

as medical care, library resources, and welfare information. The $480,000 grant awarded by the federal government for the project, however, "was used for other things" by local political leaders, Morgan said. He himself became a bane of local elites, too. He claimed that after he started a new program to provide meals for hungry children in Fayetteville, entrenched political and business elites ordered county health inspectors to shut it down, baselessly citing "unsafe" and "unsanitary" conditions in the house from which it operated.[24]

One of Morgan's fellow white VISTA volunteers also remembered that Steve Cummings, the son of the local circuit court judge who had been installed as the agency's director, "really had conflicts" with the federal workers and "the low income neighborhood people." When "EOA staff people and neighborhood people were having meetings at night," he claimed that a paranoid Cummings "would break in and accuse them of having secret meetings." By 1968, financial irregularities and suspicions of corruption finally prompted the Rockefeller administration and the federal southwest regional and national offices of the OEO to investigate the elite-run Washington County agency. One federal official noted in a memo in November 1968, "[The] Agency is shot through with corruption . . . [but the] Regional CAP is helpless to change this because of politics and the inability to prove anything illegal." To make matters worse, the official guessed that the "Vols will probably be asked to leave because of what they have exposed" and because they "were somewhat instrumental in bringing [the] investigation of the agency." Despite a dead end in the investigation, however, Director Cummings resigned the following year.[25]

Frustrated by his experience with the Washington County agency, Morgan left to take a position with the OEO's Rural Training Center in Little Rock, but he remained committed to bringing change to his hometown and surrounding areas in northwest Arkansas. Having come to believe that "you'd either be with the power structure or against them [but] couldn't be neutral," Morgan resolved to challenge elites' control over local affairs. Through the Rural Training Center, he helped spearhead a voter registration and education campaign and exposed rampant election fraud throughout the state. In rural Madison County, the home of former governor Orval Faubus, Morgan claimed that he and his associates "knocked the top off the Faubus thing of votes from dead people" after they spent "two weeks to get names off tombstones [and] put them against county voter records." "We started to penetrate with info about elected officials," he explained, "and [the power] folks raised hell." "Every so often state troopers would come in and round us up, [ask] us to identify our people [and] Hassle us about things," Morgan recalled.[26]

Intense conflict flared up in Washington County, especially between the small black community in Fayetteville and the local white political establishment. In the summer of 1969 black youths in Fayetteville "riot[ed] in the streets" one night and a "police car [was] set on fire." "After that," remembered a VISTA volunteer working in Washington County, "many of our efforts [were] stymied" to the point that poverty reformers "couldn't speak with [the] county judge or mayor." Several years later, when the feather-ruffling Morgan finally returned home to East Fayetteville in 1981, he claimed that grudge-bearing local elites had him arrested on trumped up charges of "weed" possession and had him locked away in the county jail for four months.[27]

Black activism and its role in the federal War on Poverty in Washington County, particularly in the city of Fayetteville, however, was an exception in the Arkansas Ozarks. In a region with a white population of more than 90 percent and where most counties had no black residents at all, the civil rights struggle rarely figured directly into the affairs of antipoverty programs in rural communities. Nevertheless, the public image associated with the War on Poverty and its links to African Americans' and other "radicals'" fights for civil rights left a strong impression about the programs' intentions and provided local elites with powerful ammunition to help discredit the federal reform efforts among rural whites. Earl Evans, the African American director of the OEO's Rural Training Center in Little Rock, regretted that most poor and working-class whites in Arkansas saw the federal government's War on Poverty as mostly a "special interest" program for blacks. Evans was certain that "ninety-eight percent of the [white] people don't understand the poverty program, mistakenly thinking it was only for blacks."[28]

That race was an issue that pervaded rural white Ozarkers' views of the government's War on Poverty was undeniable. More broadly, the issue of race paralleled other transformations from the old Populist ethic in the region during the postwar era, such as the rise of anti-unionism in labor relations. As historian Michael Pierce argues, many working-class whites in the rural Ozarks "came to believe that the labor movement was too closely associated with the civil rights movement, outside agitators, and an eastern elite," which helped "erode the region's pro-labor culture." Racial barriers, as we have seen, had long stood firm in the region's Populist ethic.[29]

Elsewhere in America (including parts of Appalachia), liberal poverty reformers at times succeeded in helping to unite poor and working-class blacks and whites in a "struggle for social justice for all people" against economic inequality and local elites' monopoly of power. To do so, they often worked these issues out through natives' long-entrenched cultural support for mining and other industrial labor unions.[30] In the Ozarks, however, federal VISTA volunteers working in rural communities tended to view the racism of rural whites as an inevitable and largely insurmountable obstacle ingrained in the region's backward, agrarian culture. White Boston native Bob Gorman came to all-white Newton County—the poorest and most mountainous county in Arkansas—to work in the VISTA program in the late 1960s. Gorman, who had originally been trained "to community organize in urban black communit[ies]," said that his federal supervisor in Austin, Texas, had him "reading everything about Newton Co." and the Ozarks he could find to become familiar with the supposedly peculiar culture of the area. After he arrived in the region, though fascinated by the mountain "bootleg" he had expected to find, Gorman was convinced that "we were on the leading edge of general decadence in [the] area" and was certain that the rural people there "hadn't been exposed to outsiders." He recalled that one day "2 bus loads" of mostly black children participating in a federal Upward Bound program in the Arkansas River town of Russellville came to rural Newton County for a day-long outing to explore the scenic Buffalo River. Apparently morbidly amused by rural Ozarkers' presumably isolated, anti-modern culture, Gorman claimed that the "looks on those locals' faces was like the end of the world . . . [because they] didn't have enough rope in town to hang all those kids."

Gorman believed that the black children's visit to the mountains and safe return to Russellville that day signaled a "minor silent victory" for those hill folks who remained stuck in their nineteenth-century rural culture.[31]

Gorman's assumptions about the "culturally backward" hill folks he intended to help reflected more broadly the key failure of liberal poverty reformers' efforts to win the trust and support of poor rural Ozarkers, which meant that they posed a weak challenge to local elites' highly publicized assaults on the federal government's "wasteful" and "dangerous" programs. Like many of the earliest outside reformers who went to work in Appalachia, most poverty warriors who descended on the Ozarks primarily aimed to tackle the rural region's supposedly pathological "culture of poverty" and "alter the value system of the mountain people." For the most part, as historian Thomas Kiffmeyer explains, many urban and middle-class reformers believed that the Mountain South's problems could be mostly boiled down to rural people "perpetuating their impoverishment by clinging to outdated customs, values, and traditions." This paternalistic assumption effectively "placed the burden of poverty on the poor and ignored its real sources"—namely, the destruction of the region's smallholder economy and corporate industrialization's grossly uneven consequences. It also tended to offend the proud, hardscrabble people whom reformers' programs aimed to help.[32] Unlike leaders of the farmers' organizations who had helped mobilize poor and middling backcountry folks to challenge the status quo in the late nineteenth and early twentieth centuries, poverty reformers of the 1960s and 1970s remained unable to connect with the rural dispossessed in order to rekindle a populist grassroots defiance against economic inequality and dominance by local elites.

Poverty reformers' recollections of "culture shock" when they entered the region illuminate their prevalent attitudes and assumptions about the rural poor they came to help. VISTA trainer Neal Blakely recalled that he always "tried to tell [federal poverty reformers] what kind of culture they would be working with" and that they should "understand how regional Arkansas is." When VISTA volunteer Anna Gottlieb of Illinois found out she had been assigned to Arkansas, she "seriously thought of leaving" the program altogether. "To me," she explained, "Ark was the backwards of backwards" and "just a place you were born and stuck in." Though she became good friends with her VISTA partner there, she "realized why they [program officials] didn't tell you where you were going to go until you were into training." Had she known she would be sent to rural Arkansas, she "wouldn't have gone." While rural New Yorker Carolyn Rose initially welcomed her assignment to rural Arkansas, she explained that after she arrived, "I couldn't believe I had wanted to come to this state." "Unfortunately," she stated, "I never got used to Ark." Barbara Conard, while she insisted that she endured "emotional shock, not culture shock," remembered being taken aback by the isolation-induced rural fatalism and apathy she thought she encountered. She was particularly flabbergasted when she met an impoverished woman dying of cancer and trying to care for "kids yelling and screaming" in a dilapidated shack, because the woman seemed "so submissive and so polite and so thankful" despite her tragic and unacceptable situation. California native Jane Spencer, after completing her one-year tenure as a federal social worker with the Community Resource Center in Newton County, became convinced that "family violence is accepted as a way of life among many of these mountain families" and that cultural dysfunction was the region's main problem. And John Boyle, who split time as a federal VISTA volunteer between urban Texas and northwest Arkansas, remembered "what a culture shock" he experienced in going "from inner city Houston" to the rural Ozarks. Even though he was assigned to Washington County in the most "progressive" and affluent part of the region, he found the people there exceptionally parochial, clannish, and culturally deprived.[33]

Nurses working with the federal VISTA program visit a patient in Newton County. Notice the Winthrop Rockefeller campaign poster hanging on the wall of the home. Rockefeller was governor of Arkansas from 1967 to 1971 and generally supported the War on Poverty, though he complained that states and localities should have more control over federal programs. Courtesy of Marvin Schwartz.

Federal poverty reformers working in the Ozarks were also apt to hold up what they believed was a peculiar and primitive rural culture to explain why they could not get the poor hill people whom they intended to help on board with their programs. Age-old caricatures and popular images of culturally stagnant mountaineers' knee-jerk reactions to any change and their "rugged pioneer lifestyles"—complete, that is, with the same "such attitudes that allowed the early Arkansas settlers to survive in a sparsely populated wilderness"—loomed large in how outside reformers interpreted the rural resistance they encountered. One observer of antipoverty efforts in the region stated, after all, that the federal reformers "arrived in Arkansas more or less only one hundred years after the pioneer period." By the 1960s and 1970s, apparently unaware of the region's long history of in- and out-migration, the reformer guessed that "a typical family patriarch might be the son or grandson of the original pioneer who built his cabin from trees he felled and shaped, who fed his family from the game he hunted and trapped." It stood to reason, then, that stubborn frontier attitudes remained dominant in the isolated Ozarks.[34]

Reformers might have fared better had they understood the historical dynamics of populist defiance in the region and, popular stereotypes to the contrary, the enormous economic and social changes that had transpired since the nineteenth century. In parts of Appalachia and urban black and other nonwhite ethnic communities, many national poverty warriors did, indeed, eventually "[begin] to question the validity of the cultural explanation" about the poor they were assisting and, thus, began to enjoy better success in helping mobilize grassroots community action. In Appalachia, for instance, some liberal reformers began to zero in on the industrial exploitation inflicted by King Coal and its role in that region's economic and political inequality as the primary source of poverty. "Reformers began to argue that the region should be seen as a colony of corporate energy interests," writes one Appalachian historian. Hence, despite their flaws, some reformers eventually helped ignite new waves of populist resistance and helped develop a new collective sense of working-class "Appalachian nationalism" among dispossessed natives in some places.[35] Likewise, the American civil rights struggle provided "black communities . . . a national identity movement to support and encourage their efforts," according to another historian. Meanwhile, however, "the hill culture of the Ozark and Ouachita Mountains . . . had no such external support."[36] Rural hill folks often remained "caught between . . . a reform movement . . . that thought it knew better and those industrial interests . . . that . . . dominated the region."[37]

In Appalachia the omnipresence of coal corporations delineated clear lines between the haves and have-nots, and in many black communities blatant racial discrimination literally made poverty a "black and white" issue. Identifying the real sources of problems and organizing effective solutions, however, remained far more elusive to liberal reformers in the rural Ozarks. The virtual extinction of smallholder farming and its replacement by an uneven low-wage, nonunion industrial and agribusiness economy were central to the region's problems. Federal poverty reformers working in the Ozarks, however, generally believed in the inherent superiority of "modern" urban values—even those schooled in radical organizer Saul Alinsky's *Reveille for Radicals* (1946), which called for the creation of "people's organizations" to "precipitate the social crisis by action ... by using power." They failed, then, to wrap their minds around poverty in the Ozarks, clinging instead to popular rural and hillbilly stereotypes.[38] Even after spending more than a year working in rugged and impoverished Newton County, federal Volunteer Bob Gorman, for example, candidly admitted, "I never really knew what I was there for."[39]

Reformers in the Ozarks, as we have seen, experienced firsthand and, thus, quickly came to recognize the unequal power structure and its lopsided dominance by local elites who controlled the region's economic and political order. But they also tended to mistrust the poor and common folks they were there to help, despite their sympathy for them. Convinced that these rural folks carried too much backward cultural baggage, poverty warriors held little confidence in poor and working-class Ozarkers' own abilities to actively seek change. VISTA volunteer Donna Clark, for instance, who spent time in both the Ozarks and the Delta regions of Arkansas, simply believed that "change was more difficult here [in the hill country] than in east Arkansas." She thought her work in the Ozarks was "time well spent" because "we did a few nice things for people, taught a few to read," but, overall, her experience in trying to help reform conditions of poverty amid an exceptional rural hill culture left her, she said, with "less faith in the ability to change." Social worker Fred Morrow likewise believed that Ozarkers' "resistance to change [was] related to [the] cultural level of the state." "Hill people," he claimed, "had keen awareness of having problem[s], but [the] idea of letting someone come in and help was alien to their values." Even in those cases when federal poverty warriors succeeded in getting rural people on board with programs, another reformer regretted that stubborn hill folks always insisted that "it's all on their terms."[40]

With the "backward culture" paradigm dominating most of their thinking, poverty reformers failed to tap the strong tradition of economic populism in the rural Ozarks. Instead, they tended to promote the expansion of industrial employment opportunities and the habits and values of America's urban culture as the best prescriptions for the rural Ozarks. Testifying before the Congressional Subcommittee on Rural Development in June 1967, Glen Jermstad, the director of the Arkansas Office of Economic Opportunity, explained that while "the United States is a prosperous nation with pockets of poverty . . . Arkansas is a poverty-stricken state with pockets of prosperity," and "the counties of northern Arkansas, in the Ozark mountains, represent poverty at its worst." The main reason for this, Jermstad argued, failing to acknowledge the major transformations over the previous three decades that had depleted the region's smallholder economy, was that "Arkansas is still an agricultural and rural state, and in those areas lies the problem." Rural cultural isolation, Jermstad noted, in addition to the scant availability of "modern" industrial jobs, lay at the heart of the problem. "The problem of poverty," he insisted, "is a problem of education—how to provide it, how to improve it, how to convince the poor of the advantages of getting it." "Poor soil, poor transportation, poor education, all produce poor people."[41]

To be sure, the dissipation of smallholder farming by the 1960s and 1970s had vastly eroded the rural society that had given rise to populist defiance in the late nineteenth and early twentieth centuries. Yet the vestiges of traditional populism remained evident even among some Ozarkers who strove to adapt their rural lives to the industrial and agribusiness economy of the New Ozarks. Beginning in 1962, for instance, significant numbers of rural poultry farmers in the region began to organize growers' associations to challenge vertical-integration business tactics and hegemonic control of markets by the corporate processing companies that employed them. "Major [corporate] firms such as Tyson and Arkansas Valley Industries preferred to accept the inefficiency of dealing with many individual growers rather than diminish their control over production costs," notes one Arkansas historian; so the "organization[s] died in the face of such hostility." Even so, "the idea of grower bargaining rights gained force" among many Ozarks poultry growers who continued to struggle against the uneven consequences of corporate power in their region.[42] Still, most liberal reformers seemed unable to see the similarities between such rural movements for greater economic democracy and those of "modern" urban and industrial laborers. They continued to believe that rural Ozarkers' "independent, self-reliant nature, [and] suspicio[n] of government programs and so-called new ideas," as one federal program director put it, made it nigh impossible to rally them together to improve their lives.[43]

Federal poverty reformers also missed other opportunities to rekindle the old tradition of populist activism in the rural Ozarks—namely, in neglecting the region's religious culture. With the small farm economy, the religious scene had changed remarkably in the Ozarks by the 1960s and 1970s. "Another twentieth-century casualty of rural modernization has been the country church," writes Ozarks historian Brooks Blevins, because the rapidly dwindling numbers of rural residents who remained in the region "[began] driving to nearby towns in order to join large congregations" during the post–World War II era.[44] Thus, the small and independent backcountry churches, where many rural working-class Ozarkers had drawn inspiration for their populist defiance during the late nineteenth and early twentieth centuries, had largely vanished. Even so, a significant gap between the rural "disinherited" and more affluent middle-class Christians remained visible in the Ozarks during the second half of the twentieth century, and remnants for a potential revival of populist working-class religious dissent survived.

Poverty activist John Pelkey observed the socioeconomic divisions entrenched in the religious community of the Pope County locale where he worked during the 1960s. As for the most prominent church there, an Assembly of God congregation, Pelkey noticed that "members are mostly not from low income families," and he even thought that "some look down on the low income families as trash beneath their feet." Federal poverty reformer John Lewis also noted in his journal about the barriers that existed between the well-to-do and rural poor in the region's postwar Christian culture. Lewis even confronted the managing editor of the *Arkansas Methodist* about why there seemed to be such a well-defined line between the haves—the "good, Christian folks," as he sarcastically referred to them—and the have-nots in Arkansas's mainstream church environment. The editor, he said, responded to his inquiry by saying, "Well, we've had to work hard for what we have," prompting a frustrated Lewis to simply scribble in his journal: "Come on, lady!" Yet, while liberal poverty reformers often worked successfully with African American churches to promote grassroots community activism in American cities, they proved unable—or, perhaps more accurately, unwilling—to connect with religious sentiments in the rural Ozarks. In fact, the "religious fundamentalism" of rural Ozarkers, as one federal poverty worker in the region noted, typically figured high on reformers' list of the "cultural problems" that had to be overcome.[45]

Christian leaders in the region and nationally who were political and economic conservatives, meanwhile, worked diligently and far more successfully to forge a new popular climate of religious dissent—one increasingly directed not, as in the past, against greedy corporate elites but instead at abusive liberals and a meddling federal government. The transformation of many Church of Christ congregations after World War II is a case in point. These staunchly independent fundamentalist churches that had counted "Hillbilly Socialist" Sam Faubus and many other rural populists among its members in the late 1800s and early 1900s underwent significant institutionalization and centralization during the post–World War II era. Though the Churches of Christ maintained their tradition of local congregational authority, Harding College (now Harding University), located just south of the Ozarks escarpment in White County, came to exert a heavy influence on many local churches' teachings and doctrinal beliefs throughout the region by supplying preachers, literature, and area seminars. Under the long tenure of college president George Benson, who had first saved the small institution from closing its doors during the 1930s and then grew it into one of Arkansas's largest private colleges by forging lucrative financial ties with wealthy corporate benefactors, primarily in the southwestern oil industry, Harding became a bastion of evangelical political conservatism during the postwar period, not only in the Ozarks and surrounding regions but nationally. Benson's well-funded National Education Program at Harding informed both students and the public at large about the "pernicious" federal government and its threats to free business enterprise and America's rightful place as a Christian nation. Similarly, right-wing radio evangelists, such as Billy James Hargis, warned Christians tuning in to the airwaves in the Ozarks about insidious Communist subversion in an elite-run, high-handed federal government that was forcing America to turn its back on God.[46] Churchgoers in the New Ozarks heard fewer sermons and read less in faith-based literature about the sins of material greed, oppression by rich rulers, and the "blessedness" ascribed by Jesus Christ to the poor and those who toil. Instead, they heard and read increasingly about the eminent dangers of America's liberal-induced cultural crises and path to Godlessness.

The battles waged by local elites to exert their control over federal poverty programs combined with liberal reformers' failures to tap into the Populist ethic in the rural Ozarks to leave conservative opponents of federal social programs a near free reign in public debates about the role of government. In 1980, Carroll County Judge Wayne Farwell and several area businessmen joined the editor of the *Carroll County Tribune* and the owners of the local television and radio stations to launch a vigorous "grass-top" campaign to dismantle the Ozark Institute (OI), the nonprofit antipoverty agency based in the town of Eureka Springs. In accordance with the Comprehensive Employment and Training Act (CETA), which had been signed into law by President Nixon in 1973, the U.S. Labor Department had recently approved an $822,799 grant to the OI to help conduct regional job and skills training, community cooperative and sustainability projects, and welfare awareness campaigns for the rural poor. Judge Farwell derided the OI programs as a "duplication of services" and insisted, "If we are going to spend money for this purpose, let's use our long established institutions to administer it and not create a new one which will cost many thousands of extra dollars for administration." "Being in public office for 3½ years has made me more aware of the many government giveaway programs and frankly it scares me to death," Farwell added. "I would like to see all, and I mean all, of these programs abolished, then build back the few we really need," he continued. "I keep thinking that if we ever reach the point where we have more riders than we have pushers, we are in big trouble, and I think we have about reached that point."[47]

Prominent Berryville resident and local folk culture enthusiast Lanny Gibson echoed Farwell, lamenting that "this growth called bureaucracy is a fire-breathing dragon like Grendel in *Beowulf,* or it may be a club-wielding Cyclops, or a snaky-haired Gorgon that turns all who look at it to stone, or a Hydra that doubles each time it's cut, or that creature with many eyes I can't think of right now."[48] The owner of the local television station, Clyde Payne—an urban Illinois native who once explained in a local newspaper article, "I got fed up with the rat-race and high falutin' living up around Chicagoland, so I tossed everything into my covered wagon and struck out for the Ozarks"—likewise warned rural and small-town Ozarkers about the OI's "hippie" director, Edd Jeffords, whose philosophy, he suggested, was that "after a few puffs on the peace pipe, everything will be rosy." Payne described a verbal confrontation he once had with Jeffords, a native of eastern Arkansas, in which he claimed the hot-tempered OI director rabidly barked at him: "Once a Damyankee, always a Damyankee." Payne objected and declared that, in fact, "in just a short time [in the Ozarks] . . . I had become converted to an Orthodox Confederate." Payne insisted that the liberal Jeffords, whom he referred to as "Gen U.S. Grant," was actually the real "Damyankee Traitor."

> Since that day, when I met old U.S. Grant, he has come pretty far. He's set up his Union Headquarters in a downtown building and staffed it with his Damyankee friends, and most of us Confederates don't even know it. And instead of him dealing in that $500 and $1,000 stuff, he's throwing it away by the millions! And still, he hasn't told ANYONE (nor has anyone asked) just where the money is coming from. His latest brain-child is to conscript 80 or 90 of his Damyankee friends, and in just 6 weeks teach them how to grow grass . . . at a cost of a million bucks.

"I'm a hard-working, taxpaying converted Confederate who can't seem to qualify for welfare and food stamps," Payne continued. "So I'm warning you again, my Confederate friends—if you want a few coins left in your pockets for jingling, you'd better start doing some thinking and throw in with the judge [Farwell] and me."[49]

Beginning in June 1980, local tourism booster Jane Girkin made use of the local radio station and area newspapers to start a petition drive to demand that

Arkansas's first-term governor, the young and "liberal" Bill Clinton, utilize his state veto power to kill the federal CETA grant to the OI. By the first of October, Girkin and fellow petition carriers had organized a "swell of protest" and garnered thirteen hundred signatures from area residents. *Tribune* staff writer and local historian and folk-culture aficionado Jim Lair, who was a native of southern Arkansas, declared that the local "protest movement" against this "proposed waste" had been a "refreshing experience" for him. Lair had "witnessed people getting involved in what they feel is right," and he felt strongly that "we need more citizen involvement if we are going to turn around much of the thinking that is present in our nation today."[50]

The local protest movement combined with emerging Republican political campaigns in Arkansas to stir a swarm of controversy around the OI and its federal grant, which even prompted an FBI investigation into the organization's affairs. Accordingly, Governor Clinton quickly sought to distance his administration from the issue, promising local residents, "I'll stop the CETA grant to the Ozark Institute" immediately upon any findings of wrongdoing. Aside from a handful of minor citations regarding organizational signatures on federal paperwork by the wrong personnel, the FBI found no irregularities or corruption within the OI. Nevertheless, Governor Clinton, who was neck-deep in an increasingly fragile re-election campaign, ultimately denied state approval for the OI's 1981 CETA grant anyway and refused to comment further on the matter. Faced with a firestorm of public ridicule and stripped of most of its federal funding by regional political leaders, the OI was forced to close its doors altogether in 1982.[51]

By the 1980s, the Populist ethic had undergone a remarkable transformation in the Arkansas Ozarks. Most rural people who remained in the Ozarks had entered the tumultuous and anxiety-ridden post–World War II era still thinking that the federal government ought to play a role in helping to improve conditions for their families and communities. The unflinching faith of policymakers—both locally and in Washington—in corporate industrial growth and urban-oriented development, however, actually widened the gap between the rural dispossessed and the more affluent beneficiaries of the New Ozarks political economy. Assuming that local political elites knew best about how to fix problems on the ground if only they were provided with ample resources, federal reformers, in their deference to America's political tradition of "local control," overlooked that tradition's undemocratic potential. It guaranteed that local elites with their own visions and interests possessed significant control over federal programs and an insiders' privilege for framing the dominant themes in public discourse about the "failures" and "successes" of reform efforts. This meant that a distant federal "bureaucracy" in Washington usually absorbed most of the blame for "failures," while local political and business elites took the credit for reform programs' "successes" and attributed any growth to their own visionary and bootstrap efforts.

Widespread disappointment over the limits of federal development programs fused with growing animosities toward the government's "grassroots" antipoverty efforts that aimed to address social and economic problems "from the bottom up." Frustrated local elites who were at first bypassed by these more "direct" federal programs quickly established a powerful discourse of opposition. They tended to make far better use of tying their messages to the region's popular sensibilities and anxieties than the liberal reformers who came to help—despite their major deviations from the historic roots of working-class populism in the rural Ozarks. The constant and ultimately successful political assaults by local elites to gain control of federal poverty programs thwarted reformers' original designs for expanding rural opportunities at the grassroots. At the same time, most liberal reformers working in the region came with preconceived notions that stereotyped rural people and their culture, often in humiliating ways. They misunderstood the historical dynamics of Ozarks society and, consequently, fumbled any chances they may have had to help mount a populist defense for economic democracy in rural communities to counter New Ozarks elites' vociferous condemnation of federal programs and "Big Government" liberals. In this vacuum in the political discourse, many rural working-class Ozarkers by the 1980s had joined local business elites in applauding Ronald Reagan's contention, "Government is not the solution to our problems. Government is the problem."[52] This New Ozarks defiance represented a sharp break from their rural working-class ancestors who had often collided with local elites and supported the old Populist belief "that the power of government—in other words, of the people—should be expanded . . . as rapidly and as far as the good sense of an intelligent people and the teachings of experience shall justify, to the end that oppression, injustice, and poverty shall eventually cease in the land."[53]

CONCLUSION
POPULIST DEFIANCE—THEN AND NOW

In March 2009, Mountain Home resident Bill Smith—a self-described "Ozark Guru" who proudly lists "Hillbilly Slang" as his primary language—advertised plans for the newly founded Ozark Tea Party to host a local rally on April 15. The rally was scheduled in conjunction with national Fair Tax activists' "Nationwide Tax Day Tea Party," a demonstration organized to demand the abolition of all federal income taxes. A nonnative, Smith was an Air Force veteran, an ordained minister, and the owner of a business consulting firm who had come to the Ozarks most recently from Kansas. He proclaimed his and fellow tea partiers' goals for "upholding the rights granted by God & guaranteed by the U.S. Constitution, traditional family values, 'republican' principles/ideals, transparent & limited government, free markets, liberty, school choice & individual freedom." Vowing to be the "silent majority no more" and excited that their "revolution is brewing," Ozark Tea Party organizers were organizing this anti-tax rally for the purposes of "supporting the free market and honoring our veterans." To help make their case, they asked Ozarkers to bring homemade signs, tea bags, and American flags with them to the rally. "Just as our founding fathers did at the Boston Tea Party," Smith declared, "Americans from across the country are coming together on April 15th to protest the Governments [sic] wasteful spending." Tea partiers in the Ozarks also organized similar rallies in Fayetteville, Rogers, and Springdale in the northwest corner of the state.[1]

Fellow activist and Mountain Home resident Richard Caster likewise urged the region's people to recognize that "every Generation needs a Revolution," as the venerable Thomas Jefferson had put it, and that "this is our time, this is our American Revolution." Caster was the eighteen-year-old son of entrepreneurial parents who had moved to the Ozarks from California in the 1970s. He proudly reminisced about his first taste of political activism as a nine-year-old making Republican buttons with his crayons for the Bush-Cheney campaign. Caster was a manager at his father's chain restaurant and was pursuing a business degree at the local community college, hoping someday to "open an insurance company, retire at 50 and travel the country in an RV." He was later elected to the county quorum court by local voters, making him the youngest elected official in Arkansas. Caster implored Ozarkers to ask themselves whether they would help to "take this opportunity and fight to bring America Back to its founding Principles of limited Government, A Free Market, and a Capitalistic system." "Or will we let the Far Left Liberals in our nation continue to take us down the road to socialism?" he asked. A conservative Catholic who believed that "we need to get a backbone back in our faith and back in politics," Caster hoped that the Tea Party rally in Mountain Home, along with others like it throughout the nation, would help begin to rescue America from its dangerous path of national decline under newly elected President Barack Obama and his fellow "Big Government Liberals." "If your [sic] ready for Real change please join us," he pleaded.[2]

According to their own count, about fifteen hundred people from northern Arkansas and southern Missouri attended the Ozark Tea Party's tax-day rally at the town square in Mountain Home, located, somewhat ironically, only a few miles from two of the federal government's New Deal–era dams and lakes. When the young organizer Richard Caster took to the stage to kick off the event and asked those in attendance how they were doing, one man hollered out above the rest of the noisy crowd, "We're broke!" After a few introductory remarks from Caster, Pastor Sam Bailey of the Twin Lakes Baptist Church led the Tea Party protestors in prayer and declared that "liberty is a gift from God." Then they sang the National Anthem and recited the Pledge of Allegiance before a young woman read a patriotic poem to honor the veterans of the U.S. military. Subsequently, Mickey Pendergrass, the owner of the local Century 21 real estate firm in Mountain Home and a local political leader, gave a speech in which he demanded that federal and state lawmakers immediately get to work on legislation to cancel all capital-gains and estate taxes. Finally, Tea-Party Republican Karen Hopper, the local state representative, an administrator at Mountain Home's state-funded community college, and a board member of the area chamber of commerce, topped the day off with a fiery speech. "Like Samuel Adams and Paul Revere who participated in the first great tea party," Hopper declared, "we are tired of politicians who believe that spending will solve all of our problems." "Like them, we are tired of a government that punishes those who practice responsible financial behavior and rewards those who do not," she continued. "Think about it," said Hopper, "maybe our congressmen and congresswomen will think twice about how they vote, because that last tea party sparked a revolution."[3]

Like the national Tea Party movement, members and supporters of the Ozark Tea Party and similar groups were particularly disgusted with federal social programs, with many viewing them as little more than wasteful handouts for nonwhite minorities. The Ozarks Minutemen, a self-described Tea Party group headquartered in Springfield, Missouri, for instance, stands for "Secure Borders, Lower Crime Rates, Lower Taxes, Less Crowded Schools, Lower Health Care Costs, Increas[ing] Working Wages," and, above all, "STOP[PING] THE TIDE OF ILLEGAL IMMIGRANTS COMING INTO THE OZARKS!"[4]

One Tea Party meeting in Mountain Home caught the attention of regional and national media in June 2012 when Inge Marler, a Yugoslavian-born retiree and member of the Ozark Tea Party's steering committee, told a "welfare" joke that she later claimed she had found on the internet:

> A black kid asks his mom, "Mama, what's a democracy?"
> "Well, son, that be when white folks work every day so us po' folks can get all our benefits."
> "But mama, don't the white folk get mad about that?"
> "They sho do, son. They sho do. And that's called racism."

According to a local reporter who recorded audio of the event, the crowd of about five hundred roared with laughter and applause. "There were no objections to the 'joke' . . . and no one spoke with disapproval," he wrote. After the comments went "viral," Caster, the Ozark Tea Party's chairman, issued a formal statement to the press apologizing for Marler's offensive comments and explaining that she had resigned from the party's steering committee. Caster went on in his statement, though, to "ask the media to continue to do their jobs and discover the truth wherever it lies" and provided internet links to "recent indiscretions from leaders on the Left," with labels such as "Occupy Wall Street Rapes" and "Barney Frank's Racist Joke."[5]

Like the Populist movement of the late 1800s and early 1900s, tea partyism bore strong marks of anti-establishmentarianism. Like the rural populists, tea partiers spoke with anti-elitist rhetoric about the need to clean house in America's government institutions. But this was *not* the same kind of anti-establishmentarianism and anti-elitism that had inspired the working-class defiance of backcountry Ozarkers who joined the Brothers of Freedom, or the

Bruces and their moonshining comrades, or the Harps and other rural draft resisters during World War I, or the smallholders on Hutchinson Mountain who resisted federal tick eradication, or the small farm families who hoped that the New Deal's expanded liberal state might finally help bring better economic democracy to rural and working-class Americans. Twenty-first-century tea partyism, instead, had much more in common with the corporate industrial and agribusiness visions of business elites with whom rural populists had sparred for so long. Their particular defiance against federal power was motivated by many of the same concerns that had mobilized the more recent elite-led resistance to federal poverty programs in the 1960s and 1970s. Initially emerging most prominently from larger "growth centers" like Mountain Home and the economic oasis of Washington and Benton Counties, it was conservative business elites and their supporters in the twenty-first century who launched and led a Tea Party movement that aimed to guard their local control in the low-wage industrial-, tourism-, and agribusiness-based order that, with lots of federal assistance, had finally replaced smallholder rural life in the Ozarks during the post–World War II era. Tea partyism sprang from a newer fountain of Ozarks defiance. In fact, its specific agenda of political resistance and antigovernment defiance sought to tear down many of the same federal powers that the region's rural forefathers had helped create.[6]

The unique dynamics of rural defiance against federal power in the Arkansas Ozarks during the late 1800s and early 1900s, differed very markedly, indeed, from those of the late 1900s and early 2000s, despite the prevalence of stereotyped cultural myths that may suggest otherwise. When rural Ozarkers entered the twentieth century, they were not divorced from the rest of the world in isolated mountain hollers but, rather, were right in the thick of America's Gilded Age economic, social, and political developments. Faced with rising inequalities and rural working-class dispossession, populist Ozarkers called for public power to acquire brand new roles, particularly interventions in the corporate political economy that they hoped would promote their ideals of fairness, equal opportunity, and liberty. Their resistance to federal power did not usually stem from some simple ideological or cultural aversion to the institution of government itself. Instead, what they resented most was an imbalanced status-quo system that they believed had been high-jacked by the rich and powerful few, including *local* elites, to selfishly serve their own "special interests" at the expense of everyday working people like themselves.

Popular narratives of rural people clashing with government authorities typically pit reform-minded outsiders against homogenous, egalitarian hill people who wanted nothing more than to be left alone. But confrontations over federal power in the Ozarks often had more to do with *local* clashes between the region's well-to-do and well-connected business elites and its poor and working-class inhabitants in the rural backcountry. Rural smallholders and other working people's defiance of federal authority was commonly born out of their frustrations with inequalities and resentment of town businessmen, prosperous farm owners, and other local elites who disproportionately controlled most applications of government power in the region and used it to advance a corporate political economy that burdened smallholder farm communities. Federal reformers' routine delegations of authority and resources to the "local control" of regional elites persistently obstructed rural populists' demands for economic democracy and helped ensure many *intraregional* conflicts throughout the first half of the twentieth century.

By contrast, the popular antigovernment critiques of federal power that are commonly associated with the region today arose more recently in a New Ozarks society and political economy that supplanted smallholder communities during the second half of the twentieth century. After thousands of rural working people who had been most disposed to the Populist ethic left the Ozarks during World War II and the postwar decades, a significant wave of "population replacement" by nonnatives mostly from the urban and suburban Midwest began sweeping into the region by the 1970s, a demographic change that has persisted largely unabated into the second decade of the twenty-first century. During the 1940s and 1950s, except for the prosperous anomalies of Washington and Benton Counties, the Ozarks region lost nearly one-third of its population. Between 1960 and 1990, however, even while many rural natives continued to leave, the large influx of Midwestern middle-class newcomers produced overall population increases of at least 25 percent in all but one of the fifteen primary Ozarks counties. New Ozarks "winners" like Baxter County, in addition to Washington and Benton Counties, experienced aggregate population gains that exceeded 200 percent. These "fundamental demographic, social, and even cultural transformations," asserts historian Brooks Blevins, ought to prompt "a reevaluation of the meaning of rural community."[7] Indeed, this reevaluation should include a reconsideration of what this significant change means for our narratives about rural political culture and sentiments about federal power.

The post-smallholder society of the New Ozarks lured nonnative entrepreneurs to light-industrial-, agribusiness-, retirement-, and tourism-based business ventures primarily in the region's growth centers but also to "cheap" real-estate investments throughout the depopulated countryside. New in-migrants, a large number of whom were retirees, frequently pointed to some "combination of aesthetic appeal, low-cost living, inexpensive land and housing, and absence of severe pollution and criminal activities," and especially "low taxes," as key attractions.[8] Some newcomers represented the American counterculture movement, and these idealistic "back-to-the-landers" came to the Ozarks seeking an "unspoiled" and "natural" abode.[9] But far more in-migrants arrived to the region with more "conservative" lifestyles and ideals. During this era of suburbanization and "white flight" from American cities, the "lily whiteness" of the Ozarks served as a magnet to many middle-class whites from the Midwest who were uncomfortable with the increased racial and cultural diversity of their urban neighborhoods during the postwar decades. Like the back-to-the-landers—albeit obviously for different reasons—many of these "conservative" Midwesterners were drawn to the region, at least in part, by romanticized myths of Ozarks isolation and "heritage." Seeking to escape a "liberalizing" America, they joined many native Ozarks business elites to forge a rapidly growing New Right, government-loathing political culture in the region by the turn of the twenty-first century.[10] Rural stereotypes notwithstanding, *change* had shaped new popular sentiments about federal power in the Arkansas hill country.

Though "the modern Ozarks bears little resemblance to the region before World War II," historians have generally neglected to account for this fundamental change.[11] Historians who are apt to emphasize historical continuity between today's New Right, antigovernment conservatism and rural culture in the late 1800s and early 1900s overlook glaring evidence that reveals far more change than their works usually allow for. Most specifically, they miss the significance of the Populist ethic and the primacy of *local* conflicts that, more than anything, shaped many of rural Ozarkers' biggest stands against federal power during the first half of the twentieth century.

The smallholder society that gave birth to and once sustained rural Ozarkers' populist defiance has now been mostly extinct for the better part of fifty years. This fact, especially when considered with other changes that have been transforming the Ozarks since the mid-1900s, may seem to indicate that the likelihood is slim to none for a resurgence in the foreseeable future of a Populist ethic that again sees an important role for government in helping to curb and mitigate inequalities, including *local* unevenness. The ever-strengthening antigovernment political culture in the region today that seems so fixated on the blunders of Washington might certainly suggest so. But if this book has shown us anything, it is that circumstances and ideas do change, even if they go unnoticed or are misunderstood by most observers. Moreover, an important premise of this history has been that rural people and their experiences were not all that "exceptional" but actually held much in common with nonfarm working people in more urban places, even if they at times failed to recognize those similarities. At its core, the Populist ethic that was once so strongly etched in the hearts and minds of rural Ozarkers was far too powerful and flexible to be confined to the particular grievances of small farmers in rural communities in the bygone days of the late 1800s and early 1900s.[12]

Even in the unlikely political climate of today's New Ozarks, many rural and working people have at times demonstrated a willingness to go against the grain of their political leaders' conservative ideological positions, demanding that public services and regulatory power respond to their needs. In 2011 and 2012, for instance, hundreds of people in rural communities across the region protested when the financially troubled U.S. Postal Service announced that it planned to close "roughly a third" of Arkansas's post offices, primarily in rural areas it claimed had "too little workload" and produced too little revenue to justify their operating costs. Many rural Ozarkers met at community centers, in churches, and on front porches to draw up petitions, insisting that federal leaders do something to keep their local postal services available. Others wrote letters, made phone calls, or visited their political representatives about the issue. Stanley Morrison, a fifty-nine-year-old logger and a local justice of the peace in Stone County, helped lead the protest to keep his community's post office open; he explained, "There are those who have been downtrodden so long, they can't get back up. [But] there are others who've been downtrodden so long they decide to fight back."[13]

The "swift" swarm of protest against rural post office closures quickly pressured many of the region's conservative political leaders to take a stand on the issue, including U.S. Senator John Boozman. When Boozman's office was flooded with letters, petitions, and phone calls demanding that he fight to keep rural post offices open, the senator decided to make an "apparent departure from small-government orthodoxy." The grassroots pressure quickly put Boozman to work on a legislative proposal that would have banned the Postal Service from closing any rural post office in a community that did not have access to another within ten miles. "There are times when it's not as profitable," Boozman said, explaining his unlikely position, "but it's important to provide that service [anyway]."[14]

The 2014 midterm elections in Arkansas also revealed what may, perhaps, be interpreted as some surviving embers of the old Populist ethic in today's antigovernment political climate. At the polls, while voters sent ultraconservative Tea Party favorite Tom Cotton with a virtual mandate to represent them in the U.S. Senate, on the same ballot they voted by an even more lopsided margin to support a significant increase in the state's minimum wage, an initiative backed by organized labor and other progressives.[15] Sixty-six percent of Arkansas voters said yes to raising the minimum wage from $6.25 per hour to $8.50 by 2017. The proposal had been a "nonstarter" in the Republican-controlled state legislature, but as labor activists and other progressive organizers campaigned for the initiated law in the months leading up to November, pre-election polls showed that nearly 80 percent of Arkansas residents supported the proposal. This prompted a number of conservative political leaders to claim, when questioned by reporters, that they, too, supported it, even if they had previously made statements to the contrary.[16] Recent protests against rural post office closures and groundswells of support for raising Arkansas's minimum wage are but two examples that may suggest that a penchant for analyzing the personal and local consequences of unequal social, economic, and political power are, indeed, alive and well in the region today, if perhaps dormant as the Populist ethic had seemed in the 1920s. As historian and activist Michael Stewart Foley has recently shown, strong grassroots movements can emerge and become very effective, even in the most unlikely of political environments, when people localize and personalize the threats of inequality to the well-being and aspirations of their families and communities.[17]

The inability of poverty reformers to uncover a Populist ethic in the rural Ozarks in the 1960s and 1970s makes it abundantly clear that an absence of homegrown, grassroots activism, participation, and leadership is a likely recipe for failure. But, as we have seen, the age-old stereotype of some innate cultural hostility to outsiders has little basis in historical facts. Canadian-born "furriner" Isaac McCracken's seminal role in the farmers' movement in the 1880s and 1890s, and, for that matter, the strong influence of recent in-migrants from the urban and suburban Midwest in contemporary Ozarks tea partyism, should be important reminders. The difference between the failures of most federal poverty reformers to earn the trust of rural Ozarkers, on the one hand, and the successes of the farmers' revolt and today's tea partiers, on the other, is the latter movements' abilities to relate in at least some important ways at personal and local levels to rural people's lives, values, and frustrations; hence, they convinced rational rural working people that their movements—more than the present alternatives, at least—offered the best diagnoses of and plausible prescriptions for their problems.

All these issues are important to consider, especially in light of very timely developments in recent American political discourse and discussions about federal power. Indeed, pundits of varying ideological persuasions loosely—and often erroneously, in a historical sense—employed the label "populism" to describe major political winds that blew during the 2016 presidential election cycle.[18] I will leave it to future historians to dispassionately dissect the phenomenon of "anti-establishment" politician and billionaire real-estate tycoon Donald Trump, but the apparent enthusiasm for Trump among many rural and working class Ozarkers presents an opportune moment for historians and well-meaning reformers to reflect on just how useful knowing more about the past can be for bettering our understanding of the present. Historians and reformers ought to abandon old caricatures and simplistic assumptions about rural working whites and focus instead on the real, rational frustrations and their root causes in rural and working-class communities today. Instead of writing off the region's people as hopelessly backward remnants of an earlier time, they might instead look for opportunities to help rural and working Ozarkers explore new—and perhaps surprising—perspectives that their region's history may bring to their own lives in the twenty-first century. Some, for instance, may discover a better appreciation for a healthy, democratic skepticism of elites—business elites and well as political elites, including locals—and the real power they wield, where that power truly lies, and the particular interests that are promoted by that power. This history may also help give pause for thinking twice about the specific agendas of those leaders who don an antiestablishment image and shout loud, "populist"-sounding rhetoric. Some may also find it useful to consider how it was often rural white populists' active support for or passive acceptance of the antagonistic cultural "othering" of working and poor people who looked different, lived elsewhere, or otherwise seemed strange and unfamiliar that often derailed any political substance for expansions of economic democracy and community sustainability that most of them yearned for. The possibilities seem rich, indeed.

This book has also aimed to prod historians to entertain new discussions about why liberal governments' "progressive" programs have too often failed to win the support of the people they intended to help, especially in rural areas. Historians who follow James C. Scott's "high modernism" model have done excellent work in exposing the need for policymakers to avoid cookie-cutter approaches in devising and administering reform programs and in exposing how their efforts may otherwise have fared much better had they paid closer attention to practical "local knowledge" about grassroots problems and potential solutions. Nevertheless, their indictments of distant, out-of-touch policymakers in centralized bureaucracies tend to underemphasize important inequalities, competing interests, and uneven access to power at *regional* and *local* levels. Contrary to conventional views of rural resistance to government power as an outsiders-versus-locals paradigm, the story in the Ozarks was often primarily one of *local* conflict. Many clashes were between well-to-do elites who controlled government programs and used them to promote their own visions of corporate business development and smallholder working people in the back-country who rarely benefited from the "improvements" the programs promised.

This history of the rural Ozarks may suggest, then, that any hopes of employing the liberal state to successfully combat poverty and promote a more democratic political economy must do two things simultaneously. First, reform movements must understand on a "microscopic" level how social, economic, and political power is held in localities and regions and ensure that their programs actually reach the dispossessed populations they were intended for. They must circumvent and avoid "diluting" compromises with those particular structures of local power that shape real-life inequalities. While this prescription may seem easy to write for an "armchair thinker" such as myself, it is important to realize that any course of action that bypasses and, in fact, is primarily aimed at curtailing the control of local elites—similar to the War of Poverty's "maximum feasible participation" in the 1960s—would inevitably ignite the "total" resistance of powerful and resourceful defenders of the status quo.

Second, any hopes of overcoming such formidable opposition would undoubtedly require an immense, impassioned, and largely airtight democratic front that has its sights locked on the *local* sources of unevenness that affect everyday life. A deeper understanding of such *local* dynamics should prompt reformers to shun many old and baseless stereotypes about the people they aim to help and, instead, encourage them to prioritize the grassroots inclusiveness that may bring out the populist sentiments embedded deep in dispossessed populations for substantive change. Never before have all of these parts come together in the rural Ozarks, even in the seemingly fertile and likely environment of the late nineteenth and early twentieth centuries. But it is a certainty that change happens, and the spirit of protest—in whatever form it takes—will likely remain alive and well in the Ozarks.

NOTES

ABBREVIATIONS

ASCBR   Arkansas Supreme Court Briefs and Records, UALR/Pulaski
                      County Law Library Special Collections, Little Rock
Bailey Papers   Carl E. Bailey Papers, Arkansas History Commission, Little Rock
COSR   Center for Ozarks Studies Records, Special Collections, Missouri
                      State University Libraries, Springfield.
DCUS-Harrison   Records of the District Court of the United States, Western Dis-
                      trict of Arkansas, Harrison Division, National Archives and Rec-
                      ords Administration, Fort Worth, Texas
Ellis Papers   Clyde T. Ellis Papers, Special Collections, University of Arkansas
                      Libraries, Fayetteville
Faubus Papers   Orval Faubus Papers, Special Collections, University of Arkansas
                      Libraries, Fayetteville
GRDC-ES   General Records of the Department of Commerce (RG 40), Office
                      of the Secretary, Executive Secretariat's Subject File, 1953–1974,
                      National Archives and Records Administration, College Park,
                      Maryland
GRDC-OFC   General Records of the Department of Commerce (RG 40), Office
                      of Federal Cochairmen—Ozarks Regional Commission, Orga-
                      nization Meetings and Policy, 1966–69, National Archives and
                      Records Administration, College Park, Maryland

Hargis Papers	Billy James Hargis Papers, Special Collections, University of Arkansas Libraries, Fayetteville
Hayes Papers	George Washington Hayes Papers, Arkansas History Commission, Little Rock
Laney Papers	Ben Laney Papers, Arkansas History Commission, Little Rock
McMath Papers	Sidney McMath Papers, Arkansas History Commission, Little Rock
Mills Papers	Wilbur Mills Papers, Archives and Special Collections, Hendrix College Library , Conway, Arkansas
Parnell Papers	Harvey Parnell Papers, Arkansas History Commission, Little Rock
RDC-ARCO	Records of the Department of Commerce (RG 40), Annual Reports of the Commission Ozark, 1974–1980, National Archives and Records Administration, College Park, Maryland
Remmel Papers	Harmon L. Remmel Papers, Special Collections, University of Arkansas Libraries, Fayetteville
Rockefeller Papers	Winthrop Rockefeller Papers, Special Collections, UALR/Butler Center for Arkansas Studies, Little Rock
USDC-WDA	U.S. District Court, Western District of Arkansas, *Fort Smith, Arkansas, Criminal Case Files, 1866–1900*. Online database. Provo, Utah: Ancestry.com Operations, 2012
VISTA Collection	Arkansas VISTA Collection, Archives, University of Central Arkansas Library, Conway

INTRODUCTION

1. Reed, "Shooting of Gordon Kahl"; Corcoran, *Bitter Harvest*.

2. *New York Times*, July 3, 1983; Nina Richey interview.

3. Stock, *Rural Radicals*, 4, 13.

4. Moreton, *To Serve God and Wal-Mart*; Dochuk, *From Bible Belt to Sun Belt*, xx, 4, 9, 13.

5. Iggers, *Historiography in the Twentieth Century*, 108; Levi, "On Microhistory," 97–119.

6. Levi, "On Microhistory," 113.

7. Billings, Pudup, and Waller, "Introduction"; Blevins, *Hill Folks*.

8. Petty, *Standing Their Ground*, 10, 8.

9. The Ozarks has been one of the whitest regions in America since the early 1900s. Blevins, *Hill Folks*, 77, 211–12, 298n61.

10. Goodwyn, *Populist Moment*.

11. Link, *The Paradox of Southern Progressivism*; Keith, *Country People in the New South*.

12. *New Ozarks* is my adaptation of Southern historians' longtime use of a late nineteenth-century *New South* analytical conceptualization. Woodward, *Origins of the New South*; Ayers, *Promise of the New South*.

13. Scott, *Seeing Like a State*, 1–8 (quote p. 6); Stock and Johnston, *Countryside*; Jacoby, *Crimes against Nature*.

14. Li, *Will to Improve*.

15. See Scott, *Seeing Like a State*.

16. Sanders, *Roots of Reform*.

17. Petty, *Standing Their Ground*, 11.

18. Dunn, *Cades Cove*, xiv–xv.

19. Blevins, *Hill Folks*, 7; Blevins, "Considering Regional Exceptionalism," 74.

CHAPTER 1. THE "ONE-GALLUSED" CROWD ON GOVERNMENT

1. *Arkansas Gazette*, July 5, 1899; Arsenault, *Wild Ass of the Ozarks*, 3, 77.

2. Vance, "Karl Marx for Hill Billies"; Arsenault, *Wild Ass of the Ozarks*, 77–79; Arsenault, "Jeff Davis (1862–1913)."

3. Fletcher, *Arkansas*, 261.

4. Kazin, *Godly Hero*, 149.

5. Postel, "American Populist," 118.

6. Kazin, *Godly Hero*, 149.

7. Foner, *Reconstruction*, 379.

8. DeBlack, "Harnessed Revolution," 218.

9. Ibid., 218, 227, 237–39.

10. Ibid., 239; Woodward, *Origins of the New South*, 155; Moneyhon, *Arkansas and the New South*, 23–40.

11. Billings and Blee, *Road to Poverty*, 23, 105.

12. Dougan, *Arkansas Odyssey*, 282; Whayne et al., *Arkansas*, 248–49.

13. Lewis, *Transforming the Appalachian Countryside*, 7; Blevins, *Hill Folks*, 34, 81.

14. Blevins, *Hill Folks*, 47–48.

15. Hahn, *Roots of Southern Populism*; Lewis, *Transforming the Appalachian Countryside*; Weise, *Grasping at Independence*; Blevins, *Hill Folks*, 63–89.

16. Blevins, *Hill Folks*, 69–89; Fones-Wolf, *Glass Towns*, xxii–xxv.

17. Blevins, *Hill Folks*, 48.

18. Ibid., 75–82; Lewis, *Transforming the Appalachian Countryside*.

19. Henningson, "Upland Farmers," 61. The counties primarily organized by the B of F in the Ozarks were Baxter, Boone, Madison, Marion, Newton, and Searcy. The B of F also organized a number of counties in the Arkansas River Valley of west-central Arkansas and in the Ouachita Mountains of the southwestern part of the state. The Agricultural Wheel, an initially separate "sister" organization founded the same year in the Arkansas Delta, organized several counties in the eastern Ozarks. Elkins, "Arkansas Farmers Organize for Action," 231–48; Elkins, "The Agricultural Wheel," 152–75. The B of F merged with the Wheel in 1885.

20. Henningson, "Upland Farmers," 63, 79; Hild, "Brothers of Freedom."

21. Henningson, "Upland Farmers," 74–80.

22. Postel, *Populist Vision*, 4, 288.

23. Henningson, "Upland Farmers," 75, 81–84, 98.

24. *Mountain Wave*, July 22, 1892.

25. Sanders, *Roots of Reform*, 123, 131; Tindall, *Populist Reader*, 76–77.

26. Dougan, *Arkansas Odyssey*, 303–304; Whayne et al., *Arkansas*, 266–67; Barnes, *Who Killed John Clayton?*; Seagraves, "Arkansas Politics," 179–81, 248; Kazin, *Godly Hero*, 251; *Clinton Democrat*, June 10, 1897.

27. Dougan, *Arkansas Odyssey*, 304; Whayne et al., *Arkansas*, 266–69. Voter turnout dropped by nearly 20 percent between 1890 and 1892 in Arkansas. Then, the 1892 poll tax disfranchised another 15 percent of blacks and between 9 percent and 12 percent of poor whites.

28. Dougan, *Arkansas Odyssey*, 305.

29. Davis quoted in Arsenault, *Wild Ass of the Ozarks*, 218.

30. Dougan, *Arkansas Odyssey*, 309; Arsenault, "Jeff Davis, 1901–1907"; Arsenault, "Jeff Davis (1862–1913)."

31. Arsenault, "Jeff Davis, 1901–1907," 123, 130.

32. Davis quoted in Arsenault, *Wild Ass of the Ozarks*, 218.

33. Davis quoted in ibid., 167.

34. Davis quoted in Dougan, *Arkansas Odyssey*, 311; and Arsenault, *Wild Ass of the Ozarks*, 205–6, 211–13, 214.

35. Perkins, "Race Relations in Western Lawrence County," 7–14; Lancaster, "'There Are Not Many Colored People Here,'" 429–49; Lancaster, *Racial Cleansing in Arkansas*; Harper, *White Man's Heaven*.

36. Sanders, *Roots of Reform*, 129; Wagy, "Little Sam Faubus," 275; Beeby, "Introduction," xvii.

37. *Mountain Wave*, October 14, 1898, and October 8, 1897.

38. *Courier-Democrat*, March 2, 1899; *Mountain Wave*, October 8, 1897.

39. *Courier-Democrat*, April 18, 1901; *Mountain Wave*, October 1, 1897.

40. *Sharp County Record*, January 23, 1890; *Mountain Echo*, reprinted in the *Courier-Democrat*, November 17, 1898.

41. *Mountain Wave*, September 24, 1897, October 8, 1897, and November 5, 1897.

42. Ibid., October 7, 1898, and September 16, 1899.

43. Morgan, *History*, 148–49.

44. *Russellville Democrat*, November 11, 1897; *Courier-Democrat*, February 9, 1899.

45. *Mountain Wave*, October 1, 1897.

46. *Courier-Democrat*, July 25, 1901.

47. On Davis's declining margins of victory at the polls and the depreciating power of his machine, see Arsenault, "Jeff Davis, 1901–1907," 117–30.

48. Kiser, "Socialist Party in Arkansas," 121; Bissett, *Agrarian Socialism in America*, 8; Green, *Grass-Roots Socialism*.

49. Halbrook, "Review of My Membership," 202–8; Kiser, "Socialist Party in Arkansas," 139–40; Willis, *Southern Arkansas University*, 26.

50. Hahn, *Roots of Southern Populism*, 283.

CHAPTER 2. FIRST TASTES: MOONSHINERS AND G-MEN

1. *New York Times*, August 31, 1897; *Arkansas Gazette*, August 31, 1897; *Russellville Democrat*, September 2, 1897.

2. *Russellville Democrat*, October 28, 1897; *Courier-Democrat*, October 7, 1898, November 16, 1899, and November 23, 1899.

3. Shapiro, *Appalachia on Our Mind*; Batteau, *Invention of Appalachia*; Blevins, *Arkansas/Arkansaw*; Blevins, *Hill Folks*.

4. Pierce, *Corn from a Jar*, 8.

5. Johnson, *John Barleycorn Must Die*, 10–16; Hernando, *Faces Like Devils*, 119–20, 153, 156, 215.

6. Stewart, *Moonshiners and Prohibitionists*, 6.

7. J. C. Poindexter to George W. Hayes, February 2, 1915, Hayes Papers, box 2, folder 56; Arsenault, *Wild Ass of the Ozarks*, Appendix B, 266.

8. Arsenault, *Wild Ass of the Ozarks*, Table 14, 150; Kazin, *Populist Persuasion*, 86–96.

9. *Courier-Democrat*, April 18, 1901.

10. Stewart, *Moonshiners and Prohibitionists*, 172.

11. Arsenault, *Wild Ass of the Ozarks*, Appendix B, 260–70.

12. *Arkansas Gazette*, October 5, 1897.

13. Kirkpatrick, "Washington County."

14. Arsenault, *Wild Ass of the Ozarks*, Appendix B, 260–70.

15. Orr, "Sharp County"; Sanders-Gray, "Marion County."

16. Hahn, *Roots of Southern Populism*.

17. Thompson, *Spirits of Just Men*, 131.

18. Hogue, *Back Yonder*, 265–66.

19. Ibid., 263.

20. Ibid., 263, 266.

21. Stapleton, *Moonshiners in Arkansas*, Introduction.

22. On government-subsidized developments in eastern Arkansas, see Whayne, *New Plantation South*.

23. Hogue, *Back Yonder*, 264.

24. Thompson, *Spirits of Just Men*, xxvii.

25. Manuscript Census, Winston County, Alabama, 1860; Manuscript Census, Shoal Creek Township, Cherokee County, North Carolina, 1870; Manuscript Census, Archey Valley Township, Van Buren County, Arkansas, 1880; "Legend of Harve Bruce"; Ancestry.com, *Arkansas Confederate Pension Records, 1891–1935*.

26. Manuscript Census, Wheeler Township, Van Buren County, Arkansas, 1860; Risener, "Original Grantee's Land"; *Bruce v. State*, Transcript of Testimony, ser. IV, box 15, folder 684 (1900), ASCBR, 105.

27. Johnston, "Searcy County." On Bruce's Little Rock and Oklahoma connections, see *Bruce v. State*, Transcript of Testimony, 71, 133. Turner Skidmore testified that he and Bruce had first begun operating their still about twelve months before federal

marshals confronted them in the summer of 1897 (p. 61). Longtime friend, Mr. Sutton, who had grown up with Bruce back east and now resided in the area and went to church with him, testified in court that Bruce's reputation was "very good up to the time he started making wild cat liquor" (pp. 88–89).

28. Blakley, "John Thomas Burris"; Manuscript Census, Griffin Township, Pope County, Arkansas, 1880.

29. Stapleton, *Moonshiners in Arkansas*, Introduction, 5.

30. *Russellville Democrat*, August 26, 1897.

31. *Bruce v. State*, Transcript of Testimony, 47–50.

32. Ibid., 126–27; Stapleton, *Moonshiners in Arkansas*, 1.

33. *Bruce v. State*, Transcript of Testimony, 127; *Arkansas Gazette*, September 7, 1897.

34. *Bruce v. State*, Transcript of Testimony, 127–28; Stapleton, *Moonshiners in Arkansas*, 2; *Arkansas Gazette*, September 7, 1897.

35. *Bruce v. State*, Transcript of Testimony, 126, 140–41; Stapleton, *Moonshiners in Arkansas*, 2.

36. "Benjamin Franklin Taylor," 123–24; Manuscript Census, Mountain Township, Searcy County, Arkansas, 1860; Manuscript Census, Calf Creek Township, Searcy County, Arkansas, 1870; Campbell, "Some Early Calf Creek History," 307.

37. *Arkansas Gazette*, January 4, 1880, and January 16, 1880; "Benjamin Franklin Taylor," 124–25.

38. "Benjamin Franklin Taylor," 125; Ancestry.com, *U.S. Civil War Pension Index*; "MM Taylor, et al vs. CT Stone & AJ Stone, his wife," 407; Campbell, "Some Early Calf Creek History"; *Arkansas Gazette*, August 31, 1897, and September 7, 1897; *Marshall Republican*, July 1, 1897.

39. Manuscript Census, Sylamore Township, Stone County, Arkansas, 1880; Hill, *State of Oklahoma*, 299–300.

40. *U.S. v. John F. Tubbs*, 1897, jacket no. 414; and *U.S. v. Lit Dodson*, 1897, jacket no. 289, USDC-WDA.

41. *Bruce v. State*, Transcript of Testimony, 14, 28–29, 36, 42, 47, 107–8.

42. Ibid., 47, 51, 53; *Arkansas Gazette*, September 7, 1897.

43. *Bruce v. State*, Transcript of Testimony, 15, 30.

44. Ibid., 109–10, 117, 130. Bruce maintained throughout his trial that he had no direct interest in this particular still, insisting that it belonged only to Milsap and Church. He explained that he was only visiting his friends while hiding out from the federal officers and that he had gone there to seek medical treatment for a cough from Dr. Church, Alva's father, who lived nearby. Milsap and Church supported his claim, though some witnesses testified that they knew Bruce, Milsap, and Church to be partners in the liquor business. The prosecution suggested that Bruce, Milsap, and Church had conspired to cover up Bruce's involvement in the distillery while serving time together in federal prison at Fort Leavenworth before the murder trial began, probably because Bruce was already wanted on other charges and had agreed to take the rap for all the shooting. Indeed, one might speculate that since Bruce and Skid-

more had shut down their own distillery when Burris and the feds discovered their operation during the preceding weeks, they may well have formed a partnership and consolidated their markets with their longtime friends who remained hidden from authorities and continued to do business. See pages 107, 117, 128–29, 143, 154–55.

45. Ibid., 64, 68, 75, 82–83, 85–87, 90–92.

46. Ibid., 34, 37–38, 118, 131–32. A transcript of Bruce's testimony was also printed in the *Courier-Democrat*, November 23, 1899.

47. *Bruce v. State*, Transcript of Testimony, 64, 66, 68; *Arkansas Gazette*, September 7, 1897, and September 1, 1897. Some observers erroneously assumed at first that another local moonshiner, Ki Marcum, was responsible for killing Taylor and Dodson.

48. *Bruce v. State*, Transcript of Testimony, 132–33.

49. Ibid., 141.

50. Ibid., 102–3,

51. Ibid., 110–12; *Mountain Wave*, November 26, 1897; *Annual Report of the Attorney General of the United States, 1899*, 290.

52. *Arkansas Gazette*, September 3, 1897.

53. *Arkansas Gazette*, September 5, 1897.

54. *Mountain Wave*, September 24, 1897.

55. *New York Times*, September 18, 1897, December 7, 1897, and December 18, 1897.

56. Stapleton, *Moonshiners in Arkansas*, 4.

57. *Mountain Wave*, September 24, 1897.

58. *Arkansas Gazette*, October 7, 1897.

59. *Russellville Democrat*, October 21, 1897.

60. *New York Times*, October 30, 1898.

61. *Russellville Democrat*, November 4, 1897. For other noteworthy raids in the area and elsewhere in the Arkansas uplands, see *Russellville Democrat*, October 21, 1897; *Arkansas Gazette*, October 10, 1897; and Stapleton, *Moonshiners in Arkansas*, 5–28.

62. *Russellville Democrat*, September 16, 1897.

63. *Arkansas Gazette*, October 2, 1897.

64. *Mountain Wave*, November 26, 1897.

65. Stapleton, *Moonshiners in Arkansas*, 36–37.

66. Remmel to Wilson, April 19, 1899, Remmel Papers, series 1, box 1, folder 3.

67. *Courier-Democrat*, October 7, 1898; *Mountain Wave*, October 7, 1898; *Bruce v. State*, Transcript of Testimony, 138.

68. *Courier-Democrat*, March 30, 1899; *Annual Report of the Attorney General, 1899*, 290–91.

69. *Courier-Democrat*, November 23, 1899, and November 16, 1899; Arsenault, "Jeff Davis (1862–1913)"; Arsenault, *Wild Ass of the Ozarks*, 70.

70. *Courier-Democrat*, November 23, 1899; *Mountain Wave*, November 18, 1899; quotation from *Arkansas Gazette* in *Courier-Democrat*, November 23, 1899.

71. *Arkansas Gazette*, October 2, 1897; *Courier-Democrat*, November 23, 1899; *Bruce v. State*, Transcript of Testimony, 132.

72. *Courier-Democrat*, November 23, 1899.

73. *Courier-Democrat*, November 30, 1899.

74. *Bruce v. State*, Opinion of the Supreme Court of Arkansas, June 23, 1900, 68 Ark. 310; *Conway Democrat*, August 17, 1900; Vance, "A Karl Marx for Hill Billies," 180–90; Davis quoted in Arsenault, *Wild Ass of the Ozarks*, 192.

75. *Conway Democrat*, August 17, 1900.

76. Ibid.; Stapleton, *Moonshiners in Arkansas*, 4; "Legend of Harve Bruce."

77. Quotations in Kazin, *Godly Hero*, 306 and 46, respectively.

78. Draft registration for Grover Cleveland Bruce in Ancestry.com, *World War I Draft Registration Cards*; quotations in Kazin, *Godly Hero*, 149, 56, and 20, respectively.

79. Henningson, "Upland Farmers and Agrarian Protest," 81, 100.

80. Arsenault, *Wild Ass of the Ozarks*, 148, 154.

81. Ibid., 158–62.

82. *Courier-Democrat*, November 23, 1899; Davis quoted in Arsenault, *Wild Ass of the Ozarks*, 167.

83. "Captain Benjamin Franklin Taylor."

84. *Daily Courier-Democrat*, October 17, 1982; "Legend of Harve Bruce."

85. Brown, "The Moonshiner Who Got Away with Murder."

86. Bruce, "Legend of Harve Bruce." Shane Bruce also posted the 1982 *Daily Courier-Democrat* article on his blog. Robert A. Heinlein (1907–1988) was an American science fiction writer from Butler, Missouri, whose stories emphasized themes of individualism, self-reliance, and nonconformity. H. L. Mencken (1880–1956) was an influential journalist and social critic from Baltimore who radically championed individual freedom against oppressive governments. Ironically, some of his best-known publications harpooned rural populists, especially in the South, and referred to Arkansas as the "apex of moronia," prompting the state legislature to pass a resolution in 1931 to pray for the atheist Mencken's soul. On Mencken and the South, see Hobson, *Serpent in Eden*.

87. Sanders, *Roots of Reform*, 7–8; Seagraves, "Arkansas Politics, 1874–1918," 408, 411.

CHAPTER 3. "SILK-HATTED FELLERS" AND THEIR WAR

1. Wagy, "Little Sam Faubus," 263–76.

2. Webb, *Born Fighting*, 253–56.

3. Wagy, "Little Sam Faubus," 276.

4. Keith, *Rich Man's War*, 4; Senn, "'Molders of Thought,'" 280–90.

5. Lawson, *Commonwealth of Hope*.

6. Webb, *Born Fighting*; Tindall, *Emergence of the New South*, 48; Keith, *Rich Man's War*, 6; Bissett, *Agrarian Socialism in America*, 4, 8.

7. Keith, *Rich Man's War*, 9–10, 60.

8. Ibid., 9–10, 60, 116.

9. Tindall, *Emergence of the New South*, 40–44; Smith, "Tom Watson," 293–326.

10. Niswonger, "James Paul Clarke," 105–6; Arsenault, "Jeff Davis, 1901–1907," 130; Dougan, *Arkansas Odyssey*, 376; Niswonger, "William F. Kirby," 252–63. Kirby, however, also supported the use of dragnets to apprehend urban draft evaders in New York City. Sealander, "Draft Evasion," 37–38n6.

11. *Mountain Wave*, April 8, 1898.

12. *Mountain Wave*, November 4, 1899.

13. Kazin, *Godly Hero*, 254–55; Keith, *Country People*, 161.

14. Willis, "Cleburne County Draft War," 25n3. The national average of deserters and delinquents was 12.24 percent of total inductees.

15. Keith, *Rich Man's War*, 135–61; Keith, *Country People*, 143–69.

16. *Fayetteville Democrat*, May 30, 1918.

17. Ibid., May 30, 1918.

18. Ibid., June 27, 1918.

19. Ibid., August 22, 1918.

20. Ibid., September 19, 1918.

21. Adams, "Polk County Rebellion"; Sealander, "Draft Evasion," 41; *Fayetteville Democrat*, August 22, 1918. On the Green Corn Rebellion, see Green, *Grass-Roots Socialism*, 359–66; and Bissett, *Agrarian Socialism in America*, 149–55.

22. *Mountain Wave*, November 9, 1917, February 8, 1918, March 8, 1918, April 12, 1918, and July 26, 1918.

23. *Leslie News*, June 22, 1917.

24. Walser, "In re—Leslie News, Leslie, Arkansas. Disloyal Newspaper," report no. 71793, October 24, 1917, U.S. Bureau of Investigation Case File Archives, www.fold3.com/image/#975423.

25. *Arkansas Gazette*, June 6, 1918; *Mountain Wave*, June 7, 1918, and August 9, 1918.

26. Quoted in Deatherage, "World War I Draft Evasion," 9.

27. Manuscript Census, District 10, Lewis County, Tennessee, 1850; District 3, Lewis County, Tennessee, 1860; Big Flat Township, Searcy County, Arkansas, 1870; Locust Grove Township, Stone County, Arkansas, 1880.

28. Manuscript Census, Campbell Township, Searcy County, Arkansas, 1900; Campbell Township, Searcy County, Arkansas, 1910; Personal Assessment Records, 1911 and 1919, Searcy County Courthouse.

29. For a more thorough discussion of the war's impact on the farm economy in the Ozarks, particularly on cattle farming, see chapter 4.

30. Warren, *Yellar Rag Boys*, 1–19; Johnston, "Arkansas' 1861 Peace Society," 13–29; Worley, "The Arkansas Peace Society of 1861," 445–456; Worley, "Documents," 82–111.

31. Personal Assessment Records, 1892 and 1911, Searcy County Courthouse; Manuscript Census, Campbell Township, Searcy County, Arkansas, 1910.

32. Pat Halstead interview; Keith, *Rich Man's War*, 76–83.

33. Bissett, *Agrarian Socialism in America*, 85–104.

34. Hardy Adkisson, Charley Bliss Adkisson, and Leo Martin draft cards, Ancestry. com, *World War I Draft Registration Cards*.

35. Willis, "Cleburne County Draft War," 24–39; Keith, *Rich Man's War*, 189–90; *Arkansas Gazette*, July 8–21, 1918. The *New York Times* (July 8, 1918) erroneously reported the number of fatalities and that Adkisson and his son were killed.

36. Russell, *Finished Mystery*, 51.

37. Beckford, *Trumpet of Prophecy*, 1–20; Holden, *Jehovah's Witnesses*, 7–19; Abrahams, "Charles Taze Russell," 57–70. Russellites began calling themselves "Jehovah's Witnesses" in the 1930s.

38. Abrahams, "Charles Taze Russell," 59–64. According to Abrahams, Russell supported the nationalization of railroads, "the remonetization of silver, the single tax, the imposition of an inheritance tax, and general land reform," among other Populist measures, as well as some socialist ideas. Nevertheless, he always made clear that these could only be temporary solutions, since he believed "the union among money, politics, and religion . . . was too great for the poor and powerless to break." "The only real hope for deliverance, the Jehovah's Witnesses were told, lay in the millennium."

39. *Arkansas Gazette*, July 20, 1918; Manuscript Census, Benton Township, Conway County, Arkansas, 1850; Slave Schedules, Benton Township, Conway County, Arkansas, 1850; Manuscript Census, Muddy Bayou Township, Conway County, Arkansas, 1860; Slave Schedules, Muddy Bayou Township, Conway County, Arkansas, 1860; Manuscript Census, Muddy Bayou Township, Conway County, Arkansas, 1870; Piney Township, Van Buren County, Arkansas, 1880. Sampson Adkisson and his family's rising prosperity during the 1850s was typical of other families in the Arkansas River Valley. Duncan, "'One negro, Sarah,'" 326–27.

40. Ancestry.com, *Arkansas, County Marriages Index, 1837–1957*.

41. This, of course, is not intended to reduce religious faith purely to economic determination. Recent religious historians and sociologists have done important work to refute such simplistic explanations. Deborah McCauley, for instance, maintains that a more nuanced "status power"—"the power of self-definition, or control over the means for creating a distinct style of life"—was far more central to mountaineers' dissenting religious culture than simple economic poverty (*Appalachian Mountain Religion*, 206). After all, the Adkissons, at least by the standards of the local community, were relatively better off than most of their closest neighbors. Still, they faced uncertainty about their future, and Russell's spiritual teachings may have given them a sense of control and security. Sociologist Andrew Holden notes that conversion to millenarian beliefs "can be seen as a retreat to the certainties of fundamentalism by a people who are threatened by the loss of a stable sense of self" (*Jehovah's Witnesses*, 40).

42. *Adkisson v. State*, transcript no. 2398, p. 226, ASCBR.

43. Manuscript Census, Mount Vernon Township, Faulkner County, Arkansas, 1900; Piney Township, Cleburne County, Arkansas, 1900; *Adkisson v. Arkansas*, transcript, 40; Berry, "Cleburne County"; Handley, "Settlement across Northern Arkansas," 280–81; Lewis, "Railroads," 297–316.

44. Manuscript Census, Township, Cleburne County, Arkansas, 1910; Personal Property Assessments, 1915, 1917, and 1918, Cleburne County Courthouse; *Adkisson v. Arkansas*, transcript, 222.

45. Personal Property Assessments, 1918, Cleburne County Courthouse; Leo Martin draft card; *Adkisson v. Arkansas*, transcript, 138, 214, 224–25.

46. Personal Property Assessments Book, 1918, Cleburne County Courthouse. Sweeten resided in neighboring Cadron Township.

47. Beckford, *Trumpet of Prophecy*, 9; *Adkisson v. Arkansas*, transcript, 158–70.

48. *Adkisson v. Arkansas*, transcript, 154–73, 216; Circuit Court Docket, Book 4 and Book 5, Cleburne County Courthouse.

49. Blevins, *Arkansas/Arkansaw*, 73.

50. *New York Times*, September 6, 1897.

51. *New York Times*, January 21, 1923.

52. Keith, *Country People in the New South*, 152.

53. Manuscript Census, City of Heber Springs, Cleburne County, Arkansas, 1910; Circuit Court Docket, book 5, Cleburne County Courthouse; Personal Property Assessments, 1918, Cleburne County Courthouse; Frauenthal, "Max Frauenthal (1836–1914)."

54. Jeanette Keith finds that many Southern elites demanded federal intervention when faced with local draft resistance. She asks: "Were white southerners loyal to states' rights and white supremacy as a matter of principle, or expediency? Were states' rights and white supremacy things that mattered intrinsically to white southerners, or merely slogans used to cloak the things that really mattered? When war mobilization presented southern white elites with the necessity of deciding whether to stand by states' rights and white supremacy, or to further other interests, what did they choose?" Keith, *Rich Man's War*, 8.

55. *Arkansas Gazette*, July 10, 1918, July 11, 1918, July 13, 1918, and July 20, 1918; Willis, "Cleburne County Draft War," 32–34.

56. Willis, "Cleburne County Draft War," 31–32; *Arkansas Gazette*, July 9, 1918.

57. *Arkansas Gazette*, July 9–12, 1918; Willis, "Cleburne County Draft War," 30, 34–35n41.

58. *Arkansas Gazette*, July 13, 1918.

59. *Arkansas Gazette*, July 13–17, 1918; Willis, "Cleburne County Draft War," 36–37.

60. *Arkansas Gazette*, July 14, 1918.

61. Ibid.; Willis, "Cleburne County Draft War," 39.

62. *Arkansas Gazette*, August 21, 1918; *State v. Matt Simmons, Jess Blakey, Columbus Blakey, and James Blakey*, case no. 269; *State v. Leo Martin, Jno Penrod, and Thos. Adkisson*, case no. 271; *State v. Bliss Adkisson, et al.*, case no. 272; *State v. Tom Adkisson, Bliss Adkisson, and Hardy Adkisson*, case no. 273, Spring 1919; *State v. Hardy Adkisson*, case no. 379, fall 1920, Cleburne Circuit Court, Cleburne County Courthouse; *Adkisson v. State*, 142 Ark. 15, January 26, 1920; *New York Times*, September 19, 1921; *Laurel (Mississippi) Daily Leader*, June 22, 1921.

63. *Kansas City Star*, February 19, 1919; *Arkansas Gazette*, September 25, 1918; Arthur Keeton draft card, Ancestry.com, *World War I Draft Registration Cards*.

64. *Kansas City Star*, February 19, 1919.

65. Ibid.; Manuscript Census, District 18, Rutherford County, Tennessee1870 and 1880; Grant Township, Newton County, Arkansas, 1900.

66. *Kansas City Star*, February 19, 1919; *Arkansas Gazette*, September 25, 1918.

67. *Kansas City Star*, February 19, 1919; "Uncle Sam's Little War in the Arkansas Ozarks," *Literary Digest*, March 8, 1919, 107–11. The *Literary Digest* article was essentially a reprint of the *Kansas City Star* article.

68. On Kansas City newspapers' sensational coverage of the bizarre Connie Franklin murder story in Stone County, Arkansas, in 1929 and their "irresponsible treatment of a place and people" through "stereotypes and preconceived notions," see Blevins, "Arkansas Ghost Trial," 254–71; and Blevins, *Ghost of the Ozarks*, 2, 9, 28–29, 37, 38, 156, 157, 160, 232n12.

69. *Kansas City Star*, February 19, 1919.

70. Manuscript Census, Van Buren Township, Newton County, Arkansas, 1850; Mill Creek Township, Newton County, Arkansas, 1860, 1870, and 1880; Grant Township, Newton County, Arkansas, 1910, 1920, and 1930; Elijah Harp service record, Ancestry. com, *American Civil War Regiments*; James Wesley Harp draft card, Ancestry.com, *World War I Draft Registration Cards*. The 1930 census listed twenty-seven-year-old Garret Harp as "son inv [invalid]."

71. *Kansas City Star*, February 19, 1919; Tina Farmer interview.

72. Manuscript Census, unlisted township, Marion County, Arkansas, 1850; Washington Township, Boone County, Arkansas, 1860 and 1870; Blythe Township, Boone County, Arkansas, 1880; Richland Township, Newton County, Arkansas, 1900; Crittenden and Hubert townships, Cherokee County, Oklahoma, 1910; Bryan Township, Boone County, Arkansas, and Plumblee Township, Newton County, Arkansas, 1920; John A. Slape Pension Records, Ancestry.com, *Arkansas, Confederate Pension Records*; G. W. and Mary A. Slape Record of Marriage, July 19, 1877, Ancestry.com, *Arkansas County Marriages Index, 1837–1957*; *Kansas City Star*, February 19, 1919.

73. *State v. Paul Curtis, et al.*, 1922, transcript, Independence County Courthouse; transcription of original by Susan Mosier (in author's possession), 40. Hereinafter cited as *State v. Curtis*, Mosier transcription.

CHAPTER 4. THE DAMN GOVERNMENT'S TICK TROUBLE

1. Personal Assessment and Tax Book, 1921, Independence County Courthouse; Manuscript Census, Greenbrier Township, Independence County, Arkansas, 1920; Eddleman, "Who Killed Grandpa Charley?" 2; Haygood, "Cows, Ticks, and Disease," 551–64; Strom, *Making Catfish Bait*, 7–19.

2. *Arkansas Democrat*, March 21, 1922, and March 22, 1922; "Tick Inspector Is Shot from Ambush," *Arkansas Gazette*, March 21, 1922; *Newport Weekly Independent*, March 24, 1922; *Arkansas Gazette*, March 22, 1922; Eddleman, "Who Killed Grandpa Charley?" 2, 4; *State v. Curtis*, Mosier transcription, 4–6.

3. Strom, *Making Catfish Bait*, 5.

4. Ibid., 3, 4, 106; Strom, "Texas Fever," 49–74; Dougan, *Arkansas Odyssey*, 389; Eddleman, "Who Killed Grandpa Charley?" 2.

5. Weise, *Grasping at Independence*, 10.

6. Another murder occurred in Echols County, Georgia, in February 1923. Strom, *Making Catfish Bait*, 1, 67, 72–74, 95, 178; Strom, "Editorials and Explosions," 197–214.

7. Strom, *Making Catfish Bait*, 2; Dinwiddie and Lenton, "Notes on the Cattle Tick," 212 14.

8. Strom, *Making Catfish Bait*, 2, 5, 24; Dinwiddie and Lenton, "Notes on the Cattle Tick," 214.

9. Strom, *Making Catfish Bait*, 2–3, 39, 48.

10. Dinwiddie and Lenton, "Notes on the Cattle Tick," 199.

11. Blevins, *Hill Folks*, 96.

12. Vincenheller, "Cattle Tick Eradication"; Hope, *Dip That Tick*, 10.

13. Blevins, *Hill Folks*, 95; Hope, *Dip That Tick*, 10; Strom, *Making Catfish Bait*, 2–3.

14. Link, *The Paradox of Southern Progressivism*; Keith, *Country People in the New South*; Strom, *Making Catfish Bait*.

15. Postel, *Populist Vision*; Sanders, *Roots of Reform*.

16. Blevins, *Hill Folks*, 43.

17. *Fayetteville Democrat*, August 10, 1916.

18. *Arkansas Gazette*, July 20, 1918.

19. Blevins, *Hill Folks*, 95; Blevins, *Cattle in the Cotton Fields*, 63; Strom, *Making Catfish Bait*, 67–68.

20. Dinwiddie and Lenton, "Notes on the Cattle Tick," 211. Dipping opponents in Alabama were at times referred to as "seconds" by eradication supporters, reflecting "their lower-class status in the community." Blevins, *Cattle in the Cotton Fields*, 62.

21. Strom, *Making Catfish Bait*, 39–40, 56, 62; Hope, *Dip That Tick*, 13.

22. Dinwiddie and Lenton, "Notes on the Cattle Tick," 213–14.

23. On drovers in Alabama, see Blevins, *Cattle in the Cotton Fields*, 46.

24. Wolf, *Life in the Leatherwoods*, 33.

25. *Mountain Echo*, June 2, 1921.

26. Dinwiddie and Lenton, "Notes on the Cattle Tick," 214.

27. USDA, "Prices Received," 38.

28. USDA, *Yearbook, 1921*, 44, 691.

29. *Newark Journal*, September 22, 1911; *Batesville Guard*, March 29, 1912; Mosier, "1922 'Tick War,'" 4–5.

30. Vincenheller, "Cattle Tick Eradication," 23–24.

31. On opposition to stock laws, see Hahn, *Roots of Southern Populism*, 58–63, 239–68.

32. Strom, *Making Catfish Bait*, 93; *Davis v. State*, 126 Ark. 260, Supreme Court of Arkansas, November 13, 1916; *Cazort v. State*, 130 Ark. 453, Supreme Court of Arkansas, October 1, 1917.

33. Fite, *Cotton Fields No More*, 94–96; Shideler, *Farm Crisis*, 10–19; Strom, *Making Catfish Bait*, 129.

34. USDA, "Prices Received," 38.

35. *Batesville Guard*, November 8, 1916.

36. Shideler, *Farm Crisis*, 37.

37. USDA, "Prices Received," 38.

38. Fite, *Cotton Fields No More*, 102–3.

39. Strom relegates the postwar agricultural crisis's part in the escalation of violence to a passing sentence. She instead emphasizes that "in a nation as violent as the United States, the federal determination to implement eradication combined with yeoman intransigence almost inevitably led to escalation." Strom, *Making Catfish Bait*, 178.

40. Mosier, "1922 'Tick War,'" 6–7; "Tick Eradication Laws," 11.

41. USDA, "Prices Received," 38.

42. Mosier, "1922 'Tick War,'" 7; *State v. Curtis*, Mosier transcription, 4, 25.

43. *Arkansas Democrat*, March 22, 1922; *Arkansas Gazette*, March 24, 1922.

44. Dougan, *Arkansas Odyssey*, 378; Strom, *Making Catfish Bait*, 90; *Arkansas Democrat*, March 22, 1922.

45. Manuscript Census, Otter Creek Township, Kiowa County, Oklahoma, 1910; Bissett, "Socialist Party."

46. Kiser, "Socialist Party in Arkansas," 140; Bissett, *Agrarian Socialism in America*, 108, 142, 145.

47. *Batesville Guard*, November 10, 1920.

48. *State v. Curtis*, Mosier transcription, 6ff.

49. *Arkansas Democrat*, March 22, 1922; *State v. Paul Curtis*, case nos. 952 and 953, 1915, and *State v. Paul Curtis*, nos. 431 and 432, 1916, Circuit Court Record Book G, Independence County Courthouse; *State v. Curtis*, Mosier transcription, 1–2, 55–58.

50. *Arkansas Democrat*, March 26, 1922; *Arkansas Gazette*, March 26, 1922; *State v. Curtis*, Mosier transcription, 6ff.

51. *State v. Curtis*, Mosier transcription, 20, 25–26, 29, 32–33, 36, 39.

52. Eddleman, "Who Killed Grandpa Charley?" 13.

53. *Arkansas Gazette*, March 26, 1922.

54. *Newark Journal*, April 20, 1922; Circuit Court Record Book H, Independence County Courthouse; Mosier, "1922 'Tick War,'" 20–21.

55. Susan Mosier interview; Mildred Thomas interview; Brian Jeffery interview; Eddleman, "Who Killed Grandpa Charley?" 19.

56. *Arkansas Democrat*, March 23, 1922; *Arkansas Gazette*, March 28, 1922.

57. Strom, *Making Catfish Bait*, 177; *Arkansas Democrat*, April 3, 1922; *Arkansas Gazette*, April 5, 1922, and April 9, 1922. Dave Wyatt had a personal property tax valuation of $2,430 in 1921. Compare this with the $720 assessment of W. F. Grady, the local merchant and most prosperous resident of Relief Township, the township where the murder suspects resided. Personal Assessment and Tax Book, 1921, Independence County Courthouse.

58. *Arkansas Gazette*, April 12, 1922; *Newark Journal*, April 13, 1922; *Newport Independent Weekly*, April 28, 1922.

59. *Arkansas Democrat*, April 2, 1922.

60. Paul Curtis draft card, Ancestry.com, *World War I Draft Registration Cards*; *State v. Curtis*, Mosier transcription, 40.

61. Strom, *Making Catfish Bait*, 43–44.

62. Waller, *Feud*, 58, 39.

63. *State v. Curtis*, Mosier transcription, 25; Manuscript Census, Relief Township, Independence County, Arkansas, 1920; Personal Assessment and Tax Book, 1921, Independence County Courthouse.

64. Personal Assessment and Tax Book, 1917, 1918, 1919, Independence County Courthouse.

65. Ibid., 1920, 1921.

66. *State v. Curtis*, Mosier transcription, 25–26; *Newark Journal*, April 20, 1922. Lambert seemed keenly aware of the broader controversy over tick eradication. Having corresponded with both Jeffrey and his superior, he had likely heard the standard line from officials that dipping would prove beneficial to cattlemen in the end. All testimony said that he not only called the meeting and held it at his barn, but also that he gave a speech (although no one "could remember" what he said) and joined those "opposed to dipping" who were called to congregate together. Lambert claimed that he did this only because he wanted to file an injunction to suspend dipping because he "fear[ed]" the dipping opponents but said he was "pretty close friends" with fellow suspect James McGee, an openly ardent opponent of dipping who helped him call the meeting.

67. Personal Assessment and Tax Book, 1917, 1918, 1919, Independence County Courthouse; *State v. Curtis*, Mosier transcription, 38–40, 47.

68. Personal Assessment and Tax Book, 1920, 1921, Independence County Courthouse.

69. Ibid., 1917, 1918, 1919, 1920, 1921.

70. Ibid. Census records list Hembry as a farm laborer in 1910 and a general farmer in 1920. Manuscript Census, Relief Township, Independence County, Arkansas, 1910, 1920.

71. Personal Assessment and Tax Book, 1917, 1918, 1919, 1920, 1921, Independence County Courthouse.

72. *State v. Curtis*, Mosier transcription, 21–25, 28.

73. Personal Assessment and Tax Book, 1917, 1918, 1919, 1920, 1921, Independence County Courthouse.

74. Ibid.; Jeffery interview. Jeffrey resided in nearby Greenbrier Township. Manuscript Census, Greenbrier Township, Independence County, Arkansas, 1920.

75. *Arkansas Democrat*, April 2, 1922.

76. *Melbourne Times*, April 20, 1923.

77. Waller, *Feud*; Blevins, "Arkansas Ghost Trial," 251.

78. *State of Arkansas v. George Schroggins*, case no. 331, 1915, Circuit Court, Independence County Courthouse.

79. Waller, *Feud*, 42–52, 73–76.

80. On game and fish laws, Sutton, *Arkansas Wildlife*, 61–66. On liquor-law enforcement, the *Arkansas Gazette* reported on April 18, 1922, that sixty of seventy-six grand jury indictments in Independence County involved prohibition laws.

81. USDA, "Prices Received," 38. Ancestry.com combines neighboring Liberty Township with Relief in the 1920 census in its database, but the two townships together experienced a 20 percent population loss between 1920 and 1930.

82. Kirby, *Rural Worlds Lost*, 309–33.

83. Manuscript Census, Relief Township, Independence County, Arkansas, 1930.

84. Ibid.

85. Ibid., 1920, 1930. The Hollands lived in White County in 1930. Manuscript Census, Harrison Township, White County, Arkansas, 1930.

86. Blevins, "Strike and the Still," 405–25.

87. Dougan, *Arkansas Odyssey*, 388–408.

88. Kazin, *Populist Persuasion*, 106.

CHAPTER 5. BRING ON THE DAM PROGRESS

1. Truman quoted in South Shore Foundation, "Pictorial History."

2. Woodrell, "How Much of the Ozarks Is in Me?" 4.

3. *Mountain Wave*, September 21, 1934.

4. Johnson, "'All Thoughtful Citizens'"; In Johnson, *Arkansas in Modern America*, Johnson explains that "owing to an extraordinarily high personal exemption in the income tax schedule, the only individuals subject to taxation were those earning the equivalent of 500 percent of the Arkansas per capita income" (9).

5. Reprinted in *Mountain Wave*, September 23, 1932.

6. *Mountain Wave*, April 26, 1935. Throughout the next several pages, I cite a disproportionate number of opinions expressed in Searcy County's *Mountain Wave*, though its political positions generally represented those of most other newspapers in the region. The *Wave*, though it tended to support the Democratic Party during the 1930s, may represent popular opinions in the Ozarks especially well, because that Searcy County remained one of the few competitive two-party areas in Arkansas. Sympathetic to Democrats but struggling financially amid the Depression, the paper may have made special efforts to appeal to rural readers across party lines.

7. *Mountain Wave*, November 18, 1932, February 9, 1934, and June 9, 1933; J. H. Whithen to Gov. Parnell, February 10, 1931, Parnell Papers; Malone, *Hattie and Huey*.

8. *Mountain Echo*, August 28, 1930, quoted in Blevins, *Hill Folks*, 110; Johnson, *Arkansas in Modern America*, 9–11.

9. Blevins, *Hill Folks*, 110.

10. Wagy, "Little Sam Faubus," 280–81.

11. *Mountain Wave*, December 29, 1933, and January 5, 1934.

12. *Mountain Wave*, August 25, 1933 and November 16, 1934.

13. *Mountain Wave*, February 23, 1934 and June 22, 1934.

14. *Mountain Wave*, January 19, 1934.

15. *Mountain Wave*, October 5, 1934 and March 23, 1934.

16. *Mountain Wave*, December 8, 1933.

17. Lawson, *Commonwealth of Hope*, 3, 6.

18. *Mountain Wave*, March 2, 1934;

19. Daniel, *Breaking the Land*; Blevins, *Hill Folks*, 112–14.

20. Mountain Wave, October 13, 1933. Interestingly, many white tenant farmers who settled in the Missouri Bootheel and eastern Arkansas after the turn of the twentieth century migrated from the Ozarks because "the process of corporate consolidation and monopoly power . . . had wrecked the lives of these migrants in the hills." Dispossessed farmers (white and black) in these Delta areas formed the Southern Tenant Farmers' Union and put up the most notable resistance in America against big agriculture and its supporting government programs during the 1930s. Roll, *Spirit of Rebellion*, 18.

21. *Mountain Wave*, December 22, 1933.

22. Wallace, quoted in Thompson, *Spirits of Just Men*, 139, 141.

23. Roberts, "Client Failures," 370–71.

24. *Kansas City Star*, December 30, 1942.

25. Blevins, *Hill Folks*, 112.

26. *U.S. v. J. N. Pangle and N. E. Pangle*, Civil Action no. 20, April 1940; and *U.S. v. Floyd Pumphrey and Argie Pumphrey*, Civil Action no. 60, October 1941, DCUS-Harrison.

27. Roberts, "Client Failures," 371–74, 384–86.

28. Thompson, *Spirits of Just Men*, 144, 25.

29. Ibid., 141–42.

30. Brinkley, *End of Reform*, 265–67.

31. *Mountain Wave*, August 31, 1934.

32. *Mountain Wave*, December 15, 1933.

33. "President Signs a Bill," undated clipping from *Mountain Echo*, Ellis Papers, series 2, box 5, folder 35; "The Ice Is Breaking," June 30, 1939, Bailey Papers, box 18, "Flood Control" folder; "Reservoirs for Arkansas," June 6, 1938, Bailey Papers, box 24, "Flood Control" folder; *Mountain View Herald*, January 20, 1939; Yount, "Clyde Taylor Ellis."

34. "White River Authority Bill No Mean Measure," undated clipping from *Arkansas Democrat*, Ellis Papers, box 4, folder 18; *Herald-Democrat*, January 26, 1939; Shiras, "Norfork Dam," 152; "Statement of Clyde Ellis," July 13, 1941, Ellis Papers, box 5, folder 34.

35. Mrs. C. W. Gray to Ellis, July 11, 1939, Ellis Papers, box 5, folder 31.

36. *Arkansas Gazette*, June 17, 1939; *Daily Echo*, August 19, 1940; "White River Development to Be Urged," unknown clipping, August 30, 1940, Ellis Papers, box 4, folder 19; "Local Citizens Enjoy Visit in Washington," undated clipping from *Mountain Echo*,

Ellis Papers, box 4, folder 17; "Anthology," undated clipping from *Baxter Bulletin*, Ellis Papers, box 4, folder 18; Tom Shiras to Ellis, February 11, 1941, Ellis Papers, box 5, folder 32.

37. "Ediscope," unknown and undated clipping, Ellis Papers, box 4, folder 19.

38. *Globe-Democrat*, May 11, 1941. On Missouri conservationists' opposition to other dams, see Payton and Payton, *Damming the Osage*, 168–73.

39. Johnson, *Arkansas in Modern America*, 73.

40. Ellis to Arthur T. Brewster, June 16, 1939, Ellis Papers, box 5, folder 31.

41. Shiras, "Norfork Dam," 152.

42. "Statement of Clyde Ellis," July 13, 1941, Ellis Papers, box 5, folder 34.

43. *Baxter Bulletin*, March 8, 1940.

44. *Baxter Bulletin*, July 11, 1941.

45. *Baxter Bulletin*, March 21, 1941; *Mountain Echo*, April 2, 1941.

46. Cecil E. Keiter to Ellis, June 14, 1939, and Marvin Morgan to Ellis, October 26, 1939, Ellis Papers, box 5, folder 31.

47. Ben Dearmore to Ellis, June 13, 1939, and John Q. Adams to Ellis, August 31, 1939, Ellis Papers, box 5, folder 31.

48. S. L. Scott to Ellis, July 25, 1939, Ellis Papers, box 5, folder 31.

49. Ellis to Ralph Rea, October 24, 1939, and Rex Bodenhammer to Ellis, October 26, 1939, Ellis Papers, box 5, folder 31.

50. Ellis to T. F. Kern, February 6, 1941, Ellis Papers, box 5, folder 32.

51. *Baxter Bulletin*, March 26, 1941.

52. Eli W. Collins to Ellis, Ellis Papers, box 5, folder 34.

53. *Harrison Daily*, June 13, 1941.

54. Arkansas *Gazette*, June 22, 1941.

55. *Baxter Bulletin*, August 22, 1941.

56. Ibid. Before the Norfork project, the thirty-nine-year-old Amyx was a construction contractor in Missouri. The thirty-year-old Martin had been a farm laborer in Baxter County. Manuscript Census, City of West Plains, Howell County, Missouri, and Greenwood Township, Baxter County, Arkansas, 1940.

57. Pierce, "Orval Faubus," 99; Pierce, "Labor Movement."

58. Robert R. Blecker to McMath, January 31, 1949, McMath Papers, series I, box I, folder 3.2.

59. Shiras, "Norfork Dam," 155.

60. *Arkansas Democrat*, October 1, 1944.

61. John Zachary to Laney, May 4, 1945 and Laney to John Zachary, May 7, 1945, Laney Papers, box 3, folder 53-1.

62. Mrs. Geo. W. Scott to Faubus, November 9, 1964, Faubus Papers, box 466, folder 12.

63. J. M. Gasset to Ellis, March 31, 1941, Ellis Papers, box 5, folder 32.

64. Ellis to J. M. Gasset, April 5, 1941, Ellis Papers, box 5, folder 32.

65. Ibid.

66. J. M. Gasset to Ellis, February 2, 1942, Ellis Papers, box 5, folder 33. Ellis did run for the U.S. Senate but lost to incumbent John McClellan. After he left Congress in 1943, he became the first general manager of the National Rural Electric Cooperative Association, a newly formed lobbying group that promoted the interests of the New Deal's rural electrification programs. Ellis held this position until he retired in 1967, in the meantime earning a national reputation as "Mr. Rural Electrification." Yount, "Clyde Taylor Ellis."

67. Shiras, "Norfork Dam," 156.

68. G. H. Hand to Ellis, May 22, 1939, and Ellis to G. H. Hand, June 1, 1939, Ellis Papers, box 5, folder 31.

69. H. E. Rand to Ellis, July 13, 1941; T. F. Kern to H. E. Rand, August 13, 1941; H. E. Rand to Ellis, November 5, 1941; J. R. Crume Jr. to H. E. Rand, November 18, 1941, Ellis Papers, box 5, folders 32 and 34.

70. T. F. Kern to Ellis, March 6, 1941, Ellis Papers, box 5, folder 32. As late as November 1942, the Acting District Engineer wrote Ellis to explain that "the original Government survey is greatly in error" and to inform him that the Corps had had to file yet another petition of condemnation in federal court to acquire more needed lands. Maj. G. R. Schneider to Ellis, November 25, 1942, Ellis Papers, box 5, folder 32.

71. R. S. Hensley to Ellis, February 4, 1942, and Ellis to R. S. Hensley, February 9, 1942, Ellis Papers, box 5, folder 33.

72. Geo. L. Bell to Ellis, June 6, 1941, and T. F. Kern to Ellis, June 20, 1941, Ellis Papers, box 5, folder 32.

73. *Baxter Bulletin*, August 28, 1941.

74. *Harrison Daily Times*, October 6, 1940, October 9, 1940, and October 10, 1940.

75. *Harrison Daily Times*, April 3, 1941; *Mountain Echo*, April 2, 1941; Civil Action no. 55, October 1941, DCUS-Harrison.

76. Rex Bodenhammer to Ellis, November 4, 1942, Ellis Papers, box 5, folder 33.

77. Murphy, *Higden*, 2–16.

78. Ibid., 130–31.

79. Ibid., 147–48.

80. Ibid., 1, 148–50.

81. Ibid., 1, 150–51; Kennedy, "Address."

82. Shiras, "Norfork Dam," 157.

83. Doyle Hurst interview.

84. Mulloy, "Mountain Home"; Blevins, *Hill Folks*, 192.

85. Garbacz, "Ozarks," 418–21; Payton and Payton, *Damming the Osage*, 258–59.

86. Blevins, *Hill Folks*, 192.

87. Harlin Pierson interview.

88. Jewell Tilley interview.

89. Doyle Hurst interview.

90. Garbacz, "Ozarks," 421.

91. Payton and Payton, *Damming the Osage*, 300. A major political fight erupted during the 1960s and 1970s between local dam supporters in Searcy and Newton Counties

and a group of conservationists in northwest Arkansas over the Corps' proposal to construct a dam on the Buffalo River. Conservationists, led by Neil Compton and the Ozark Society, won the battle and successfully lobbied the National Park Service to protect the free-flowing stream as a national river, raising the ire of most dam supporters even more, and that of many of local landowners as well. Compton, *Battle for the Buffalo River*; Pitcaithley, *Let the River Be*.

CHAPTER 6. GROWTH POLITICS AND RURAL DISAPPOINTMENT

1. Martha Wagner to McMath, January 29, 1952, McMath Papers, series I, box 2, file 12, folder 3.

2. Lester, "Sidney Sanders McMath," 210–15.

3. McMath to Martha Wagner, February 12, 1952, McMath Papers, series I, box 2, file 12, folder 3.

4. *Wall Street Journal*, November 13, 1965.

5. Hodgson, *America in Our Time*, 12, 18.

6. Quoted in Isserman and Kazin, *America Divided*, 111.

7. Quoted in Thomas, *Appalachian Reawakening*, 126.

8. Thomas, *Appalachian Reawakening*, 127.

9. Blevins, "Wretched and Innocent," 266.

10. Ozarks Regional Commission (ORC), *Ozarks Region*, 1–2. These figures are based on the 125 counties in Arkansas, Missouri, and Oklahoma initially included in the ORC.

11. Nielson, "Comparison," 65. In 1960, 44.4 percent of Ozarks families were deemed low income (less than $3,000 per year), while that figure was 30.7 percent in Appalachia, as defined by the ARC.

12. ORC, *Ozarks Region*, 6.

13. Bonnie Perkins interview.

14. Blevins, *Hill Folks*, 147–78.

15. Hamilton, *Trucking Country*; Moreton, *To Serve God and Wal-Mart*, 12.

16. Brake, "'Commendably Democratic'?"

17. ORC, *Ozarks Region*, 10; *Wall Street Journal*, November 13, 1965.

18. Brake, "'Commendably Democratic'?"

19. Matusow, *Unraveling of America*, 33.

20. Thomas, *Appalachian Reawakening*, 129; Eller, *Uneven Ground*, 57–60; Whisnant, *Modernizing the Mountaineer*, chap. 3.

21. Wilson, *Communities Left Behind*.

22. Thomas, *Appalachian Reawakening*, 130–32; Whisnant, *Modernizing the Mountaineer*, 78–80; Eller, *Uneven Ground*, 60. Historian Bethany Moreton emphasizes the large doses of government-assisted economic redistribution that flowed to the Ozarks during the postwar era to help transform the region into part of the Sun Belt. Her focus on "Wal-Mart Country," however, ignores the profoundly uneven distribution of these resources within the region. Moreton, *To Serve God and Wal-Mart*, 4–5, 24–48.

23. Wilson, *Communities Left Behind*, 111; *New York Times*, July 24, 1961.

24. *New York Times*, July 24, 1961.

25. The AIDC was established in March 1957. Wilson, *Communities Left Behind*, 13.

26. *New York Times*, July 24, 1961.

27. Ibid.; Wilson, *Communities Left Behind*, xvii, 112.

28. Wilson, *Communities Left Behind*, 112.

29. Eller, *Uneven Ground*, 67–75; Whisnant, *Modernizing the Mountaineer*, 128–32.

30. Eller, *Uneven Ground*, 85–86.

31. *Tulsa World*, February 2, 1965.

32. *Human Events*, February 27, 1965.

33. Tower to J. W. Birkhead, May 15, 1964, Hargis Papers, box 64, folder 1; *New York Times*, January 30, 1965 and September 19, 1964.

34. *Tulsa World*, February 2, 1965.

35. Murphy, "Regional Commission System," 180; Nielson, "Comparison," 37–40; Eller, *Uneven Ground*, 177; "Summary Minutes of the Federal Advisory Council on Regional Economic Development," April 3, 1969, GRDC-ES, box 181.

36. *Post-Dispatch*, August 1, 1966.

37. *Post-Dispatch*, September 3, 1966; "Statement of Governor Warren E. Hearnes," Mills Papers, box 431, folder 6.

38. Ozarka Regional Development Association, Board of Directors Meeting Minutes, December 8, 1965; Faubus to Conner, March 4, 1966, both in Mills Papers, box 431, folder 7.

39. Ozarka Regional Development Association, Board of Directors Meeting Minutes.

40. Hurst to Mills, September 7, 1967, Mills Papers, box 431, folder 3.

41. "Ozarks Regional Commission—Economic Facts," n.d., Mills Papers, box 431, folder 1.

42. Dickens to Mills, October 8, 1966, Mills Papers, box 431, folder 5; "Ozarks Regional Commission—Economic Facts."

43. Dickens to Mills, October 8, 1966.

44. Bullock to Mills, June 11, 1965, Mills Papers, box 431, folder 7.

45. "U.S. Disputes Faubus' Thinking on Ozarka," unknown clipping, April 16, 1966, News Clippings: Ozarks Regional Commission, COSR, box 8, folder 28.

46. Johnson quoted in Brands, *Strange Death of American Liberalism*, 97.

47. McCandless to Mills, October 10, 1967, Mills Papers, box 431, folder 3.

48. Rockefeller's political ascendancy was an anomaly amid the rise of the Republican Party in the old Confederacy during the 1960s. Most historians point to whites' resentment of the black civil rights movement as the key to the Republican Party's rise in other southern states, but Rockefeller's "belief in racial equality became well-known" in Arkansas, and he defied a number of the conservative, limited-government principles among many leading voices of the GOP's right wing by calling for higher taxes and government assistance to promote economic growth and public education. The wealthy,

New York-born grandson of John D. Rockefeller had headed the Arkansas Industrial Development Commission during Faubus's administration, and he made economic development the centerpiece of his gubernatorial campaign in 1966. His success at the polls reveals the hope among Arkansas voters in the potential for new economic development to bring widespread prosperity in the state. Dillard, "Winthrop Rockefeller."

49. "Briefing on the Ozarks Regional Planning Commission," Rockefeller Papers, box 92, file 2b.

50. Gordon, "Ozarks Regional Commission," 11.

51. Ibid., 11–12; Nielson, "Comparison," 66.

52. *Congressional Record*, S1776, February 18, 1969. Even considering the Appalachian program's higher population, the ARC received $75.22 to spend per resident in 1973, while each of the other five regional commissions' funding represented only $7.77 per resident. Gordon, "Ozarks Regional Commission," 10–11.

53. Ibid., 63–64; "Hearnes Urges Support for Ozark Region Unit," unknown clipping, December 3, 1970, News Clippings: Ozarks Regional Commission, COSR, box 8, folder 28.

54. *New York Times*, April 8, 1973; Gordon, "The Ozarks Regional Commission and Its Impact in Arkansas," 11–12.

55. Ralph Mecham to Maurice Stans, May 27, 1969, GRDC-ES, box 181.

56. Gordon, "Ozarks Regional Commission," 11–12; *New York Times*, March 12, 1971; *Post-Dispatch*, April 1, 1973, and February 14, 1973; "Ozarks Commission Dropped from Budget," unknown clipping, January 31, 1973, News Clippings: Ozarks Regional Commission, COSR, box 8, folder 28.

57. ORC, *Economic Development Action Plan*, ii; Eller, "Modernization," 214. On the "true geographic Ozarks region," see Rafferty, *Ozarks*, xiv, 2–3, 12–13.

58. Gordon, "Ozarks Regional Commission," 64–65.

59. *New York Times*, March 12, 1971.

60. Eller, *Uneven Ground*, 7.

61. E. A. Emerson to Faubus, November 29, 1965, and E.A. Emerson to Faubus, December 6, 1965, Faubus Papers, box 481, folder 3.

62. ORC, *Ozarks Region*, 7.

63. *Wall Street Journal*, November 13, 1965.

64. Ralph Mecham to Maurice Stans, October 20, 1969; "Minutes of the Secretary's Conference on the Regional Economic Program," June 20–21, 1969, GRDC-ES, box 181.

65. Morley to Faubus, September 7, 1966; "Regional Planning for Economic Development," Rockefeller Papers, box 36, file 1.

66. Eller, *Uneven Ground*, 192–93.

67. Quoted in Schwartz, *In Service to America*, 108.

68. *Ozarks Regional Commission Listing*, 2.

69. Gordon, "Ozarks Regional Commission," 33, 50; Blevins, *Hill Folks*, 213; *Ozarks Regional Commission Listing*, 2–10; Eller, "Modernization," 215.

70. W. R. Braden to Faubus, March 7, 1966, Faubus Papers, series 13, subseries 3, box 481, folder 5.

71. McClellan to Morton, December 2, 1975, RDC-ARCO, box 1.

72. Commerce's EDA was also created by the Public Works and Economic Development Act of 1965 to replace the old Area Redevelopment Administration. Though the EDA and the Title V regional commissions were separate programs, they often worked together closely on development projects.

73. *New York Times*, December 16, 1973; Gordon, "Ozarks Regional Commission," 50; *Ozarks Regional Commission Listing*, 3.

74. Piland, *History of Ozark County*, 30–31; *Ozarks Regional Commission Listing*, 23.

75. Tinnon to Opitz, March 15, 1967, Mills Papers, box 431, folder 5.

76. Meeting minutes, December 23, 1968, GRDC-OFC, box 2.

77. "Summary Minutes of the Federal Advisory Council on Regional Economic Development," April 3, 1969; Meeting minutes, January 7, 1969, GRDC-OFC, box 2.

78. Harley W. Ladd to Iuen, October 2, 1975; Perry to Iuen, February 3, 1981; Al Pollard to Iuen, February 2, 1981, RDC-ARCO, box 2.

79. *Iola Register*, May 4, 1979.

80. "Expensive Vanity," photocopy, RDC-ARCO, box 2.

81. Moreton, *To Serve God and Wal-Mart*, 30–48; Blevins, *Hill Folks*, 213–18.

82. E. L. Stewart Jr. to Robert E. Ruddy, October 12, 1972, RDC-ARCO, box 4.

CHAPTER 7. THE WAR ON POVERTY AND A NEW RIGHT RESISTANCE

1. Desmarais and Jeffords, *Uncertain Harvest*, 52–62.

2. Ibid., 52–55.

3. Ibid., 53–55.

4. Postel, "American Populist and Anti-Populist Legacy."

5. Lo, "Astroturf versus Grass Roots," 98–99.

6. Eller, "Modernization," 209–10.

7. *Arkansas Democrat*, April 8, 1964.

8. Bob Adkisson interview notes, VISTA Collection, series 1, box 1, folder 5; Schwartz, *In Service to America*, 61–64.

9. Eller, "Modernization," 207, 209–10; McKee, "'This Government Is with Us,'" 33; Faubus to Wilbur Mills, May 8, 1964, Faubus Papers, box 482, folder 5.

10. Schwartz, *In Service to America*, 3.

11. Alexander to Faubus, May 11, 1964, Faubus Papers, box 482, folder 5; Schwartz, *In Service to America*, 100.

12. Rock to Faubus, May 26, 1964, Faubus Papers, box 482, folder 5.

13. *Arkansas Newsletter*, May 1964.

14. A. F. Burgess to Orval Faubus, November 28, 1964, and attached *Reader's Digest* articles, Faubus Papers, box 482, folder 6; Katz, *Undeserving Poor*.

15. Schwartz, *In Service to America*, 64–67, 72; Bob Adkisson interview notes.

16. Orleck, "Introduction," 15.

17. Stutchman to "Gov. Laney," n.d. and Faubus to Stutchman, September 3, 1964, Faubus Papers, box 482, folder 6. Stutchman apparently thought she was writing her letter to Ben Laney, the ardent states' rights Arkansas governor who had served from 1945 to 1949 and had joined the southern Dixiecrat revolt, perhaps indicating her strong views on race.

18. Dillard, "Winthrop Rockefeller"; Shriver to Rockefeller, November 8, 1967, Rockefeller Papers, box 322, file 56.

19. Rockefeller to Rochelle Stanfield, October 11, 1967, Rockefeller Papers, box 322, file 56.

20. Orleck, "Introduction," 17.

21. Eller, "Modernization," 213.

22. Rockefeller to Walter Richter, September 29, 1967, Rockefeller Papers, box 322, file 56.

23. Schwartz, *In Service to America*, 197–99; *Arkansas Gazette*, November 29, 1969, and February 5, 1970.

24. Schwartz, *In Service to America*, 161–65; Bobby Morgan interview notes, VISTA Collection, series 1, box 1, folder 1.

25. Charles Johnson interview notes, VISTA Collection, series 1, box 1, folder 6; "WASHCO-EOA—Steve Cummings," November 1968, VISTA Collection, series 1, box 1, folder 6.

26. Schwartz, *In Service to America*, 166–167; Bobby Morgan interview notes.

27. Paul Williams interview notes, VISTA Collection, series 1, box 1, folder 6; Bobby Morgan interview notes.

28. On black population, see Blevins, *Hill Folks*, 212; Schwartz, *In Service to America*, 49.

29. Pierce, "Orval Faubus," 113.

30. Kiffmeyer, "Looking Back," 378–81.

31. Bob Gorman interview notes, VISTA Collection, series 1, box 1, folder 5.

32. Kiffmeyer, "Looking Back," 364–70; O'Conner, *Poverty Knowledge*.

33. Neal Blakely interview notes; Anna Gottlieb interview notes; Carolyn Rose interview notes; Barbara Conard interview notes; Community Resource Center: Jane Spencer interview notes; John Boyle interview notes, VISTA Collection, series 1, box 1, folder 6.

34. Schwartz, *In Service to America*, 464–65.

35. Kiffmeyer, "Looking Back," 373, 381.

36. Schwartz, *In Service to America*, 464.

37. Kiffmeyer, *Reformers to Radicals*, 14.

38. Orleck, "Introduction," 12.

39. Bob Gorman interview notes.

40. Donna Clark interview notes; Fred Morrow interview notes; John Boyle interview notes, VISTA Collection, series 1, box 1, folder 6.

41. Glen L. Jermstad, untitled position paper presented to the Subcommittee on Rural Development of the U.S. House of Representatives, June 26, 1967, Rockefeller Papers, box 322, file 56.

42. Johnson, *Arkansas in Modern America*, 192–93.

43. Community Resource Center: Jane Spencer interview notes.

44. Blevins, *Hill Folks*, 202–3.

45. John Pelkey interview notes, VISTA Collection, series 1, box 1, folder 6; Lewis, *Vista Diary* (n.p., 1969–1970), 2–3, VISTA Collection.

46. Harrell, *Churches of Christ*, 115–75; Dochuk, *From Bible Belt to Sun Belt*, 60–66, 112–14, 128–34, 237, 256, 270–71; Moreton, *To Serve God and Wal-Mart*, 164–68, 171.

47. *Carroll County Tribune*, September 12, 1980.

48. Ibid. Gibson self-published a folk-humor book, *The Magic of Scrub Holler: Ozark Mountain Life*, in 2001.

49. *Eureka Springs Times-Echo*, October 23, 1980. Ironically, Carroll Countians, along with others in parts of northwest Arkansas, had been bitterly divided between pro-Confederate and pro-Union sympathies during the Civil War. Miller, "Carroll County."

50. *Carroll County Tribune*, October 3, 1980.

51. *Carroll County Tribune*, September 12, 1980; *Southwest Times Record*, October 7, 1980; Blair, "William Jefferson Clinton," 264–65.

52. Reagan quoted in Orleck, "Introduction," 7. Of the fifteen primary counties in the Arkansas Ozarks, Reagan won all but two in 1980; Jimmy Carter carried only Izard and Stone Counties. Carter had won all but two counties, Benton and Baxter, in 1976. "1980 Presidential General Election Results—Arkansas" and "1976 Presidential General Election Results—Arkansas," *Dave Liep's Atlas of U.S. Presidential Elections*.

53. Quoted in Sanders, *Roots of Reform*, 131.

CONCLUSION

1. "Ozark Tea Party—Mountain Home, Arkansas," posted at http://www.fairtaxnation.com/profiles/blogs/ozark-tea-party-mountain-home, March 26, 2009; "Dr. Bill Smith," biographical profile, https://www.linkedin.com/in/ozarkguru; "Resume: Dr. Bill Smith (Ozark Guru)," http://agora-assoc.com/smithresume.html.

2. "Ozark Tea Party—Mountain Home, Arkansas"; "Student Begins His Political Career in Mountain Home," December 4, 2010, http://www.arkansas-catholic.org/news/article/2371/Student-begins-his-political-career-in-Mountain-Home; "Mary Ann Caster, Real Estate Agent, Gilbert Realty Co.," http://www.gilbertrealty.com/marylist.htm.

3. "Ozark Tea Party in Mountain Home AR," video posted at http://www.youtube.com/watch?v=9RoOzTSaH6Q; "Karen S. Hopper," http://www.arkansashouse.org/member/232/Karen%20S.-Hopper.

4. "Ozarks Minutemen," http://ozarksminutemen.com.

5. Cook, "Racism in the Tea Party," http://talkbusiness.net; Parker, "Arkansas Racism, Tea-Party Style," https://www.washingtonpost.com/blogs/she-the-people/post/arkansas-racism-tea-party-style/2012/06/15/gJQAHQIfeV_blog.html?utm_term=.c1492785dd86; Brantley, "Tea Party Leader on Racist Joke," http://www.arktimes.com/ArkansasBlog/archives/2012/06/15/tea-party-leader-on-racist-joke-yes-but;

Celock, "Inge Marler, Arkansas Tea Party Leader, Makes Racist Joke at Event," and Celock, "Inge Marler, Arkansas Tea Party Leader, Resigns after Racist Joke," http://www.huffingtonpost.com/2012/06/15/inge-marler-arkansas-tea-party-richard-caster_n_1600376.html.

6. Postel, "American Populist and Anti-Populist Legacy"; Postel, "Tea Party in Historical Perspective"; Nugent, *Tolerant Populists*.

7. Blevins, "Retreating to the Hill," 475–88; Blevins, *Hill Folks*, 193–205.

8. Blevins, "Retreating to the Hill," 476, 480.

9. Phillips, "Hipbillies and Hillbillies," 89–110.

10. Blevins, *Hill Folks*, 204–6.

11. Ibid., 217.

12. For an excellent treatment of the Populist movement in an urban working-class setting, see Pierce, *Striking with the Ballot*.

13. *New York Times*, January 4, 2012.

14. Ibid.; "John Boozman for Senate Campaign News Conference, July 6, 2010," https://www.c-span.org/video/?294383–1/john-boozman-senate-campaign-news-conference.

15. "November 4, 2014, Arkansas General Election and Nonpartisan Runoff Election: Official Results," http://results.enr.clarityelections.com/AR/53237/149792/Web01/en/summary.html.

16. Ibid.; "Tom Cotton Says He Will Vote for Minimum Wage Hike 'As a Citizen,'" September 5, 2014, http://www.huffingtonpost.com/2014/09/05/tom-cotton-minimum-wage_n_5772246.html; "Four States Vote to Raise Minimum Wage," November 5, 2014, https://www.nytimes.com/2014/11/05/upshot/election-results-2014-minimum-wage.html?ref=2014-midterm-elections.

17. Foley, *Front Porch Politics*.

18. Packer, "Populists"; Goldberg, "Sanders and Trump"; Postel, "American Populist and Anti-Populist Legacy." For an excellent comparison and contrast of the original Populism and pundits' loose application of "populism" to candidates in the 2016 presidential race, see Postel, "Trump and Sanders."

BIBLIOGRAPHY

MANUSCRIPT COLLECTIONS

Arkansas History Commission, Little Rock, Arkansas
    Ben Laney Papers
    Carl E. Bailey Papers
    George Washington Hayes Papers
    Harvey Parnell Papers
    Sidney McMath Papers
Cleburne County Courthouse, Heber Springs, Arkansas
    Circuit Court Records
    Personal Property Tax Records
Hendrix College Archives and Special Collections, Conway, Arkansas
    Wilbur Mills Papers
Independence County Courthouse, Batesville, Arkansas
    Circuit Court Records
    Personal Property Tax Records
Missouri State University Special Collections, Springfield, Missouri
    Center for Ozarks Studies Records
National Archives, College Park, Maryland
    General Records of the Department of Commerce (RG 40)
    U.S. Bureau of Investigation Case File Archives (RG 65)
National Archives, Fort Worth, Texas
    U.S. District Court Records (RG 21)

Searcy County Courthouse, Marshall, Arkansas
    Personal Property Tax Records
University of Arkansas at Little Rock Special Collections, Butler Center for Arkansas
    Studies, Little Rock, Arkansas
    Winthrop Rockefeller Papers
University of Arkansas Special Collections, Fayetteville, Arkansas
    Billy James Hargis Papers
    Clyde T. Ellis Papers
    Harmon L. Remmel Papers
    Orval Faubus Papers
    Ozark Institute Records
University of Central Arkansas Archives, Conway, Arkansas
    Arkansas VISTA Collection

GOVERNMENT PUBLICATIONS

Dinwiddie, R. R., and W. Lenton. "Notes on the Cattle Tick and Tick Fever of Cattle."
    Bulletin No. 101. Fayetteville: Arkansas Agricultural Experiment Station, 1908.
Kennedy, John F. "Address by President John F. Kennedy, Dedication of Greer's Ferry
    Dam, Heber Springs, Arkansas, October 3, 1963." Reprinted in the program of the
    Greer's Ferry Dam 50th Anniversary Dedication Ceremony. U.S. Army Corps of
    Engineers. October 3, 2013.
Ozarks Regional Commission. *Ozarks Region: An Opportunity for Growth*. Washington,
    D.C.: Ozarks Regional Commission, 1967.
———. *Ozarks Regional Commission Economic Development Action Plan*. Washington, D.C.:
    Ozarks Regional Commission, 1976.
*Ozarks Regional Commission Listing: Technical Assistance Projects, Demonstration Projects, Supple-
    mental Grant Projects Completed or in Progress, FY 1968-FY 1979*. N.p., N.d. (Available at John
    Vaughan Library, Northeastern Oklahoma State University, Tahlequah, Oklahoma).
"Tick Eradication Laws." *Bulletin No. 160*. Fayetteville: Arkansas Agricultural Experi-
    ment Station, 1919.
U.S. Congress. *Congressional Record*, S1776. February 18, 1969.
U.S. Department of Agriculture. "Prices Received by Farmers for Beef Cattle: United
    States and States Monthly and Annual Average, 1909–59." *Statistical Bulletin No. 265*.
    Washington, D.C.: USDA Agricultural Marketing Service, 1960.
———. *United States Department of Agriculture Yearbook, 1921*. Washington, D.C.: GPO, 1922.
U.S. Department of Interior. Office of the Census. *Seventh Census of the United States,
    1850: Population*. Manuscript Schedules.
———. *Seventh Census of the United States, 1850: Slaves*. Manuscript Schedules.
———. *Eighth Census of the United States, 1860: Population*. Manuscript Schedules.
———. *Eighth Census of the United States, 1860: Slaves*. Manuscript Schedules.
———. *Ninth Census of the United States, 1870: Population*. Manuscript Schedules.
———. *Tenth Census of the United States, 1880: Population*. Manuscript Schedules.

————. *Twelfth Census of the United States, 1900: Population.* Manuscript Schedules.

————. *Thirteenth Census of the United States, 1910: Population.* Manuscript Schedules.

————. *Fourteenth Census of the United States, 1920: Population.* Manuscript Schedules.

————. *Fifteenth Census of the United States, 1930: Population.* Manuscript Schedules.

————. *Sixteenth Census of the United States, 1940: Population.* Manuscript Schedules.

U.S. Department of Justice. *Annual Report of the Attorney General of the United States, 1899.* Washington, D.C.: GPO, 1899.

U.S. Department of War. *Final Report of the Provost Marshall to the Secretary of War on the Operation of the Selective Service to July 15, 1919.* Washington, D.C.: GPO, 1920.

Vincenheller, W. G. "Cattle Tick Eradication in Northwest Arkansas." *Bulletin No. 93.* Fayetteville: Arkansas Agricultural Experiment Station, 1907.

COURT RECORDS

Adkisson v. State. 1920. Arkansas Supreme Court Briefs and Records. UALR/Pulaski County Law Library Special Collections, Little Rock, Arkansas.

Bruce v. State. 1900. Arkansas Supreme Court Briefs and Records. UALR/Pulaski County Law Library Special Collections, Little Rock, Arkansas.

Cazort v. State. 1917. Arkansas Supreme Court Briefs and Records. UALR/Pulaski County Law Library Special Collections, Little Rock, Arkansas.

Davis v. State. 1916. Arkansas Supreme Court Briefs and Records. UALR/Pulaski County Law Library Special Collections, Little Rock, Arkansas.

State v. Bliss Adkisson, et al. 1919. Cleburne County Circuit Court. Cleburne County Courthouse, Heber Springs, Arkansas.

State v. George Schroggins. 1915. Independence County Circuit Court. Independence County Courthouse, Batesville, Arkansas.

State v. Hardy Adkisson. 1920. Cleburne County Circuit Court. Cleburne County Courthouse, Heber Springs, Arkansas.

State v. Leo Martin, Jno Penrod, and Thos. Adkisson. 1919. Cleburne County Circuit Court. Cleburne County Courthouse, Heber Springs, Arkansas.

State v. Matt Simmons, Jess Blakey, Columbus Blakey, and James Blakey. 1919. Cleburne County Circuit Court. Cleburne County Courthouse, Heber Springs, Arkansas.

State v. Paul Curtis. 1915. Independence County Circuit Court. Independence County Courthouse, Batesville, Arkansas.

State v. Paul Curtis. 1916. Independence County Circuit Court. Independence County Courthouse, Batesville, Arkansas.

State v. Paul Curtis, et al. 1922. Preliminary Justice of the Peace Hearing. Independence County Courthouse, Batesville, Arkansas. Transcription of original by Susan Mosier in possession of author.

State v. Tom Adkisson, Bliss Adkisson, and Hardy Adkisson. 1919. Cleburne County Circuit Court. Cleburne County Courthouse, Heber Springs, Arkansas.

U.S. v. Floyd Pumphrey and Argie Pumphrey. 1941. U.S. District Court, Western District of Arkansas, Harrison Division. National Archives at Fort Worth, Texas.

U.S. v. J. N. Pangle and N. E. Pangle. 1940. U.S. District Court, Western District of Arkansas, Harrison Division. National Archives at Fort Worth, Texas.

U.S. v. John F. Tubbs. 1897. U.S. District Court, Western District of Arkansas. Jacket no. 414. National Archives at Fort Worth, Texas.

U.S. v. Lit Dodson. 1897. U.S. District Court, Western District of Arkansas. Jacket no. 289. National Archives at Fort Worth, Texas.

NEWSPAPERS AND PERIODICALS

Arkansas Democrat (Little Rock)
Arkansas Farmer (magazine)
Arkansas Gazette (Little Rock)
Arkansas Newsletter (magazine)
Batesville Guard
Baxter Bulletin (Mountain Home)
Carroll County Tribune (Berryville)
Clinton Democrat
Courier-Democrat (Russellville)
Daily Echo (Eureka Springs)
Eureka Springs Times-Echo
Fayetteville Democrat
Globe-Democrat (St. Louis, Missouri)
Harrison Daily Times
Herald-Democrat (Siloam Springs)
Human Events (magazine)
Iola Register (Kansas)
Joplin Globe (Missouri)
Kansas City Star (Missouri)
Laurel Daily Leader (Mississippi)
Leslie News
Literary Digest (magazine)
Marshall Republican
Melbourne Times
Mountain Echo (Yellville)
Mountain View Herald
Mountain Wave (Marshall)
Newark Journal
Newport Weekly Independent
Reader's Digest (magazine)
Russellville Democrat
Sharp County Record (Evening Shade)
Southwest Times Record (Fort Smith)

St. Louis Post-Dispatch (Missouri)
New York Times (New York)
Wall Street Journal (New York)

ORAL HISTORY INTERVIEWS

Farmer, Tina. Interview with author. September 19, 2012.

Halstead, Pat. Interview with author. August 30, 2012.

Hurst, Doyle. Interview with Aaron Williams. April 19, 1999. Published in *South Shore Memory Project Archives*, http://ozarkhistory.com/archive/SouthShore/t-Doyle%20Hurst.htm.

Interview Notes. Arkansas VISTA Collection. University of Central Arkansas Archives, Conway.

Jeffery, Brian. Interview with author. July 17, 2010.

Mosier, Susan. Interview with author. May 25, 2010.

Perkins, Bonnie. Interview with author. November 20, 2006.

Pierson, Harlin. Interview with Tracey Chandler. April 9, 1999. Published in *South Shore Memory Project Archives*, http://ozarkhistory.com/archive/SouthShore/t- Harlin %20Pierson.htm.

Richey, Nina. Interview with author. August 2, 2012.

Thomas, Mildred. Interview with author. May 28, 2010.

Tilley, Jewell. Interview with Brad Goeke. February 10, 1999. Published in *South Shore Memory Project Archives*, http://ozarkhistory.com/archive/SouthShore/t-J.Tilley.htm.

BOOKS AND ARTICLES

Abrahams, Edward H. "Charles Taze Russell and the Jehovah's Witnesses, 1879–1916." *American Studies* 18 (Spring 1977): 57–71.

Arsenault, Raymond. "Jeff Davis, 1901–1907." In Donovan, Gatewood, and Whayne, *Governors of Arkansas*, 115–30.

———. *The Wild Ass of the Ozarks: Jeff Davis and the Social Bases of Southern Politics*. Philadelphia: Temple University Press, 1984.

Ayers, Edward L. *The Promise of the New South: Life after Reconstruction*. New York: Oxford University Press, 1992.

Barnes, Kenneth C. *Who Killed John Clayton? Political Violence and the Emergence of the New South, 1861–1893*. Durham. N.C.: Duke University Press, 1998.

Batteau, Allen W. *The Invention of Appalachia*. Tucson: University of Arizona Press, 1990.

Beckford, James A. *The Trumpet of Prophecy: A Sociological Study of Jehovah's Witnesses*. New York: Wiley, 1975.

Beeby, James M. "Introduction: Populism in the American South." In Beeby, *Populism in the South Revisited*, ix–xxi.

———, ed. *Populism in the South Revisited: New Interpretations and New Departures*. Oxford: University Press of Mississippi, 2012.

"Benjamin Franklin Taylor." *Searcy County Ancestor Information Exchange* 16 (February 2007).

Billings, Dwight B., and Kathleen M. Blee. *The Road to Poverty: The Making of Wealth and Hardship in Appalachia*. New York: Cambridge University Press, 2000.

Billings, Dwight B., Mary Beth Pudup, and Altina L. Waller. "Introduction: Taking Exception with Exceptionalism: The Emergence and Transformation of Historical Studies of Appalachia." In *Appalachia in the Making: The Mountain South in the Nineteenth Century*, edited by Mary Beth Pudup, Dwight B. Billings, and Altina L. Waller, 1–24. Chapel Hill: University of North Carolina Press, 1995.

Bissett, Jim. *Agrarian Socialism in America: Marx, Jefferson, and Jesus in the Oklahoma Countryside, 1904–1920*. Norman: University of Oklahoma Press, 1999.

Blair, Dianne D. "William Jefferson Clinton 1979–1981, 1983–1992." In Donovan, Gatewood, and Whayne. *Governors of Arkansas*, 261–75.

Blevins, Brooks. *Arkansas/Arkansaw: How Bear Hunters, Hillbillies, and Good Ol' Boys Defined a State*. Fayetteville: University of Arkansas Press, 2009.

——. "The Arkansas Ghost Trial: The Connie Franklin Case and the Ozarks in the National Media," *Arkansas Historical Quarterly* 68, no. 3 (Autumn 2009): 245–71.

——. *Cattle in the Cotton Fields: A History of Cattle Raising in Alabama*. Tuscaloosa: University of Alabama Press, 1998.

——. "Considering Regional Exceptionalism: The Case of the Ghost of the Ozarks." *Missouri Historical Review* 107, no. 2 (January 2013): 63–76.

——. *Ghost of the Ozarks: Murder and Memory in the Upland South*. Urbana: University of Illinois Press, 2012.

——. *Hill Folks: A History of Arkansas Ozarkers and Their Image*. Chapel Hill: University of North Carolina Press, 2002.

——. "Retreating to the Hill: Population Replacement in the Arkansas Ozarks." *Agricultural History* 74, no. 2 (Spring 2000): 475–88.

——. "Revisiting Race Relations in an Upland South Community: LaCrosse, Arkansas." In *History and Hope in the Heart of Dixie: Scholarship, Activism, and Wayne Flynt in the Modern South*, edited by Gordon E. Harvey, Richard D. Starnes, and Glenn Feldman, 5–25. Tuscaloosa: University of Alabama Press, 2006.

——. "The Strike and the Still: Anti-Radical Violence and the Ku Klux Klan in the Ozarks." *Arkansas Historical Quarterly* 52, no. 4 (Winter 1993): 405–25.

——. "Wretched and Innocent: Two Mountain Regions in the National Consciousness." *Journal of Appalachian Studies* 7, no. 2 (Fall 2001): 257–71.

Brands, H. W. *The Strange Death of American Liberalism*. New Haven, Conn.: Yale University Press, 2001.

Brinkley, Alan. *The End of Reform: New Deal Liberalism in Recession and War*. New York: Vintage, 1995.

Campbell, B. T. "Some Early Calf Creek History." *Searcy County Ancestor Information Exchange* 4 (December 1994).

Cohen, Lizabeth. *A Consumers' Republic: The Politics of Mass Consumption in Postwar America*. New York: Vintage, 2003.

Compton, Neil. *The Battle for the Buffalo River: A Twentieth-Century Conservation Crisis in the Ozarks*. Fayetteville: University of Arkansas Press, 1992.

Corcoran, James. *Bitter Harvest: Gordon Kahl and the Posse Comitatus; Murder in the Heartland*. New York: Viking Penguin, 1990.

Daniel, Pete. *Breaking the Land: The Transformation of Cotton, Tobacco, and Rice Cultures since 1880*. Urbana: University of Illinois Press, 1985.

DeBlack, Thomas. "'A Harnessed Revolution': Reconstruction in Arkansas." In Whayne, DeBlack, Sabo, and Arnold, *Arkansas: A Narrative History*, 205–39.

Desmarais, Ralph, and Edd Jeffords, eds. *Uncertain Harvest: The Family Farm in Arkansas*. Eureka Springs, Ark.: Ozark Institute, 1980.

Dochuk, Darren. *From Bible Belt to Sun Belt: Plain-Folk Religion, Grassroots Politics, and the Rise of Evangelical Conservatism*. New York: Norton, 2011.

Donovan, Timothy P., Willard B. Gatewood Jr., and Jeannie M. Whayne, eds. *The Governors of Arkansas: Essays in Political Biography*. 2nd ed. Fayetteville: University of Arkansas Press, 1995.

Dougan, Michael B. *Arkansas Odyssey: The Saga of Arkansas from Prehistoric Times to Present*. Little Rock, Ark.: Rose, 1994.

Duncan, Georgena. "'One negro, Sarah . . . one horse named Collier, one cow and calf named Pink': Slave Records from the Arkansas River Valley." *Arkansas Historical Quarterly* 69, no. 4 (Winter 2010): 325–45.

Dunn, Durwood. *Cades Cove: The Life and Death of a Southern Appalachian Community, 1818-1937*. Knoxville: University of Tennessee Press, 1988.

Edwards, Robert. "A Jeffersonian Distillation: The Environment of Politics." *Ozarks Watch* 4, no. 1 (Summer 1990): 22–24.

Elkins, F. Clark. "Arkansas Farmers Organize for Action, 1882–1884." *Arkansas Historical Quarterly* 13, no. 3 (Autumn 1954): 231–48.

———. "The Agricultural Wheel: County Politics and Consolidation, 1884–1885." *Arkansas Historical Quarterly* 29, no. 2 (Summer 1970): 152–75.

Eller, Ronald D. "Modernization, 1940–2000." In Straw and Blethen, *High Mountains Rising*, 197–220.

———. *Uneven Ground: Appalachia since 1945*. Lexington: University Press of Kentucky, 2008.

Fite, Gilbert C. *Cotton Fields No More: Southern Agriculture, 1865–1980*. Lexington: University Press of Kentucky, 1984.

Fletcher, John Gould. *Arkansas*. John Gould Fletcher Series 3. 1947. Reprint, Fayetteville: University of Arkansas Press, 1989.

Foley, Michael Stewart. *Front Porch Politics: The Forgotten Heyday of American Activism in the 1970s and 1980s* (New York: Hill and Wang, 2013).

Foner, Eric. *Reconstruction: America's Unfinished Revolution, 1863–1877*. New York: Perennial, 2002.

Fones-Wolf, Ken. *Glass Towns: Industry, Labor, and Political Economy in Appalachia, 1890-1930s*. Urbana: University of Illinois Press, 2007.

Garbacz, Christopher. "The Ozarks: Recreation and Economic Development." *Land Economics* 47, no. 4 (November 1971): 418–20.

Gibson, Lanny. *The Magic of Scrub Holler: Ozark Mountain Life*. N.p.: self-published, 2001.

Goldberg, Johan. "Sanders and Trump: Two Populist Peas in a Pod?" *National Review*, August 19, 2015.

Goodwyn, Lawrence. *The Populist Moment: A Short History of the Agrarian Revolt in America*. New York: Oxford University Press, 1978.

Green, James R. *Grass-Roots Socialism: Radical Movements in the Southwest, 1895–1943*. Baton Rouge: Louisiana State University Press, 1978.

Hahn, Steven. *The Roots of Southern Populism: Yeoman Farmers and the Transformation of the Georgia Upcountry, 1850–1890*. New York: Oxford University Press, 1983.

Halbrook, William E. "A Review of My Membership in the Farmers Union." *Arkansas Historical Quarterly* 15, no. 3 (Autumn 1956): 202–8.

Hamilton, Shane. *Trucking Country: The Road to America's Wal-Mart Economy*. Princeton, N.J.: Princeton University Press, 2008.

Handley, Lawrence R. "Settlement across Northern Arkansas as Influenced by the Missouri and North Arkansas Railroad." *Arkansas Historical Quarterly* 33, no. 4 (Winter 1974): 273–94.

Harper, Kimberly. *White Man's Heaven: The Lynching and Expulsion of Blacks in the Southern Ozarks, 1894–1909*. Fayetteville: University of Arkansas Press, 2012.

Harrell, David Edwin, Jr. *The Churches of Christ in the Twentieth Century: Homer Hailey's Personal Journey of Faith*. Tuscaloosa: University of Alabama Press, 2000.

Harrington, Michael. *The Other America*. New York: Macmillan, 1962.

Haygood, Tamara Miner. "Cows, Ticks, and Disease: A Medical Interpretation of the Southern Cattle Industry." *Journal of Southern History* 52, no. 4 (November 1986): 551–64.

Hernando, Matthew. *Faces Like Devils: The Bald Knobber Vigilantes in the Ozarks*. Columbia: University of Missouri Press, 2015.

Hill, Luther B. *A History of the State of Oklahoma*. Vol. 2. Chicago: Lewis, 1910.

Hobson, Fred C., Jr. *Serpent in Eden: H. L. Mencken in the South*. Chapel Hill: University of North Carolina Press, 1974.

Hodgson, Godfrey. *America in Our Time: From World War II to Nixon—What Happened and Why*. New York: Doubleday, 1976.

Hofstadter, Richard. *The Age of Reform: From Bryan to F.D.R.* New York: Vintage, 1955.

Hogue, Wayman. *Back Yonder: An Ozark Chronicle*. 1932. Reprint. Edited by Brooks Blevins. Fayetteville: University of Arkansas Press, 2016.

Holden, Andrew. *Jehovah's Witnesses: Portrait of a Contemporary Religious Movement*. London: Routledge, 2002.

Hope, Holly. *Dip That Tick: Texas Tick Fever Eradication in Arkansas, 1907–1943*. Little Rock: Arkansas Historic Preservation Program, 2005.

Iggers, Georg G. *Historiography in the Twentieth Century: From Scientific Objectivity to the Postmodern Challenge*. Hanover, N.H.: Wesleyan University Press, 1997.

Isserman, Maurice, and Michael Kazin. *America Divided: The Civil War of the 1960s*. New York: Oxford University Press, 2008.

Jacoby, Karl. *Crimes against Nature: Squatters, Poachers, Thieves, and the Hidden History of American Conservation*. Berkeley: University of California Press, 2001.

Johnson, Ben F., III. "'All Thoughtful Citizens': The Arkansas School Reform Movement, 1921- 1930." *Arkansas Historical Quarterly* 46, no. 2 (Summer 1987): 105–32.

———. *Arkansas in Modern America, 1930–1999*. Fayetteville: University of Arkansas Press, 2000.

———. *John Barleycorn Must Die: The War against Drink in Arkansas*. Fayetteville: University of Arkansas Press, 2005.

Johnston, James. "Arkansas' 1861 Peace Society." *Arkansas Family Historian* 29, no. 1 (March 1991): 13–29.

Katz, Michael B. *The Undeserving Poor: America's Enduring Confrontation with Poverty*. 2nd ed. New York: Oxford University Press, 2013.

Kazin, Michael. *A Godly Hero: The Life of William Jennings Bryan*. New York: Anchor, 2006.

———. *The Populist Persuasion: An American History*. New York: Basic, 1995.

Keith, Jeanette. *Country People in the New South: Tennessee's Upper Cumberland*. Chapel Hill: University of North Carolina Press, 1995.

———. *Rich Man's War, Poor Man's Fight: Race, Class, and Power in the Rural South during the First World War*. Chapel Hill: University of North Carolina Press, 2004.

Kiffmeyer, Thomas. "Looking Back to the City in the Hills: The Council of the Southern Mountains and a Longer View of the War on Poverty in the Appalachian South, 1913- 1970." In Orleck and Hazirjian, *War on Poverty*, 359–86.

———. *Reformers to Radicals: The Appalachian Volunteers and the War on Poverty*. Lexington: University Press of Kentucky, 2008.

Kirby, Jack Temple. *Rural Worlds Lost: The American South, 1920–1960*. Baton Rouge: Louisiana State University Press, 1987.

Kiser, G. Gregory. "The Socialist Party in Arkansas, 1900–1912." *Arkansas Historical Quarterly* 40, no. 2 (Summer 1981): 119–53.

Lancaster, Guy. *Racial Cleansing in Arkansas, 1883–1924: Politics, Land, Labor, and Criminality*. Lanham, Md.: Lexington, 2014.

———. "'There Are Not Many Colored People Here': African Americans in Polk County, Arkansas, 1896–1937." *Arkansas Historical Quarterly* 70, no. 4 (Winter 2011): 429–49.

Lawson, Alan. *A Commonwealth of Hope: The New Deal Response to Crisis*. Baltimore, Md.: Johns Hopkins University Press, 2006.

Lester, James E. "Sidney Sanders McMath, 1949–1953." In Donovan, Gatewood, and Whayne, *Governors of Arkansas*, 210–15.

Levi, Giovanni. "On Microhistory." In *New Perspectives on Historical Writing*, edited by Peter Burke, 97–119. University Park: Pennsylvania State University Press, 2001.

Lewis, Helen M., and Edward E. Knipe. "The Colonialism Model: The Appalachian Case." In Lewis, Johnson, and Askins, *Colonialism in Modern America*, 9–32.

Lewis, Helen M., Linda Johnson, and Donald Askins, eds. *Colonialism in Modern America: The Appalachian Case*. Boone, N.C.: Appalachian Consortium, 1978.

Lewis, John. *A Vista Diary*. N.p., 1969–1970. (Available in Arkansas VISTA Collection, University of Central Arkansas Archives, Conway, Arkansas).

Lewis, Ronald L. "Railroads, Deforestation, and the Transformation of Agriculture in the West Virginia Back Counties, 1880–1920." In Pudup, Billings, and Waller, *Appalachia in the Making*, 297–320.

———. *Transforming the Appalachian Countryside: Railroads, Deforestation, and Social Change in West Virginia, 1880–1920*. Chapel Hill: University of North Carolina Press, 1998.

Li, Tania Murray. *The Will to Improve: Governmentality, Development, and the Practice of Politics*. Durham, N.C.: Duke University Press, 2007.

Lichtenstein, Nelson, and Elizabeth Tandy Shermer, eds. *The Right and Labor in America: Politics, Ideology, and Imagination*. Philadelphia: University of Pennsylvania Press, 2012.

Link, William A. *A Hard Country and a Lonely Place: Schooling, Society, and Reform in Rural Virginia, 1870–1920*. Chapel Hill: University of North Carolina Press, 1986.

———. *The Paradox of Southern Progressivism, 1880–1930*. Chapel Hill: University of North Carolina Press, 1992.

Lo, Clarence Y. H. "Astroturf versus Grass Roots: Scenes from Early Tea Party Mobilization." In Rosenthal and Trost, *Steep*, 98–130.

Malone, David. *Hattie and Huey: An Arkansas Tour*. Fayetteville: University of Arkansas Press, 1989.

Matusow, Allen J. *The Unraveling of America: A History of Liberalism in the 1960s*. New York: Harper and Row, 1984.

McCauley, Deborah. *Appalachian Mountain Religion: A History*. Urbana: University of Illinois Press, 1995.

McKee, Guian A. "'This Government Is with Us': Lyndon Johnson and the Grassroots War on Poverty." In Orleck and Hazirjian, *War on Poverty*, 31–62.

"MM Taylor, et al. vs. CT Stone & AJ Stone, his wife." *Searcy County Ancestor Information Exchange* 7 (February 1998).

Moneyhon, Carl H. *Arkansas and the New South, 1874–1929*. Fayetteville: University of Arkansas Press, 1997.

Moreton, Bethany. *To Serve God and Wal-Mart: The Making of Christian Free Enterprise*. Cambridge, Mass.: Harvard University Press, 2009.

Morgan, W. S. *History of the Wheel and Alliance and the Impending Revolution*. Fort Scott, Kan.: Rice, 1889.

Mosier, Susan. "The 1922 'Tick War': Dynamite, Barn Burning, and Murder in Independence County." *Independence County Chronicle* 41 (October 1999–January 2000).

Murphy, Karen Potter. *Higden . . . A Place in the Heart: Life before Greer's Ferry Lake*. N.p.: Create Space Independent Publishing Platform, 2013.

Murphy, Robert T. "The Regional Commission System." *Public Administration Review* 33, no. 2 (March/April 1973): 179–84.

Niswonger, Richard L. "James Paul Clarke, 1895–1897." In Donovan, Gatewood, and Whayne, *Governors of Arkansas*, 101–6.

———. "William F. Kirby, Arkansas's Maverick Senator." *Arkansas Historical Quarterly* 37, no. 3 (Autumn 1978): 252–63.

Nugent, Walter T. K. *The Tolerant Populists: Kansas Populism and Nativism.* 2nd ed. Chicago: University of Chicago Press, 2013.

O'Conner, Alice. *Poverty Knowledge: Social Science, Social Policy, and the Poor in Twentieth-Century U.S. History.* Princeton, N.J.: Princeton University Press, 2001.

Orleck, Annelise. "Introduction: The War on Poverty from the Grass Roots Up." In Orleck and Hazirjian, *War on Poverty,* 1–30.

Orleck, Annelise, and Lisa Gayle Hazirjian, eds. *The War on Poverty: A New Grassroots History, 1964–1980.* Athens: University of Georgia, 2011.

Packer, George. "The Populists." *New Yorker,* September 7, 2015.

Payton, Leland, and Crystal Payton. *Damming the Osage: The Conflicted Story of Lake of the Ozarks and the Truman Reservoir.* Springfield, Mo.: Lens and Pen, 2012.

Perkins, Blake. "Race Relations in Western Lawrence County, Arkansas." *Big Muddy: A Journal of the Mississippi River Valley* 9, no.1 (2009).

Petty, Adrienne Monteith. *Standing Their Ground: Small Farmers in North Carolina since the Civil War.* New York: Oxford University Press, 2013.

Phillips, Jared M. "Hipbillies and Hillbillies: Back-to-the-Landers in the Arkansas Ozarks during the 1970s." *Arkansas Historical Quarterly* 75, no. 2 (Summer 2016): 89–110.

Pierce, Daniel S. *Corn from a Jar: Moonshining in the Great Smoky Mountains.* Gatlinburg, Tenn.: Great Smoky Mountains Association, 2013.

Pierce, Michael. "Orval Faubus and the Rise of Anti-Labor Populism in Northwestern Arkansas." In Lichtenstein and Shermer, *Right and Labor in America,* 98–113.

———. *Striking with the Ballot: Ohio Labor and the Populist Party.* DeKalb: Northern Illinois University Press, 2010.

Piland, Shirley Carter, ed. *A History of Ozark County, 1841–1991.* Gainesville, Mo.: Ozark County Genealogical and Historical Society, 1991.

Pitcaithley, Dwight T. *Let the River Be: A History of the Ozark's Buffalo River.* Santa Fe, N.M.: Southwest Cultural Resources Center of the National Park Service, 1978.

Postel, Charles. "If Trump and Sanders Are Both Populists, What Does Populist Mean?" *American Historian,* February 2016, 14–17.

———. "The American Populist and Anti-Populist Legacy." In *Transformations of Populism in Europe and the Americas: History and Recent Tendencies,* edited by John Abromeit, 116–35. London: Bloomsbury, 2016.

———. *The Populist Vision.* New York: Oxford University Press, 2007.

———. "The Tea Party in Historical Perspective: A Conservative Response to a Crisis of Political Economy." In Rosenthal and Trost, *Steep,* 25–46.

Pudup, Mary Beth, Dwight B. Billings, and Altina L. Waller, eds. *Appalachia in the Making: The Mountain South in the Nineteenth Century.* Chapel Hill: University of North Carolina Press, 1995.

Rafferty, Milton D. *The Ozarks: Land and Life.* 2nd ed. Fayetteville: University of Arkansas Press, 2001.

Randolph, Vance. *The Ozarks: An American Survival of Primitive Society*. New York: Vanguard, 1931.

Rayburn, Otto Ernest Rayburn. *Ozark Country*. New York: Duell, Sloan and Pearce, 1941.

Reuter, Frank. "Family Farms in Northwest Arkansas." In Desmarais and Jeffords, *Uncertain Harvest*, 52–62.

Roberts, Charles Kenneth. "Client Failures and Supervised Credit in the Farm Security Administration." *Agricultural History* 87, no. 3 (Summer 2013): 368–90.

Robins, Ruby. "Nine Decades of Progress: 1900–1991." In Piland, *History of Ozark County*.

Roll, Jarod. *Spirit of Rebellion: Labor and Religion in the New Cotton South*. Urbana: University of Illinois Press, 2010.

Rosenthal, Lawrence and Christine Trost, eds. *Steep: The Precipitous Rise of the Tea Party*. Berkeley: University of California Press, 2012.

Russell, Charles Taze. *The Finished Mystery*. Studies in the Scriptures, Series VII. Brooklyn, N.Y.: International Bible Students Association, 1918.

Sanders, Elizabeth. *Roots of Reform: Farmers, Workers, and the American State, 1877–1917*. Chicago: University of Chicago Press, 1999.

Schwartz, Marvin. *In Service to America: A History of VISTA in Arkansas, 1965–1985*. Fayetteville: University of Arkansas Press, 1988.

Scott, James C. *Seeing Like a State: How Certain Schemes to Improve the Human Condition Have Failed*. New Haven, Conn.: Yale University Press, 1998.

Senn, Gerald. "'Molders of Thought, Directors of Action': The Arkansas Council of Defense, 1917–1918." *Arkansas Historical Quarterly* 36, no. 3 (Autumn 1977): 280–90.

Shapiro, Henry D. *Appalachia on Our Mind: The Southern Mountains and Mountaineers in the American Consciousness*. Chapel Hill: University of North Carolina Press, 1978.

Shideler, James H. *Farm Crisis, 1919–1923*. Berkeley: University of California Press, 1957.

Shiras, Frances. "Norfork Dam." *Arkansas Historical Quarterly* 4, no. 2 (Summer 1945): 150–58.

Smith, Zachary. "Tom Watson and Resistance to Federal War Policies in Georgia during World War I." *Journal of Southern History* 78, no. 2 (May 2012): 293–326.

Stapleton, Isaac. *Moonshiners in Arkansas*. Independence, Mo.: Zion's, 1948.

Stewart, Bruce E. *Moonshiners and Prohibitionists: The Battle over Alcohol in Southern Appalachia*. Lexington: University of Kentucky Press, 2011.

Stock, Catherine McNicol. *Rural Radicals: Righteous Rage in the American Grain*. Ithaca, N.Y.: Cornell University Press, 1996.

Stock, Catherine McNicol, and Robert D. Johnston, eds. *The Countryside in the Age of the Modern State: Political Histories of Rural America*. Ithaca, N.Y.: Cornell University Press, 2001.

Straw, Richard A., and H. Tyler Blethen, eds. *High Mountains Rising: Appalachia in Time and Place*. Urbana: University of Illinois Press, 2004.

Strom, Claire. "Editorials and Explosions: Insights into Grassroots Opposition to Tick Eradication in Georgia, 1915–1920." *Georgia Historical Quarterly* 88, no. 2 (Summer 2004): 197–214.

——. *Making Catfish Bait out of Government Boys: The Fight against Cattle Ticks and the Transformation of the Yeoman South.* Athens: University of Georgia Press, 2009.

——. "Texas Fever and the Dispossession of the Southern Yeoman Farmer." *Journal of Southern History* 66, no. 1 (February 2000): 49–74.

Sutton, Keith, ed. *Arkansas Wildlife: A History.* Fayetteville: University of Arkansas Press, 1998.

Thomas, Jerry Bruce. *An Appalachian Reawakening: West Virginia and the Perils of the New Machine Age, 1945–1972.* Morgantown: West Virginia University Press, 2010.

Thompson, Charles D., Jr. *Spirits of Just Men: Mountaineers, Liquor Bosses, and Lawmen in the Moonshine Capital of the World.* Urbana: University of Illinois Press, 2011.

Tindall, George B. *The Emergence of the New South, 1913–1945.* Baton Rouge: Louisiana State University Press, 1967.

——, ed. *A Populist Reader: Selections from the Works of American Populist Leaders.* New York: Harper Torchbooks, 1966.

Trivellato, Francesca. "Is There a Future for Italian Microhistory in the Age of Global History?" *California Italian Studies* 2, no.1 (2011).

Vance, Rupert. "A Karl Marx for Hill Billies." *Social Forces* 9, no. 2 (December 1930): 180–90.

Wagy, Tom. "Little Sam Faubus: Hillbilly Socialist." *Arkansas Historical Quarterly* 53, no.3 (Autumn 1994): 263–89.

Waller, Altina L. *Feud: Hatfields, McCoys, and Social Change in Appalachia, 1860–1900.* Chapel Hill: University of North Carolina Press, 1988.

Warren, Luther E. *Yellar Rag Boys: The Arkansas Peace Society of 1861 and Other Events in Northern Arkansas, 1861 to 1865.* Marshall, Ark.: Weaver, 1993.

Webb, James. *Born Fighting: How the Scots-Irish Shaped America.* New York: Broadway, 2004.

Weise, Robert S. *Grasping at Independence: Debt, Male Authority, and Mineral Rights in Appalachian Kentucky, 1850–1915.* Knoxville: University of Tennessee Press, 2001.

Willis, James F. *Southern Arkansas University: The Mulerider School's Centennial History, 1909–2009.* Magnolia, Ark.: Southern Arkansas University Foundation, 2009.

——. "The Cleburne County Draft War." *Arkansas Historical Quarterly* 26, no. 1 (Spring 1967): 24–39.

Wilson, Gregory S. *Communities Left Behind: The Area Redevelopment Administration, 1945–1965.* Knoxville: University of Tennessee Press, 2009.

Whayne, Jeannie M. *A New Plantation South: Land, Labor, and Federal Favor in Twentieth-Century Arkansas.* Charlottesville: University Press of Virginia, 1996.

——. "Prosperity Eluded: Era of Transition, 1880–1900." In Whayne, DeBlack, Sabo, and Arnold, *Arkansas: A Narrative History*, 240–71.

Whayne, Jeannie M., Thomas A. DeBlack, George Sabo III, and Morris S. Arnold, eds. *Arkansas: A Narrative History.* Fayetteville: University of Arkansas Press, 2002.

Williams, John Alexander. *Appalachia: A History.* Chapel Hill: University of North Carolina Press, 2002.

Wolf, John Quincy. *Life in the Leatherwoods.* Edited by Gene Hyde and Brooks Blevins. Fayetteville: University of Arkansas Press, 2000.

Woodrell, Daniel. "How Much of the Ozarks Is in Me?" In "Reading Group Guide" of *Daniel Woodrell, The Death of Sweet Mister*, 2001. New York: Back Bay, 2012.

Woodward, C. Vann. *Origins of the New South, 1877–1913*. Baton Rouge: Louisiana State University Press, 1951.

Worley, Ted R. "Documents Relating to the Arkansas Peace Society of 1861." *Arkansas Historical Quarterly* 17, no. 1 (Spring 1958): 82–111.

———. "The Arkansas Peace Society of 1861: A Study in Mountain Unionism." *Journal of Southern History* 24, no. 4 (November 1958): 445–56.

UNPUBLISHED THESES, DISSERTATIONS, AND PAPERS

Adams, J. Brett. "The Polk County Rebellion." Unpublished conference paper, Third Annual Ozarks Studies Symposium, West Plains, Missouri, September 2009.

Brake, Elizabeth. "'Commendably Democratic' and 'Intensely Practical'? Federal Farm Policy Administration and the County ASCS Committees." Unpublished conference paper, Southern Historical Association 77th Annual Meeting, Baltimore, Maryland, October 2011.

Deatherage, Todd. "World War I Draft Evasion and the Ozark Mountain Draft Wars." Unpublished student paper, University of Arkansas, 1989.

Eddleman, Janice Bufford. "Who Killed Grandpa Charley? The Independence County Tick War and the Murder of Charles Jeffrey." Unpublished research paper, n.d.

Gordon, Leland P., Jr. "The Ozarks Regional Commission and Its Impact in Arkansas." Unpublished graduate internship paper, University of Arkansas, 1973.

Henningson, Randy. "Upland Farmers and Agrarian Protest: Northwest Arkansas and the Brothers of Freedom." MA thesis, University of Arkansas, 1973.

Nielson, Ann. "A Comparison of the Regional Planning Approaches of the Appalachian and Ozarks Regional Commissions." MA thesis, University of Oklahoma, 1970.

Seagraves, Joe T. "Arkansas Politics, 1874–1918." PhD dissertation, University of Kentucky, 1973.

Sealander, Judith. "Draft Evasion in the South during the First World War." MA thesis, University of Arkansas, 1973.

INTERNET SOURCES

Ancestry.com. *American Civil War Regiments*. Provo, Utah: Ancestry.com Operations, 1999.

———. *Arkansas Confederate Pension Records, 1891–1935*. Provo, Utah: Ancestry.com Operations, 2011.

———. *Arkansas, County Marriages Index, 1837–1957*. Provo, Utah: Ancestry.com Operations, 2011.

———. *Fort Smith, Arkansas, Criminal Case Files, 1866–1900*. Provo, Utah: Ancestry.com Operations, 2012.

———. *U.S. Civil War Pension Index: General Index to Pension Files, 1861–1934*. Provo, Utah: Ancestry.com Operations, 2000.

———. *World War I Draft Registration Cards, 1917–1918*. Provo, Utah: Ancestry.com Operations, 2005.

Arkansas Secretary of State. "November 4, 2014, Arkansas General Election and Nonpartisan Runoff Election: Official Results." http://results.enr.clarityelections.com/AR/53237/149792/Web01/en/summary.html.

Arsenault, Raymond. "Jeff Davis (1862–1913)." *Encyclopedia of Arkansas History and Culture* http://www.encyclopediaofarkansas.net/encyclopedia/entry-detail.aspx?entryID=98.

Barro, Josh. "Four States Vote to Raise Minimum Wage." November 5, 2014. *NYTimes.com*. https://www.nytimes.com/2014/11/05/upshot/election-results-2014-minimum-wage.html.

Barth, Jay. "Democratic Party." *Encyclopedia of Arkansas History and Culture*. http://www.encyclopediaofarkansas.net/encyclopedia/entry-detail.aspx?entryID=593.

Berry, Evalena. "Cleburne County." *Encyclopedia of Arkansas History and Culture*. http://www.encyclopediaofarkansas.net/encyclopedia/entry-detail.aspx?entryID=756.

Bissett, Jim. "Socialist Party." *Encyclopedia of Oklahoma History and Culture*. http://www.okhistory.org/publications/enc/entry.php?entry=SO001.

Blakley, Dee. "John Thomas Burris." *Shakin' the Family Tree*. http://wc.rootsweb.ancestry.com/cgi-bin/igm.cgi?op=GET&db=sharpchick&id=156.

Bobic, Igor. "Tom Cotton Says He Will Vote for Minimum Wage Hike 'As a Citizen.'" September 5, 2014. *HuffingtonPost.com*. http://www.huffingtonpost.com/2014/09/05/tom-cotton minimum-wage_n_5772246.html.

Brantley, Max. "Tea Party Leader on Racist Joke—Yes, But . . ." http://www.arktimes.com/ArkansasBlog/archives/2012/06/15/tea-party-leader-on-racist joke-yes-but.

Brown, Norman W. "The Moonshiner Who Got Away with Murder . . . And Escaped the Hangman's Noose." *True West Magazine*.com. February 24, 2015. http://www.truewestmagazine.com/the-moonshiner-who-got-away-with murder.

Bruce, Shane. "The Legend of Harve Bruce (My Great Grandpa)." *Bludgeon and Skewer*. Posted May 10, 2012. http://bludgeonandskewer.blogspot.com/2012_05_01_archive.html.

"Captain Benjamin Franklin Taylor." In *Ancestors of Jody Lawrence Drewry: Notes*. http://www.angelfire.com/ut2/jldrewry/Jody/pafn07.htm.

Celock, John. "Inge Marler, Arkansas Tea Party Leader, Makes Racist Joke at Event." http://www.huffingtonpost.com/2012/06/14/inge-marler-tea-party-arkansas-leader -racist joke_n_1597334.html.

———. "Inge Marler, Arkansas Tea Party Leader, Resigns after Racist Joke." http://www.huffingtonpost.com/2012/06/15/inge-marler-arkansas-tea-party-richard caster _n_1600376.html.

Cook, Michael. "Racism in the Arkansas Tea Party." http://talkbusiness.net/2012/06/racism-in-the-arkansas-tea-party.

Dave Liep's Atlas of U.S. Presidential Elections. http://uselectionatlas.org/RESULTS.

Dillard, Tom W. "Winthrop Rockefeller (1912–1973)." *Encyclopedia of Arkansas History and Culture.* http://www.encyclopediaofarkansas.net/encyclopedia/entry-detail.aspx ?search=1&entryID=122.

"Dr. Bill Smith." Biographical profile. https://www.linkedin.com/in/ozarkguru.

Dumas, Ernest. "Bullfrog Valley Gang." *Encyclopedia of Arkansas History and Culture.* http:// www.encyclopediaofarkansas.net/encyclopedia/entry-detail.aspx?entryID=7378.

Frauenthal, Jeannie. "Max Frauenthal (1836–1914)." *Encyclopedia of Arkansas History and Culture.* http://www.encyclopediaofarkansas.net/encyclopedia/entry-detail.aspx ?search=1&entryID=3184.

Hanson, Aprille. "Student Begins His Political Career in Mountain Home." *Arkansas Catholic.org.* December 4, 2010. http://www.arkansas-catholic.org/news/article/ 2371.

Hild, Matthew. "Brothers of Freedom." *Encyclopedia of Arkansas History and Culture* http:// www.encyclopediaofarkansas.net/encyclopedia/entry-detail.aspx?entryID=6990.

"John Boozman for Senate Campaign News Conference, July 6, 2010." *C-SPAN.org.* http://www.c-span.org/video/?294383-1/john-boozman-senate-campaign-news - conference.

Johnston, James J. "Searcy County." *Encyclopedia of Arkansas History and Culture.* http:// www.encyclopediaofarkansas.net/encyclopedia/entry-detail.aspx?entryID=806.

"Karen S. Hopper." State House of Representatives profile. http://www.arkansashouse .org/member/232/Karen%20S.-Hopper.

Kirkpatrick, Matthew B. "Washington County." *Encyclopedia of Arkansas History and Culture.* http://www.encyclopediaofarkansas.net/encyclopedia/entry-detail.aspx ?entryID=813.

"The Legend of Harve Bruce." *OakSpringsMountainRanch.com.* http://oakspringsmoun-tainranch.com/Legend_of_Harve_Bruce.html.

"Mary Ann Caster, Real Estate Agent, Gilbert Realty Co." *GilbertRealty.com.* http:// www.gilbertrealty.com/marylist.htm.

Miller, C. J. "Carroll County." *Encyclopedia of Arkansas History and Culture.* http://www .encyclopediaofarkansas.net/encyclopedia/entry-detail.aspx?entryID=752.

Mulloy, Clement. "Mountain Home (Baxter County)." *Encyclopedia of Arkansas History and Culture.* http://www.encyclopediaofarkansas.net/encyclopedia/entry-detail.aspx ?search=1&entryID=826.

Orr, Nancy. "Sharp County." *Encyclopedia of Arkansas History and Culture.* http://www .encyclopediaofarkansas.net/encyclopedia/entry-detail.aspx?entryID=809.

"Ozark Tea Party in Mountain Home AR." Video posted at http://www.youtube.com/ watch?v=9R0OzTSaH6Q.

"Ozarks Minutemen." http://ozarksminutemen.com.

Parker, Suzie. "Arkansas Racism, Tea Party Style." https://www.washingtonpost.com/ blogs/she-the-people/post/arkansas-racism-tea-party-style/2012/06/15/gJQAHQI feV_blog.html?utm_term=.99fc2303f9ff.

Pierce, Michael Pierce. "Labor Movement." *Encyclopedia of Arkansas History and Culture*. http://www.encyclopediaofarkansas.net/encyclopedia/entry-detail.aspx ?entryID=4235.

Reed, Bernard. "Shooting of Gordon Kahl." *Encyclopedia of Arkansas History and Culture*. http://www.encyclopediaofarkansas.net/encyclopedia/entry-detail.aspx ?search=1&entryID=5483.

"Resume: Dr. Bill Smith (Ozark Guru)." http://agora-assoc.com/smithresume.html.

Risener, Lynn Banard. "Original Grantee's Land, Van Buren County, Arkansas: Township 11N, Range 17W." http://www.rootsweb.ancestry.com/~arvanbur/LandRecords/111.

Sanders-Gray, Sherry. "Marion County." *Encyclopedia of Arkansas History and Culture*. http://www.encyclopediaofarkansas.net/encyclopedia/entry-detail.aspx?entryID =789.

Smith, Bill. "Ozark Tea Party—Mountain Home, Arkansas." Advertisement posted at *FairTaxNation.com*. March 26, 2009. http://www.fairtaxnation.com/profiles/blogs/ ozark-tea-party-mountain-home.

South Shore Foundation. *A Pictorial History of Bull Shoals Dam and the Town of Bull Shoals*. Flippin, Ark.: South Shore Foundation, 2002. Online at http://www.southshore.com/ bsdam.htm.

———. *South Shore Memory Project Archives*. http://ozarkhistory.com/archive.

Yount, Shelia. "Clyde Taylor Ellis (1908–1980)." *Encyclopedia of Arkansas History and Culture*. http://www.encyclopediaofarkansas.net/encyclopedia/entry-detail.aspx?search =1&entryID=2532.

INDEX

J. BLAKE PERKINS, a native of the Arkansas Ozarks, is an assistant professor of history at Williams Baptist College.

THE WORKING CLASS IN AMERICAN HISTORY

The University of Illinois Press
is a founding member of the
Association of American University Presses.

Composed in 10.25/13 Marat Pro
with BarberinoCleanTT display
by Lisa Connery
at the University of Illinois Press
Manufactured by Sheridan Books, Inc.

University of Illinois Press
1325 South Oak Street
Champaign, IL 61820-6903
www.press.uillinois.edu